BREAKING THE CYCLE

Debbie—

In addition to your superb chapter,
thank you for your generosity, insight
and personal support throughout
this endeavor —

Rod

BREAKING THE CYCLE

RODERICK VON LIPSEY

ST. MARTIN'S PRESS
NEW YORK

ISBN 0-312-16253-7

Library of Congress Cataloging-in-Publication Data

Breaking the cycle : a framework for conflict intervention / [edited
    by Roderick K. von Lipsey].
        p.   cm.
    Includes bibliographical references and index.
    ISBN 0-312-16253-7
    1. Intervention (International law)   2. International police.
3. Conflict management   4. Conflict management—Case studies.
I. Von Lipsey, Roderick K.
JX4481.B67   1997
327.1'72—DC20   96-28136
                                                          CIP

Interior Design by Harry Katz

First edition: May, 1997
10   9   8   7   6   5   4   3   2   1

Contents

PART ONE
INTERVENING WITH A CONCEPTUAL FRAMEWORK

PART TWO
CASE STUDIES IN INTERVENTION

PART THREE
BREAKING THE CYCLE

Foreword

LES GELB

In the first chapter of this book, Rod von Lipsey refers to the "cyclical nature" of international conflict. He is right; conflicts are cyclical, with repeating patterns of tension—religious, economic, diplomatic, and so on—emerging and reemerging in shifting contexts over time. Foreign relations are often self-confounding by nature; rarely can we resolve a dilemma without planting the seed of another, or reigniting one from the past. We in the business of thinking about foreign policy, then, face the challenge of trying to determine generally usable and distilled approaches to understanding and resolving (or managing) conflicts that can be applied to most situations around the world and across time.

This challenge is met elegantly and admirably in *Breaking the Cycle*. Von Lipsey and his fellow authors tell us how not to intervene in each and every case, but how to think about conflict situations in general, and intervention in particular. In effect, the authors lay out a paradigm for analyzing what kind of situation is emerging, its stage of development, and what approaches might be used to dismantle it. Von Lipsey summarizes the essence of his paradigm and its purpose in the chapter entitled "Lessons Learned," in which he writes that "the Intervention Cycle provides a point of departure with which to assess the appropriate tasks and tools of intervening to mitigate, resolve, or prevent violent intergroup conflict." But the Intervention Cycle does not simply describe the different instruments of diplomacy available to manage and resolve conflict. Instead, it is itself one of those instruments.

This book picks up on several crucial points that are overlooked too often and too easily in analyses of intergroup conflicts. Von Lipsey makes the worthy observation that "the most important, and frequently overlooked, aspect of conflict intervention only begins when the shooting stops." The case studies presented in *Breaking the Cycle* illustrate the truth of this assertion, and make many others. From the studies, for example, we realize that, while quelling violent conflict is a top priority in every situation, it is sometimes the easiest step in the peacemaker's byzantine path. Each case also reflects the importance and validity of some of von Lipsey's other arguments: that the diplomat must always be sensitive to the internal structures that—damaged as they may be—remain in each state after a period of conflict; and that continued support for those structures is vital to the process of financial, social, and political regeneration.

The significance of *Breaking the Cycle* has everything to do with the generation of new ideas. It is a particularly gratifying work because it is one of the first products of the Council on Foreign Relations' thinking on the next generation. Von Lipsey and his colleagues are scholars of the next generation in foreign policy thinking. Theirs represents a new set of concerns and approaches to foreign relations—a set that is not characterized by the singularly focused mind frame of the cold war era. This next generation's interests seem more humanitarian and less political than those of its predecessors; the authors' good work is an outgrowth of general apprehension about social and political injustice and violence rather than a distrust of or desire to change a specific political system. They are concerned more with policies that help people than ways to promote or control particular forms of government.

In the end, *Breaking the Cycle* helps us to come to terms with the rules and rhythms of the new post–cold war world. They are rules that are being influenced by young leaders like the authors of this book. Rod von Lipsey is only 37 years old, but he has already generated two books' worth of novel approaches to a few age-old problems. He engaged the Council in his dialogue on foreign policy when he served as our International Affairs Fellow. With any luck, he and his co-authors will continue to inspire thought and provide fresh insight into U.S. foreign policy as they work to define their own generation, and begin to shape the next.

LES GELB
August 1996

Preface

RODERICK VON LIPSEY

As this work neared completion, the always controversial subject of conflict intervention became a politically charged and unpopular theme in American political discourse. This seemed ironic, especially in a state whose historic declaration of principles holds certain truths "self evident," and whose history contains numerous examples of selfless, even if also a few selfish, attempts to spread those principles far and wide in order to achieve the goal of global freedom, accord, and prosperity.

The experiences of the first half-decade of post–cold war euphoria did much to dampen American enthusiasm for intervening abroad with the hope of bringing peace and plenty to societies steeped in conflict. To some, the familiarity of the lost cold war paradigm began to look less distasteful than the shocking and complex offspring born in the Balkans, the Horn of Africa, and broad regions of the former Soviet Union.

This work seeks to take a few steps back from the political discourse surrounding the issue of intervention and to look at the patterns of recent conflicts with the hope of finding some heuristic framework with which to describe what is occurring. *Breaking the Cycle* is neither intended to encourage nor discourage decisions to intervene, but rather to help guide the process of intervention decision making. The Intervention Cycle developed in this book illustrates the relationship between levels of conflict in a society; it is a descriptive and user-friendly tool with which the remedy to conflict becomes much more apparent, even if no less difficult.

During the course of writing this book, various descriptive architectures were proposed and tested; however, we found none to be simpler and more descriptive than that contained herein. In short, the Intervention Cycle passes the "back-of-the-envelope" test: it is simple enough to be descriptive and easily remembered, yet it enables its reader to focus discussion and consideration on the key elements and dynamics of conflict intervention.

Breaking the Cycle and the Intervention Cycle framework cannot solve the difficult tasks associated with conflict intervention; nor is it likely to persuade those opposed to intervention that it is a task from which we cannot nor should not walk away. It does, however, argue strenuously for the use of a comprehensive, guided approach to helping societies threatened with unabated conflict by effectively linking the purpose and tasks of an intervention with the means and mechanisms available to break the cycle of violence.

Part 1 of this book outlines the theory and application of the Intervention Cycle. Part 2 presents a diverse set of recent case studies of intervention that are representative of the wide array of challenges faced by those who live in this world of uncertainty and change. The cases, as seen through the eyes of an equally diverse set of talented and accomplished colleagues, illustrate the complexity of intergroup conflict from the perspectives of infantry officers, intelligence analysts, journalists, political theorists, security experts, and diplomats. However, through the lens of the Intervention Cycle the authors— and the reader—are able to identify clearly a common reference point from which, it is our hope, the magnitude and direction of resolution efforts in each individual conflict might emanate.

Among the many people and institutions to whom I am deeply grateful for supporting, inspiring, and encouraging this project, my co-authors, the Council on Foreign Relations, the Joint Center for Political and Economic Studies, and the United States Marine Corps are second only to my wife, Kori Schake, whose intellectual support and personal forbearance made this work possible.

RODERICK VON LIPSEY
June 1996

PART ONE

Intervening with a Conceptual Framework

■ ■ ■ ■ ■ ■

CHAPTER 1

The Intervention Cycle

Roderick von Lipsey

A prominent feature of the post–cold war global landscape is intergroup conflict. It manifests itself as "ethnic," religious, economic, or cultural clashes all over the world in increasingly familiar places such as Bosnia, Gaza, Somalia, Rwanda, Chechnya, and Nagorno-Karabakh. Just in the last five years, dozens of states, international organizations, and treaty groups have poured their resources into the mitigation and resolution of major intergroup conflicts in over twenty countries. Scores of additional states are experiencing similar struggles on a smaller scale; no state is immune.

Among the world's most stable countries, within NATO alone, Canada faces a secessionist threat by the Québecois, the Belgians seek compromise between the Flemish and Walloons, the British struggle with Northern Ireland, the Turks battle the Kurds, the Greeks feud with the Macedonians, and so on. In Mexico, historic fault lines along ethnic and economic fissures spilled violence and bloodshed in Chiapas and Chihuahua. And in the United States, riots shook Los Angeles and rekindled racial and ethnic tensions in the heart of America's "melting pot." The prominence of these conflicts and their drain on the political, economic, and human capital of individual states and international organizations make the resolution and prevention of conflict—*intergroup* conflict—a timely and important issue.

This work contributes to the study of intergroup conflict by exploring potential underlying causes; identifying possible mechanisms for their resolution; and presenting a conceptual framework that brings together the various disciplines, tasks and mechanisms that must be applied during interventions that seek to defuse this seemingly intractable problem. That framework, presented in the form of the Intervention Cycle, graphically represents the cyclical nature of intergroup conflict, outlines essential intervention tasks, and allows the ready identification of goals for any contemplated or ongoing intervention. Most important, this work provides the would-be interventionist—be it a single state, coalition, or international organization—a guide with which to select and shape the mechanisms employed at any stage of conflict. That guide can shape intervention efforts in a manner that achieves the greatest effect in defusing conflict and breaking the too frequently escalating cycle of conflict and intervention.

I. TERMS OF REFERENCE

The literature on intervention, peacekeeping, and intergroup conflict cuts across so many disciplines and involves so many organizations with so many terminologies that confusion can easily result from the imprecise use of terms. For the sake of clarity, this chapter will commence with a short discussion of several terms of reference that include:

- intervention
- prevention
- mitigation
- resolution
- peacekeeping
- peace enforcement
- peace making
- intergroup conflict

A clear differentiation and scrupulous adherence to the resulting definitions of these terms as they are used throughout our discussion, will aid the fullest comprehension of the Intervention Cycle as a framework for conflict intervention.

A. Intervention, Prevention, Mitigation, and Resolution

The concept of intervention, as discussed in this work, refers to the deliberate actions taken by individual states, organizations, or a coalition of states in the international community to assist other states or national entities in the favorable resolution of pressing matters of humanitarian, regional security or international economic interest. For the sake of conceptual integrity, the word "intervention" is assumed to be benign, that is, absent of political, legal, or ideological inference. Further, the purpose of this work is to provide a framework with which to intervene *to do good*—as opposed to inflicting further harm upon societies and states stressed by and threatened with intergroup conflict.

Those who choose to intervene to solve intergroup conflicts find the need to carry out a range of constructive activities that, although related, are discrete in terms of their focus of effort and scope of operations. Prevention is the preemption of the least desired and final manifestation of unresolved intergroup conflict—violence. Conflict always bubbles beneath the surface of relationships between states and groups. This is especially true when groups inside a state identify themselves outside the parameters of a collective state identity. To the extent that this natural tension can be managed, or kept from erupting into violence, the prevention of conflict can be achieved. Preventative measures, then, are successful only to the extent that they keep violence from occurring. When we speak of the prevention of conflict, we are referring to the employment of those measures and mechanisms that reduce tensions, deter lawlessness, or coerce cooperation between individuals, groups, and the state in such a way as to prevent the occurrence of violence.

When the preventative measures fail and violence does occur, those who wish to intervene in order to restore peace are faced with two tasks: mitigation and resolution. Mitigation refers to the reduction or minimization of violent acts. Thus, mitigative measures are employed only after the outbreak of violence in order to restore calm. They traditionally employ, for example, the interposition of neutral forces to restore a peaceful or nonviolent condition within which the root causes of conflict may be resolved.

Although mitigation can often prevent or contain the spread of violence vis-à-vis bordering regions, the measures employed are distinctively different from those used during prevention. Mitigation normally targets a specific group in order to compel restraint. These efforts are not particularly well-suited to the prevention of conflict on a broad scale because even if dissuasive, they rarely compel the active support of nonviolent alternatives to conflict resolution between all parties.

Once a peaceful environment has been achieved through mitigative measures or by mutual consent, exhaustion, or defeat, another set of actions must be taken to eliminate the sources of conflict. We refer to these as resolution measures. The distinction between resolution and prevention is fundamental to understanding the Intervention Cycle. Specifically, measures taken to resolve conflict, especially after that conflict manifests itself in an outbreak of violence, differ from preventative measures in two respects: First, resolution measures normally include some fundamental change to the status quo. For example, resolution may involve the extension of certain rights or privileges, the modification of borders, the payment of restitution, the granting of amnesty or asylum, and/or the taking of some form of retribution against parties to the conflict. In contrast, preventative measures normally employ mechanisms that seek to preserve the (new) status quo (state boundaries, ethnic diversity, etc.) while reducing tension and eliminating the underlying causes of future conflict.

Second, resolution measures normally require a broad and deep commitment of resources from parties internal to the conflict. Participation, not mere acquiescence from the disputing groups, is essential to a full resolution. However, the destructive and debilitating nature of violent conflict also generally necessitates external support for the successful implementation of resolution measures. Prevention, on the low end of conflict, reduces the need for external intervention and supports those internal mechanisms and initiatives that are fundamental to maintaining intergroup cohesion.

B. The Intervention Cycle

The relationship between prevention, mitigation, and resolution forms the basis of the Intervention Cycle. The Intervention Cycle illustrates the relationship between levels of conflict; the outbreak of violence; the application of measures that seek to prevent, mitigate, or resolve conflict; and the mechanisms/agencies and related tasks employed at various stages of the cycle to intervene—that is, to facilitate or deter—in the cyclical progression.

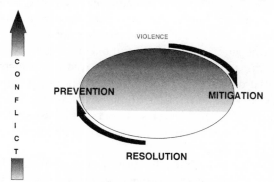

Figure 1. The Intervention Cycle

The Intervention Cycle is graphically depicted as a circle superimposed on a vertical axis (Figure 1). Levels of conflict progress vertically up the axis from low to high, with the outbreak of violence occurring at the uppermost point of the vertical axis and the top of the corresponding circle. When conflict manifests itself as a violent outbreak at the circle's zenith, the process of mitigation allows it to subside as we move clockwise through the cycle. Resolution occurs when conflict reaches the nadir. Prevention, if appropriately applied, stems the reescalation of conflict on the left side of the circle, allowing conflict to reach a steady state of normal societal tensions (between approximately seven and nine o'clock) and stopping the cyclical flow back toward violence at the circle's zenith. The failure to prevent conflict becomes apparent when violence recurs, repeating the cycle of intervention with renewed attempts to mitigate and resolve conflict.

The Intervention Cycle can be applied to conflict on both the macro- and microlevels. On the macrolevel, a region torn apart by armed intergroup conflict may find itself stuck in the mitigation phase of the cycle. However, on the microlevel subelements of the same regional conflict may be involved in resolution or prevention. Further, the cycle applies equally to conflict between armies or individuals. Thus, the manifestation of intergroup conflict in America led by the Radical Right is as germane to the Intervention Cycle as is a war in the Balkans. The only difference is scale.

Figure 1 outlines the basic cycle and the correlation of the intervention principles discussed. In the following sections, the specific tasks inherent to the prevention, mitigation, or resolution of conflict will be added. Before proceeding with that discussion, however, attention turns to the concept of intergroup conflict.

C. Intergroup Conflict

In the study of conflict, there exists a variety of modifiers that seek to describe the not-so-new, but terribly prevalent, manifestations of turmoil between states and substate elements spanning the spectrum of intensity from minor unrest to all-out warfare. Rather than attempting to classify conflict narrowly as "ethnic," "religious," "social," "economic" or otherwise, this work seeks a definition that is broadly inclusive: intergroup conflict. This widely applicable term underscores the relevance of the Intervention Cycle to a host of substate conflict phenomena. Most conflicts prevalent in the current international environment occur between groups.[1]

Intergroup conflict is not a new phenomenon. It has been known for years, yet referred to in different terms, such as ethnic conflict, *jihad,* holy war, civil war, civil unrest, civil disobedience, or, quite simply, crime. However, in the past an empire, bloc, dominant ideology, or state structure retained control over broad areas of conflict, providing a framework with which to define it in these more convenient and traditional terms.[2]

Recent experience suggests that the manifestation of conflict that we must be prepared to preempt in the current and future course of world events occurs outside of one of these convenient frameworks. Further, intergroup conflict, as opposed to interstate conflict, poses more complex problems to those who wish to intervene because it requires a more sophisticated application of solutions. For example, recent events in Rwanda between two tribal clans were affected by the cross-border activities of clan members in neighboring

Zaire, Burundi, and Uganda without the express involvement of the political elite or state infrastructures of these sovereign entities. The international community that first sought to contain the outbreak of violence within the political borders of Rwanda, however, soon realized that these administrative boundaries were quickly traversed by violence and intragroup affinities.

This neither implies the irrelevance of resolving conflict between states, nor lessens the responsibility borne by each state in the prevention of intergroup conflict; rather it illustrates that the focus of conflict intervention effort must often reach below, and beyond, the state level. The impact of intervention must be felt at, what those in American politics have come to describe as, the grassroots level. This poses a problem for both the state and the traditional mechanisms of conflict intervention—international organizations—in that neither have been fully prepared to handle intergroup conflict.

International forums are best equipped to address conflict at the state level, precisely because they are comprised of representatives of sovereign states, not groups or elements of ethnic, religious, or social derivation. However, state boundaries were not generally drawn along ethnic, religious, or cultural lines; thus, these artificial borders have little or no meaning to those who become a party to this type of conflict. Therefore, as will be discussed in more detail later, the key challenge for states is to impart relevance to their borders via the mechanisms of prevention in order to achieve social enfranchisement. International organizations can provide the assets for conflict mitigation and resolution; however, the key to breaking the cycle of intergroup conflict resides within the state and those internal mechanisms adopted for conflict prevention.

Just as in the conflict between the Hatfields and McCoys of American folklore—where the scale of violence ranges from name calling to a shooting war—states and international fora must be prepared to defuse a range of intergroup conflict that traverses the same scale. Of course, the most apparent, troublesome, and destructive manifestation of intergroup conflict is violent, armed struggle.

Conflict that occurs at levels below this threshold is more difficult to recognize and is of a domestic nature—that is, these lower levels of conflict do not result in the tumultuous upheaval of vast segments of the population, widespread killing, massive flows of refugees and immigrants, and disruption of regional stability.[3] Thus, the primary focus of this work is the mitigation of violent conflict, and the application of those mechanisms that treat this most devastating form of intergroup conflict.

D. Peace: Keeping, Enforcement and Making

Peacekeeping is the focus of much of the intervention activity around the world today. Books, journals, magazines, and newspapers have discussed this issue extensively; however, there remains some lack of discipline with which its terms of reference are discussed. The result is often the absence of a clear linkage between the peacekeeping mechanisms employed and their efficacy with respect to nature of the task at hand.

Thus, before commencing a broad discussion of intervening in an inter-group conflict, it is essential to place the tasks associated with peacekeeping within the conceptual framework of the Intervention Cycle. To do so we must clearly define the terms, "peacekeeping," "peace enforcement," and "peacemaking"—three tasks with specific political, legal, and military differentiation that are often lumped together under the terms, "peacekeeping," "peace operations," or alternatively, "operations other than war."

Peacekeeping, in its most narrow interpretation, is the use of neutral forces between, and with the consent of, previously warring parties for the maintenance of an existing cease-fire or cessation of hostilities. Peacekeeping in the context of this narrow definition is mitigative in nature; it provides a stable environment in which the resolution of conflict may be achieved. It may involve the interposition of neutral forces to police or maintain law and order in a narrowly proscribed area of interface among willing participants in a resolution process. Preferably, contending forces have been disarmed, confined to their barracks, or otherwise physically separated prior to the commencement of the peacekeeping operation.[4] Peacekeeping activities are normally associated with those actions authorized under Chapter VI of the UN Charter.

Peace enforcement involves the forcible interposition of parties external to the conflict between warring factions in order to facilitate the cessation of hostilities, deter renewed aggression, and create an environment conducive to the declaration of a cease-fire and commencement of resolution measures. Unlike peacekeeping, peace enforcement requires neither the consent of the (previously) warring parties nor, necessarily, the cessation of hostilities. The political, military, and legal implications of peace enforcement are tantamount to an international declaration of war against one or more parties to the conflict, with the hope of forcibly separating the factions and enforcing such a separation with military strength. These operations are normally referred to under Chapter VII of the UN Charter.

Peacemaking, a less often used term, describes some of the activities associated with the initial phases of what some call "nation building." Peacemaking entails the employment of resolution mechanisms that seek the redress of wrongs, establishment of mutually accepted boundaries, and restoration of political and governmental infrastructures. Unlike peacekeeping and peace enforcement, the activities commenced under the heading peacemaking require substantial commitment by the parties to the conflict under the facilitating good offices of international bodies or organizations. Two sides can agree, or be coerced, to cease violent conflict; however, the making of peace requires more than acquiescence. It requires full and active participation. The actual tasks inherent to peacemaking are resolutionary; these will be discussed in great detail in Section 3. Having completed an overview of key terms to be employed in this work, the discussion returns to analysis of the three primary tasks framed by the Intervention Cycle: conflict mitigation, resolution, and prevention.

II. INTERVENING TO MITIGATE CONFLICT

Those who intervene to mitigate conflict face an overwhelming chore. The quest to achieve the cessation of violent conflict and the peaceful resolution of intergroup differences is fraught with political, economic, and social implications of staggering proportions. The voyage is costly, both in terms of lives and resources; the process is treacherous; and success may only be measured in the passage of time. However, those who enter this quest with a clear understanding of its requirements will be able to do more good than harm. This section presents an outline of the tasks inherent to the mitigation of conflict.

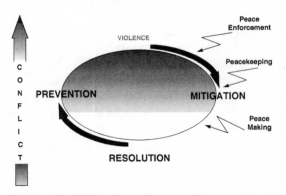

Figure 2. The Intervention Cycle with Peace Operations Overlay

A. Peace Operations

The full range of tasks conducted by those who intervene to mitigate conflict is described by the term, "peace operations." Figure 2 identifies the three types of peace operations and their relationship to the Intervention Cycle. The significance of their placement on the cycle relates not only to the discrete mission focus of each task, but also to the comparative level of conflict between parties to the dispute (as defined by the vertical axis to the right of the cycle).

Peace enforcement enters the cycle near the zenith of violence with the intended effect of facilitating mitigation. Due to the level of active conflict, it is combative in nature. Peacekeeping of a traditional nature complements a previously established pattern of mitigation; that is, with a cease-fire in place, conflict has subsided to a level that peacekeepers hope to preserve and further encourage. Finally, peacemaking enters into the cycle at the commencement of the resolution phase.

The distinction the Intervention Cycle makes with regard to peace operations is that they are clearly identified as mitigating tools. Contrary to commonly held perceptions, peace operations alone are not sufficient for the resolution or the prevention of intergroup conflict. Although the localized effect of peace operations may have some preventative value, their focus and impact lay primarily in the area of conflict mitigation. As such, the types of peace operations described in this section, and prevalent in real-world interventions, are poorly suited to conflict resolution. For, once the cease-fire has been established, more difficult work must begin. Having clearly identified the phase of conflict affected by peace operations, the discussion turns to the specifics of each particular mission.

B. Forcibly Restoring Peace

Not only is each task associated with peace operations unique, the resources, equipment, profession of peace workers and their intervention skills vary profoundly. Peace enforcement requires the skills, equipment, and professional orientation of warriors. In scope (even if not in principle) the forcible restoration of peace among warring parties is a combat operation. To treat it otherwise would be a grave mistake.

Working with perhaps only the consent of the international community, peace enforcement interposes armed troops between members of warring factions by directly exposing them to combat conditions. In this respect peace enforcers fundamentally differ from the types of personnel required to perform peacekeeping, peacemaking, or other forms of conflict intervention. Peace enforcers require the ability and propensity to employ combat skills directly. This state of readiness makes them effective at enforcement; consequently, the same forces utilized for enforcing the peace are inappropriate or poorly suited to the tasks of peacekeeping or peacemaking. Their propensity to employ combat skills can, and should, rule them out as suitable providers of the follow-on functions associated with peacekeeping and peacemaking.

The combative nature of peace enforcement requires forces tasked with this mission to retain the command, control, communications, coordination, intelligence tools, and effectiveness of a combat organization. Further, the rules of engagement prescribed for peace enforcers must be permissive— that is, peace enforcement commanders must be authorized to use force in carrying out their mission until all parties have acceded to the cessation of hostilities and a transition to traditional peacekeeping activities can be made. This permissive engagement policy is crucial to establishing the credibility of the enforcement effort between groups engaged in violent conflict.

Peace enforcement is not unconstrained warfare; however, parties to the conflict must not suffer from the delusion that peace enforcers may be fired upon, impeded, or harassed at will. This only prolongs the conflict, increases the number of casualties, and blurs the lines of distinction between enforcer and partisan.

Neither is peace enforcement neutral intervention. Working without the consent of one or more parties to a conflict—the definition of peace enforcement—makes peace enforcement forces partisan from the perspective of an aggrieved and unyielding combatant. If peace enforcement occurs with the willing agreement of only one side, those who conduct the intervention may be perceived as favoring that side and belligerent toward the other. The perception of one-sidedness may be impossible to overcome but it will be reinforced should the intervening body apply its rules of engagement unevenly between the parties.

Leaders of peace enforcement forces should have the authority to negotiate with belligerent parties, not for the permission to carry out the enforcement mission, but rather to limit the amount of force required to achieve a peaceful environment. Further, these negotiations should be conducted in such a manner that they are separate from, yet coordinated with, other political, humanitarian, or military negotiations conducted by intervening parties. This degree of separation is essential to differentiate clearly what is negotiable (noncombatant personnel access, humanitarian relief efforts, political concessions) from what is not negotiable (the free movement of forces, their supplies and noncombatant representatives of international fora). This close coordination is also required to ensure that a parallel plan of political engagement is formulated and implemented as soon as a peaceful environment has been (re)established.

Peace enforcement missions should be clearly identified and tightly constrained to the restoration of a peaceful environment. The use of force is specifically authorized in this endeavor and rules of engagement should reflect a tactically sound approach to the mission. Incremental applications of force and the use of threats should be specifically avoided in this process, as these are political expedients that undermine the military credibility and capability of the enforcement mission. Where the political will to support such conditions is lacking, military intervention should not be contemplated. The use of military forces or assets to conduct peripheral humanitarian operations is certainly possible; however, there should be no impression that such efforts alone will mitigate conflict.

At this stage of the Intervention Cycle the parties to the conflict are in the active pursuit of their goals through violent means. Only the decisive application of force can counter force until such time as parties to the conflict determine that either: (1) one side has won (or victory is imminent); (2) all parties have exhausted their ability/willingness to continue fighting; (3) no further gains can be made through the use of force; or (4) the political, economic, or tactical risks of the continued use of force outweigh any tactical or strategic advantages. Political dialogue and humanitarian engagement at this stage of conflict is, in fact, important and effective. However, these efforts should be viewed with a full understanding of their limitations and risks. During this stage of armed and violent struggle, political engagement may facilitate dialogue between the leaders of the belligerent parties and establish relationships with and between parties and their interlocutors that will be of primary importance during the resolution process. An uneven engagement of the parties, or signs that peace is a "negotiable" item for the interested party, however, may undermine enforcement efforts and prolong the conflict. Further, in those cases where the international community has identified a party as being at fault, the chimera of neutrality must be lifted. In this case, engagement should accurately reflect the resolve and commitment with which the intervening parties are willing to engage in the enforcement process. Where that resolve and commitment is lacking, peace enforcement operations should not be undertaken. Rather, the key elites of all parties should be politically engaged, morally persuaded, or economically coerced until a cease-fire occurs and peacekeeping operations can be contemplated.

C. Keeping the Peace

While conflict rages between groups, those interested in its resolution normally appeal to other parties, states, or international fora for assistance. The desired assistance may take several forms—military, economic, political, diplomatic, or humanitarian. As the potential providers of such assistance coordinate an appropriate response, unilateral efforts by humanitarian organizations or development agencies, for example, are likely to respond to the crises that flourish on the periphery of the conflict. The next chapter discusses these efforts to assuage the medical emergencies, refugee flows, and other corollary problems associated with violent intergroup conflict in some detail. However, the initial focus of the regional or international response should be containing the violence—keeping the peace where violent conflict has not yet erupted.

Even in those cases where enforcement action is contemplated, immediate efforts to stem the spread of conflict will be important. Employing deterrent measures, similar to the use of U.S./UN monitoring forces on the border between the Yugoslav Republic of Serbia and Montenegro and the Former Yugoslav Republic of Macedonia, may help stem the widening of the area of violent conflict while coordinated intervention efforts are constructed. Coercive measures may also be employed within the area of conflict, should there exist peripheral areas of nonviolent confrontation. However, these efforts are not peace operations, per se; rather, they are redoubled preventative measures directed at containing the spread of violent conflict.[5]

As efforts to limit the conflict—to keep the peace where it does exist—are implemented, those who seek to intervene must make a decision on their willingness and ability to conduct peace enforcement. If there exists neither sufficient resolve nor capacity to do so with decisive force, planning and coordination should focus on the appropriate diplomatic, political, or economic incentives that may induce a cease-fire agreement between the parties. Humanitarian relief efforts may be coordinated outside of the area of conflict or in those areas where deterrence and coercion have been successful.[6] However, these efforts should not take precedence over the greater task of coordinating a concerted effort that is ready immediately to engage in keeping the peace, where and when it is established.

The transition from peace enforcement to peacekeeping must not be viewed as amorphous. It occurs after the formal and demonstrated implementation of a cease-fire, disengagement of partisan forces, and receipt of consent from all parties for the interposition of peacekeeping forces. Absent these critical factors, intervention must be treated as peace enforcement or delayed until such conditions exist. If brought about through enforcement efforts, the transition to peacekeeping should also include the transfer of peace operation responsibility to a neutral party (or from the combat-oriented structure of military forces to police forces).

Upon the completion of enforcement operations, peace enforcers should be separated from the other parties and withdrawn; when practicable, some component may be held in reserve for use should fighting resume. However, separation or removal of enforcement forces, though potentially costly and inconvenient for those conducting the intervention, is important. That is because during the conduct of peace enforcement, these forces were party to the violence and are likely viewed as belligerent by the party that did not consent to the enforcement operation. They may be required to conduct these operations again should fighting resume, and should retain the readiness posture and efficacy of their combat mission orientation.

Additionally, the transition in types and training of forces from combat to constabulary is a key aspect of this transition. Peacekeeping, in its traditional sense, requires a police force. In skills, equipment, and professional orientation, keeping the peace requires persons trained in the maintenance of law and order. Working under the mutual consent and accepted rules of both parties, the peacekeeper provides a neutral law enforcer with the mandate to support the will of those political elites or governmental leaders who are party to the conflict—that is, to maintain peace while diplomacy works to resolve the conflict.

Police and, to a lesser extent, military forces are suited to this task. The use of police forces is preferable due to their training in law enforcement and ingrained appreciation for the restricted use of force. The use of police forces clearly distinguishes the mission of peacekeeping from that of peace enforcement by providing less opportunity for their mission to "creep" toward enforcement should violence resume. In those cases where "muscular peacekeeping" (commonly referred to as "UN Chapter Six-and-a-half") operations are contemplated, the precepts of peace enforcement must apply until there is real peace to be kept. Again, should the political will to enforce peace be lacking, interested parties should acknowledge their inability or unwillingness to impose peace forcibly upon the area of conflict and resist the temptation to straddle the fence between peace enforcement and peacekeeping.

Upon commencement of peacekeeping activities, a stable and peaceful environment will exist for the insertion of humanitarian, medical, developmental, and diplomatic missions. The focus of effort, however, should remain the mitigation of conflict; for the resumption of hostilities will quickly reverse other efforts and endanger those participating in relief-type activities. Mitigating conflict will require the reestablishment of the rule of law and the aggressive maintenance of the terms of the cease-fire agreement.

Peacekeeping must retain, to the greatest extent possible, the air of neutrality. The terms of the cease-fire should include the separation of combatant forces; any attempt to violate that separation should be restrained with impartiality. Access to humanitarian assistance and other services must be closely coordinated to ensure balanced application. Disparities along these lines will exacerbate tensions and undermine the peace agreement. The engagement of political and military elites in the peacekeeping process is essential. They must be part of keeping the peace by exercising restraint over partisan forces and loyalists. Further, they must understand that the termination of the assistance missions will be the first casualty of resumed hostilities. All parties, to include those handling the intervention, must understand that peace-keeping is not possible unless there is peace to be kept.

D. Making Peace

The culmination of conflict mitigation and the shift toward resolution occurs during the peacemaking process. Here the building blocks of peace are selected and arranged in such a manner as to define where the foundation of the resulting state(s) will be laid. The signing of a formal peace treaty signifies only the breaking of ground; the toils and labor of construction lay ahead.

To arrive at the ground breaking, however, the architects of peace must design the structure, gain approval for the plans, locate the construction materials, and, finally, fund the project. This metaphor captures the essence of the peacemaking process. As the level of conflict subsides among the parties they are brought together at the negotiating table to draft a settlement agreement. This agreement will determine the architecture of the new state. In Section 1 it was noted that the resolution of conflict requires a change in the status quo. The dysfunctional structure of the preconflict society and state contributed to the outbreak of violence. To resolve that dysfunction, certain elements of the structure will require change; that change must be negotiated during the peacemaking process. To do so, the diplomatic resources and imagination of intervening parties, the expert technical assistance of development organizations, and the financial resources of international financial institutions must be brought to bear on the problem.

Outside of the negotiating room, the reestablishment of the rule of law is being supervised by peacekeepers. During the peacemaking process, technical assistance teams should facilitate the turnover of routine law enforcement activities to a reconstituted or newly created civilian police force. The visibility of international or neutral party peace forces may be reduced, while law enforcement, judicial, and legislative activities are (re)constituted on the state and local level. Likewise, military forces must be reoriented, disbanded, or combined as appropriate to neutralize the resumption of forceful conflict resolution.

One of the more difficult tasks undertaken during the peacemaking process will be reaching decisions with respect to amnesty, war crimes prosecution, and human rights violations that occurred during the period of violent conflict. The making of peace will require patience, leadership, and the sustained support of intervening parties. Most importantly, however, this phase of the Intervention Cycle marks a significant shift in the focus of effort: peace enforcement may be imposed upon parties to a conflict; peacekeeping requires only passive acceptance. However, the making of peace will require their full cooperation and commitment. Intervening organizations, through their good offices, diplomatic resources, and other means of assistance must assure that all participants to the conflict are engaged in the drafting of the peace agreement—and fully understand the implications of its entry into force.

During the peacemaking effort all parties must be vigilant for signs of reescalating conflict and tensions. Peacekeepers may need to retain a degree of visibility throughout the process and well into resolution; just as peace enforcers were retained on stand-by during the transition from enforcement to peacekeeping. The extent and duration of each peace operation can only be determined by progress on the ground. As such, the process is likely to be filled with twists, turns, setbacks and reversals. However, with the road map of the Intervention Cycle the path of conflict mitigation is clearly marked. Efforts that are not focused on the mitigation of conflict may be gratifying politically or morally; however, they will wind up being costly—and perhaps inconsequential.

Once conflict has been mitigated and a nonviolent environment established, progress on the road to permanent peace can be accelerated by the enfranchising efforts that will be discussed below. Enfranchisement—the bringing together of groups, individuals, and the state into a process of mutual benefit—combines with peacemaking to form the core of conflict resolution.

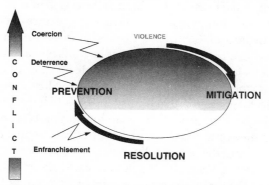

Figure 3. The Intervention Cycle with Prevention Overlay

III. INTERVENING TO RESOLVE CONFLICT

It is unfortunate that the most important, and frequently overlooked, aspect of conflict intervention begins with resolution, or at the stasis of reduced societal tension. This generally occurs at or around the six o'clock position of the Intervention Cycle (Figure 3). At this stage, the need for intervention appears lowest and calm generally prevails. This is also the time at which those who intervened to mitigate violence are rightfully anxious to claim success and withdraw. Ironically, however, this is the point at which international organizations, especially those that bring the expertise and key tools with which civil and political societies are rebuilt, are needed most. Rather than a time of disengagement, this is a time of focused effort toward the enfranchisement of all individuals, groups, and parties to the conflict back into an overarching structure of society—preferably the state.

During the resolution process, the tools of intervention must change. However, the intensity and determination of those who seek to resolve intergroup conflict must persevere if the cycle is to be broken. The firestorm of violent conflict has passed; however, the framework of society, its means of sustenance, and the tools of reconstruction lay among the debris. The surviving state and/or parties to the conflict are normally too weak or too divided to pick up the pieces alone. Reconstruction, development, financial assistance, and, most importantly, continuing support for internal political engagement are vital resources for the resolution process.

Resolution involves more than the cessation of violence; it requires the incremental breakdown of those barriers that impede communication and discourage the peaceful discussion of intergroup grievances. This traditionally entails connecting them to each other through the overarching structure of an intervening body. Resolution requires a considerable degree of participation from all parties to the conflict as well as the good offices of a neutral body that seeks to facilitate their transition from a state in conflict to a state in peace.

The conditions for such participation include a degree of enfranchisement, buying into the process, by those who seek the redress of wrongs or the address of particular grievances that formed the basis of the original conflict. Although resolution begins with the peacemaking process—and usually culminates with the pomp and circumstance of a treaty-signing ceremony— it is not complete until the parties fully commit to the process of peacefully resolving their disputes. The highly publicized Israel-Palestine handshake on the south lawn of the White House in September 1993 symbolized the climax of a peacemaking effort. However, the continued violence and souring of relationships between Israel and the PLO over the following year suggested a failure to complete the resolution process. Resolution failed to occur because the parties to the conflict did not become fully enfranchised in a system of political dialogue that represented the interests of all parties, nor did they continue to progress in the discussion and rectification of the underlying causes of the Israel-Palestine conflict. In short, one or more of the parties remained disenfranchised.

A. The Disenfranchised

Intergroup tension often arises from a lack of shared concerns or values. From the perspective of a state or national structure, the lack of shared concerns or values by subelements within a state or nation can lead to disenfranchisement. That disenfranchisement represents a lack of political, economic, or social stake in the present and future well-being of the state; it is the predominant factor in intergroup conflict within the state. Left untouched, disenfranchisement will undermine the state's foundation.

When individuals or groups of individuals feel enfranchised in a process or system they feel empowered. That empowerment stems from their ability to agree or disagree, vote or abstain, participate or not participate in the leadership and destiny of that system. In some manner, all members feel that they benefit from this enfranchisement. On the traditional level of "nations," this means that individuals feel that they have a voice in the making of national laws and policies and the selection of the nation's leadership. Further, true enfranchisement means that these individuals not only feel empowered, they feel a sense of commitment to the preservation of the system or reference group.

On the other hand, individuals who feel excluded from the political or economic well-being of states normally seek an affiliation with others who share their values or interests. This often means an immediate family, tribe, clan, or village; the extent of the affiliation is constrained by the degree to which the groups remain homogenous with respect to values. In many cases the only values that unite a group of disenfranchised individuals pertain to race, economics, geography, history, or religion. From this devolution of common values—from the state to an interest group—comes a concern for preserving only those things perceived to be of value to the group or capable of increasing the group's power relative to others within the society. That preservation of narrowly defined interests works to the detriment of broader affiliations required for stability within the society and the state.

With any degree of disenfranchisement there will be conflict. That conflict may take the form of political activism, not unlike the American civil rights movement of the late 1950s through the 1960s, or interclass struggles that manifest themselves in civil unrest. Civil unrest can, of course, quickly ignite into mass violence and economically motivated crimes such as looting, carjacking, destruction of property, and robbery—a situation not unlike the riots that occurred in Los Angeles in the spring of 1992. If the extent of disenfranchisement reaches a great enough proportion, that is individuals or groups feel absolutely no stake in the system, there no longer exists a check against the upward spiral of violence. The contemporary economically and politically motivated violence in Chiapas serves as another example of this kind of intergroup conflict escalation on a local level. The application of deterrence measures or force, by the police or the military, serves only to rechannel or temporarily contain the conflict that seethes beneath the surface.

Actions taken to resolve and prevent conflict seek to find ways to maximize the extent to which individuals and groups feel that they have a stake in the system—any system. Through the application of measures that stem the disenfranchisement of groups and individuals, conflict can be most effectively prevented by shoring up the foundation of the state with the support of its citizens. This should be the central thrust of conflict resolution and the early stages of prevention.[7]

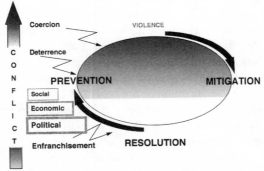

Figure 3a. The Intervention Cycle with Enfranchisement Categories

B. Enfranchising: Politically, Economically, and Socially

The concept of enfranchisement contains three specific elements: political, economic, and social, as depicted in Figure 3a. Each serves a unique and important role in the resolution of conflict. The last element, social enfranchisement, also defines the critical point of transition between resolution and prevention on the Intervention Cycle. Under optimal circumstances, efforts to achieve all three elements of enfranchisement should be undertaken concurrently. However, under real-world conditions where resources are limited and intervention efforts must be prioritized, the order of enfranchisement should be political, economic, and then social. While the full enfranchisement of groups and individuals should be the long-term goal of all states, economic and social enfranchisement will be especially elusive and, perhaps in the latter case, realistically unattainable. Political enfranchisement will be the key to long-term stability and the achievement of a viable and sustainable state structure.

(1) Political Enfranchisement. Political enfranchisement provides individuals or groups a stake in the political system, meaning that there is a perceived value in the preservation of that system because it works to the benefit of its participants. For states that have experienced violent conflict prior to or during the conflict mitigation process, political enfranchisement is of utmost importance for maintaining reduced intergroup tension.[8] Newly formed states, or those in which intergroup cleavages are becoming more apparent due to massive immigration, economic disparities, demographic changes, or localized phenomena need to revisit the issue of political enfranchisement as a fundamental tool for restoring intergroup stability.

The process of resolution provides a smooth transition from peacemaking to this type of enfranchisement due to the political nature of the peacemaking process. In the context of post–cold war conflict, the "victors" and "vanquished" take on less absolute characteristics than one might find in traditional zero-sum warfare scenarios. Negotiation is more prevalent than surrender; thus, the relative degree of success or failure of warring factions is normally reflected in the peace treaty; territorial, political, and/or economic concessions form the core of a negotiated settlement.

In the settlement agreement, however, trouble areas are normally highlighted, not resolved. Parties have not necessarily bought into the settlement when hands shake and the ink dries. Rather, the process of enfranchisement begins when the terms of the agreement are enacted and parties follow through with the routine political engagement of each other and their constituencies. Those who wish to ensure success should work toward the seamless implementation of the settlement agreement along with the development of routinized political engagement among the key elites of each group, and eventually within and among the groups themselves.

The primacy of political enfranchisement is, perhaps, a simple statement of the obvious; for states are political structures. As such, they will cease to exist if the members feel no stake in the preservation of a political system. The leadership of many states that find themselves in the throes of intergroup conflict continue their attempts to preserve political systems or mechanisms that no longer enfranchise their membership. Alternatively, these leaders should focus on the establishment or reinvigoration of those mechanisms that will support the resolution of the conflict.

Some of the mechanisms of polities that can inculcate enfranchisement include:

- legal (or constitution-based) mechanisms for the preservation of individual, minority, indigenous, and cultural rights (such as a bill of rights);

- political frameworks for the protection of religious, cultural, or linguistic heritage and expression (such as the adoption of multiple "official" languages);
- representational governments that include specific provisions for proportionality (such as district or cabinet seat allocations to minority parties); and
- judicial and structural checks on majority power.

Support for the creation or restoration of these mechanisms must be part of the conflict intervention plan adopted by states or organizations that seek to facilitate the resolution process.

Note that when these mechanisms are incorporated and political participation is afforded to all members of the polity on an equal basis, conflict will not magically disappear. Individuals and groups will continue to struggle for relative power or for the prevalence of their views. This point should not dissuade continued engagement, nor—as may be the case with UN intervention in Somalia—should intervening organizations unknowingly support or undermine a particular group, party, or faction. Long-term success will be achieved to the extent that these struggles are constrained within the developing negotiation structure.

In other words, preserving the political system must be made of some, even if not equal, benefit to all major participants. Alternatives, while possible, must be made less attractive to the broadest section of the populace. To the extent that this broad section of the population includes all extant forms of political and other minorities, as well as other self-defining entities, conflict will be minimized. And to the extent that political enfranchisement can be maximized, the more successfully states will avoid the occurrence or recurrence of the type of violent conflict that specifically seeks to destroy the state's structure.

Any discussion of political enfranchisement is, of course, heavily weighted toward democracy-based models. Despite the number of recent studies on the effect of democratization on the stability of lesser-developed and newly emergent states, the view of democratization in itself as a destabilizing force is questionable. Rather, it is the transition and consolidation stages of democracy that lend themselves to a degree of instability. The root cause of that instability is the failure of nascent democratic systems to politically enfranchise its citizens.[9] Further, the democracy-based model most accurately reflects the dynamics of multiethnic or multicultural group states.

Traditional authoritarian regimes may also provide a degree of political enfranchisement that stems from individual perceptions of having a political stake in the ruling regime. Those regimes often serve as guarantors of stability, protection, status, or power for a relatively homogeneous social structure that feels internally and/or externally threatened. These regimes often appear stable and politically enfranchised, even to the extent that authoritarian preferences appear among citizens. However, as the ruthless (and unobserved) repression of minority groups, political activists, and other "threats" to the authoritative status quo becomes less feasible, the pool of disenfranchised grows to proportions that will eventually foment intergroup conflict and confrontation. Examples of this process include Khrushchev's Soviet Union, Pinochet's Chile, Tito's Yugoslavia, and, perhaps, contemporary China.

As new democracies form in the aftermath of authoritarian demise, political secession, or violent division, their leaders and international supporters must work vigorously to employ mechanisms that will assure individuals and groups a stake in the political future of the state. There must be a sense that each individual and group has the ability to participate in a system that works at least partially to their benefit, even if the results are not immediately tangible. It is the participation itself that is key; the power of newfound political expression must not be underestimated.

Finally, in the long-term view, political expression must manifest itself in the preservation of those values relevant to the individuals or groups concerned. Thus, there is no ideological weight attached to types of political systems that may be adopted by various cultures. One may be able to develop, for example, an argument for various shades of autocratic or nonsecular polities or cite a range of democracy-based formulae that work to the benefit of their constituents. For this discussion of political enfranchisement, the method of selecting political leadership is less important than retaining the consensus of the ruled. That consent will only be retained to the extent that the political structure preserves those ideas, expressions, and liberties deemed valuable by the participants. And to the extent that the values of a subsection of individuals are not protected, there will be conflict within the state. Accordingly, to the extent that a polity maximizes political enfranchisement, the destabilizing force of intergroup conflict can be minimized.

The discussion turns now to the next level of enfranchisement—economic—a much more complex and elusive element of conflict resolution.

(2) Economic Enfranchisement. Economic enfranchisement follows political because of its prominent, albeit secondary, importance. Political enfranchisement appears to be a sufficient condition for long–term stability within a state, which does not seem to be true of economic enfranchisement. For, lacking political credibility with its members, a state structure will generally fail, but lacking economic credibility, it will be fractious, even if some states survive. Thus, to the degree that individuals or groups of individuals feel that

they have a role in both the political and economic mainstream of a state—
that is the state ensures access to the "common wealth," economic class
cleavages appear soluble, and opportunities for economic mobility are present—conflict will remain at manageable levels.

Economic enfranchisement should not be seen as a panacea. It can neither
be expected to abolish the extremes of poverty and affluence, nor to offset
structural inequities such as land distribution. Rather, it strives to provide all
members of the society the ability to be both upwardly and downwardly
mobile according to employment opportunities, market forces, and personal
initiative. This is neither a new concept nor one unknown to political leaders
of several postmodern states.

State leaders in the post-Westphalian era have understood the importance
of economic enfranchisement on the level of state-to-state relations. In this
century, the European Coal and Steel Community, the Marshall Plan, and the
General Agreement on Tariffs and Trade stand as continental, hemispheric,
and global examples of this recognition. On a substate level economic
enfranchisement is equally important. It forms the basis of the relationship
between individuals and the state as a financial structure and guarantor of
economic relevance.

The development of communism was Marx's attempt to limit the degree of
disenfranchisement experienced by those individuals who did not share in the
distribution of wealth during the industrial revolution. Marxism attempted to
eliminate the disparities of individual access to the means of economic production and the distribution of wealth. Keynesian economics sought to limit the
degree of postwar disenfranchisement via government economic and monetary
policies that stimulate employment. Though utilized by vastly different political systems, both of these ideologies recognized the importance of some form
of individual economic relevance to the preservation of a stable polity.

The term economic enfranchisement transcends the notion of day-to-day
participation in the financial life of a state economy. It is a degree of empowerment that changes the individual-state relationship from ward-provider to
partnership. It allows individuals the ability to seek a direct correlation
between personal input and economic output in the form of goods, services,
and earnings. It affects every facet of existence from employment, food, shelter, clothing, transportation, education, and medicine to raising our children.

Earlier, the notion of an individual stake in the economic well-being of the
state was described as having access to the economic mainstream as well as the
ability to be both upwardly and downwardly mobile according to employment opportunities, market forces, and personal initiative. What is meant by
this rather provocative statement is that the economic system of the state

affords an opportunity for access to all members of the state without regard to ethnicity, religion, cultural heritage, or other constraints on participation. The ability to succeed or fail comes equally to all. This is, of course, good in theory but nearly impossible to achieve.

Employment opportunities are based upon a wide range of factors: education, communications skills, experience, geographic location, and market forces, to name a few. Most of these determinants are related to individual skills; thus, not all members of a state will be able (or wish) to compete on an even basis for all employment opportunities. The key, however, is that no qualified members of the state are specifically excluded from the job market. This means that anyone able to gain and hold employment is entitled to the requisite compensation and can access those things afforded by their resultant economic status. Regardless of race, gender, religion, or ethnicity, the fruits of labor are legal tender that provide access to housing, nutrition, medical care, education, financial services, and all goods and services available in the market. But what of those who lack employment or are underemployed?

The test of the system revolves around the role of the state, specifically in its provision of access to its economic lifeblood for the poor or disadvantaged. Here, the burden upon the state is to provide an opportunity—for all those who wish to be enfranchised—to improve their lot. In order to play this role, however, the state requires the forbearance of taxpayers to provide or underwrite services for those who are unable to do so. The resultant system of social welfare (which might appear to have nothing to do with economic enfranchisement) is thus held hostage to the wishes of the politically enfranchised members of the state.

This is one of the reasons that economic enfranchisement was described as both elusive and secondary to political enfranchisement. It relies upon forces within the state structure that cannot be established without a solid foundation of intergroup tolerance and political accommodation. Without the political structure, tolerance, and accommodation that result from efforts to achieve political enfranchisement, these economic goals are nearly impossible to achieve. Not only the state, but those within it, must participate in the full economic enfranchisement of the membership.

Where sufficient political support is lacking, internal and external financial institutions have some ability to infuse ready capital for short-term access. However, one must not confuse simple access with enfranchisement. *Access* merely implies an ability to take short-term advantage of goods or services available in the market; *enfranchisement* implies an ability to participate in the shaping of the economy—taking advantage of its successes and suffering through its failures.

On the other hand, where the only structural barrier to financial enfranchisement is the lack of capital, international financial institutions, regional development banks, private lending institutions, and volunteer organizations that specialize in microloans, business education, and other development tools may be employed with a significant degree of effectiveness.

In the final analysis, economic enfranchisement is an essential successor to political enfranchisement. It is not, however, automatic. Egalitarian policies are required across the spectrum of goods and services offered by both the state and the private sector. Mechanisms that assure these policies can only be put into place by political systems that are broadly representative. These are polities that strive to afford equal protection and equal opportunities to all members of the state. Further, once these policies are in place, economic enfranchisement requires placing individuals into the system via employment and the provision of those services that enable full workforce participation, such as education, access to health care, housing, and nutrition.

In a free market of goods, services, labor, and access to capital, the playing field will not, of course, be level. Some will prosper and others will not; economic stratification is an inevitable by-product. Economic-based conflict will be minimized, however, to the extent that this by-product is self-selective, in other words, those in lower stratum will be able to identify and avail themselves of mechanisms through which their own efforts can improve their status.

The bar has been set quite high on this economic "high hurdle"; in fact, there are few states that can meet these ideals. However, to the extent that these principles are embodied, conflict will be minimized. And to the extent that states fail to scrutinize continually their own efforts to eliminate political and economic inequities there will be conflict. The intensity and scope of that conflict depends on the degree to which our third and final franchise, social, creates a consensus for the preservation of the state structure.

(3) Social Enfranchisement. This last form of enfranchisement marks the transition between resolving intergroup conflict and prevention. Successful conflict resolution—which breaks the cycle of recurrent intergroup conflict— allows the state to reach a point of stability somewhere between the seven and nine o'clock positions on the Intervention Cycle. That is because political and economic disparities are never fully eliminated in even the most egalitarian systems. However, the addition of this third element, social enfranchisement, provides a self-checking mechanism within the polity that encourages peaceful resolution of grievances and a general consensus to stem—or prevent—violent conflict before it causes systemic collapse.

Intergroup conflict can be attenuated to the extent that the members of society share a common social identity. This common social identity is most difficult to achieve in multiethnic or multireligious group states—especially in those states whose population includes indigenous groups who became members of a state structure only by way of postcolonial administrative incorporation, annexation, or military conquest. However, even in those cases where full political and economic enfranchisement is difficult in the near term, the inculcation of a common, or state, identity can be of stabilizing value.

Traditional sociology holds that members of various groups will assimilate over time into the general population of a political entity. Through that process of assimilation, group identity becomes of lesser importance to individuals than their identity as part of a whole or collective society.[10] Regardless of the means by which traditional affiliations are abandoned or subjugated, for long-term stability it is essential that new and durable affiliations be formed between a state and the individuals that it serves. The state's success will depend on the degree to which individual allegiance will encourage support for the peaceful resolution of intergroup conflict and preservation of the state structure. For this reason social enfranchisement is the final step in the resolution of conflict and the first step toward prevention.

Social enfranchisement is tertiary to political and economic enfranchisement because it depends upon these factors for its foundation. For this type of enfranchisement to occur on the state level, there must exist a set of values and interests shared by all members of the society that transcend ethnicity, religion and the like. Those values were earlier described as political and economic stakes; when fully embraced by individuals, these stakes become of greater importance than those prescribed via ethnicity, religion, or any other discriminating factor.

This final level of enfranchisement is the most difficult to achieve; in some cases it is, perhaps, impossible to realize. It requires the state to enmesh its individual members so fully that cohesive bonds of group identity become secondary to a collective self-affiliation with the state.[11] To the extent that individuals can be co-opted into the preservation of a collective identity—one that approaches the confluence of both "nation" and state—the structure of the state can be consolidated and conflict resolved.

C. Resolution

The resolution phase of the Intervention Cycle begins with efforts at peacemaking and ends with enfranchisement; it is a formidable process with a wide array of discrete tasks. Those who wish to intervene during this crucial phase must clearly understand the dynamics of the societal relationships that are being nurtured: relationships between individuals, groups, the state, and each other.

Unlike the mitigation process, resolution cannot be imposed upon parties to conflict. Intervening mechanisms must compel the full and voluntary participation of all parties; the relative advantage of continued negotiation and dialogue must exceed any benefit of continued violence or belligerence. The selection of such mechanisms, and the allotment of sufficient time and resources to gain the willing participation of all parties, requires careful analysis and patience. No set formula can meet the requirements of varied cultural, geographic, and situational needs. Rather, an understanding of the resolution process and its components must be applied to ensure a sustained, coherent effort across the spectrum of diplomatic, political, economic, and social remedies. Recent experiences in Somalia and Bosnia, for example, underscore the drain on political, economic, and military capital that accompanies the transition from conflict mitigation to resolution, as well as the need for a conceptual understanding of both the sequence and timing of various forms of intervention effort.

The resolution process attempts to defuse the sources of intergroup conflict within the society by first applying the diplomatic and moral suasion of neutral, international fora in order to bring the parties together in a peaceful dialogue. As the parties to the conflict realize the relative advantages of their participation in this process—treaties, restoration of commerce, infrastructure repair, and monetary benefits—the scope of the political negotiations can expand in a manner that directly correlates the extension of benefits to their willingness to participate in compromise and conciliation. The seeds of true political enfranchisement are often overlooked during the negotiation process; as a result, intervening parties are often frustrated by the failure of their efforts to bear fruit.

For example, an agreement among the political elites of Israel and Palestine should not only tangibly benefit West Bank and Gaza Palestinians and Jewish settlers, it should lead to an expanded scope of political dialogue. Such a dialogue must include all parties to the conflict: the Palestine Liberation Organization (PLO), Islamic Resistance Movement (HAMAS) and other major Palestinian/Islamic organizations on one side, and the Labor, Likud, and other Israeli parties on the other in order to sow the seeds of political enfranchisement. The failure to link peacemaking with political enfranchisement will result in a breakdown of the resolution process and stymie efforts to cultivate the broad and inclusive dialogue required to resolve the underlying causes of the intergroup conflict.

Resolution—peacemaking and enfranchisement—is what was once referred to as successful *nation building*. Despite the term's fall from favor, nation building is an important aspect of resolving intergroup conflict. The focus of resolution is the breakdown of impediments to intergroup cooperation and the reconstruction of infrastructures that facilitate political and economic empowerment at the grassroots level. The attempt to closely correlate nations with states—social enfranchisement—is the crowning achievement of nation building when broad and diverse segments of the population are brought together through shared values of political and economic opportunity and preservation of the state.

IV. INTERVENING TO PREVENT CONFLICT

In this section, the preventative application of enfranchisement, deterrence, and coercion will be discussed as they relate to spiraling conflict among and between groups and the state.

Prevention employs those mechanisms that reduce tension between parties in such a way as to preempt violence. It lies on the left side of our Intervention Cycle and, metaphorically speaking, on the back burner of world attention. Successful prevention is anticlimactic: there is no crisis worthy of global fixation when prevention has been successful, nor are the warning signs of impending violence easily identifiable from a great distance. In short, successful prevention fails the "CNN test"; it will rarely become a headline on the evening news.

Yet, the warning signs of rising intergroup conflict are strikingly clear to those who are on the scene or paying close attention. As efforts to enfranchise groups and individuals politically or economically ebb and flow in degree of success, states often overlook key indicators of impending failure. One of the most common, and important, indicators of the failure to enfranchise the state's membership is the (re)emergence of fractious groups—many of whom will seek to play their "ethnicity card."

Other warning signs of intergroup conflict are more obvious: racially motivated crimes, hate crimes, mass protests, class actions. As the level of conflict in society increases, governments are compelled to do things such as crack down on crime, get tougher with criminals, increase police presence, and build more prisons. These activities generally fall in the category of "deterrence" (Figure 3). External interventions, when appropriate, often employ monitoring activities that establish the watchful eye of an external party that hopes to dissuade violent acts via moral suasion and symbolic presence.

When deterrent measures fail and states are no longer able to deter intergroup violence, they resort to coercion, or forceful measures such as martial law, border closing, or militia patrols, with the hope of reducing crime and violence. International intervention is often applied in the form of coercive political or economic sanctions in those cases where the government or key state officials are the perpetrators of violent conflict or targeted persecution. These efforts are seldom effective, however, because they either fail to reduce the level of violence, exacerbate intergroup tensions, target the symptom of violence without addressing the underlying disenfranchisement, or are applied so late that violence cannot be abated except through the application of a superior violent force, or peace enforcement.

A. The Disenfranchised: Playing The Ethnicity Card

When individuals and groups feel isolated from the state's political, economic, or social activity, or life has dealt them a cruel hand of cards, they will seek some other form of affiliation. They often select ethnicity; thus the prevalence of conflicts described as ethnic in nature.

Playing the ethnicity card frequently has more to do with individuals' desire to belong to a group than with any particular racial or cultural dimension of enfranchisement. Viewed in this light, the chaotic world of ethnic conflict appears somewhat ordered. For, it is not in our nature to self-categorize neatly or exclusively; group affiliations often change as individual or collective circumstances (such as cultural, geographic, political, or economic) evolve. Further, identification with one group does not preclude affiliation with other racial, cultural, political, economic, or geographic groups. Human nature compels us to belong to at least one of these groups.

The lowest common denominator is often ethnicity, a self-selected identity of rather broad parameters, some of which may include physical characteristics, cultural or religious traditions, geographic proximity, social class, and language or blood line. Where this work has focused on the generic concept of a group, other authors have sought a more precise description of shared identities by utilizing, for example, the term "communal groups."[12] For this discussion, however, it is more important to understand *why* individuals often feel compelled to emphasize a group or ethnic identity, rather than reaching a definitive answer to the *how* or *what* of identity.

Self-identification serves as a convenient reference point for group affiliation and a barometer of social cohesion. Traditionally, self-identification coincided with a "nationality" that identified some aspects of geographic, cultural, and linguistic affiliation. Most importantly, it identified an allegiance—or a belonging—to some sovereign or overarching entity that represented the interests of its members. The fact that this allegiance is channeled away from the state should be cause for concern in societies that seek stability.

For example, support for the continued self-identification with Hutu or Tutsi tribal heritage in Rwanda accurately identified language, culture, and genealogy, yet, precluded the development of broader affiliations with the states of Burundi, Rwanda, or Zaire. In retrospect, this structurally supported delimitation of tribal affiliation enforced a tradition of political, economic, and social disenfranchisement that had disastrous—even if unintended—results. Lacking other cards with which to influence the course of political events in Rwanda, both Hutu militia and Tutsi soldiers used their common denominator of tribal group as a mobilizing force to both exploit and disrupt the political status quo.

The recent course of global upheaval illustrates the drawing power of the ethnicity card. Intergroup conflict in its many current manifestations—be they ethnic, religious, or otherwise—appears to have trumped all other forms of warfare. State or governmental affiliations alone do not fully identify the rallying causes of modern conflict. In terms of prevention, this creates a troubling paradox: this conflict results from the collapse of broader affiliations between groups of people and their state structures; however, the resolution of these conflicts is dependent upon the very state structures that have ceased to hold relevance to these groups.

This grim reality underscores the importance of state efforts to prevent disenfranchisement before conflict rises to the point of violent outbreak and the governmental collapse. Social enfranchisement provides the bridge between resolution and prevention by narrowing the gap between nation and state. To the extent that this gap can be eliminated, and a nation-state formed, conflict can be prevented.

B. Reconsidering the Nation-State

As with the term "ethnic," "nation" is open to broad variations of interpretation. We know, however, that a nation cannot be stable as a collection of groups or individuals without a common identity. Further, nationhood is a participatory and psychological phenomena: it has no prerequisite physical, religious, linguistic, or genealogical qualities for membership. Instead, members of a nation make a personal choice to become part of its collective identity. Sometimes the socioeconomic and personal benefits of embracing or eschewing a particular nationality are so overwhelming that the choice is automatic. It remains, however, a choice.

Thus, nationhood is by and large a psychological intangible. Its physical manifestations may include outward symbols such as flags and anthems; or its citizens may celebrate a shared legend through national shrines, heroes, traditions, and holidays. Usually nations have a common language among their members, and often share a common religion or set of spiritual principles. Yet, beyond these signs of allegiance, there are few tangibles that uniquely determine national status.

Note that those things normally associated with states—common governments, leaders, constitutional structures, monetary system, and so forth, have been carefully avoided. This omission is intended to underscore that the tools of government and administration are not the tools of nationality. A concrete example of this separation may be found in the European Union's Maastricht Treaty as originally conceived. The framers clearly sought European political and economic unity; however, that unity sought to preserve the distinctive nationalities of the member states. Had Maastricht been implemented to its fullest extent, the structures of statehood, the control of monetary instruments, and the political and economic enfranchisement of Europeans would still have been accomplished without the creation of a European nation.[13]

The cohesive force of nationality has long been viewed as a positive force in the world. However, recent works on the emergence of a rising tendency toward negative forms of nationalism (or as Kaplan writes, tribalism[14]) have underscored the centrifugal power of group identities in the post–cold war world. These forces are not new; rather, we are challenged by the destruction of the East-West bloc paradigm that provided an artificial framework with which to constrain these disintegrating forces. Lacking that structure, our current challenge is the identification of methods by which to canalize the power of group or national identity and direct it toward a positive development. This is the challenge for state structures that seek to remain intact as they enter the twenty-first century.[15]

In selecting focal points for the prevention of intergroup conflict, emphasis should be redirected away from the neo-Wilsonian concept of group-based self-determination, or ethnic nationalism. Ethnic nationalism is the type of nationalism that results from the fragmentation of the social structure of a state rather than the cohesive bond of enfranchisement. Lacking a check against its divisive force, however, nationalism is a perpetually self-bifurcating phenomenon that continues indefinitely. Some mechanism must emerge to fulfill the political and economic needs of the nation, or its less enfranchised members will seek a new common denominator of identification.

The concept of nation-state should be reconsidered in the context of enfranchisement-based nationality (as opposed to ethnic-based nationality). A state that is unable to provide for the political and economic needs of its citizens is nonsustainable and short-lived. Thus, the check against the divisive forces of group identity is the creation of an enfranchisement-based collective identity that provides each member with the durable qualities of political and economic stakes in the system.

Unfortunately, many of the mechanisms currently employed by the international community to prevent intergroup conflict inadvertently sustain them. For example, some international fora may have provided premature political recognition to national elements in the rush to post-Soviet independence; likewise, other organizations have provided economic assistance to substate elements, extending them a sense legitimacy that may have stymied efforts to reconcile the conflict within the state.

Rather than empowering splinter groups by immediately entering into direct negotiation with individual leaders, international organizations should seek to intervene by supplying the state structure with the tools required to provide political and economic enfranchisement to its substate elements. Where the state structure does not exist or is incapable of such action, all competing faction leaders must be brought into and engaged in dialogue with the intervening party.[16]

In concert with the principle of reenfranchisement, intervening parties and organizations must underscore the benefit of utilizing and recognizing the state's structure or an inclusive resolution forum as the central channel through which political and economic remedies may be obtained. Bolstering these structures will strengthen or establish the funnel through which aid, relief, and other forms of assistance can be evenly distributed. Such support will also institutionalize the practice of political negotiation and compromise as a paradigm for future conflict resolution and government activity.

Without the ability to enfranchise individuals and groups under a common structure, there are few checks against the upward spiral of conflict that can ultimately consume society and the state. Those who lack political and economic stakes in the system will seek some other form of social affiliation through which they can fulfill their need for affinity. The paradox is that the resultant identity—the *ethnic* nation, for example—will remain durable only to the extent that it provides political and economic enfranchisement. Without these it, too, will disintegrate. Thus, only when all three factors, political, economic, and social, are combined under one structure will the society reach a point of stability and be able to prevent conflict. The resultant stable state resembles—not surprisingly—a nation-state. The difference, however, is that this nation-state is predicated upon a psychological tie to a system of political, economic, and social benefit for its citizens, rather than an ethnic-based relationship of the lowest common denominator.[17] In the long term, this means that the prevention of intergroup conflict requires maximizing political and economic enfranchisement under the imprimatur of a common, socially cohesive identity. That socially cohesive identity strives toward the attainment of a collective *state* nationality under which the mechanisms of the state become the mechanisms of the nation.

C. Deterring Intergroup Conflict

The lofty goals of enfranchisement can appear daunting, if not unrealistic, in the conflict-torn real world. Yet the alternative, a perpetually self-dividing set of ethnic, tribal or religious entities, is wholly unattractive and dangerously volatile.

As the global consensus of state foreign policy priorities shifts away from strengthening spheres of influence to creating market opportunities, stable state structures become increasingly important. Global treaties between these states, even if domestically controversial, are vital to the interests of industrialized and developing nations. Regional instability, even in those areas once deemed remote, exacts human, political, and economic tolls across the globe. And recent experience demonstrates to the global community that resolving conflict *after* it erupts is costly, difficult and resource-intensive. Thus, the prevention of conflict appears to be an increasingly appealing, if not urgent, option.

While the process of enfranchisement seeks long-term solutions to conflict, short-term deterrents to violence must be sought in order to preserve the forward momentum. Law enforcement is the most common form of maintaining order within society. The concept of law exceeds the institution of police and includes legislative and judicial mechanisms as checks and balances to the process of law-giving and enforcement. When laws are seen as legitimate—that is, the result of a politically enfranchising process—they serve as a tremendous deterrent to the use of violence in the resolution of conflict.

International laws can be instrumental in the resolution of conflict between states. However, they are recognized as legitimate only to the extent that states feel enfranchised in the process of international law making. Those states participating in setting the rules feel the greatest sense of responsibility to follow them and to compel others to do likewise. Those who feel the rule-making process has not considered their interests feel little or no compulsion to follow them. This is also true on the level of societies. Those who feel a part of the rule-making process (even if not on the prevailing side of the discourse) will look upon the outcome of law making as legitimate.

But what of self-interests? This concept is best understood when discussed on the international level. The second-order dynamic of self-interest and risk/gain, two important issues with respect to deterrence, is most often discussed in the state-to-state environment. Although equally valid on the level of social (or group-to-group) interaction, the interplay between the rule of law and self-interest is most familiar when discussed within the foreign policy context of national interest.

Through the prism of national interests, most states agree to abide by those laws that are not offensive to their own pursuits up to a certain threshold. Beyond that threshold (for example, those dubbed "vital" interests) the state feels no sense of political or moral compunction to abide by the rules, laws, or opinions of international bodies, even those in which they participate, because the prospective gain of unilateral interest outweighs the real or perceived risk of noncompliance. This concept of voluntary compliance with international law is generally accepted on a universal scale with regard to external matters. However, few states would agree to accept the terms of an international law within their own domestic confines.

The deterrent effect of law within society goes only as far as the vital interests of constituent groups are protected and/or the risk of violation is greater than the gain of noncompliance. In other words, law will deter only those who feel that they have a stake in the maintenance of law and order. Moreover, to the extent that violating the law for individual gain is not counterbalanced by a significant risk of punishment, those who have little or no stake in upholding the law will choose the path of personal gain. This leaves those who wish to intervene for the purpose of deterring violence within societies two primary alternatives: (1) the use of law enforcement to deter violence among those who have a stake in preserving the system of law/the state (the enfranchised); or (2) the use or threatened use of force against those who have no stake in preserving the status of law/the state.

The implications of these alternatives are far reaching. First, it follows that the tools of deterrence must be selected based upon the degree of enfranchisement within the society or, in the case of states, the international community. The less a state has been able to enfranchise groups and individuals, the more draconian the means of deterring intergroup conflict and violence tend to be. Second, deterrent measures are generally effective only to the degree that the risk of noncompliance exceeds potential gain.

Those who wish to intervene to deter intergroup conflict must therefore assess the degree of legitimacy of the deterrent measure as regarded by those being deterred. Police officers in many urban areas are finding that they have little or no deterrent value among those for whom there is neither respect for their authority nor fear of the likely punishment. Similarly, UN observation forces are harassed, fired upon, and ignored in areas in which the parties to conflict neither recognize the UN's legitimacy in representing their interests nor fear the consequences of such harassment. It follows, then, that the deterrence value of police officers walking the beat or UN observers roving the countryside is limited to those areas in which the society shares the value of law and order or has interests in the realm of international community membership.

Likewise, the penalties of continued conflict must outweigh the potential gain. For example, the loss of voting rights, loss of revenues or finance, or other restrictions on personal or group freedoms must counterbalance the potential gains of fomenting violent unrest, assaults, crime, and the like. This, however, underscores the paradox of deterrence: as intergroup conflict increases, the need for applying deterrent measures increases. Yet, these deterrent measures lead to further alienation and erosion of intergroup cohesion by punishing the disenfranchised. Thus, deterrent measures alone are ineffective at reducing intergroup conflict. They must be applied in conjunction with redoubled efforts at political and economic enfranchisement.

This point is often lost upon those called upon to deter conflict at home and abroad. In the United States, for example, some initially sought to add 100,000 more police officers without implementing complementary programs that would work to recapture those disenfranchised who resorted to violence. Likewise, in Northern Ireland, British soldiers were called upon for decades to deter violence between Protestant and Catholic parties for whom no political forum existed, nor incentives created to promote nonviolent alternatives. Abroad, as political factions are isolated, marginalized, or otherwise removed from a UN resolution process, UN monitors often stand by powerless and are fired upon at will by the perpetrators of political violence.

Deterrence is placed on the Intervention Cycle at the same level of conflict as peacekeeping, which in an earlier discussion was described as a function requiring the consent of all parties. Similarly, deterrence requires that the parties to a conflict share at least some interest in preserving law and order, if not the current structure of the state. It requires some degree of enfranchisement to be effective before, during, and after its implementation. Deterrence must also compel compliance by making the consequences of violent behavior less attractive than the short-term political, economic, or social gains of conflictual activity. This is, however, a slippery slope. The power to compel, when utilized, must be followed up with efforts to reenfranchise. Otherwise, the gap between those who have a political or economic stake in enforcing the laws of society and those who do so only in response to deterrent measures will widen. Once that gap widens too greatly, the state or the international community will be forced to implement coercive measures that, even if effective in preventing violent conflict, will adversely affect all parties, guilty and innocent.

D. Resorting to Coercion

As intergroup conflict mounts and deterrent measures fail, the intervention of last resort is coercion. As such, it is placed near the apex of conflict on the Intervention Cycle. The forceful measures of coercion seek to drive up the cost of violent acts and modify the behavior of society in such a manner that regular deterrence can again be effective. Coercive measures may be targeted against specific, or elite, members of fractious groups; alternatively, coercive measures may be applied across the board. Through mechanisms such as the United Nations Security Council (UNSC) or Regional Security Organizations, the international community may see fit to apply targeted or general coercive measures such as embargoes, travel restrictions, or financial levies; internally, states often resort to extralegal or emergency measures.

When considering this measure of last resort, states and international organizations must have a clear understanding of the targeted group, targeted behavior, desired effect, and condition for removal of the selected method of coercion. Much like the use of armed force, coercion is a blunt instrument that cannot be wielded without some collateral damage. Therefore, it is a measure that should neither be undertaken wantonly, nor with the impression that coercive measures will adversely affect only those whose behavior they seek to modify.

Because coercive measures seek forcibly to modify behavior or restrict an individual or group's freedom, they run afoul of normal constitutional or legal standards of state or international behavior. As such, they require special and deliberate consideration by those who seek their implementation. The emerging norm of international behavior for the application of coercive measures such as sanctions, embargoes or travel/immigration restrictions is the use of the UN, regional organizations such as the Organization for Security and Cooperation in Europe (OSCE), EU, or the International Court of Justice as legitimizing sources of international opinion and judicial oversight. Measures within states that do not involve the implementation of constitutional emergency powers often require the dissolution of legislatures or the declaration of extraconstitutional measures such as a "state of emergency," or martial law. These actions, unless carefully deliberated and implemented with absolute clarity of purpose, will be more inflammatory than preventative. With this caution in mind, some guidelines for the use of coercion are essential. These include:

Target Group. Coercive measures should target the individual or groups whose behavior must be modified in order to reduce the level of conflict or prevent the outbreak of violence. As such, a clear determination of the target group's vulnerability to coercive measures must be made. For example, restrictions on the purchase, sale, or transfer of necessary items, such as fuel and energy products, may be ineffectual if the target group either has (a) no real dependence on these commodities for its existence; (b) sufficient supplies to ration resources for extended periods; and/or (c) sufficient funds to obtain fuel from alternative sources at unlimited cost. Moreover, restrictions that are ineffectual on the target group are likely to be very effective on some unintended segment of the population, either the enfranchised upon whom the state relies for continued popular support, or those who have neither excess supplies nor sufficient capital to leverage illicit supply sources. Further, even if the selected coercive measure is successful in adversely affecting the target group, those responsible for implementation must consider the collateral damage to other groups within the society.

Targeted Behavior. The use of coercive measures to target the modification of a particular behavior is germane to preventing the outbreak of violence. The most obvious danger of this approach may be an increase in the level of conflict; this, in some cases, is unavoidable. However, the associated risk of increased conflict is counterbalanced by the effective suppression of the egregious behavior. For example, stopping human rights abuses from being committed may warrant the arrest or disarmament of partisan police or paramilitary forces. However, if the incarceration of those forces is abusive, or allows their opponents to begin acts of retribution, the targeted behavior will not have been prevented, but rather shifted from one group to another. Thus, the behavior targeted by coercive measures must be eliminated across the board.

Desired Effect. Often those faced with mounting conflict and the threat of violent outbreak will grasp for coercive measures without a clear understanding of the desired effect. In other words, they fail to answer the question, "what is the effect of coercion on the target group once the targeted behavior is modified?" For example, on the international level, sanctions are imposed upon a country in order to isolate its ruling elite from interaction with the community of nations and to generate dissatisfaction within the general public. Their aim is to effect a change in policy, or to pressure the resignation or departure of the ruling elite. This is a tall order, but, not unfamiliar to the post–cold war world.

One must carefully consider the effect of these sanctions beyond the cessation of uranium enrichment or chemical weapons production, for example, especially if the targeted group is the ruling elite and the targeted behavior is belligerence or the development of weapons of mass destruction. For, if in the process of behavior modification, the target group becomes more radical, polarized, belligerent, or popular, the net effect of the sanctions may actually be increased conflict and a greater propensity for violence. The risk of achieving something other than the desired effect of coercive measures cannot be eliminated. However, measures should be selected on the basis of their ability to limit that risk, and a plan should be developed for dealing with such a contingency.

Condition for Removal. Finally, those who choose to implement coercive measures must clearly identify conditions for removal. Preferably these conditions will be enumerated at the outset of coercive action in order to present real incentives for behavior modification. In all cases, those who contemplate the use of force, even if coercive and nonphysical, must have a clear understanding of when the force has achieved the desired result among the target group. For, if the incentives for compliance have been removed, the continued and excessive use of coercion can lead not only to increased intergroup conflict, but to the resumption of the targeted behavior.

Inherent to all of these guidelines for the use of coercion is the precept that these measures are taken as a last resort and that they are limited in scope and duration. The need to resort to coercion indicates that the degree of disenfranchisement within the society has risen beyond the point at which deterrent measures can be effectively employed. In other words, where the social fabric is already badly torn further pressure may cause irreparable damage. To the extent that this irreparable injury can be limited to the target group, total disenfranchisement can be avoided and simple deterrence will allow redoubled efforts to knit society back together. When coercive measures lead to total disenfranchisement, there is no internal check to violent upheaval and the state, in its current manifestation, will cease to exist.

The Intervention Cycle graphically depicts what occurs when prevention fails. An unbroken cycle leads to the renewed outbreak of violence and the requirement to consider renewed efforts at mitigation. During mitigation, the human, political, and economic price of intervention swells to staggering proportions. Here, those who were once resolved to intervene for the cause of humanity and justice must take a deep breath and reconsider their individual and collective abilities.

V. INTERVENING WITH A CONCEPTUAL FRAMEWORK

This section returns to the Intervention Cycle to discuss its utility as a conceptual framework for conflict intervention. The cycle depicted in Figure 4 identifies the full range of interventionist missions—peace operations, enfranchisement, deterrence, and coercion—and correlates them with their functional nature as mitigative, resolutionary, and preventative steps of conflict intervention.

Those parties interested in intervening—preventing intergroup conflict or mitigating and resolving conflict that has turned violent—must enter into this cycle with a clear vision of what they wish to achieve, what stage of the cycle they wish to affect, and which mechanisms are appropriate. Quite often, military forces are committed to a situation that calls for peace enforcement or peacekeeping; however, once the level of violence has subsided, the mechanisms suited to resolution are often not put into play. Likewise, economic assistance is often applied to an area of minor instability with the hopes of achieving "development" absent the enfranchisement of the major groups of individuals who do, or will, form the core of intergroup conflict.

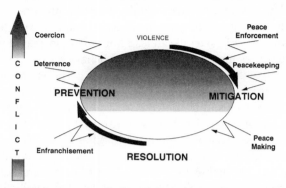

Figure 4. The Intervention Cycle with Prevention and Mitigation Overlays

The Intervention Cycle provides a conceptual template around which to place tasks, mechanisms, and organizations in order to differentiate their focus of effort and efficacy. To illustrate this utility, consider the following example: In response to a hypothetical conflict in southern Europe, NATO forces, acting under the authority of a UN Chapter VII mandate, intervene between warring factions. The Intervention Cycle indicates that NATO's military forces can be used with effectiveness in this peace enforcement mission; however, upon their successful mitigation of the conflict, multinational or UN-sponsored police forces should replace those combat forces. This change in force composition mirrors the change in both the intervention task and the relationship between the parties to the conflict. Further, a change in peace operation rules of engagement should naturally accompany the commencement of the resolutionary process in order to facilitate the resumption of normal law-and-order–related police activities.

Our hypothetical conflict has gained the attention of numerous states, international organizations, and other interested parties such as relief organizations and nongovernmental organizations (NGOs). Each has some degree of equity in addressing some aspect of the intergroup conflict problem—massive refugee flows, conflict containment or security concerns, humanitarian crisis, political turmoil, economic devastation, trade interruption, and so on. Each task must be addressed in a coherent fashion and should be prioritized according to its focus of effort as depicted on the Intervention Cycle. When there is sufficient resolve and capability to undertake direct intervention, those mechanisms that directly address conflict mitigation—such as containment, enforcement, and monitoring activities—

should be implemented as soon as possible, take priority over nonmitigation measures, and set the course for interparty political dialogue.

This statement should come as no surprise; for in the case of violent intergroup conflict in which there has been no cessation of hostilities, attempts at conflict mitigation by intervening parties lacking both enforcement capability and commitment are rarely successful at reducing the level of violence.[18] In practical terms, this means that the forces sent forward to perform peace enforcement tasks must be able to bring decisive combat power to bear on localized zones of confrontation in order to deter hostile action by any party to the conflict. Without this ability to deter hostile acts, the warring factions will continue to pursue tactical advantages of opportunity, whether or not they seek to influence the course of the ongoing political negotiations. Until the level of conflict has receded to the point at which the parties are willing to reach settlements based upon political rather than armed confrontation, diplomatic efforts are highly inefficient.

Once political engagement has become possible, one of the first issues at hand will be the identification and resolution of the grievances between the parties. As outlined earlier, many of these grievances will require deep concessions. The previous discussion of the changed nature of victor and vanquished in the post–cold war era acknowledged that intervention interrupts armed conflict at a point short of total war. However, the by-product prevention of total war is the elimination of total victory; settlement requires negotiation and compromise. Resolution cannot be imposed; rather it must be reached in an inclusive and participatory manner. International bodies that can provide neutral fora, as well as political and economic incentives, are most effective in engaging the parties at this juncture.[19]

The ongoing peace operation must transform itself from enforcement to peacekeeping to peacemaking as mitigation progresses; however, appropriate measures must be implemented to ensure that peace forces retain the ability to apply decisive force on a localized basis. In practical terms, this may require the implementation of demilitarized zones, the confiscation of heavy weapons, or the institution of confidence-building measures that deter local military exploitation of tactical opportunities. Further, as the enforcement mission's combat forces are withdrawn and replaced with police forces, a credible combat response capability must be retained on call. This capability will help ensure that the mitigative process continues to facilitate the implementation of political mechanisms without total military victory or the defeat of either party.

During the mitigation process, efforts to treat the humanitarian consequences on the periphery of the conflict—in those areas where violence is not occurring—may commence. Mitigating the loss of life and suffering of those dislocated by the fighting is an important and compelling task, as long as those efforts neither detract from the primary mission of stopping the violence, nor provide an additional issue for intergroup contention (such as unbalanced aid delivery or the provision of succor to combatants). Continued violence will only increase the humanitarian toll.

On the microlevel of Intervention Cycle application, relief efforts may proceed during the mitigation phase. Moreover, these efforts may even move on to the resolution and prevention of a specific humanitarian concern. Using our hypothetical scenario, a medical relief organization such as Médecins Sans Frontières (MSF) may be able to mitigate the suffering of cholera through distribution of antidiarrheal medication, resolve the spread of infection by dispensing cholera vaccines, and with the assistance of U.S. Army engineers, prevent a recurrence of the disease by providing a potable water source and instituting sanitation measures. As long as these microlevel efforts do not detract from the main focus of the intervention—the *mitigation* of intergroup conflict—they may occur simultaneously with the NATO peace enforcement effort occurring on the macrolevel.

As the resolutionary process is implemented, political mechanisms are implemented beyond the level of dialogue between the key elites who are party to the conflict. Political enfranchisement of individuals and groups should immediately commence with, for example, the intervention of NGOs to begin the process of political consensus building, voter registration, and democratization programs. This is also the stage at which military-to-military contact programs and foreign assistance programs engage to foster political tolerance and "professionalize" armed forces.

International financial institutions (IFIs) play a role in the resolutionary process by providing economic development incentives at the state level to remedy structural impediments to political and economic enfranchisement. These impediments may take the form of capital and infrastructure shortfalls that prevent the development of a robust economy or impair the free flow of goods and services. However, our conceptual model underscores that IFIs and donors must follow through to ensure that states implement programs that facilitate the economic enfranchisement of individuals at community levels. This is an area in which there is growing awareness by both IFIs and NGOs, implemented under the rubrics of "economic development," "empowerment zones," and special "economic areas."

Likewise, the OSCE and human rights organizations can then engage monitors to record what, if any, human rights violations are associated with residual intergroup conflict and social disenfranchisement. Even if these monitors are only preventative on a local scale, they serve as a feedback mechanism to identify low levels of conflict that may be acted upon before they erupt into widespread violence. The feedback of the monitors serves as a "report card" by which interventionists and states can assess the effectiveness of their mitigative or preventative measures, and facilitate timely action to prevent the recurrence of violence.

Using the Intervention Cycle as a model, the appropriate response to a reeruption of violence would be, of course, the application of mitigative measures. This is the process on the right side of our cycle. Without the use of this conceptual template, many would seek to intervene immediately with the application of more extensive political or economic measures, possibly ignoring the requirement to stop the violence (by force, if necessary) and resolve the underlying problem before continuing with enfranchisement efforts. As noted earlier, this process may occur on a micro- or macrolevel; thus both efforts may occur simultaneously. The key, however, is the application of a remedy that is appropriate to the task at hand. When conflict mitigation is called for, preventative measures are ineffective.

And finally, after mechanisms for political and economic enfranchisement have been put into place successfully, the state will face the challenge of socially enfranchising the public into an identity of national pride, perhaps using its success at uniting disparate groups as its rallying cry. The process— whether by assimilation into the system of the state, or by individual adoption of a national identity, or by incorporating extant groups into a system of mutual benefit—will vary according to the political structure, history, and homogeneity of the state. Whatever mechanisms are developed during the resolution process, their successful employment over time will start the enfranchisement process moving forward toward the goal of real and effectual nation building.

VI. CONCLUSION

The conceptual framework of the Intervention Cycle provides a common point of departure for the discussion of intervening in an ongoing or developing intergroup conflict. An important aspect of the Intervention Cycle is that it clearly differentiates between the tasks and mechanisms of mitigation and prevention. They differ intrinsically and are depicted as conceptual opposites. Further, the Intervention Cycle clearly illustrates that prevention will not follow mitigation unless the underlying causes of the conflict are resolved. Without resolution, the parties are stuck on the right side of the cycle and conflict will ebb and flow according only to the effectiveness of the mitigative forces in place. Moreover, the template indicates that without achieving political enfranchisement, economic development efforts are likely to fail. They will serve only to exacerbate intergroup conflict unless all parties are politically co-opted into a system of mutual benefit.

The Intervention Cycle also illustrates that the outbreak of violent intergroup conflict, regardless of its duration or degree, is evidence of underlying problems of disenfranchisement that cannot be solved by the application of force, nor through the tougher enforcement of sanctions (coercion) or increases in police or military patrols (deterrence). Rather, it suggests that the violence, once abated, can only be prevented with a redoubling of political, economic, and social measures. Violence is only the symptom; disenfranchisement is the cause. Those organizations that bring the tools of political empowerment and economic development to the problem are the ones best suited to a long-term solution.

And finally, the Intervention Cycle emphasizes that political methodologies are not mitigative in nature. Enforcement and police actions mitigate conflict; politicians only resolve the underlying causes once mitigation has occurred and all parties to the conflict are ready to participate in the resolutionary process. A premature shift in emphasis from mitigation to resolution could prove disastrous, a point that is borne out in many failed interventions experienced in recent years.

The cycle can be applied on both a micro- and macrolevel; for within widespread outbreaks of intergroup conflict, there will be pockets of relative calm. Likewise, the effectiveness of peace operations is often limited to localized areas of presence. Thus the process of mitigation, resolution, and prevention can exist concurrently on a microlevel while at the macrolevel another phase of the cycle is in play. This concept is equally useful to the soldier, police officer, politician, and relief worker; all four may be engaged simultaneously at different phases of conflict intervention.

The cycle is also, unfortunately, reversible. Once intergroup conflict has been mitigated and resolved, the failure to glean political, economic, and social progress—either through, for example, the continued postponement of internal elections or the continued application of external economic sanctions—will push the cycle forward and allow the reescalation of conflict to the extent that deterrent measures or coercion are unable to check the upward spiral of violence.[20] That reescalation will not only change the required focus of effort for the intervening parties, but will be an indicator of the relative degree of effectiveness of those enfranchising measures heretofore employed.

As one surveys the array of intervention tools available, be they security, political, or financial organizations, it will be crucial to identify clearly their area of intersection with the cycle. The failure to do so could be costly, if not fatal, in the long term. After determining the desired effect of the contemplated intervention, it is also important to take into consideration those factors that will allow the cycle to progress or regress, as appropriate. For example, during the implementation of resolutionary measures, there remains a need for heightened vigilance by those parties involved in the peacemaking mission to ensure that confrontations are minimized, as well as for the initial engagement of those key elites who form the basis of the political structure to be implemented or contested.

This type of coordination is all too often overlooked by the interventionist, and the parties to dispute resolution are often too heavily engaged in the process to be able to exercise this degree of vigilance. Further, intervening organizations or parties are often poorly suited to the performance of the adjacent function on the Intervention Cycle, which has surely been the case in a number of failed interventions during which the initial phases of the operation were hailed as unmitigated successes.

The use of the Intervention Cycle as a conceptual framework should contribute to the effective coordination of intervening mechanisms by clearly correlating the ends and means of intervention while ensuring that they are applied in a sequence that facilitates the accomplishment of the critical tasks at hand.

NOTES

1. This includes the civilization conflict theory forwarded by Samuel P. Huntington in his essay, "The Clash of Civilizations?" Huntington defines the civilization as, "the *highest* cultural grouping of people and the *broadest* level of cultural identity. . . . " [emphasis added] Even within Huntington's "civilizations" it is ethnic or group identity—the lowest common denominator of cultural affinity—which is most germane to the study of conflict resolution and preventative measures. See, Samuel P. Huntington, "The Clash of Civilizations?" in *Foreign Affairs*, 72, no. 3, (Summer 1993), p. 24.

2. The absence of absolute power over citizens as exercised by traditional authoritarian regimes, the collapse of the bloc system, and the waxing trend of self-identification/individual empowerment among world polities all contribute to the rising trend of conflicts that manifest themselves in entities other than state structures. These alternative structures often seek ethnicity as the lowest common denominator—thus the term "ethnic" conflict has come to the forefront of modern usage.

There are many works on the subject of ethnicity and ethnonational identity; a discussion of the contextual importance of these works is beyond the scope of this writing. It is important to note that many of the wars and conflicts experienced in the twentieth century have ethnic conflict on some scale as their basis. However, in the post–cold war era this phenomenon is less salient; conflict between nonethnic elements has been at the root of war in Europe, Asia, Africa, the Middle East—and to a lesser extent—even in the Americas.

A close look at causal factors identifies many other common denominators to those small wars that currently dot the globe. Their prevalence and degree of complexity lay at the root of our interest in their resolution and prevention; therefore, the use of the inclusive term "intergroup" allows broader consideration. Thus, wherever possible in this work, the word "ethnic" is avoided and the nondescriptive term "group" is used to describe a shared identity (physical, cultural, geographic, religious, linguistic, sanguineous, or otherwise self-defined) that unites one body of people and provides for them a point of differentiation from others.

Because of this broad interpretation of group affinities, it is also essential to avoid the unqualified use of the words "ethnic" or "nation" unless describing an ethnically homogenous state or a substate element of self-ascribed national identity. In those cases that refer to traditional governmental structures or sovereignties whose relations with neighbors are defined by a series of internationally recognized borders, the word "state" will be used. That is because nations, by our definition, are most commonly substate elements—or ethnic groupings.

3. Major General William A. Stofft and Dr. Gary L. Guertner present a useful depiction of this scale in their "Spectrum of Ethnic Conflict," in Annex A of their monograph on ethnic conflict. Stofft and Guertner depict a range of activities from nonviolent protest through human rights violations to regional conflict and propose responses that range from nonintervention through diplomacy to peace enforcement, respectively. Their discussion of military intervention in ethnic conflict provides a superb "quick-look" assessment of appropriate roles and missions for armed forces. See Major General William A. Stofft and Dr. Gary L. Guertner, *Ethnic Conflict: Implications for the Army of the Future.* Strategic Studies Institute. Carlisle Barracks, PA: U.S. Army War College, 1994.

4. According to a U.S. Central Intelligence Agency study dated July 29, 1992, p. 2, cited by Raymond W. Duncan and G. Paul Holman Jr., *Ethnic Nationalism and Regional Conflict: The Former Soviet Union and Yugoslavia.* Boulder, CO: Westview Press, 1994, p. 11.

5. Misinterpreting the distinction between coercion (the prevention of violent conflict) and enforcement operations can be disastrous. "Pockets" created by UN safe areas within the contested state of Bosnia created a potentially disastrous mix of peace enforcement, peacekeeping, and humanitarian assistance. Coercion in peripheral areas more closely resembles efforts undertaken in the Vojvodina and Kosovo Provinces of Serbia to prevent further conflict. Deterrent and coercive measures will be further discussed in Section 4 of this chapter.

6. The risk to humanitarian and medical relief personnel in these areas is significant; therefore the use of military force to provide for their safety may be

directed. This can become problematic for both the military and the relief personnel. Deborah Kobak's Rwanda essay will discuss two problems recently observed when the area of conflict widens to include (or surround) the locale of these efforts. Its April Oliver's Somalia case study will discuss how U.S. forces sent to ensure the unimpeded delivery of humanitarian relief became caught up in a greater conflict during the transition from the United Nations International Task Force (UNITAF) to the second United Nations Operations in Somalia (UNOSOM II). Likewise, Kobak will note how relief efforts in bordering regions became a staging ground for partisan activities—leading to the eventual withdrawal of several relief missions.

7. Or stated differently, "Key sources of conflict are deeply rooted in the economic, social and political conditions . . . in which multiethnic and communal groups find themselves living." See W. Raymond Duncan and G. Paul Holman Jr., *Ethnic Nationalism and Regional Conflict: The Former Soviet Union and Yugoslavia.* Boulder, CO: Westview Press, 1994, p. 197.

8. In South Africa, for example, this reduced state of conflict occurred immediately after the election of President Mandela. During a visit in the months immediately following the election, I was personally struck by the sway and allure of politics, especially among young black adolescents. Full of hope, lacking economic enfranchisement, and facing a long and arduous road toward becoming part of South Africa's vitality, dreams and aspirations of becoming political leaders were in full bloom among these youth—and with more tangible evidence of possibility. Other authors have documented the importance of political enfranchisement among ethnic and indigenous populations in a more scientific manner; see T. R. Gurr, *Minorities at Risk: A Global View of Ethnopolitical Conflicts.* Washington, DC: United States Institute of Peace Press, 1993, pp. 323-24.

9. Marina Ottaway of the U.S. Overseas Development Council wrote an essay on African and Eastern European experiences with democratization and ethnic conflict that reaches a similar conclusion. Her study of the liberalization and democratization process in the former authoritarian regimes of Czechoslovakia, Yugoslavia, Ethiopia, and South Africa points out that it was the transition to democracy that provided an opening to the forces of ethnic nationalism. Before democracy could be consolidated, these political systems failed, in varying degrees, to recognize the rights of minorities and accommodate them within the system. Ottaway's essay supports our emphasis on the primary necessity for political enfranchisement. See Marina Ottaway, *Democratization and Ethnic Nationalism: African and Eastern European Experiences.* Washington, DC: Overseas Development Council, 1994.

10. Scholars often point to the American experience as the quintessential example of assimilation and social enfranchisement. However, it must be noted that there are others who point out that the validity of the American experience is less applicable to the rest of the world because of its lack of indigenous peoples in large numbers and the overwhelming incentive to immigrants for abandoning their traditional affinities in order to "become American." See Walker Connor,

Ethnonationalism: The Quest for Understanding, Princeton NJ: Princeton University Press, 1994.

11. In the Navajo Nation, for example, we find an interesting paradox between ethnic nationalism and United States citizenship. The Navajo Nation is fiercely independent and protective of its indigenous rights as T'aa Dine Native Americans. However, there exists a deep and profound patriotism among the Navajo with respect to their American citizenship. Examples of that intense loyalty are perhaps best illustrated by stories regarding the Navajo "Code Talkers" who served in the United States Marine Corps during World War II.

12. T. R. Gurr identifies communal groups in his extensive study of ethnopolitical conflict. He emphasizes the psychological collective identity of these groups, which he bases on cultural traits and "lifeways." See Ted Roberts Gurr, *Minorities at Risk: A Global View of Ethnopolitical Conflicts,* Washington, DC: United States Institute of Peace Press, 1993.

13. In fact, the deterioration of support for the goals of Maastricht is highly illustrative. The Single Europe Act fell well short of being able to co-opt large segments of the population into the adoption of one self-identifying "nationality"; thus, no extent of political or economic enfranchisement could overcome the deeply rooted sentiments (and symbols) of nationalism and cultural heritage that currently prevail within the European Union. Some authors point out that European ethnic allegiances were even strengthened by the globalization of economies. See, Stephen Iwan Griffiths, *Nationalism and Ethnic Conflict: Threats to European Security,* SIPRI Research Report no. 5. Stockholm International Peace Research Institute. New York: Oxford University Press, 1993, pp. 126-27.

14. See Robert D. Kaplan, "The Coming Anarchy," in *The Atlantic Monthly,* 273, no. 2, February 1994.

15. A recent volume of *Foreign Affairs* contains two provocative essays that dispute our point in two respects. The first, "In Defense of Liberal Nationalism," by Michael Lind, proposes the "correspondence of cultural nation and state," and outlines the progression of enfranchisement in the opposite order presented in this work. According to Lind, "First comes the nation state, then a liberal constitution reinforced by a liberal political culture, and only then, if at all, democracy." Lind's article may argue persuasively for the acceptance of the end result of disenfranchisement, however, it fails to address the root causes. His theory holds true only under the assumption that a nation has some concrete set of homogenous factors that will not further subdivide absent the enfranchising mechanisms discussed in detail above. In the second essay, "Nations Without States," by Gidon Gottlieb, the author proposes the "deconstruction and rearrangement" of the existing international order into one in which the standing of "national communities" is afforded certain diplomatic and constitutional recognition. This is an intellectually interesting argument; however, it falls short on practicability. See *Foreign Affairs,* 73, no. 3 (May/June 1994), pp. 87-112.

16. The danger of isolating particular faction leaders became particularly evident during the UN intervention in Somalia. Under UNOSOM II, influential Somali fac-

tion leader Mohamed Farah Aideed was singled out with disastrous results as the target of a manhunt. Singling out Aideed would have been appropriate only if the UN were willing to intervene without attempting to remain neutral. Targeting Aideed alienated his loyalists, strengthened rivals, and undermined domestic and international support for the political dialogues required for resolution. Richard K. Betts provides an important, thoughtful, and provocative discussion of neutral interventions in his essay "The Delusion of Impartial Intervention," *Foreign Affairs*, 73, no. 6 (November/December 1994), pp. 20-33.

17. T. R. Gurr provides an in-depth discussion of the role of communal (ethnic) groups within the context of global state structures that reaches similar conclusions. "A more constructive and open-ended answer [to the place of communal groups within states] is . . . both recognizing and strengthening communal groups within the existing state system." Our concepts of political and economic enfranchisement achieve these same goals, while social enfranchisement creates the same type of psychological "nationality" that Gurr explores in his works. See Gurr, *Minorities at Risk*, pp. 323-24.

18. Esther Brimmer's case study on Haiti will discuss this point vis-à-vis the Carter-Nunn-Powell diplomatic mission to Haiti, carried out in the eleventh hour of a United States–led UN-authorized peace enforcement operation. There, the imminent arrival of United States combat forces—demonstrated enforcement capability—swayed Haiti's illegitimate rulers into accepting a peaceful departure, thus paving the way for a rapid transition from peace enforcement to peacekeeping.

19. One of the most compelling arguments against the development of a UN peace enforcement capability (standing army) is the incongruous nature of that task vis-à-vis the UN's traditional role as an "honest broker" and humanitarian assistance agency. UN peace enforcement activities, and their dilution of UN efficacy in its central roles of mediation and humanitarian assistance, will be discussed in greater detail in Chapter 2.

20. An example of this may be found in the HAMAS-sponsored terrorist incidents in Israel and Gaza during September, October, and November 1994. The sustained political and economic disenfranchisement of Gaza Palestinians, even after their jubilant receipt of autonomy, caused a reescalation of conflict. To date, both the Israeli and Palestinian authorities see the employment of draconian border control and law enforcement measures as necessary to control or contain violent conflict. These measures are essentially deterrence and coercion enacted to forestall undermining the resolution process, and are likely to continue until a process of real political enfranchisement, that includes all factions, commences.

CHAPTER 2

Intervening Mechanisms

Roderick von Lipsey

During two post–world war periods of this century, the leaders of global powers sought to establish international institutions that could prevent future conflict. They attempted to do so by constructing treaty organizations upon the bedrock of mutually accepted principles of peaceful coexistence, national self-determination, and the sanctity of state sovereignty. During this third postwar period, the post–cold war period, the search continues. Today, however, both the nature of international institutions and the construct of the world's states have changed; ethnic, religious, economic, and ideological fissures have been revealed in our human foundation. And through the erosion of spheres of influence, blocs, alliances, and other topical layers of common interest, the roots of intergroup conflict have been laid bare before us on every continent across the globe.

Once in vogue, the idea of national self-determination, or the division of states along monoethnic or religious borders, has revealed itself as increasingly impractical and, in fact, undesirable. As a result of the natural yearnings sparked by the idea of self-determination, and fanned by the flames of prejudicial practices and disenfranchisement within state structures, conflicts between states have been subsumed by the prevalence of conflict between groups. The intractable nature of ethnic, religious, and other forms of intergroup conflict and its human, political, and economic tolls propels us forward in the search for preventative and resolutionary mechanisms. As conflict manifests itself into an ever increasing number of localized struggles, a plethora of international, regional, governmental, and private institutions and organizations emerges to tackle the challenges posed by both the conflict and its offshoots—famine, disease, refugees, economic ruin, and infrastructural collapse.

Nongovernmental organizations (NGOs), specialized councils and commissions, international financial institutions (IFIs), and private volunteer organizations (PVOs) have taken on a greater portion of the intervention duties traditionally carried out by the UN or unilaterally by interested parties. Conflict intervention has become a more decentralized problem as many of the mitigation, resolution, and prevention functions outlined in the Intervention Cycle are relegated to these independent and specialized mechanisms. Some of this decentralization reflects the breakdown of great power spheres of influence and the economic and physical limitations caused by the sheer number of emerging conflicts.

A significant portion of that decentralization, however, is due to the special nature of conflict as it occurs between groups rather than between states. Those mechanisms that serve the purpose of preventing conflict between states are designed for conflict prevention, mitigation, or resolution at a level that often cannot adequately address the needs of substate elements. Governmental leaders—the representatives of states—have generally found themselves unprepared and poorly equipped to solve these problems on a wide scale and cross-border basis. Further, states often face the dilemma that actions that relieve one group are often taken at the expense of another. For example, relief programs in one region are paid for by increased taxes in another.

Traditionally, international organizations such as the UN and the Organization for Security and Cooperation in Europe (OSCE, formerly CSCE) provide avenues of dialogue and mechanisms for conflict prevention among states. Moreover, international security and other treaty organizations like NATO, the Commonwealth of Independent States (CIS), Western European Union (WEU), Organization of African Unity (OAU), or Organization of American States (OAS), provide structural mechanisms that deter the outbreak of violence against member states and/or mitigate disputes between them. Substate ethnic, religious, geographic, or economic groups and subnational clans, tribes, communal groups, sects, castes, or refugees, however, receive no direct representation in these fora. Yet the resolution of their concerns are of primary importance to their organizational members.

Therefore, discussing the mitigation, resolution, and prevention of conflict in broadly inclusive terms, requires an exploration of a broad range of intervening mechanisms, or organizations (Table 1). Many of these have not previously been seen as playing an essential and global role in conflict intervention. Due to their number and the degree of specialization involved, it will be impossible to present a comprehensive overview of all those mechanisms available. This chapter will, however, discuss the general categories of mechanisms available as they relate to the framework of the Intervention Cycle presented in Chapter 1.

Understanding the relationship between intervening mechanisms and intervention tasks is vital. In the face of conflict or disaster there will be tremendous pressure to do something. Often, the resulting pressure to form an ad hoc intervention results in confusion: organizations that appear most suited to the particular humanitarian or security intervention task can be pre-empted by those less suitable, yet more convenient. A clear and common frame of reference should contribute to the more effective matching of tasks and mechanisms, as well as provide some degree of subjective assessment on the likelihood of the success of a proposed intervention.

As the number of intervention organizations increases, and the lines of distinction between them blur, careful consideration must be given to the efficacy of a particular organizational genre at each phase of the Intervention Cycle. The organizations are designed to intervene—politically, economically, militarily, or socially—with the purpose of providing relief from some particular aspect of conflict. However, in this world of burgeoning intervention challenges and commitments, few guidelines are available with which to coordinate their efforts. The efficacy of resources requires a framework with which these intervention mechanisms can be prioritized in a manner that focuses on the achievement of a particular set of intervention tasks. The Intervention Cycle, with its clear depiction of the three essential intervention missions—mitigation, resolution, and prevention—may provide such a framework.

The following sections of this chapter will be devoted to the intervention focus of international organizations, special councils and commissions, NGOs, IFIs, and PVOs, their relation to the broader intervention mission at hand, the optimal sequence of their application, and their overall efficacy at each phase of the Intervention Cycle. The purpose is to clarify the issue of conflict intervention for those whose agencies or organizations are responsible for recommending or implementing policies that seek to end intergroup conflict and prevent its recurrence.

I. INTERNATIONAL ORGANIZATIONS AND INTERVENTION

International organizations provide an infrastructure that is central to all aspects of conflict mitigation, resolution, and prevention. They serve as metaphoric funnels through which diplomatic, economic, humanitarian, and reconstruction aid may be directed toward the root causes of conflict, and later provide forms around which state structures can be recast. Further, due to their international nature, significant number of specialists, and assumed lack of competing political motivations, national elements are often more willing to subject themselves to the scrutiny of international organizations than to accept the intervention efforts of bordering states or regional organizations.[1]

The UN Security Council (UNSC) plays an important role with respect to international organizations and conflict intervention. This most powerful—and controversial—body of the UN is the forum tasked with arbitration and decision making on issues of high visibility and global impact. The UNSC performs this role on the behalf of the international community (as seen through the eyes of its permanent members) and serves primarily as a legitimating body whose resolutions provide the imprimatur of a united and international will to intervene.[2] When serving in this capacity, the UNSC becomes the de facto approving authority for intervention by other international mechanisms, including subelements of the UN itself, and gives the green light for the commencement of intervention activities, even in those states lacking formal ties to the organizations themselves.[3]

This section will briefly explore some of those international organizations and other mechanisms involved in conflict intervention within the context of the first two primary missions outlined by the Intervention Cycle, mitigation and resolution. To provide additional structure for this discussion and broader applicability to future organizational developments, Table 2 depicts the intervening mechanisms as they have been separated into five organizational genres: aggregate, security, humanitarian, developmental, and economic. Aggregate organizations bring multiple intervention capabilities to the table via their individual mix of security, humanitarian, developmental, financial, and economic subsets. The latter genres are more narrowly defined and self-descriptive in terms of their functions. However, each genre has particular strengths that may become of primary value at one particular phase of the cycle and then rendered essentially useless (or even counterproductive) at another. Thus, each of the genres will be discussed under the heading of their discrete and essential intervention mission: the mitigation and resolution of conflict.

A. International Organizations in Conflict Mitigation.

As discussed in Chapter 1, the tasks inherent to the mission of conflict mitigation are broadly defined under the term "peace operations." A glance at those organizations outlined in Tables 1 and 2 reveals that the majority of them are not those normally associated with peace operations. However, upon further reflection, one realizes that a large number of them are involved in virtually every real world intervention scenario. How, then, do they—or *should* they—fit together?

The primary mission focus during this phase of the Intervention Cycle should be conflict mitigation. Those tasks performed should contribute to the preemption of an ongoing violent confrontation and/or the establishment of an atmosphere conducive to a transition to the resolutionary process. The mitigative tasks discussed under the terms peace enforcement and peacekeeping were those that directly addressed one specific *symptom* of intergroup conflict: violence. Violence is not the only symptom present at this stage of intervention, but it is the most essential symptom for treatment.

TABLE I
SAMPLE INTERVENTION ORGANIZATIONS

African Development Bank	North Atlantic Treaty Organization
Amnesty International	Organization for African Unity
AmeriCARES	Organization for Security and
CARE	Cooperation in Europe
Commonwealth of Independent States	Peace Corps
European Bank for Reconstruction	Project Hope
and Development	Salvation Army
European Union	Save the Children
Human Rights Watch	United Nations
InterAction	United Nations Development Program
International Rescue Commission	United National International
International Committee of the Red	Children's Education Fund
Cross/Red Crescent	Western European Union
International Monetary Fund	World Bank
Médecins Sans Frontières	

TABLE 2
SAMPLE INTERVENTION ORGANIZATIONS BY MECHANISM

Security	Aggregate	Humanitarian	Developmental	Economic
NATO	CIS	Amnesty Int'l	Peace Corps	Banks
OSCE	EU	AmeriCARES	Project Hope	IMF
OAU	InterAction	CARE	UNDP	World Bank
WEU	Red Cross	MSF	UNICEF	
	UN	Salvation Army	World Food Program	
		UNHCR	Save the Children	

As the wave of violent conflict sweeps across a polity it brings with it a host of problems. Humanitarian disaster in the form of starvation, disease, famine, and displaced persons, as well as economic disruption and the destruction of local facilities and life-sustaining infrastructure whirl in the vortex of violent intergroup conflict. Treatment of these problems, as important and heartrending as they may be, is secondary to the essential task of mitigating violence.

Few policymakers would risk uttering so harsh a reality; however, it must be kept in mind that mitigating humanitarian disaster is of secondary importance to mitigating the violence that causes it, for continued violence will bring prolonged suffering and tragedy. Mitigating violence must be the primary focus of interventions that seek to enable resolution. In cases where sufficient resources do not exist or there lacks sufficient political will to commit the appropriate mechanisms to mitigate intergroup violence, intervention for purely humanitarian reasons can limit the immediate extent of human suffering. However, this path should not be pursued under the impression that humanitarian intervention alone will resolve or foreshorten the conflict.

Thus, when intervening with the purpose of mitigating conflict in the absence of a cease-fire or other truce, peace enforcement troops must be the first mechanism applied to stop the violence. In most cases a successful cessation will require the application of superior force against force. Where a cease-fire agreement is in place and there exists consent of all parties, peace-keeping forces may be introduced. However, should violence resume, the peacekeeping mission must be immediately withdrawn or superseded by enforcement action from a combat force.

Stopping the violence and preventing its recurrence are the first and most essential tasks during the mitigation phase of the intervention cycle. Without these, other forms of intervention will be premature and likely to fail. If there is insufficient resolve or an inadequate force to conduct these tasks, then violent conflict must ebb of its own accord; one party becomes the victor, key elites reach a compromise (which in most cases comes after tactical advantages can no longer be exploited for additional leverage), or all parties exhaust their resources and seek a peaceful resolution. Only then can the next phase of intervention commence.

It is important to reinforce this point and clarify the overall application of the Intervention Cycle. Remember from the previous chapter's discussion, that the Intervention Cycle can be applied simultaneously on a macrolevel (general) and microlevel (local). That is, various stages of intervention can take place on a microlevel, within the larger context of a particular conflict intervention. During the mitigation phase of the cycle, this means that concurrent with the introduction of forces that are capable of stopping violent activities, the local use of mechanisms that mitigate some other offshoot of intergroup conflict may also be appropriate, as long as these activities do not detract from the larger mission of mitigating conflict.

For example, in localized areas where violence is not occurring efforts may commence to treat the humanitarian consequences of the conflict. Such efforts could stem the loss of life and suffering of those dislocated by the fighting. In fact, as long as these efforts do not detract from the overall mission—the *mitigation* of intergroup conflict—attempts may be made to resolve and prevent the future recurrence of some localized problems.

On the macrolevel real success in resolving and preventing the humanitarian emergency cannot precede the overall mitigation of violence. If left unabated, violent conflict will soon threaten successful disease prevention and will cause renewed displacement, facility destruction, and humanitarian suffering—restarting the process from the beginning. Failed intervention attempts in Somalia and Bosnia were replete with localized successes. Localized humanitarian success in the case of Rwanda diverted international attention away from the primary mission of conflict mitigation, resolution, and prevention between the Hutu and Tutsi and resulted in a failure to "break the cycle." The need to reintervene lays ahead.

Even from a purely humanitarian perspective, stopping violence provides the most effective means of mitigation. Other measures may occur concomitantly, such as the provision of emergency medical assistance, emergency rations, essential medication, and shelter when available. However, it is essential to underscore that these measures are purely aimed at mitigating one of the symptoms of intergroup conflict. It would be a mistake to proceed on with measures that seek fully to resolve the humanitarian emergency prior to mitigating the violence. This is an important point to be considered by those responsible for prioritizing the flow of intervention equipment, materials, and supplies on the macrolevel. The Intervention Cycle framework illustrates that such an action may not only be counterproductive to the successful accomplishment of the intervention mission at hand, it may be tremendously costly and eventually ineffective.

With this point in mind, one must consider the intervention capability of each international organization and prioritize them in accordance with their focus of effort and capability with respect to the mission of conflict mitigation. Of the five types of organizations available for consideration (aggregate, security, humanitarian, developmental, and economic), security and aggregate organizations are the most effective in the initial phases of conflict mitigation. Concurrently, humanitarian organizations can work to alleviate the suffering of those displaced by violence and societal upheaval. However, the previous discussion shows how these organizations can obliquely affect conflict mitigation by undermining security efforts or prolonging the conflict on the macrolevel.

The discussion now turns to consideration of each organizational genre's role during the mitigation phase of conflict intervention.

(1) Security Organizations. Security organizations are those mechanisms that were traditionally associated with balance-of-power blocs or regional defense structures. Though considered by some to be increasingly irrelevant, they play a crucial and primary role in conflict mitigation. The North Atlantic Treaty Organization (NATO) is the largest and most robust of this genre and the last to retain a standing, active force structure. Other international organizations in this category retain readily constituted security components, such as the Commonwealth of Independent States (CIS) and Western European Union (WEU). Also, a number of other regional organizations could sponsor ad hoc force coalitions and make them available as needed, such as the Organization of American States (OAS) and Organization of African Unity (OAU). And finally, specialized multinational coalitions, such as the Euro-Corps and the Baltic Brigade are included in this category due to their separable nature from other security infrastructures, which allows them to retain their multinational characteristic and military capability while exercising an expanded degree of political autonomy from other treaty or security infrastructures.

As depicted in Figure 5, security organizations are best suited to the early stages of mitigating violence when peace enforcement operations are required to impose by force the separation of warring factions. Security organizations or ad hoc, UN-mandated coalition forces under major power command provide the combat capability required for peace enforcement.

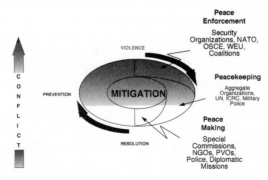

Figure 5. The Intervention Cycle with Mitigation Tasks and Mechanisms

Formal and active force structures, such as NATO, WEU, CIS, or (perhaps in the future) the OSCE provide the most responsive conflict intervention capability due to their standing operational command linkages and deployment readiness. Additionally, these organizations or coalitions in which participants are likely to bring the resources of command and control, logistics, and intelligence that are essential to enforcement actions. Unilateral action by military powers may also be effectively employed for enforcement operations. However, the international legal and political implications of unilateral action must be taken into consideration.

(2) Aggregate Organizations. Aggregate international organizations are, metaphorically speaking, jacks of all trades. These are organizations whose structures enable them to carry out some combination of emergency medical services, humanitarian and disaster relief, developmental and economic assistance, and, in some cases, security-related functions on a global scale. The UN and the International Committee of the Red Cross/Red Crescent (ICRC) are two of a very small number of organizations that provide a variety of services that may be applied across a broad spectrum of intervention missions. However, by their truly aggregate nature, care must be taken to ensure that the mechanisms employed by these organizations are suited to the particular task at hand. Further, due to their size and degree of operational diversity, "fiefdoms" often develop within the organization, resulting in the loss of centralized control and coordination of the various mechanisms available. When this occurs, it can render the aggregate organization a loose collection of individuals acting independently while under the same organizational name and headquarters.

For example, many consider the UN capable of peace operations across the full spectrum of mitigative tasks. Although extremely useful for consentual peacekeeping and peacemaking operations, recent cases in Somalia and Bosnia illustrate the limits to the effective use of UN (blue helmet) forces for peace enforcement operations. That is because the ad hoc nature of UN force structure, lack of organic equipment, and bifurcated lines of command and control render UN forces unresponsive, inflexible, and relatively ineffective as combatants. Semirestrictive rules of engagement can allow fighting forces to retain efficacy as peace enforcers; however, the violent nature of unabated conflict requires combat efficiencies not found within the UN structure.

Further, the efforts of subelements of the UN—for example, the High Commissioner for Refugees (UNHCR), the World Health Organization (WHO), the Development Program (UNDP), the Department of Peacekeeping Operations (UNDPKO), and special envoys appointed to represent the secretary general and UNSC—often confound each other's efforts, especially in those areas where violent conflict coincides with humanitarian emergency, natural disaster, and UN relief efforts in the so-called developing world. If the UN is given the additional task of performing security-related functions, such as peace enforcement, it is placed in the conflicting position of being both the "good" and "bad cops." This conflict not only erodes the efficacy of its mitigation efforts, it undermines the UN's ability to provide its unique good offices and vital development services during the resolution and prevention phases of intervention.

Figure 5 shows that aggregate organizations such as the UN and ICRC commence their mitigative efforts in the early stages of peace enforcement. In fact, some representatives of aggregate (and other) organizations are likely to be present prior to the arrival of security forces. This is either due to prior or ongoing humanitarian or development efforts, or a failed preventative intervention (to be discussed further below). Perhaps the most difficult task for those personnel present at the commencement of mitigation efforts is making the transition in the focus of effort, or making the decision to suspend and/or relocate their activities. Although aggregate organizations, especially the UN, play a nearly continuous role throughout the Intervention Cycle it is important to understand the relationship of their ongoing efforts to the primary intervention task at hand. Note from the depiction in Figure 5 that their role is limited while peace enforcement tasks are being conducted, and expands to fullest proportions during the peacekeeping to peacemaking transition. When mitigation tasks are primary, aggregate organizations must yield the priority of effort to security organizations. As security organizations incrementally succeed in reducing the level of violent conflict, the aggregate organizations' role increases proportionally, reaching its peak after enforcement efforts are concluded and police-type peacekeeping operations have commenced. The handover from security organizations to aggregate organizations cannot occur prior to the implementation of a durable cease-fire agreement and separation of combatant forces. Additionally, the mechanisms of enforcement operations—the combat units employed by the security organization—should be included in the category of "combatants" for the purposes of separation. Thus the responsibility for further conduct of peace operation missions should be handed over from the enforcement organization to the UN or to military police-type elements of (preferably) an unrelated organization or national force.

(3) Humanitarian Organizations. Perhaps the most wrenching offshoot of intergroup conflict is its humanitarian toll: the debilitation of civil society and the destruction of its life-sustaining infrastructure. Thus, humanitarian assistance organizations often form the first wave of intervention; relief organizations respond to the crises posed by refugees and displaced persons fleeing the initial outbreak of violence. Moreover, since intergroup conflict can arise as a

result of the social disruption and economic collapse caused by natural disasters, humanitarian assistance agencies may be on scene at the outbreak of violent conflict.

There is no mystery behind the prevalence of intergroup conflict in areas suffering from the hardships of natural disaster, famine, drought, or some other precipitous event. The social and economic interruption that often result exacerbate already present societal cleavages and forms of disenfranchisement. That speeds the onset of violent conflict and accelerates the cycle. Thus, there are many examples of intervention that began as humanitarian assistance missions and devolved into some form of peace operation or law enforcement interventions. Even in those cases where violent conflict erupts due to causes other than natural disaster, humanitarian need is often the most compelling reason for intervention. Thus, there will be a humanitarian component present at the onset of virtually every intervention. It must be properly anticipated, balanced, and coordinated between intervening security and humanitarian organizations and other parties.

Lifesaving intervention by international organizations is a relatively new phenomenon. Prior to the mid-1960s few international humanitarian aid organizations existed outside of the Red Cross and UN. However, the postwar demise of colonial empires, especially on the African continent, substantially reduced the political and economic incentives for the former colonialists to intervene in the amelioration of the effects of drought, famine, and other natural disasters in their former surrogate states. In response to these natural disasters and their staggering human toll, private volunteer organizations such as MSF and nongovernmental organizations such as CARE, and Project HOPE took on the challenge of saving lives and improving conditions in the so-called Third World. Continued unrest, change, and natural disasters in the densely populated regions of the postcolonial world made the demand for their services one of continual increase. Today, hundreds of these organizations operate around the world, and the need for them continues to outpace their growing capacity.

Therefore, when intergroup conflict reaches proportions at which international organizations feel compelled to intervene politically, militarily, economically, or otherwise, their involvement will likely come on the heels of a private or nongovernmental response. Representatives or workers from the ICRC, International Rescue Commission (IRC), World Food Program (WFP), WHO, MSF, CARE and Human Rights Watch, among others, are likely to have arrived prior to the first wave of intervention. If not, they will soon follow. Quite often, the presence of these caregivers can complicate the main thrust of intervention, especially during the conflict mitigation phase.

From the perspective of the mitigation phase of the Intervention Cycle, NGOs, PVOs, and relief agencies will complicate, and yet support, the efforts of security organizations to mitigate violence. Their independent and nominally apolitical construct, as well as the nature of their services allow them physical access to areas contested by opposing forces, often even at the height of the conflict. This is at once a blessing and a curse—a blessing in that relief organizations are often able to apply food and medical relief to those in greatest need; a curse in that they often find themselves caught in both the literal and figurative cross-fire of intergroup conflict and become impediments to mitigation efforts. Interventions that enter the cycle near the apex of violence, or peace enforcement operations, must seek immediately to separate humanitarian efforts from enforcement operations. Enforcement operational plans must take into account the preexisting humanitarian relief efforts and presence of relief workers. When possible, planning should include coordination with the parent agencies to locate and identify personnel and facilities, as well as arrange for their relocation or evacuation, if necessary. This type of coordination should reduce the danger to innocent third parties as well as preclude the opportunity for belligerents to use volunteers and noncombatants as shields or hostages to thwart enforcement efforts.

For example, although it was not conducted in conjunction with enforcement operations, the evacuation of relief workers and UN observers from Kigali, Rwanda, and subsequent establishment of safe zones and refugee camps on the periphery of conflict at the height of the Hutu-Tutsi clashes provides an example of optimal separation. On the other hand, the attempt at combining peace enforcement with humanitarian assistance in Bosnia— with the same forces and without physically isolating the mission areas— provides an example of what ensues when this degree of physical and mission-oriented separation fails to occur.

Because it is nearly impossible to isolate the various intervention mechanisms and tasks from each other, the U.S. government—through the efforts of the State Department's Office of Foreign Disaster Assistance, the Defense Department's Office of Humanitarian Affairs, and the Joint Chiefs of Staff— has promoted the development of Joint Coordination Centers that work in conjunction with a military command center and the Disaster Assistance Response Team to coordinate the efforts of governmental organizations, NGOs, PVOs, aggregate, and security organizations on a local level. However, the ability to control the efforts and effectively coordinate the vastly different tasks of conflict intervention and humanitarian relief on a wide-scale basis is unlikely in the near term. This is especially true in an atmosphere of ad hoc crisis response; for, neither individual organizations nor states are likely to provide the bulk of both relief and security forces. A broad application of the Intervention Cycle could prove helpful to on-scene humanitarian aid coordinators, organizations, and donor-states when making the difficult decisions a crisis presents.

(4) Developmental Organizations. Developmental efforts, like those sponsored by UNDP, Project HOPE, the UN Children's Fund (UNICEF), and the UN Education, Scientific and Cultural Organization (UNESCO), as well as the U.S. Peace Corps provide technical assistance for agriculture, education, health and sanitation program development, urban and rural technical assistance, and cultural programs. In the mitigation phase of conflict intervention, there is little work for these organizations until violence has abated and humanitarian assistance efforts have been able to commence.

Concurrent with the distribution of humanitarian aid, developmental organizations are able to begin initial assessment of the assistance requirements for those regions affected by the conflict or the influx of refugees or displaced persons. These agencies and organizations play a key role in the reconstruction of civil society and its infrastructural supports. Premature commencement of development efforts, however, may impede mitigation efforts by establishing a contested status quo, engaging illegitimate elements of local leadership, and subjecting development volunteers to the hazards of partisan fighting.

With this in mind, developmental organizations are not depicted in the Intervention Cycle during the mitigation phase. They best serve conflict resolution and are thus assumed to be distant observers, planning for and anticipating engagement upon the cessation of hostilities.

(5) Economic Organizations. Economic Organizations serve no direct operational role in the mitigation of violent conflict. However, their ability to affect the fundamental issues that foment intergroup conflict make them an important consideration during the mitigation phase of the Intervention Cycle. The terms of a negotiated settlement between the key representatives of belligerent parties, intervention organizations, and international fora will normally include some combination of political remedies and economic incentives or disincentives. Examples of the economic tools include: loan guarantees, development project funding, trade concessions/sanctions, exchange rate linkages, cash payments, and payments-in-kind (oil, gas, and foodstuffs, for example). The particulars of such a settlement normally mirror some discernible subset of political and economic problems that predate the outbreak of the conflict (i.e., disenfranchisement). Thus, organizations such as the World Bank, International Monetary Fund (IMF), and other international financial and trade organizations are particularly well-suited to the analysis and prescription of remedial economic and fiscal measures.

During the course of political interventions aimed at the mitigation of intergroup conflict, the issue of monetary incentives, either via project financing, trade, loan guarantees, or direct capital investment, will likely be broached. Extant economic disparities within the state will have either caused or exacerbated regional or intergroup tensions. Even if economic problems were only a minor factor, the outbreak of widespread violence can topple state structures and interrupt vital lines of communication—those transportation, commerce, and information systems that link disparate regions and peoples in the former or besieged state—leading to economic disaster and/or collapse.

The reestablishment of these lines of communication are of both practical and symbolic importance to states or, if a breakup has occurred, the successor regime(s) immediately upon the cessation of hostilities. On the practical side, these lines are required for the distribution of essential food, supplies, humanitarian aid, and, eventually, resumption of trade and commerce. Symbolically, there must be some tangible sign of benefit for those required to make various concessions in order to reach a peace agreement. Thus, monetary incentives and support for structural rehabilitation are of tremendous importance to the aggrieved party or parties, especially if trade sanctions or embargoes are levied as part of the external response to the conflict.

Further, with the outbreak of violence, states normally divert precious financial resources from their intended programs and governmental functions to military and security expenditures. As a result, those internal mechanisms with the capacity to resolve intrastate conflict often become the first casualties of the conflict. The reestablishment of these internal mechanisms—parliament, state legislature, city and regional governments, councils, courts, police departments, and so forth—is essential during the resolution phase, and normally requires some economic support in addition to political willpower. That support (or the promise thereof) plays an important role in the negotiation process that strives to mitigate the conflict.

Although direct economic incentives are normally associated with an intervening state government or regional group (like the EU), international organizations such as the World Bank, IMF, and the regional development banks play a critical role in identifying both potential projects and the recipients of financial remedies to intergroup conflict. Working in conjunction with the developmental organizations discussed above, IFIs can identify broad-based measures that support the (re)construction of key elements of a state's civil and political societies, as well as provide incentives for peaceful conflict resolution, thereby contributing to conflict mitigation.

In the following section on conflict resolution, the role of the IFIs becomes increasingly important, reaching its peak during the preventative phase of the Intervention Cycle. During the mitigation phase, however, IFIs primarily provide technical advice and assistance. Further, in conjunction with developmental organizations, they are able to evaluate and identify economic remedies that may help facilitate the commencement of the resolutionary process. To the extent that the conflict is based on economic cleavages within the state or society, their remedy proposals can be translated into political incentives for the cessation of hostilities and the pursuit of nonviolent alternatives.

In summary, security and aggregate organizations are of primary importance during the mitigation phase of the Intervention Cycle. They are best equipped for and focused on the implementation of active and direct measures that can mitigate intergroup conflict and create an atmosphere under which the root causes may be addressed. Humanitarian organizations perform the important task of mitigating the loss of life and human suffering associated with the societal breakdown and infrastructural collapse that follows in the path of violent conflict. And finally, developmental and economic organizations carefully assess the factors leading to the disenfranchisement of parties to the conflict and analyze prescriptive remedies for rebuilding civil and political societies during later phases of intervention.

This set of observations may support efforts to assign overall responsibility for intervention effort coordination to the security or aggregate organizations performing the primary mitigation task (peace enforcement, and peacekeeping, for example). This highly structured approach assumes, of course, that humanitarian, private, and diplomatic organizations can and will abide by this hierarchical assignment of coordination responsibilities. Mandating organizations such as the UN or OSCE may consider a clear delineation of intervention "command relationships" in the area of operation that extends beyond the appointment of a primarily political or diplomatic mission of the special envoy.

B. International Organizations in Conflict Resolution

In some respects, the method by which conflict is mitigated determines both the pace and scope of resolution onset. More specifically, conflict mitigation that comes as the result of vigorous enforcement action—or the forcible separation of parties and imposition of a settlement to armed conflict—is likely to require a more exhaustive, protracted, and supervised process of resolution than, for example, conflict mitigated by the mutual consent of all major participants. In the former case, the resolutionary process will likely commence via the formal and centralized communications channels of those key elites who participated in the negotiation process with the international community. In the latter scenario, mitigation by mutual consent, the process may commence through a broader network of officials and agencies whose contact with parties to the conflict have grown out of informal relationships formed during the period of mitigation.

Prior to and during enforcement actions, high-level negotiators engage the key elites of both parties across negotiating tables. However, as unwilling partners to the mitigation of conflict, it very unlikely that the partisan factions have extensively engaged each other at working levels. For example, warring military forces, having been forcibly separated, are less likely to have routinized localized truces for casualty exchanges, nor taken other similar actions that require some degree of contact and communication between forces. Similarly, local civic leaders—village elders, city mayors, doctors, or lower-level public utility officials—are unlikely to have engaged or attempted to engage local faction leaders to take measures to limit the effect of the conflict on noncombatants or the sick and wounded.

In the enforcement heavy scenario, the lack of this type of low-level contact will make the resolutionary process a slower activity. It will be highly dependent on the leadership of key elites and the work of neutral actors such as international or regional organizations to foster communication and interaction at these lower levels, with the caveat, of course, that these international or regional actors are not the same as those used for the enforcement action.[4] Further, since physical separation by interpositional forces was likely to have been used during the enforcement action, there has been little or no contact between the parties without the presence of a neutral party facilitator. This resolution process will likely require the continued presence of that third party, since negotiation and direct compromise has never been established between the members of partisan groups.

In those cases where conflict mitigation requires more supervision than enforcement, lower levels of communication are likely to have been established between parties to the conflict, and the degree of physical separation between the parties is likely to have been significantly less. Local leaders and officials from all parties to the conflict are more likely to have some knowledge of each other and issues of mutual interest. This linkage significantly reduces the requirement for third-party presence in all facets of the resolutionary process and at every level of political and social interchange, enabling a more timely transition to a broad-based resolutionary process.

We have spent little time discussing the role of negotiations in the Intervention Cycle. That is because negotiations are not an end in and of themselves; rather, they are simply one of the tools used at each stage of the cycle both by parties to the conflict and by external actors. Accordingly, both the composition and complexion of the negotiations and negotiators will change to conform to the task at hand, be it mitigation, resolution, or prevention. During the resolution stage, the role of the intervention mechanisms is heavily skewed toward conducting negotiations. That is because the task of resolution is primarily political; it contains extensive legal, economic, and social implications that must be negotiated and not imposed upon parties.

Those international efforts to limit (and, one hopes, eliminate) the effects of humanitarian disaster and infrastructural destruction that were of secondary importance during the mitigation of violence, come to the forefront during at the beginning of the resolutionary phase (see Figure 6). In fact, some may argue that the facilitation of these efforts should be the main focus of all intervening parties, for the rebuilding of civil society will accomplish much more in the short term than the political dialogue of key elites.

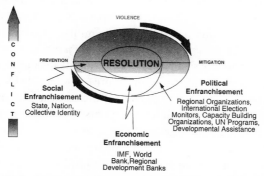

Figure 6. The Intervention Cycle with Resolution Tasks and Mechanisms

With the successful mitigation of violent conflict, the role of international organizations in conflict resolution will evolve along the lines that follow:

(1) Security Organizations. The same security organizations that played a leading role in the mitigation phase, especially if peace enforcement operations were required, will participate in the resolution process. In addition to providing a ready response or contingency force, security organizations will be key participants in the negotiated resolution of underlying military and security issues.

Some of the issues that will require security organization participation include war crimes investigations, confidence building, military-to-civilian control transition, armed force "professionalization," force and weapons monitoring activities, and regional stabilization. Although some of these appear tertiary to the resolution of factors directly responsible for the recently contained violence, it is important to note that even dormant or disbanded armed forces possess tremendous powers of destabilization. They, along with the police, hold the weapons of renewed conflict. Further, states weakened by internal conflict often present a "security vacuum" at the cessation of hostilities that can, and probably will, be filled by other forces not under the control or scrutiny of the state government or intervening parties.

Since partisan forces are the likely source of instability and violent outbreak, their status warrants immediate negotiated settlement at the onset of the resolutionary process. The prosecution of those deemed to have committed war crimes poses a significant challenge to the process of resolution. Although several precedents for this type of proceeding exist, the modern paradigm appears to remain outside of the traditional context of the victor-vanquished relationship. Thus, compromise in the form of a special or general amnesty is likely to be one aspect of the resolutionary process.

Additionally, members of opposing militias must be brought under the control of civilian leadership. This will be especially difficult in those cases in which enforcement action was required or the military itself was a party to the conflict, as in a military coup or rule by military *junta*. In the first case, the requirement for a forcible separation of combatants insinuates a strong military component to the conflict and the failure of one or all sides to meet specific military objectives within or outside of the context of a political power struggle. Further, the lack of willingness to pursue peaceful avenues to intergroup conflict resolution insinuates the presence of capable (or persuasive) military leaders. In the second case, the military leaders have subsumed military objectives to political power, yet retain complete control of forces able to implement or simply impose their political preferences. In both cases, the military leaders hold significant sway over public attitudes and opinion, and are likely to remain in a position to foment unrest or the resumption of violence should the resolution process circumvent their concerns.

Security organizations are best suited to the conduct of negotiations among force leaders. Their experience with military confidence-building measures, knowledge of military objectives, and ability to credibly assuage the security concerns of all parties are key at this juncture. Further, cultural similarities—or the common esprit that bonds military professionals from foreign lands to one another—render military-to-military contacts an irreplaceable aspect of the resolutionary process.[5] Further, continued contact with professional military forces will help the process of professionalizing national forces. That is the process of instilling obedience to civil authority, disassociating the military from political debates or power struggles, and/or redirecting the military from a force of internal repression or domestic enforcement to a role of defense against external threats to state security.

And finally, the contentious issue of disarming local and national militias must be addressed. The prevailing belief among security and law enforcement professionals is that this is an improbable, if not impossible, task. Thus, security organizations must rely on confidence-building and other measures that reduce the likelihood of armed conflict or the escalatory nature of localized outbursts. Three contemporary models, Iraq, South Africa, and Haiti derive from distinctly different examples of how security organizations may approach this issue without attempting to disband or disarm militias and military units.

The Iraq model derives from the expulsion of Iraqi troops from the territory of the aggrieved party, Kuwait. After pushing Iraq's forces out of Kuwait, the enforcement coalition declined further pursuit and destruction based on a number of assessments and assumptions. Central to our discussion is the assessment that equipment losses to the Iraqi national military were sufficient to stop the targeted aggression and deter further offensive acts, while preserving sufficient military structure for legitimate defensive purposes. Iraq was forced to destroy weapons of mass destruction and long-range delivery systems, but allowed to retain sufficient force to prevent the formation of a regional security vacuum that bordering states such as Iran could be tempted to exploit. Thus, the Iraq model is roughly one of the destruction of offensive capability and retention of a purely defensive force.[6]

The South Africa model derives from the retraining and consolidation of regional militias into a single, united national defense force. Great pains were taken to allow members to retain relative degrees of seniority and responsibility during the integration, while assuring standards of training and qualification across the board. The South Africa model, then, is one of consolidation.

And finally, the Haiti model derives from the disbanding of the military and absorbing former members into a police force retraining program or attempting civilian job placements. Further, since the Haitian military had become, primarily, a tool of the ruling *junta* for the repression and/or extermination of threats to their extraconstitutional military rule, its former members were subjected to a closely monitored vetting process prior to being accepted into the police force. This process sought to ensure that those suspected of human rights abuses or possessed some other questionable affiliation were disqualified for police force service. This model is one of disbandment and reorientation. The future of a new Haitian defense force was the subject of deliberation by a special UN commission.

It is important to note that all three of these models include some elements from one or both of the others. For example, reorientation was also required for the South African forces that, although technically integrated, were used internally to enforce the restrictions of apartheid. The Iraq model required a forcible separation, in this case, the ejection of the Iraqi army from Kuwait. In this, and in the other two models, external intervention and supervision is critical to the pace, sustainment, and success of the transition process. This will be one of the key tasks for security organizations in the resolutionary process.

One additional task of security organizations is to ensure compliance with the provisions of international agreements regarding demilitarization and weapons disposal or destruction. In the latter case, highly specialized security organizations such as the International Atomic Energy Agency (IAEA) may be required to conduct intrusive inspections, supervise weapons destruction, install monitoring equipment, and perform long-term surveillance of weapons activities and treaty compliance. Resolutionary measures that stipulate this type of activity provide both the transparency required for regional stability as well as a monitoring function to warn of inflammatory behavior or the resumption of weapons programs that could signal future belligerent intentions.

Monitoring activities may also include the placement of security personnel in demilitarized zones, buffer zones, or areas of highly contentious or strategic value. These activities, while rarely effective in resolving conflicts, can deter aggression and build confidence in the international organization's ability to preserve local stability at the resolutionary stage.

In summary, as the parties to the conflict are brought together to resolve their grievances, international security organizations have a significant role. Although the greater resolution dialogue will normally be held between diplomats at national or state political levels, control over military factions and military leaders is an essential element of the process. Since disarmament is generally agreed to be an improbable or impossible task, military members will continue to possess the instruments of reescalation. International security organizations, especially those able to retain elements of impartiality during the conflict mitigation process, provide important functions for the resolutionary process.

(2) Aggregate Organizations. The resolution process is one in which the good offices of aggregate organizations become uniquely important. They facilitate the party-to-party resolution of grievances and the drafting of new architectures for the postconflict state. Further, the ability to coordinate the delivery of a vast array of goods and services to those states emerging from devastating conflict is the hallmark of aggregate organizations such as the UN and ICRC.

The diffuse, multifaceted focus of effort that hindered the use of aggregate organizations during the process of conflict mitigation may be used to some advantage during the resolution process. The ability to deliver various forms of support, from diplomatic to developmental, allows the aggregate organization to advance on several fronts simultaneously. Further, as the UN continues to develop its internal capacity for the coordination of NGOs and PVOs via the Economic and Social Committee (ECOSOC) it will become a more efficient conduit of relief and nation-building support.

While the focus of diplomatic efforts often becomes myopic during the resolution process, the aggregate organization can play a role in redirecting talks and negotiations toward other areas that will bear fruit. For example, should the leaders of the major conflict groups become fixated on the technicalities of redrawing maps—a common pitfall—the aggregate organization can redirect discussions toward civil works, agricultural development, and/or political representation. When the resolution or discussion of these various issues can be facilitated by the same organization, contentious items may be tabled temporarily and focus shifted to a separate set of issues. While such agenda changes could be attempted by negotiators from any organization, only those working under the sponsorship of an aggregate organization have the capacity to speak with authority (or summon those who can) across the full spectrum of resolutionary measures.

Because the process of resolving the underlying causes of conflict opens a Pandora's box of issues, those who choose to intervene (or to facilitate the process) should either possess or have access to a wide range of resolutionary tools. Aggregates like the UN are able to bring the diplomatic power of the UNSC, the economic power of the Bretton Woods organizations, and the developmental power of UNDP to the table during negotiations. Other actors, such as the EU, are also able to access a range of diplomatic, economic, and developmental mechanisms to the table. The danger faced by unilateral actors or multilateral contact groups is their lack of access to (and leverage over) the broad range of mechanisms required during the resolution process.

In summary, aggregate organizations reach the peak of their utility and effectiveness during the early stages of conflict resolution (Figure 6). As the issues become identified and engaged by appropriate parties, the aggregate organization facilitates progress across the full range of intervention tasks and—most importantly—preserves momentum by redirecting the emphasis from areas of impasse to areas of common interest. In the fluid and dynamic environment of conflict resolution, the versatility of the aggregate organization renders it one of the most important intervention mechanisms.

(3) Humanitarian Organizations. As the peace process progresses, conditions in and around the area of conflict become increasingly conducive to the delivery of humanitarian relief and assistance. Further, as the parties to the conflict become less engaged in partisan contests the delivery of aid becomes a less contentious issue. Delivery organizations must, however, remain vigilant to the

fair and equitable distribution of aid and emergency resources in order to avoid rekindling hostilities between factions.

During the mitigation stage of the Intervention Cycle discussion, this work urges that humanitarian efforts be restricted to areas on the periphery of the violent conflict. Through this restricted area of operations, an impartial and safe environment could be established for the treatment of those humanitarian emergencies that result from this type of intergroup struggle. However, with the declaration (and demonstrated implementation) of a cease-fire agreement, humanitarian organizations may be granted direct access to the area of the fighting. Once again, care must be taken to ensure that the efforts of any one organization or donor country does not unwittingly favor one or another party to the conflict, thereby reigniting hostilities.

Such an approach to humanitarian assistance may be considered an inhumane rationing of emergency medical assistance and essential relief. However, as emphasized in the previous chapter and borne out in actual relief experiences in Bosnia, Somalia, and Rwanda, humanitarian organizations cannot work effectively in areas of continued intergroup conflict without endangering their workers or, perhaps, prolonging the conflict. Continued fighting begets continued casualties and, in some cases, those strengthened by the succor of emergency relief recover only to continue to pursue violent partisan conflict. Aid organizations caught in the vortex of this situation often feel trapped by the threat of retaliation, should they choose to withdraw their assistance. Yet they are compelled to cease aiding parties intent upon continuing to perpetuate the violence from which the humanitarian crisis stemmed in the first place. As the funds and resources available to humanitarian organizations continue to be stretched to respond to a growing global population the threat of intergroup conflict over scarce resources increases, resulting in the decision to ration humanitarian assistance. This is accomplished by acting on the periphery of conflict until violence has abated and the intention to resolve disputes peacefully has been demonstrated.

(4) Development Organizations. Careful, yet distant, assessment of rebuilding requirements were prescribed during the mitigation phase. Upon commencement of the resolution phase of the Intervention Cycle, development organizations play key roles in prescribing the best path toward the reconstruction and reinvigoration of the state's civil society. Organizations that facilitate the redevelopment of agricultural, septic, water, electrical, and other infrastructural programs are most helpful in reestablishing public faith in the state's ability to deliver necessary services. Organizations that specialize in the reestablishment of local leadership customs—the civic, religious, and other traditional leadership figures found within various cultures—will help invig-

orate the civil and political bases of a future stable government. This work will be of paramount importance to the full resolution of the conflict at the grassroots level of the society. Further, the foundation laid by these organizations in partnership with individuals and groups within the society during this stage of conflict intervention will be that which will bear (or fail to bear) the weight of prevention in the future.

There is currently no organization capable of complete coordination of developmental efforts. The range of development tasks required to rebuild a society that has been torn apart by violent intergroup conflict is so broad that the capacity for such a task is beyond the scope of any one intervening party. However, those states and aggregate organizations that have assumed leadership roles in the intervention process can, and should, assist the state with the development and implementation of guidelines or principles with which civil and political society can be reconstructed. An example of such a set of guidelines may be found in South Africa's "Reconstruction and Development Programme," which outlined a postapartheid framework to address that state's particular social and economic problems.[7]

As development organizations utilize these guidelines during the task of rebuilding civil and political society, care must be taken to ensure that any developmental architectures created by such activities neither uproot nor replace the society targeted for assistance. Intervention by outside parties can introduce large numbers of volunteers, relief workers, and administrators along with their attendant equipment, supplies, and support requirements. This influx creates its own microeconomy and society whose impact upon the local area must be carefully assessed during both the engagement and disengagement processes of intervention. Jobs are created: cooks, drivers, laborers, equipment operators, translators, and security guards. And new social strata may emerge centered around the aid-givers, their employees, those involved in their support, and all others. These new (and temporary) social and economic conditions can sow the seeds of further divisiveness within the society, unwittingly upsetting the basis for long-term economic and political enfranchisement by creating a new cadre of elites and upsetting the cultures and traditions endemic to the region.

Thus, development agencies such as UNDP and the Agency for International Development (AID) often unwittingly create a cadre of "donor dependents" during their intervention activities. The financial and material resources that accompany developmental assistance, as well as the administration of these resources, creates unwanted yet unavoidable political and economic effects that must be managed. This may be accomplished by minimizing the direct impact through careful local hiring practices, limiting the duration of intervention activities in a particular locale, and utilizing extant or newly created developmental infrastructures that will be eventually maintained by the local population during and after the resolution process.

(5) Economic Organizations. During the resolution phase of the Intervention Cycle, economic organizations play a major supporting role. As the diplomats work toward political settlement in the state capital, citizens turn to settlement in their homes and villages. The devastation of state infrastructure that often results from violent upheaval—the loss of schools, homes, government centers, industries, highways, rail line, ports, and so forth—creates a massive need for economic assistance during the resolution phase of conflict intervention. The extent and duration of the conflict dictates not only the degree of destruction, it determines the ability of the successor state/government quickly to resume the function of governing.

As conflict subsides and the process of rebuilding commences, reconstruction and development grants, World Bank loans, and donor-nation assistance play essential roles in the process. In most cases the need will far exceed the state's capacity to identify, prioritize, fund, and manage the vast number of projects required for rebuilding or repairing its damaged infrastructure. In other cases the need will also exceed the desire of some partisan elites to equitably allocate the resources required to correct deficiencies in certain regions or functional areas. Thus, international financial organizations and donor states can find themselves in the position of taking on responsibility for making decisions or performing functions most appropriately handled by the state government.

Although expedient, this type of intervention should raise a cautionary flag in the minds of those who wish to ensure the reestablishment of a stable and sovereign state entity. Although money and resources are powerful, power is political. Thus, the support and/or reconstruction of viable political structures must take precedence over the expediency of nonhumanitarian assistance. International financial institutions and donor states/organizations should redouble efforts to ensure that their efforts are taken in conjunction with, and with the consent of, the nascent political structure and its key elites.

The Intervention Cycle discussion indicated that economic issues were of secondary importance to political issues during conflict resolution. One reason for such a value assessment is that political enfranchisement is a prerequisite to stability (in other words, the members of the state will choose to resolve conflicts via political mechanisms rather than resorting to violent measures). Another reason is that economic remedies are normally resource-intensive and effective over the long term. They require enormous sums of capital investment and time to bring into fruition (such as the rebuilding of a hydroelectric dam and power distribution system).

There are, however, short-term economic "infusions" that can support the resolutionary process. Most of these support those development priorities established by the state–international organization–NGO partnership discussed above. Short-term initiatives can be undertaken by economic organizations acting in conjunction with humanitarian and development programs with some degree of autonomy from the nascent political infrastructure. These initiatives, however, suffer from the same risks as those encountered by development organizations: locals affiliated with or directly benefiting from the implementation of the program become members of a newly created economic or class structure that changes the social status quo and risks deepening intergroup tensions. Careful coordination of economic support, developmental efforts, and a state-sponsored reconstruction framework will reduce the impact of these real, and in some cases unavoidable, disparities.

While short-term economic initiatives focus on development assistance–related funding, the drafting of a long-term economic plan commences in conjunction with government and/or transition party officials during the resolution process. The plan should balance the long-term requirements of aid donors (targets and conditions stipulated in the terms of assistance) and the long-term needs of the state (especially those suffering from massive destruction of preexisting infrastructure). To do so, economic organizations cannot raise the bar too high, nor can states set their standards too low. For example, a multiparty democratic government, full protection of human rights, and a market economy are laudable long-term goals to embrace. However, these may not be appropriate prerequisites for all forms of economic assistance. Rather, a good-faith declaration of intent with agreed-upon intervals and indices of progress measurement may suffice. Further, donors must ensure that their assistance offers are reasonably suited to the long-term needs of the state. For example, trade credits and agricultural subsidies may be of little or no value to a nomadic, semiagrarian society desperately in need of communication, transportation, and water distribution infrastructures.

As discussed earlier, the role of the economic organizations and IFIs reaches its peak during the next phase of the Intervention Cycle—prevention. During resolution, these organizations begin to support short-term developmental initiatives (microeconomic) while working in conjunction with the state to develop long-term (macroeconomic) strategies toward the development of free markets and sustainment of democratic systems. To the extent that these organizations can work within the structure of state agencies and political processes, economic forces that serve to undermine the resolution process can be limited if not translated into political support for the ongoing, yet still infant, process of politically resolving conflicts within the society.

In summary, humanitarian and developmental organizations are of primary importance during the resolution phase of the Intervention Cycle. They are suited to performing the task of rebuilding the civil and political societies of the state at the grassroots level. Although aggregate organizations and other interested parties will diplomatically engage the key elites of previously warring factions, the direct benefits of a peaceful resolution are most clearly translated into positive impact "on the ground" by these two organizations and their workers.

The negotiating tables, signing ceremonies, and the high drama of resolution are remote from the daily lives of individuals and groups who must feel the effect of resolution. It is there that humanitarian organizations can take advantage of the cessation of hostilities to put into place both temporary and enduring programs that will have an immediate impact on health and welfare. Developmental organizations can also begin the reconstruction of civil and political societies by assisting with the repair and reestablishment of local services and support systems, while assisting the state with the design of a reconstruction and development architecture that will sustain the long-term goals of political and economic enfranchisement. Although no one organization has the capacity to take overall responsibility for this range of intervention efforts, some method of coordination is required in order to assure that relief is equitably distributed, soundly applied, and appropriately supervised. Just as the center of coordination efforts shifted from the military to aggregate organizations during the mitigation phase, the center shifts from aggregate to development organizations in the resolution phase.

When the UN is involved in the resolution process, the transition from a humanitarian relief to a development focus may be considered by some to be seamless, or an in-house shift in coordination responsibility. However, even in the context of transferring coordination leads from one UN agency to another, there should be no assumptions. Stovepiping, or the narrow vertical reporting channels within some directorates and agencies, can result in little lateral communication between agencies on the ground. For example, anecdotal comments received by the author of the Rwanda case study during her research indicated that members of the same UN agency who were located on opposite sides of the Rwanda-Zaire borders had no direct contact with each other. Rather, reporting from one side of the border went to Geneva; reporting from the other side went to New York. While this may be an isolated incident, it illustrates the necessity for headquarters elements to clearly delegate and transfer coordination responsibilities to their representatives at the site of the intervention effort.

As the resolution process progresses, of course, the responsibility for coordination makes one final shift: to the state. As the Intervention Cycle begins its shift from resolution to prevention, external organizations begin to cede coordination responsibilities to the state structure, providing only those oversight and management functions required by the terms of their support. Intervening organizations can—and should—define the point of this transition in order to identify the limits of their own intervention activities and to help preclude the "donor dependency" discussed earlier.

The process of resolution will likely take longer than individual organizations or interested states remain engaged and interested. For example, in both the Cambodia and El Salvador cases, UN officials lamented the "premature" declaration of UN success; in both cases, those close to the interventions saw much more work to be done. However, with the framework in place and the building blocks of political and economic enfranchisement established, the state must be held responsible for its own success. In the next section, conflict prevention, international mechanisms that provide state governments with incentives for peacefully resolving intergroup conflict will be discussed.

II. INTERNATIONAL ORGANIZATIONS AND PREVENTION

Despite the nongovernmental nature of intergroup conflict, international organizations play a prominent role in both the prevention of and intervention in intergroup conflict when and if it becomes necessary. These institutions bring several important forces to bear on the problem: they provide membership or participatory incentives, facilitate internal and external dialogue, give transparency to internal developments, and provide the mechanisms for direct intervention, when needed. Additionally, and perhaps foremost among their attributes, is their international nature: they serve as global, regional, or multinational bodies or mechanisms that are nominally bereft of cultural, geographic, or religious biases, and are often able to credibly serve with a mantle of impartiality.

Membership to some large international organizations has an allure that alone can provide incentive for states to retain internal stability. State governments place a significant degree of equity in membership to international organizations such as the UN, the IMF, or NATO, due to the real or perceived political, economic, or military benefits—and, quite often, the status—that come along with membership. Because the retention of a formal state structure, recognized state borders, and adherence to some basic principles of internal and external behavior are prerequisites for participation, membership in international organizations often serves as a considerable incentive to the resolution of internal conflicts.

By retaining its sovereign integrity and a patina of internal stability—which requires the general pacification or enfranchisement of regional, ethnic, religious, and other groups—the state preserves its access to the benefits of membership in global fora. In contrast, states that appear to place no value in membership, "rogue" states who reject the international contract inherent in the fundamental principles of membership, are often those who are most needy of future emergency assistance.

It is often difficult to look inside states for evidence of disenfranchisement. This is especially true in those cases in which a state lacks membership in various global fora. In addition to a lack of systemic transparency, there is little or no leverage available to those on the outside who seek to correct repressive or discriminatory practices when they become apparent. We are thus forced either to wait for some external manifestation to warrant intervention or witness the collapse of the regime. However, because there appears to be some correlation between organizational membership and state stability—dysfunctional or nonexistent state structures prevail where and when violent intergroup conflict erupts—we need not find ourselves unprepared for or surprised by a need for intervention.

Institutional linkages to international fora are weakest and most tenuous in states in which recent violent conflict has occurred. Although the lack of linkages may have more to do with the nature of failed colonial or ideological empires and their offspring than with individual state failures to embrace international organizations, this correlation bears consideration. Efforts to encourage incentives for institutional membership may not only spur corrective measures within the state, they may facilitate the application of preventative measures. Further, if (re)intervention is required at some point in the future, these institutional linkages are the vehicles through which vital political, economic, and human resources can be delivered to mitigate violence and address conflict resolution.

A. Organizational Roles in Conflict Prevention

During this third phase of the Intervention Cycle, the focus of external intervention efforts should be the state. Yet, because the state must focus its preventative efforts toward individuals and groups within its borders, those who wish to intervene to do good often circumvent the bureaucratic middleman of state governments in order to provide help directly where it is needed. The preservation of this two-tiered relationship—organization/state and state/citizen—is a key element to the prevention of intergroup conflict. It should not be construed as a mere obstacle to providing relief directly to those who suffer from economic, political, or humanitarian inequities within a sovereign structure of the state.

In the previous chapter, the concept of social enfranchisement was introduced and identified as the blending of state and national identities. The long-term prevention of intergroup conflict requires the maximization of social enfranchisement, while keeping the divisive forces of nonstate ethnic, cultural, religious, or other identities under control. Interventions that unnecessarily circumvent the state and its structures undermine the concept of social enfranchisement by reinforcing the importance of an individual (e.g., refugee, displaced person, disadvantaged, tribe, clan) rather than a collective identity of the state with respect to the receipt of benefits in the form international assistance. Exacerbating these intergroup cleavages further weakens the state and could lead to increased intergroup conflict. In doing so, the cure becomes part of the disease.

It is important to reemphasize that this discussion takes place within the framework of preventative measures. Thus, the focus on preserving, strengthening, or even creating the state's capacity to cope with intergroup conflict and its various manifestations is of greatest value to the international community at this juncture and over the long term. In general, holding the state together (if only to allow it time to subdivide via political processes) will be less costly in lives, resources, and capital than allowing it to disintegrate under the centrifugal forces of intergroup conflict. With this concept in mind, the discussion now turns to a brief overview of each organizational genre and its role during the prevention phase of intervention.

(1) Security Organizations. In the prevention phase of the intervention cycle, the focus of security organizations is to affect the behavior of states, their leaders, and their policies in such a manner as to prevent the outbreak of intergroup conflict. As such, it does not necessarily involve the introduction of forces into an area of conflict, nor does it require direct action. However, there are two particular roles that stand out in recent preventative intervention experience: preventing the spillover of conflict from one region or state to another and asserting particular state values as a prerequisite or condition for membership.

The first, preventing spillover, is the strongest and most traditionally oriented role for any security organization. It is related, in both practice and principle, to the traditional mission lexicons of "deterrence," "peace through readiness," or "show of force." Placing organization member state forces on the periphery of an ongoing conflict may present an effective deterrence to the spread of violent outbreak, as the use of a small contingent of NATO military observers on the Serbia-Macedonia border or the use of CIS forces on the Georgia-Abkhazia border. The presence of these forces—and the organization they represent—can provide a physical and psychological barrier to the spread of violence and unrest.

In the second role, it is the terms and conditions of organizational membership that foster, for example, democratic government, civilian control of the military, respect for human rights, and other key aspects of political enfranchisement that can substantively contribute to the prevention of intergroup conflict. By holding (or withholding) the prospect of membership in a multilateral security organization, other states attempt to apply a form of moral suasion to the leaders of the would-be member state in order to affect their internal policies and practices. The ongoing discussion on the terms and conditions for the extension of NATO membership to former Warsaw Pact states is a case in point.

The efficacy of either of these roles, however, stems from a complicated set of conditions that, on the state-to-state level, closely resemble the interaction described in the previous chapter's discussion on the use of deterrent and coercive measures on groups or individuals. Deterrence, in the earlier context, is relatively ineffective when applied to the disenfranchised who have no stake in the state system. In the context of this relationship between international organizations and states, there is a similar condition.

Deterrence is relatively ineffective against a state that neither values the security organization (or its representatives) nor has a stake in the international system. For example, it can be argued that Pakistani forces in UNOSOM I were ineffective because Somali clans neither respected their ability as a combat force nor the UN as a body that represented their interests. Similarly, UN Protective Force (UNPROFOR) was ineffective at deterring the spread of violence in Bosnia's UN-declared safe zones once it became clear to Bosnian Serb and Muslim forces that UNPROFOR was unable or unwilling to actively enforce the sanctity of those areas. Conversely, the U.S. and Russian forces deployed on the Macedonian and Abkhaz borders respectively were regarded by local partisans as unlikely to suffer harassment without responding forcefully. More importantly, the key elites of the Serbian and Georgian states were compelled to ensure that local security forces remained in check, local unrest was minimized, and the rights of local minorities were reasonably upheld due to the real or perceived danger of drawing further U.S. (NATO) or Russian (CIS) intervention.

Moreover, the carrot of a NATO partnership or eventual membership would be ineffective should, for example, the leaders of former Soviet satellite states such as Romania or Bulgaria find no reason to value a stake in the future of the North Atlantic defense alliance. However, the responsibilities of current or prospective NATO membership has been effective in the shaping of human rights protection in areas of Central Europe where, for example, there exists a large Hungarian diaspora in Romania and Slovakia and sizable

Turk diaspora in Germany and Bulgaria. To a lesser degree, Turkey—a NATO member—has come under pressure over its treatment of its Kurdish minority. To the extent that moral suasion has been successful in that case, it has primarily been through Turkey's link with (and respect for) the Atlantic alliance and the status and benefits of NATO membership.

During the prevention phase of conflict intervention, then, security organizations play a role in shaping the policies of the state either by the proximate influence of deterrent forces or the persuasive power of their terms of membership. In cases where neither their forces nor membership hold the power of persuasion, security organizations are of little or no preventative value.

(2) Aggregate Organizations. Much like security organizations, the terms of aggregate organization membership provide some of the strongest influence over the actions of individual states. UN member-states, for example, have in theory accepted their obligation to "reaffirm faith in the fundamental human rights, in the dignity and worth of the human person, in the equal rights of men and women . . . and to establish conditions under which justice and respect for the obligations arising from treaties and other sources of international law. . . ."[8] The individual member-state willingness or ability to adopt and abide by such policies may, of course, vary. However, where the benefits of aggregate organization membership suit the interests of state governments, the lever of moral suasion may be effectively implemented.

The UN plays a special role as the archetypal aggregate organization. The demoralization suffered by the UN and its leadership in the wake of intervention failures during the early 1990s, should be of concern to those interested in preserving the beneficial aspects of aggregate organizations. Demonized by political elites in many states—whether for political gains, out of frustration over intractable conflicts abroad, the inefficiency of action by the "least common denominator," or due to ideological differences over the role of multilateralism in global affairs—the UN has been badly bruised by these attacks. Further weakened by overcommitment and decades of economic excess, the fate of the UN may turn upon changes within the structure of its headquarters, methods of operation, and leadership. Reform, while greatly needed at this time of upheaval and fundamental change in the global political, economic, and diplomatic status quo, should come in a manner that preserves the organization and its core competencies. The widespread ratification of such an expansive treaty such as the one that created the UN is quite unlikely in the current world political climate.

The benefits of an aggregate organization may be less readily apparent during conflict mitigation and resolution stages than during the prevention stage but are nonetheless, critical. During the previous stages of intervention, security, humanitarian, and developmental organizations appeared to bring real, concrete, and tangible efforts directly to bear on the situation at hand. However, when conflict has subsided to the point where the efforts of these organizations are no longer needed, their very presence would be meddlesome at best, disruptive at worst. Sovereign states, especially those emerging from a period of crisis, are eager to assert their independence and competence. The presence of assistance organizations may easily become a point of resentment for the political elite of the newly minted state.

Aggregate organizations, on the other hand, are membership oriented; therefore, "they" are "we." Through their character of belongingness, states may obtain the benefits (and, of course, must bear the responsibilities) of membership without appearing to be receiving a handout, a subsidy, or requiring further international intervention. Further, the aggregate organization provides connectivity with and participation in economic, trade, security, and other fora of extreme importance to developed and developing nations. The creation of specific international forums such as the World Trade Organization provides alternatives to aggregate organization membership however limited and unique in scope these options are. Further, UN membership provides the visibility and legitimacy required as a virtual prerequisite for membership in these other treaty or trade organizations.

During the conflict prevention stage of intervention, state policies and practices that nurture political and economic enfranchisement may be cultivated and supported through its network of programs, conferences, and commissions. Each of these programs develop out of the common need to address a problem of international proportion, such as water, natural resources, refugees and immigration, and trade. In these various fora, state representatives discuss these problems and, in theory, attempt to reach a consensus on how individual state policies can be made to work in conjunction with others in a manner that alleviates or minimizes the impact of the problem on the others. Agreements on issues such as immigration, labor, or water rights, for example, can lead to enhanced regional stability and economic development.

In those cases where individual member state practices cause harm to internal or external groups and individuals, the aggregate organization can apply deterrent or coercive measures that seek to rectify state policies or practices that threaten stability. Through its various diplomatic, financial, developmental, or security levers, the aggregate organization may exert sufficient influence on the state to prevent political or economic disenfranchisement successfully. Again, however, the efficacy of these levers are directly associated with the degree of benefit the state attaches to its status of organizational membership. In the case of the UN, that organizational membership approaches the heightened stature of global membership and legitimacy.

(3) Humanitarian Organizations. During the prevention phase of the Intervention Cycle, humanitarian organizations can normally be expected to be engaged elsewhere, such as the scene of grave humanitarian emergency or natural disaster. For those states that have recently emerged from the resolution process, it is also quite likely that the limits of humanitarian assistance resources have been met and general disengagement has been attempted.

However, even in those cases where tremendous capacity has been reconstructed within the state and the human toll has been brought under control, the prospect for humanitarian intervention remains high, especially in those regions susceptible to natural disasters or other endemic natural or environmental phenomena. As briefly discussed in the preceding chapter, natural disasters such as drought, famine, earthquakes, fires, and floods can cause or exacerbate sources of intergroup tension. The capacity of state governments to respond to the needs that arise from these occurrences can, and likely will, be quickly surpassed. Timely support—provided either directly to those in need or through the state's own response network—from humanitarian organizations can limit the stress placed on the society. This responsive humanitarian intervention will be of significant importance to the prevention of intergroup conflict.

Humanitarian organizations are naturally poised to help anywhere disaster strikes. However, the calculus for response includes the type of disaster and the ability of a particular state to meet the resultant humanitarian need. An eye toward the prevention of intergroup conflict may suggest that these organizations also factor in the extent to which one particular subset of the state (a tribal, regional, ethnic, cultural, or religious group, for example) has been singled out, either in receiving the brunt of the damage or the benefit of relief. In those cases where such inequities exist, humanitarian organizations may aid in the prevention of intergroup conflict by bolstering the state's response efforts where needed.

Further, humanitarian organizations can assist development and aggregate organizations by identifying those states whose capacity for dealing with humanitarian emergencies falls well short of their needs. This may be due to policy and spending practices in the area of public health and welfare that court disastrous consequences by causing regional or socioeconomic disparities in facilities and/or access to emergency supplies and treatment. In this way, humanitarian organizations from Human Rights Watch to CARE provide input that can help alleviate the intergroup conflict "flash points" that turn natural disasters into governmental crises.

(4) Development Organizations. The discussion of conflict resolution pointed out that the work of development organizations reaches its peak during that phase of intervention; as capacity is built within the state's architecture, fewer development related projects are required. However, there are several areas in which development organizations can—and do—remain engaged. They serve as "watch" organizations to monitor the pulse of political, economic, and social enfranchisement; they also serve as partners with regional and local organizations to maintain the perishable attributes of intergroup relationships.

For example, organizations like Amnesty International, the American Civil Liberties Union, and even private endowments such as the Ford Foundation provide continued oversight of political tolerance, social justice, human rights, and the ethics of a government. Although not commonly perceived as "development" projects or placed in the same context as road building, crop planting, and water purification, these are essential tasks in the development of stable, democratic, nation-states.

Many of the factors contributing to disenfranchisement are found in the government's practices and policies. Likewise, the inability or failure of a state's civil and political societies to address these factors allows them slowly to erode the state's foundation. Those organizations that specialize in the cultivation of healthy elements of a state's civil and political societies can play an instrumental role in conflict prevention. Their activity, however, can be easily undermined by the policies of the state.

Because the focus of these organizations is often at the substate level— labor unions, academic institutions, political parties, and so on—the state must be a willing partner in the efforts of developmental organizations. In many cases, the approval of the state government must be received in order to allow the organization to operate freely within its borders. Further, regardless of the progress made within elements of civil or political society, the state must remain responsive toward implementing the resultant policy changes or recommendations. For this reason, the effectiveness of developmental assistance is directly tied to the cooperation of the state. As a preventative mechanism, then, developmental organizations are only as effective as the state allows, leaving them with little ability to intervene in order to deter or coerce the course of state affairs. In those cases where the state is amenable to their activities, much of their work will directly strengthen the overall efforts to prevent the recurrence of intergroup conflict.

(5) Economic Organizations. The economic dynamics of the state revealed during the resolution process may provide a clear indication of those areas in which continued vigilance must be exercised to ensure continued economic

enfranchisement within the society. States in which there exists a very small minority of individuals who control the preponderance of the state's gross domestic product (GDP), for example, are much more likely to require broad-scale assistance in the form of extensive economic development and microlending programs that target individuals and communities. States with extensive rural or nomadic populations and an agrarian-based economy may require more extensive effort in the communication and transportation sectors than states in which populations are massed in coastal regions or around production centers with an industrial or service-based economy. Moreover, some states will require efforts to facilitate a total change in economic structure due to the depletion of natural resources, obsolescence of end products, or inability to compete in a global market with other suppliers of goods and services.

In these latter cases, where the traditional economic foundation of the state is no longer viable, the work of economic organizations is critical to the prevention of economic-related disenfranchisement. Working on both the state and substate levels, the economic organization can link the much needed infusion of capital to the ongoing efforts of, for example, developmental organizations and private business initiatives. Further, they can work in conjunction with civic and political organizations to ensure the development of public investment and capital-building activities that, in the future, will provide the internal resources that can prevent the need for reintervention.

In most cases, economic intervention will be initiated at the request of a state's government, either in conjunction with the conduct of its normal activities or as the result of a crisis, such as a natural disaster or famine. When IMF, World Bank, or regional development loans are sought by state governments that—from the outside—provide every indication of stability, the tasks associated with preventing intergroup conflict remain the same as in those states emerging from violent conflict. However, it is more difficult to argue in favor of, or recognize a compelling need for, the application of preventative measures. Not only are the external manifestations of intergroup conflict less apparent in the stable state, principles of sovereignty compel international fora to avoid assistance that appears ideologically linked to a particular set of values. However, in a world of constrained resources there are preventative measures that can and should be conducted with diligence in order to protect the international investment and contribute to enduring stability via policies that cultivate long-term economic enfranchisement.

Political theorists have studied and debated the cause and effect relationship between a state's economic condition and its stability. However, many economic-based analyses are weakened by their inability to be uniquely determinative; that is, they are unable to determine a unique condition to

which a given set of economic criteria will lead.[9] For the purpose of this discussion, let it suffice to say that structural impediments to economic development directly affect the ability of the state to carry out those government
and social programs that lead to long-term growth. Where there are structural
impediments to economic growth—regardless of whether the result of violent
conflict, social, political, or geographic circumstances, or some other historic
factor—economic organizations that intervene must ensure that relief efforts
in the form of capital, credit, or investment are supported by policies that will
enfranchise those groups and individuals responsible for building and/or sus-
taining the "P" in GDP. Without exercising such vigilance, the (re)creation of
economic disparities will lead to increased tension among various sectors of
the society and economic disenfranchisement.

The economic organization has tremendous leverage over the state in
need of economic assistance. Withholding, or threatening to withhold, funds
can serve as a powerful deterrent toward unsound or potentially disenfranchising monetary practices. That leverage, if used with an eye toward creating
long-term stability, may persuade the state to change offending policies.
However, the coercive value of withholding economic assistance appears, to
this author, less clearly effective. That is because, when deterrent measures are
insufficiently persuasive, the continued withholding of economic assistance
will cause further erosion of the state's infrastructure, further depletion of its
resources and, as so clearly evident in the recent use of economic embargoes
against Iraq and Haiti, may accelerate the disenfranchisement of those most
needy of economic assistance. This underscores a paradox in the use of economic mechanisms: although potentially deterrent in nature, the actual
implementation of economic sanctions will most likely exacerbate the economic cleavages present within a state structure, worsening the condition of
those who are in most need of assistance.

In summary, the economic organization can play a role in the prevention
of intergroup conflict by promoting sound monetary practices and state
policies that foster enfranchisement, as well as supporting the work of those
organizations involved in the development or strong civil and political societies. The relative strength of economic deterrence is much greater than that
of coercion, however, due to the disproportionate impact of economic sanctions upon the poor and those without access to economic resources (invest-
ment/savings) or relief (credit). This limitation to the utility of economic
mechanisms underscores the importance of those remedies that foster deepened political and social enfranchisement as means of preventing intergroup conflict.

B. Conflict Prevention

The task facing those who seek to intervene for the prevention of conflict is, as this discussion has shown, complex. Moreover, even the ability to intervene during this stage of the Intervention Cycle is called into question by the principle of sovereignty: the mere fact that a state's practices appear offensive or disenfranchising to the international community is insufficient for the violation of that state's right to conduct affairs within its own borders as it sees fit. Thus, those states whose policies appear most destabilizing may also be the ones most inaccessible to those seeking to intervene to do good. If so, then the issue of conflict prevention is hypothetical at best, impossible at worst.

Fortunately, however, there have been few instances in which an effort at conflict intervention was a state's first contact with international organizations.[10] Most states find themselves compelled to seek the assistance—or the forbearance—of some regional and international partners. Either through trade, security, ideological, or political fora, sovereign entities give up some of their absolute rights of independence in order to obtain the benefits of commerce, security, safe passage, or resource access. The Intervention Cycle suggests ways in which various international fora can contribute to the prevention of conflict by understanding its causes, promoting policies that foster enfranchisement, and exercising vigilance over the policies and practices of member states. Further, when called upon to intervene, international fora can and should have an understanding of the problem being faced, its potential causes, and the desired outcome of intervention. Without express principles, goals, and a framework upon which to approach the challenges of intervention, there can be little hope for success.

NOTES

1. See Paul Taylor, "Coordination in International Organisation," in Paul Taylor and A. J. R. Groom (Eds.), *International Organisation: A Conceptual Approach*, New York: Nichols Publishing, 1978, p. 195.
2. UNSC permanent members—China, France, Russia, the United Kingdom and the United States—are those whose role as the post–World War II "great powers" relegated them the burden of responsibility for global peace. Expansion of UNSC permanent membership to include Japan and Germany, due to their contemporary economic and military power, is currently under consideration.

   Several discussions on the legitimating value of the UNSC in conflict intervention have been written in recent years. One that is particularly helpful is Lori Fisler Damrosch (Ed.), *Enforcing Restraint: Collective Intervention in Internal Conflicts*, New York: Council on Foreign Relations Press, 1993.

3. Although this study specifically avoids debating the decision to intervene, enumerating intervention criteria, or exploring the international legal implications thereof, it does not underestimate the legitimizing power of the UNSC. Recent history provides numerous examples of states and parties seeking a UN mantle of approval under which to conduct interventions based on unilateral security interests. One such example is the United States intervention and enforcement action in Haiti which sought UNSC approval for the use of "all necessary means" to reinstate the legitimate government of Haiti's deposed president.

   Although conducted under the chimera of an international coalition, U.S. forces carried out the enforcement action unilaterally—in response to various American political, economic, security, and humanitarian interests—and subsequently turned the operation over to the UN and other intervening mechanisms at the point of transition between conflict mitigation and resolution tasks. In the Haiti case, the UNSC provided the legitimacy for the intervention, while other mechanisms—both internal and external to the UN—provided the actual implementation. This paradigm is likely to be repeated in the OSCE-led intervention in Nagorno-Karabakh, with a Russian-led body of peacekeepers providing confidence and physically separating parties to the conflict in western Azerbaijan.

4. See Chapter 1 under "Keeping the Peace."

5. For example, in an eleventh-hour attempt to avoid a military "invasion" of Haiti, U.S. President Bill Clinton dispatched a negotiating team headed by former President Jimmy Carter. That team's other key negotiator was retired Army General Colin L. Powell, former Chairman of the Joint Chiefs of Staff. Numerous postmission accounts show that Powell was tremendously effective due to his professional military reputation and stature among Haiti's military leaders and soldiers. When Powell, a fellow soldier, looked them in the eye and said it was so, there was no doubt that it was so.

6. The problems associated with attempting to adopt such a model are exceptionally clear through the lens of hindsight. Iraq has continued to prosecute an internal offensive in its northern and southern regions with great effectiveness and at considerable human cost. Further, military "exercises" in the fall of 1994 identified the requirement to create a buffer zone of physical separation between the Iraqi army and Kuwait due to its relative offensive strength against its southern neighbor. However, the model is presented to differentiate conceptual constructs of practical disarmament and reorientation; as such, it is a useful example. Other related, but less contemporary, models would include Japan and postwar Germany.

7. The South African Reconstruction and Development Programme provided an example of how states, political parties, NGOs, and research organizations can work together to develop, publicize, and work toward the implementation of a comprehensive blueprint for the resolution of violence, lack of housing, lack of jobs, inadequate education and health care, lack of democracy and a failing economy, problems that are at the root of political, economic, and social disenfranchisement. See, "A Basic Guide to the Reconstruction and Development Programme." Johannesburg: African National Congress, 1994, p. 1.

8. Preamble of the UN Charter.

9. See Adam Przeworski, "Some Problems of the Study of the Transition to Democracy," in Guillermo O'Donnell, Phillipe C. Schmitter, and Laurence Whitehead, (Eds.), *Transitions From Authoritarian Rule*, Baltimore: The Johns Hopkins University Press, 1986.

10. Even in the case of Somalia, where there was no recognized Somali government at the time of international intervention, early steps at prevention could have been undertaken during Barré's rule by Somalia's major benefactors before the civil war. Further, there are many indications that the actions taken by aid organizations and others during and subsequent to the civil war served to deepen the political, economic, and social cleavages in Somali society. See April Oliver's discussion in Chapter 4.

PART TWO

Case Studies in Intervention

■ ■ ■ ■ ■ ■

■ ■ ■ ■ ■ ■

This second section of *Breaking the Cycle* examines nine cases of conflict intervention. Diverse both in region and circumstance, these cases are intended to bring the theoretical discussion of Part 1 of this book into the context of real-world conflict. They are intended less to demonstrate the current state of the conflicts than how the use of a conceptual framework—the Intervention Cycle—lends an unprecedented clarity of purpose and depth of understanding to the discussion of intervention.

The first three cases, Bosnia, Somalia, and Rwanda, discuss the best-known and most recent international efforts to intervene at the height of unmitigated violence. The authors, from uniquely different perspectives and backgrounds, discuss the specifics of these three difficult interventions with the benefit of hindsight and through the clarifying lens of the Intervention Cycle. Their individual observations and conclusions present a compelling argument for redoubled international efforts at preventative engagement. The contributors also emphasize the need for clarity of purpose and strength of commitment required when intervening at the height of violent, intergroup conflict.

The middle four cases, Haiti, West Bank and Gaza, Nagorno-Karabakh, and El Salvador, present cases in which international intervention efforts have met with some degree of success toward mitigating violence and beginning the process of resolution. However, this equally diverse set of cases— again by colleagues of multifaceted perspectives—begins to illustrate the strength of the Intervention Cycle as a framework for identifying the discrete tasks and appropriate mechanisms for intervention. Readers will find parallels, heretofore unexpressed in works on the subject of intervention, that provide comprehension of not only the history of these cases, but the challenges yet to come.

Finally, the last two case studies, Tajikistan and Chechnya, present cautionary tales of failed prevention in an area of the world that is undergoing significant political, economic, and social change during this post-Soviet era. These final cases also illustrate the manifestation of intergroup conflict in areas where Western or international interests are less clearly engaged, yet where the course and method of preventing or mitigating widespread, violent conflict may have profound implications for the future. These less-known cases further allow the reader to take the lessons learned from the prior intervention discussions and see how the Intervention Cycle lends unusual clarity to the effects of widespread disenfranchisement and the challenges of imparting relevance to a "national" or "state" identity.

These case studies, while as varied in style, subject, and content, as the background of their authors, illustrate the utility of the Intervention Cycle framework as a conceptual tool with which to understand the dynamics of intergroup conflict, regardless of perspective, venue, or circumstance. More importantly, however, the diversity of these cases provides readers with the broadest possible overview of this important issue: how to formulate a concept for effectively intervening to mitigate, resolve, or prevent the recurrence of violent intergroup conflict.

CHAPTER 3

The Breakup of Yugoslavia

Kori N. Schake

The breakup of Yugoslavia resulted in 250,000 casualties, two million refugees, Europe's most shocking war crimes in a half-century, and a country cantonized into jealous ethnic blocs.[1] This violent dissolution of the state is all the more tragic since from 1945 to 1990 Yugoslavia had largely succeeded at the very difficult task of creating a tolerant and enfranchised society from five major ethnic groups with three different languages and religions.

The death of Premier Josip Tito, wrenching economic disruptions, and the rise of Serbian leaders who resuscitated historic grievances set in motion a spiral of disenfranchisement whose centrifugal forces polarized political discourse, reduced allegiances beyond ethnic groups, and pulled the country apart. While the Dayton Peace Accords have now halted the carnage, the enormous difficulty associated with reenfranchisement suggests that war could resume soon after the NATO Implementation Force withdraws in December 1996.

The breakup of Yugoslavia is more than a human tragedy for those involved, a moral defeat for secular humanism, and a cause to question the ideological belief that democracy produces peaceful governments. It is also a cautionary tale about the difficulties of intervention. Much could have been done by the international community to catalyze the situation in positive directions. Much was done by the international community that, the Intervention Cycle suggests and events in the former Yugoslavia demonstrate, aggravated the problems.[2]

Kori N. Schake is a Postdoctoral Scholar at the Institute on Global Conflict and Cooperation, at the University of California at San Diego. She holds a Ph.D. in political science from the University of Maryland and has previously worked for the Assistant Secretary of Defense for Strategy and Requirements and as the NATO Desk Officer in the Directorate for Strategic Plans and Policy in the Joint Staff.

One of the central reasons for late and frequently contradictory intervention by the international community was the inability to agree on the nature of the problem in Yugoslavia. The war in Yugoslavia has been explained as the inevitable dissolution of a state that never engendered a single nation, the inevitable clash of religion and culture between the Muslim and Christian worlds, a civil war of sequential secession to avoid minority status, and calculated territorial expansion.[3] Each of these interpretations warrant different types of intervention. The international community's desire to do something without reaching consensus on the nature of the problem led to choosing over time elements that remedy different diseases in order to maintain community support.

The Intervention Cycle helps to identify which of these rubrics accurately describes the dissolution of the state of Yugoslavia and the war that ensued. It suggests that Yugoslavia's dissolution was not inevitable, either as a result of the artificial nature of the state or the clash between the Muslim and Christian worlds. Yugoslavia did not have the ethnic, religious, or linguistic homogeneity that aid creation and maintenance of a state. However, it did have acknowledged borders, an economy integrated across republics, a shared historical legacy, and over 40 years of experience functioning as a state. If the international community had intervened to maintain and further political, social, and economic enfranchisement, the forces that exploded Yugoslavia could probably have been contained.

Elements of both a civil war of sequential secession to avoid minority status and calculated territorial expansion are evident in the breakup of Yugoslavia. However, just as the dissolution of Yugoslavia was not inevitable, neither was its violent breakup. The Intervention Cycle suggests that if the society had been enfranchised by the active intervention of the international community, its collapse into nationalist regimes at war over the demarcation and ethnic purification of their cantonal frontiers could have been prevented. The Intervention Cycle also suggests the great difficulty of that task, and the limited role that the use of force by the international community would play in such an effort.

This chapter applies the Intervention Cycle framework to events since 1990 to assess the efficacy of intervention. It suggests seven main findings, that (1) early intervention could have prevented the conflict; (2) elections require support for democratic principles to be stabilizing; (3) military force is inadequate for resolving intergroup conflict, that is, political, economic, and social elements are essential for reenfranchisement; (4) unity of purpose is essential for effective intervention; (5) linking intervention to issues beyond the intergroup conflict is destructive; (6) negotiation must be tied to intervention; and (7) resolving intergroup conflict is exceedingly difficult, but essential to enfranchisement.

I. THE LAND OF THE SOUTHERN SLAVS

A cursory review of Yugoslav history demonstrates the evolution of its complex ethnic and religious composition and 700 years of recurrent tension between encouraging ethnic affiliation and subordinating it to an inclusive national identity broader than ethnicity: control by the Ottoman empire from 1389 to 1878, when Russian victories secured Balkan independence; Austro-Hungarian annexation of Bosnia in 1908 until the assassination of Archduke Franz Ferdinand that began the First World War; a decade of democracy as "the Kingdom of Serbs, Croats, and Slovenes"; establishment of a Kingdom of Southern Slavs—Yugoslavia—to subordinate ethnicity and ensure the rights of non-Serbs; loose confederation from 1934 (when the king was assassinated) until the Nazi invasion of 1941. Nazi Germany occupied Serbia and established a separate fascist state in Croatia. Italy occupied Montenegro and southern Slovenia. Macedonia was partitioned between Bulgaria and Albania. Josip Tito's Communists waged a savage resistance; estimates of Yugoslav casualties are around 1.7 million, of which one million are estimated to have been killed by other Yugoslavs.[4]

In 1945, Tito reconstituted Yugoslavia as a socialist federation of six republics: Serbia, Croatia, Slovenia, Bosnia-Herzegovina, Macedonia, and Montenegro; and two autonomous Serbian provinces in Vojvodina and Kosovo. Administrative boundaries were explicitly created to prevent Serb domination of other ethnic groups.[5] Federal legislatures reflected both universal suffrage (the Federal Council) and proportional representation by region (Council of Nationalities). The constitution guaranteed equal rights for all ethnic groups and made inciting racial or religious intolerance a federal crime.[6]

In 1974 Tito attempted further to weaken the hold of ethnic and religious ties by creating representation based on occupational and interest groups.[7] Power was largely decentralized; what centralized power existed, such as the federal presidency, was exercised within agreed power sharing formulae and balanced by veto power of the republics.

These political reforms suggest that significant tensions remained among Yugoslavia's communities. The fact that minority ethnic communities commonly existed as separate enclaves suggests tolerance but a failure to create identities broader than ethnicity. Serbia and Slovenia were relatively homogenous, but Croatia and Bosnia were more ethnically and religiously heterogeneous. The population of Slovenia was 90 percent Slovene; Serbia was 85 percent Serb; Croatia was 75 percent Croat and 12 percent Serb; Bosnia was 32 percent Serb, 18 percent Croat, and 40 percent Muslim.[8] The government was actively engaged in expanding enfranchisement and was making progress, as demonstrated by the fact that nearly 25 percent of all marriages were between people of different ethnic groups.[9]

The decade from Tito's death in 1980 until the collapse of the Communist party in 1990 saw desperate, unsuccessful efforts to maintain enfranchisement through a balance of ethnic authority within Yugoslavia. Without the unifying figure of Tito or the weight of the Communist party to balance ethnicity, political and social enfranchisement quickly eroded. In addition, the 1980s saw the near collapse of the Yugoslav economy. Efforts to shift from a socialist to a market economy and increasing interdependence with the international economy caused economic upheaval, exacerbating the fragile political state of the country.[10] By 1989, inflation had increased to nearly 2,000 percent per year, unemployment remained high, foreign debt skyrocketed (simultaneously increasing the influence of international institutions and limiting the government's ability to provide services), and regional economic disparities increased.[11]

The country was collapsing: governmental authority was disintegrating, intolerance was taking strong hold in the public discourse, and the economy was bad and getting worse. All of the major indicators of disenfranchisement outlined in the Intervention Cycle were clearly evident.

The breakup of the former Yugoslavia has five phases: (1) independence of the republics from Serbia in 1991; (2) war between Croats and secessionist Serbs in Croatia in 1992; (3) stabilizing Macedonia and Kosovo in 1992; (4) war among secessionist communities in Bosnia from 1992 to 1995; and (5) cessation of fighting in 1995 due to the Dayton Peace Accords. The remainder of this chapter reviews these phases and the international community's involvement in them.

II. ESCALATING DISENFRANCHISEMENT: INDEPENDENCE FOR THE REPUBLICS

The fracturing of Yugoslav society was initiated by Serbs demanding redress for the limits Tito had placed on their power.[12] Slobodan Milosevic ran for president of Serbia in 1990 to secure for Serbs the right to live in a single state. The ferocity of Serbian rhetoric frayed the fabric of political tolerance, alarmed non-Serbs throughout Yugoslavia, and heightened their desire for independence.[13] Parties whose platforms were based on ethnicity were elected in five of the six republics (all except Macedonia). The 1990 republic elections doomed Yugoslavia's multicultural state. The democratic process fueled local and ethnic grievances and validated by majority vote exclusionary ethnic policies.

A. Prevention

The disenfranchisement of non-Serbs in the former Yugoslavia began the momentum toward violence identified in the Intervention Cycle. As the old order was collapsing, the international community did very little to assist in the establishment of a stable and peaceful new order, in large part because of preoccupation with the Persian Gulf War and dramatic changes in the international order resulting from the collapse of the Soviet Union and unification of Germany.

The Intervention Cycle suggests that the international community could have played an extremely important role in this early stage by intervening to stabilize the economy and support domestic cohesion among and within the emerging republics. Providing incentives to newly elected leaders for moderate behavior, supporting media and businesses that promoted tolerance, assisting in education for newly enfranchised electorates, targeting aid to balance increasing regional disparities, assisting in the peaceful resolution of disputes and providing peacekeeping forces along newly established borders might have encouraged alternatives to Milosevic, diminished Serb xenophobia, and made possible a peaceful transition.[14] Given the resources committed by the international community since conflict broke out, preventative intervention would undoubtedly have been the least costly alternative.

B. Deterrence

The republic elections were followed by successful referenda on secession in Slovenia and Croatia that gave the federal government until June 1991 to develop an acceptable formula for loose confederation. Unable to reach agreement with other republics on a balance of powers suitable to Slovenia and Croatia, the two republics declared their independence from Yugoslavia in July 1991. Serb president Milosevic responded by instituting economic sanctions against Slovenia and Croatia and employing the Yugoslav military in support of Serb claims that republics could only secede if Serbian populations and "Serbian lands" remained with Serbia.[15]

The Intervention Cycle suggests that once the republics declared their independence, the international community should have focused its efforts on deterring violence between the republics and redoubled its efforts at enfranchisement within republics. Instead, the international community treated the breakup as if it were preventable, although preventative measures were ineffective by this time.[16]

The Intervention Cycle suggests that economic sanctions, political isolation, or other deterrent and coercive measures including the use of force could have been applied to deter a resort to violence. Recognition should have been tied to peacefully negotiating the terms of secession and denied to any republic that resorted to force. This position, advocated by both the UN and the U.S. government, was undercut by the European Community.[17]

The employment of the Yugoslav national army to enforce Serbia's claim in Slovenia completed the delegitimization of Yugoslav federal authority. The army's failure to prevent Slovenia's secession probably emboldened other republics to fight for their independence. Thus, the battle over Slovenian independence validated both the republics desire for independence and the recourse to violence to achieve it.

III. THE WAR IN CROATIA

While Slovenian independence was a political and economic loss to Serbia, independence of Croatia would be much more difficult to accept since Croatia had a substantial Serbian population. During 1991 negotiations on Croatian independence, the Yugoslav navy bombarded the Croatian cities of Vukovar and Dubrovnik. With the support of the Yugoslav army, Croatian Serbs living in Kraijina (the area contiguous to Serbia) went to war against Croatia for the right to be part of the Serbian state.

A. Failed Deterrence and Coercion

The Intervention Cycle notes that deterrence is only successful when the deterrent measures are considered legitimate and the losses accrued through noncompliance exceed the potential gain. Short of military intervention, the international community probably could not have prevented conflict between Serbia and Croatia after Slovenian independence.

However, had the international community forcefully intervened at this critical juncture to punish Serbian aggression in Croatia, it could have possibly coerced a halt to violence. Many of the tools later employed by the international community would have been valuable coercive measures and may have modified aggressive behavior before the parties to the conflict became committed to their war aims. For example, strikes against Yugoslav Navy ships shelling Dubrovnik—continuing until the shelling ceased or all the ships had been sunk—would have identified the target group and behavior and clearly signaled the desired effect and the condition for removal outlined in the Intervention Cycle as conditions for effective coercion.

Instead, the international community sought to remain neutral and negotiate the cessation of violence. Coercing the parties into peaceful resolution of the dispute may have derailed neutral negotiations; but the "neutral" negotiations conducted by the International Conference on the Former Yugoslavia reinforced Serb political and military advantages.

The early inaction of the international community diminished the value of its future threats of involvement and encouraged the Serbs to believe they could conduct aggression with impunity.[18] In retrospect, the shelling of Vukovar and Dubrovnik appears to be zero hour in the Intervention Cycle, the point at which the parties to the conflict in Croatia became committed to violence.

B. Mitigation

The evidence of atrocities committed against civilians in Croatia mobilized the international community to intervene in the former Yugoslavia in late 1991. Four initiatives were undertaken: (1) expulsion of Serbia from the Conference on Security and Cooperation in Europe for violating international norms of behavior; (2) economic embargo of Serbia led by the European Community; (3) establishment of a war crimes tribunal by the UN; and (4) UN arms embargo against all the Yugoslav republics.

The first three initiatives sought to isolate and punish Serbia. Serbia was clearly identified as the aggressor and sanctioned for its resort to force by the same organizations professing neutrality in negotiations. These sanctions were an important step in applying punitive or coercive measures against Serbia and building the foundation for a broader-based intervention. The Intervention Cycle suggests that these sanctions may have been more effective had they been applied prior to the outbreak of widespread violence. However, these initiatives ran counter to the international community's professions of neutrality. They also were undertaken too late. By this time, however, Serbia no longer held a stake in maintaining peace in the former Yugoslavia.

Political and economic tools might have been effective earlier in the course of the conflict, but by the spring of 1992 only the use of force would have likely mitigated the conflict. These tools remain important in demonstrating the unity of purpose in the international community, particularly in leading up to the use of force; thus they remain powerful elements of a broader politico-military strategy. However, by the time that parties to the conflict are committed to violence, political and economic tools alone cease to be adequate to deter or coerce behavior.

The arms embargo was aimed at limiting the violence of the war, but in practice it aided the Serbs. Since the Yugoslav army possessed most of the weaponry, they could—and did—arm Serbs in the other republics. An arms embargo might have been a useful tool at other points in the Intervention Cycle. However, put to use once fighting had broken out, the embargo had the worst combination of effects: it punished the victims of Serb aggression by limiting their ability to defend themselves, shifted the strategic balance in favor of Serbia winning the war, and sent mixed signals of intent.[19] None of these actions dissuaded Serbians from pursuing a greater Serbia by force. Indeed, Bosnian Serb forces had already accomplished much toward this end by early 1992.

C. Peace Operations

The Intervention Cycle suggests that a successful intervention would have required deploying to Croatia a combat force capable of compelling accession to the will of the community. The military mission of the international force could have been moving organized Yugoslav military forces back across the Serbian border, halting arms shipments to Kraijina Serbs, and restoring a secure environment within Croatia. Accomplishing these missions would have delegitimized the use of force in the conflict.

The Intervention Cycle also suggests that having accomplished this mission, the military forces should have been replaced with peacekeeping forces drawn from different nations or a different organization than the enforcement force. While peacekeeping forces were deployed in the area of conflict, negotiations could begin about the terms for establishing order in the society. When the society was sufficiently stable to make the transition from peacekeeping forces to a localized police force to maintain civil order, resolution of the underlying sources of conflict could be addressed and the civil society reconstructed.

None of this occurred in Croatia. Instead, the community deployed a UN military force in Croatia to monitor human rights and support delivery of humanitarian assistance. Military forces were interjected into a conflict the international community had no intention of resolving in order to mediate the effects of the war. The UN subsequently added over 40 Security Council resolutions to this mandate that further obscured the force's mission and degraded its ability to carry out the assigned tasks. The forces were billed as neutral, even though their tasks prevented the Serbs from achieving their war aims.

The situation remained a stalemate until the spring of 1995, when Croatia resumed its military campaign. The international community acquiesced while Croats drove Serbs out of Western Slavonia and Kraijina.[20] The area is now at peace only through expulsion of non-Croats from territory held by Croatian forces: 15,000 Serb refugees were forced out of Western Slavonia in May 1995, and nearly 200,000 Serbs fled Kraijina in August, the largest forced migration of the Yugoslav wars.[21] Croats continue to prevent the return of Muslim and Serb refugees alike.[22] In the wake of this ethnic cleansing, the boundaries between Croatia and Serbia largely stabilized consistent with ethnic distribution.

Instead of resolving the source of the conflict, the international community chose methods of intervention intended to soften the effects of the conflict on civilians. However, the Intervention Cycle suggests that unless the international community intervenes forcefully to stop the violence, these efforts will not be successful. Humanitarian efforts should be subordinated to the military mission of establishing a stable environment when—and if—there is sufficient will and commitment to stop the violence.

IV. KOSOVO AND MACEDONIA

Preventing conflict in Kosovo and Macedonia are the success stories of international involvement in the former Yugoslavia. In both cases, successful intervention prevented the outbreak of violence and reenfranchisement efforts are underway to resolve the source of intergroup conflict.

In the case of Kosovo, Presidents Bush and Clinton successfully deterred the outbreak of violence.[23] Both publicly warned Milosevic that Serbia would be held accountable for any violence that occurred in Kosovo. While Kosovo remains tense, arms flows appear to have ceased and calm currently prevails.

Macedonian independence was not seriously contested by the former Yugoslav republics. Although there were tensions between Slavs and the Albanian minority in Macedonia, and an unemployment rate of 45 percent, Macedonia faced its greatest threat from outside powers, particularly Greece (pressing a rival claim to Macedonian heritage).[24] Macedonia's relative success lies in three factors: timing, Western interest, and enfranchisement. The community's attention was already focused on the Balkans as enfranchisement in Macedonia was fraying. Greek efforts to isolate Macedonia politically and economically, and Turkey's support for Macedonia, threatened a Balkan war in which two NATO allies were involved on opposing sides. Macedonia posed the most direct threat to the interests of the West.

The international community dispatched a peacekeeping force to monitor activity in Macedonia (including a substantial U.S. contingent), pressured Greece and Turkey to moderate their involvement, tied aid to respect for minority rights in Macedonia, and made diplomatic relations contingent upon negotiated resolution of issues outstanding with its neighbors.[25] These preventative measures succeeded in avoiding intergroup conflict in Macedonia.

In addition to preventing the outbreak of violence, the intervention succeeded in assisting enfranchisement. The Macedonian government made significant concessions to its minority population to better incorporate them into Macedonian society, and to assure political power commensurate with their representation in the broader community.[26] The Intervention Cycle suggests that the international community should continue to assist with further political and economic enfranchisement measures to create a stable political bedrock that fosters an identification beyond ethnicity.

V. THE WAR IN BOSNIA

A. Missed Opportunities for Prevention

As Slovenia escaped into Western Europe and Croatia battled secessionist Serbs, the international community did very little to prevent war in Bosnia. The Bosnian government begged the UN to deploy a preventative peacekeeping force in the fall of 1991. It is a major failure of the international community that the opportunity was not taken to send a force capable of enforcing peace to preserve a stable environment and reinforce enfranchisement.

Instead, the Bosnian Serbs, with support from Serbia, declared Serbian autonomous regions within Bosnia, established a Bosnian Serb parliament, and began the war for secession from Bosnia. Only when Sarajevo fell siege to Bosnian Serb artillery in early 1992 and Bosnian Serbs began using violence to coerce Muslims and Croats to leave their homes did attention turn to this most destructive phase of the breakup of the former Yugoslavia. By then, the parties to the conflict were already committed to violence to achieve their political goals; indeed, that violence was well underway before the international community intervened.

B. Peacekeeping

As in Croatia, the international community chose not to enforce the cessation of violence in Bosnia. Instead of enforcing its will, the international community chose to ameliorate only the effects of that violence.[27] The international community did intervene in 1992 with a UN military force to assist delivery of humanitarian aid, and a NATO force to restrict overflight. In 1993-1994, the community employed both forces to protect UN safe areas.

These conflicting elements of the military forces' burgeoning mandates badly muddled the intervention. The blame for UNPROFOR and NATO's failings rests directly on the nations—the United States among them—that created a contradictory mandate, burdensome administrative and political restrictions on the military forces, and denied the UN the forces required by the missions. These same nations then used UNPROFOR's limitations as an excuse for failing to take more significant action to establish peace in Bosnia.[28]

The Intervention Cycle suggests that UNPROFOR should have been withdrawn and replaced with military troops empowered to enforce compliance with the UN mandates. The intervention should not have been undertaken with the pretenses of neutrality and consent.[29] It also suggests that the international community should not have intervened without a much stronger sense of common purpose. The institutional competition that produced the UN and NATO "dual key" arrangement and concern by the European Community and Russia about NATO involvement further diminished the effectiveness of the intervention.[30] The international community created an interlocking web of military operations, some of which claimed to be neutral while others were intentionally punitive and directed at the Serbs. Enforcement and peacekeeping operations should be sequential because their concurrent prosecution does not communicate a clear signal of the community's intentions.

In August 1992, the UN and the European Community sponsored an international effort under mediators Cyrus Vance and Lord Owen to negotiate an end to the Yugoslav crisis. The London Conference advocated the territorial integrity of Bosnia, delivery of humanitarian aid, and opposed recognition of forcible territorial gains. What the London Conference did not do, however, was impose a just settlement, insure the territorial integrity of Bosnia-Herzegovina, force compliance with the delivery of humanitarian assistance, or reject forcible territorial gains.[31] The lengthy duration of the Vance-Owen process, in which the diplomatic efforts were not backed up by forceful mitigation, actually served to legitimate Serbian gains, since they controlled disputed areas throughout the negotiating process and few punitive measures were imposed on them as long as they participated in the negotiations.

In January 1993, the Vance-Owen process ceded the goal of a multiethnic Bosnia and began carving up Bosnia into ethnic cantons. Focusing on the division of territory had two very negative effects in the former Yugoslavia: it rewarded aggression and reinforced ethnicity.[32] Bosnia might have been saved by establishing boundaries purposely not intended to reflect ethnic control of the territory or providing nonterritorial incentives for cooperation, such as the promise of international assistance, admission into international organizations, and economic aid.[33]

C. Attempts at Mitigation

Although unwilling to mobilize to a peace enforcement effort, in the summer of 1992 the international community considered shedding the pretense of neutrality for direct use of force against the Serbs. There was a belief that the use of military forces in nearly any capacity would "send a signal to the Serbs," quelling Bosnian Serb aggression and halting Serbian support. The Intervention Cycle suggests that signaling a willingness to intervene might be effective earlier in the cycle (in the deterrence and coercion phases) but it will not be effective once the parties to the conflict are committed to violence. By the time the international community considered the use of force against them, the Bosnian Serbs had basically achieved their territorial objectives.

Subsequent military interventions (expanding air strikes, strengthening UNPROFOR, deploying a European reaction force, and aggressively utilizing NATO to signal international resolve) were all negated by the fundamental contradiction in Western action: attempting to sustain neutral activities (like delivery of aid and negotiating cease fires) while punishing one party to the conflict. The international community did not harmonize its political and military objectives.[34]

The Intervention Cycle identifies two ways besides intervention to arrive at conflict mitigation: victory and exhaustion. In late 1994, the former Yugoslavia appeared to be stabilizing as a result of both factors.[35]

Five new factors emerged from the conflict to prevent Bosnian Serb consolidation of their gains into a stable settlement: (1) clandestine arming of the Bosnian army; (2) collusion between the Croat and Bosnian forces; (3) an effective offensive by those forces to roll back Bosnian Serb gains and "simplify" the negotiating map; (4) sanctions against Serbia to increase incentives for Belgrade to constrain the behavior of Bosnian Serbs; and (5) international outrage over tactics employed by the Bosnian Serbs in the spring of 1995 (which included taking UN peacekeepers hostage during airstrikes in May, chaining UN forces to high value military targets such as bridges to impede NATO airstrikes, attacking UN safe areas of Srebrenica, Zepa, Tuzla, and Gorazde in July, recommencing the shelling of Sarajevo, preventing the exodus of Muslims, and executing Muslim men).[36]

Changes in the political dynamics also gave new impetus to settlement efforts: the beginning of the U.S. presidential campaign, and combined UN and European desire to terminate UNPROFOR. In the United States, President Clinton's desire to resolve Bosnia before elections and congressional action to unilaterally lift the arms embargo against Bosnia gave new incentives for serious diplomatic efforts.[37] NATO domination of operations, manipulation of UN forces by all of the parties to the conflict, waning support of force contributors, and the $2 billion annual cost of UNPROFOR had reduced UN interest by the summer of 1995.[38]

D. Toward Resolution

These factors resulted in a summer 1995 peace initiative that finally coupled military force with an overarching political objective: peace consistent with extant territorial holdings. The UN consolidated its forces in more defensible positions (facilitated by the gains of Croatian and Bosnian military offensives), and NATO expanded its airstrikes from proportional to punitive attacks against the Bosnian Serb military.[39]

In return for eased sanctions, Serbian president Milosevic committed to restrain Bosnian Serbs and enforce the agreement.[40] The Bosniac-Croat Federation, the Serbs, and the international community accepted a partition along ethnic lines consistent with territorial control.[41]

The peace initiative succeeded in producing an agreement among the Croats, Serbs, and Bosnian government on November 21, 1995.[42] The Dayton Peace Accords and the Basic Agreement on Eastern Slavonia adhered to the Vance-Owen principle of 51 percent of territory for the Federation (Croats and Muslims) and 49 percent to the Bosnian Serbs.[43]

The peace agreement stated that the Federation of Bosnia and Herzegovina "will continue as a sovereign state within its present internationally-recognized borders," although the state will be comprised of two entities: the Bosniac–Croat Federation and the Serb Republic.[44] Bosnian Croats had extensive rights of confederation with Croatia, and Bosnian Serbs, while denied the right of confederation, were given a "parallel special relationship" with Serbia.

The Dayton Accords commit the parties to numerous elements intended to bolster enfranchisement: creating conditions for and holding free elections in September 1996, establishing the free movement of peoples and return of refugees, cooperating with investigation of war crimes, participating in confidence and transparency building measures, and negotiating an arms control regime.[45]

The Dayton peace agreement included a detailed timetable of military tasks, including withdrawal of forces behind cease-fire lines, establishment of demilitarized zones, withdrawal of heavy weapons into monitored holding points, and withdrawal of all foreign forces. The parties also agreed to enforcement of Dayton's military aspects by a 60,000 troop NATO Implementation Force (IFOR).[46] Elements of UNPROFOR that were not folded into IFOR were withdrawn.

The Dayton Accords include taskings to the UN and CSCE to lead aid, return of refugees, interim law enforcement, training and monitoring of Bosnian police, arms control negotiations, and certification of conditions for holding elections. As the Intervention Cycle recommends, these activities are subordinate to enforcement tasks until violence has been halted.

The Dayton Accords were an enormous achievement toward peace in the former Yugoslavia. They committed the parties to the conflict not only to a cease-fire, but to a detailed schedule of demobilization, confidence building, and civilian reenfranchisement that, if implemented, would diminish intergroup conflict in the former Yugoslavia. The Accords acknowledge a fundamental tenet of the Intervention Cycle: military force can stabilize a country careening toward or already consumed with violence, but only rebuilding the civilian institutions and reenfranchising the population can create a stable peace. However, if enfranchisement is not undertaken with alacrity, the accords could result in the complete separation of Bosnia.

D. Resolution?

NATO's Implementation Force made significant progress toward creating a stable and secure military environment in Bosnia.[47] The parties to the conflict have met nearly all of the military requirements; IFOR has credited them with good faith in all areas except encouraging freedom of movement.[48]

The major challenges to the successful implementation of the Dayton Accords are not the military tasks, however. The major challenges are those areas outside the IFOR mandate: return of prisoners of war, war crimes trials, return of refugees, and creating civilian institutions that can reenfranchise the Bosnian population.

All parties continue to hold prisoners, disrupt repatriation of refugees and restrict opposition political activities.[49] The Bosnian Serbs have yet to account for the 7,000 prisoners taken during the fall of Srebrenica in August of 1995. Of the 57 suspects indicted by the International War Crimes Tribunal, only four are in custody; President Karadzik and General Mladic continue at liberty in Bosnian Serb territory.[50] Arbitration over the status of the town of Brco is behind schedule and could ignite Croat-Serb fighting, and the U.S. plan to arm and train the Bosniac-Croat Federation could still undermine regional stability.[51] Further, as of May 1996, only 300 of the 1,970 UN police had arrived, putting public order at risk as tensions rise over the return of territory and refugees.[52]

Perhaps the most difficult challenge inherent in the Dayton accords is encouraging the return of refugees. Resettlement is the key to reenfranchisement because the construction of multiethnic civil institutions and patterns of cooperation essential to reconstruction of a multiethnic society depend on it.

The Intervention Cycle suggests that building commonality at the local or regional level would move the society in a positive direction. The international community has intervened in this way to create and support the Bosniac-Croat Federation. The community convinced Bosnian Croats and Muslims of their common interest in opposing the Bosnian Serbs, and used that as the basis for combined military operations. The Federation continues to meet its minimum objective, which is to prevent conflict between Bosnia and Croatia. However, despite considerable effort to bring them together, the Federation has not succeeded in integrating governmental or military functions. Nor has it given the

Muslim and Croat populations the confidence to return to their homes or share local control; Mostar has become two separate Croat and Muslim cities.[53]

Repairing war damage, providing developmental assistance, and creating functioning justice and law enforcement systems are essential to peace in Bosnia and merit the same funding and attention as military tasks.[54] Unless enfranchisement is dramatically accelerated, the uncertainty of law enforcement and freedom of movement, potential for collapse of the Bosniac-Croat Federation, withdrawal of IFOR looming in December 1996, and "scorched earth policies being implemented by all sides" as territory is vacated, the Dayton Accords may result in complete cantonment, with Bosnian Croat territory absorbed into Croatia, Bosnian Serb territory united with Serbia, and encroachment by both Croatia and Serbia on the remaining Bosniac territory.[55]

Although it certified Bosnia's readiness for elections (under intense U.S. pressure), the OSCE is rightly concerned that unless the civil mandate makes significant additional progress, elections could serve, as they did in 1991, to fracture rather than reenfranchise the society and pose a serious challenge to peace when IFOR withdraws.[56]

VI. LESSONS FROM THE FORMER YUGOSLAVIA

Five years of intergroup conflict and international intervention in the former Yugoslavia have resulted in relatively peaceful independence for Slovenia and Macedonia, but violent establishment of ethnic states in Croatia and Serbia, and within partitioned Bosnia. What are the lessons of intervention in the breakup of Yugoslavia?

A. Prevention Works

Preventative measures to strengthen enfranchisement, provide aid, and monitor military activities can be useful in signaling the involvement of the international community and deterring a recourse to violence. Such efforts were successful in Kosovo and Macedonia. The international community missed a pivotal opportunity to prevent the outbreak of violence elsewhere in Yugoslavia, however. The use of deterrence and coercion in order to halt the conflict close to inception, targeting any faction that resorted to force may have prevented the resort to force. The attacks on Vukovar and Dubrovnik appear to have been particularly promising times to intervene. Had the international community identified the stage of intergroup conflict occurring in Serbia, Croatia, and Bosnia, and intervened effectively, a multiethnic state might have been preserved and enormous destruction prevented. The difficulty with prevention is, of course,

that it requires resources—money, political commitment, and military forces—
that are scarce commodities.

B. Elections Can Be Destabilizing

As elections were shaping up in 1991, political dialogue became a polar-
izing force. Intervention to assist in the development of the electoral process,
training of new political leaders, creation of multiethnic political alliances,
ability to highlight issues with intergroup appeal, and support free media
could have significantly diminished the attraction of extremist candidates,
encouraged protection for minority rights, and assisted peaceful change.[57]
Elections alone do not constitute democracy; they can even serve to further
disenfranchisement. The Yugoslav republic elections of 1991 demonstrate that
creation of a civil society respecting the principles of democratic governance
is essential for elections to be a productive force. Because the civil aspects of
the Dayton Accords have not taken root, the September 1996 Bosnian elections risk repeating this mistake.

C. Military Force Is Not Enough

The Intervention Cycle illustrates that appropriate intervention mechanisms are not necessarily military forces. In the former Yugoslavia, however,
intervention was neither early nor effective enough to broaden the spectrum of
options. Military force had to be employed to halt intergroup violence before
other tools could become effective again. Military forces alone are an inadequate
tool for the essential tasks of resolution, because they cannot reenfranchise the
society. The mechanisms that can assist in those tasks must be undertaken
with the same commitment in order for the cycle of conflict to be broken.

The international community used force poorly in the former Yugoslavia,
threatening too much and doing too little.[58] The international community
professed interests and actions beyond their real willingness to intervene in
the former Yugoslavia, which gave hope to the victims of aggression that the
West would eventually come to their aid and reduced their willingness to
make concessions during negotiations. Moreover, symbolic uses of military
force only highlight the limits of community interest.[59] Demands made by the
international community were only honored when tied to effective uses of
military force.[60]

D. Unity of Purpose is Essential

The divisions among states seeking to intervene in Yugoslavia resulted in
contradictory political and military efforts. The UNPROFOR experience

demonstrates that the international community cannot build successful interventions without a unified politico-economic-military strategy pursued by the institutions and states involved. This was not achieved until the Bosnian Serb attack on UN safe areas and shelling of Sarajevo in the summer of 1995, four years into the intervention. Agreement on the limits of the international community's interest in a collapsing society is also necessary to keep intervention policy consistent with the resources being committed to the endeavor.

The international community should not have undertaken UN Chapter VI (traditional peacekeeping) and Chapter VII (enforcement) operations simultaneously. These contradictory operations sent mixed signals about the community's intent and ensured ineffective operations. The community should have paid more attention to the practical effect of ostensibly neutral actions, such as the arms embargo; these actions were not neutral in practice. The international community could also been more scrupulously neutral in their enforcement.[61] Punitive measures should be directed at behavior, irrespective of which participants in the conflict display the behavior. By responding to Serbian aggression with NATO airstrikes but not preventing Bosnian government attacks from the UN Protected Areas or Croat ethnic cleansing in Kraijina, the community undermined its ability to intervene effectively.

E. Linkage Is Detrimental

Nations that intervened in Yugoslavia used the opportunity to establish precedents for their own preferred institutional order. In many ways their intervention diminished the prospects of international cooperation and timely action to solve Yugoslavia's strife. The intervention heightened Russian concerns about their own role in the post–cold war order and burdened the issue of local aggression in the former Yugoslavia with broader institutional competition between the United Nations, the European Community, the Conference on Security Cooperation in Europe, and NATO.[62]

F. Negotiation Must Be Tied to Intervention

During the four years of warfare, as Yugoslavia was torn into ethnic cantons, international negotiators were at work seeking a territorial settlement. The international community's unwillingness to impose a solution gave little incentive to those winning military victories (first the Serbs, then the Bosnian Serbs, then the Muslim-Croat Federation) to accept a settlement. The focus on delineating territory aggravated the crisis by emphasizing ethnicity in negotiation, and creating a zero-sum dynamic of territorial trade-offs. The complexity of the maps made monitoring and peacekeeping such a challenging task that it further reduced international willingness to forcibly impose an agreement forcibly. In the end, the 1995 military victories of the Bosnian-Croat Federation were rewarded in the Dayton Accords. The Intervention Cycle suggests, and the breakup of the former Yugoslavia attests, that if no party is willing to enforce a cessation to hostilities, resolution will likely take the form of a simple legitimization of the military gains made during the war.

G. Resolution Is Difficult

Finally, Yugoslavia demonstrates the enormous challenge of truly resolving conflicts. What the Intervention Cycle terms reconciliation can also be described as nation building, enfranchising all elements of the population into the political and economic system and creating a community broader than ethnicity. Building successfully functioning societies, particularly multicultural societies, is an enormous challenge, especially once communities are broken. The demands on interventionists to do good rather than damage are enormous, in terms of knowledge about the society and how to structure an effective integrated politico-economic-military plan.

The Dayton Accords acknowledge that essential nation building must occur to reenfranchise a society pulled apart by the centrifugal forces of ethnic conflict; however, the accords cede multinational communities that are essential to resolution. The Intervention Cycle suggests that the ethnic cantonment upon which the Dayton Peace Accords are built will not serve as a stable basis for future resolution and prevention.

While we in the international community did much that was wrong in the former Yugoslavia, those who would intervene to do good should not see the breakup of Yugoslavia as a demonstration that intervention cannot succeed. Yugoslavia was an extremely complex, multicultural state whose dissolution occurred at a time when the international community itself was changing dramatically. It was the first state to collapse in Europe since World War II; in the early 1990s the international community and its institutions were simply unprepared for the challenges that were posed by the dissolution of Yugoslavia.

NOTES

1. Cheryl Bernard, "Bosnia: Was It Inevitable?" in Zalmay M. Khalilzad (Ed.), *Lessons from Bosnia*, (Santa Monica, CA: RAND, 1994), p. 24.
2. Susan L. Woodward, *Balkan Tragedy: Chaos and Dissolution After the Cold War* (Washington, DC: The Brookings Institution, 1995), p. 18.
3. See: Mark Thompson, *A Paper House: The Ending of Yugoslavia* (NY: Pantheon, 1993); Samuel O. Huntington, "The Clash of Civilizations," *Foreign Affairs*, 72,

no. 3 (Summer 1993); Charles G. Boyd, "Making Peace with the Guilty: The Truth About Bosnia," *Foreign Affairs* 74, no. 5 (September/October 1995); and Misha Glenny, "Heading Off War in the Southern Balkans," *Foreign Affairs* 74, no. 3 (May/June 1995).

4. Fred Singleton, *A Short History of the Yugoslav Peoples*, (Cambridge: Cambridge University Press, 1985), pp. 26, 97, 110, 206, 211.

5. Marko Milivojevic, *Descent Into Chaos: Yugoslavia's Worsening Crisis*, (London: Institute for European Defence and Strategic Studies, 1989), p. 9.

6. Glenn E. Curtis (Ed.), *Yugoslavia: A Country Study* (Washington, DC: Library of Congress, December 1990), pp. xxvi, 70-71.

7. Local delegations were created in six areas: social workers, peasants and farmers, liberal professions, state officials and soldiers, territorial constituencies, and sociopolitical organizations. See Fred Singleton, *Yugoslav Peoples*, p. 260.

8. Glenn Curtis, *Yugoslavia*, p. 293; Central Intelligence Agency Directorate of Intelligence, *Bosnia and Herzegovina: Recent Changes in Ethnic Distribution* (Washington, DC: Intelligence Research Paper, April 1993); Susan Woodward, *Balkan Tragedy*, pp. 226-227.

9. Statement by President Bill Clinton, November 21, 1995 (Washington, DC: The White House, 1995).

10. Susan Woodward, *Balkan Tragedy*, pp. 47-82.

11. Glenn E. Curtis, *Yugoslavia*, p. 163.

12. For supporters of this view, see remarks of Secretary Perry in "For the Record," *The Washington Post*, March 17, 1995; Art Pine, "U.S. Reports Progress in Effort to Keep Croatia From Ousting UN," *Los Angeles Times*, March 10, 1995, p. 12; Margaret Thatcher, et. al., *Wall Street Journal*, September 2, 1994.

13. Warren Zimmerman, "The Last Ambassador: A Memoir of the Collapse of Yugoslavia," *Foreign Affairs*, 74, no. 2 (March/April 1995), p. 5.

14. David Owen, *Balkan Odyssey*, (New York: Harcourt Brace & Company, 1995), pp. 342-344; Susan Woodward, *Balkan Tragedy*, p. 18. An excellent account of the elections and the prominent role played by the controlled media in fomenting nationalist sentiments is Misha Glenny, *The Fall of Yugoslavia: The Third Balkan War*, (London: Penguin Books, 1992), pp. 10-21, 38-45.

15. The Yugoslav Army officer corps was predominantly Serbian. Estimates of Serb representation range from 50-80 percent. Marko Miliojevic, *Descent Into Chaos*, p. 28.

16. Secretary James Baker's June 21, 1991 meetings with the main political actors, in which he advocated a unified state and opposed secession without negotiated agreement, are illustrative of continuing preventative approaches. Warren Zimmerman, "The Last Ambassador," p. 12.

17. Lord Carrington cautioned "Milosevic has warned that military action would take place there if Croatia and Slovenia were recognized . . . [and that] this might well be the spark that sets Bosnia-Herzegovina alight." David Owen, *Balkan Odyssey*, p. 343.

18. Warren Zimmerman, "The Last Ambassador," p. 14.

19. The Serb forces' central advantage is in equipment because the Croatian and Bosnian forces have greater numbers of troops.
20. The United States endorsed the military campaign as a way to "simplify the map" for peace negotiations. "Richard Holbrooke, Bosnia Wrangler," *The Economist,* September 16, 1995, p. 36.
21. "Bosnia's Real Lesson, *The Economist,* September 9, 1995, p. 20; Charles G. Boyd, "Making Peace," p. 23; David Owen, *Balkan Odyssey,* pp. 342-53.
22. Boutros Boutros-Ghali, "Further Report of the Secretary-General Pursuant to Security Council Resolutions 1025 (1995) and 1026 (1995)," February 6, 1996 (New York: United Nations #S/1996/83), para 5.
23. James M. Steinberg, "Turning Points in Bosnia and the West," in Zalmay M. Khalilzad, (Ed.), Lessons, p. 8; Secretary of Defense William Perry, quoted in "Perry Aghast Over Lifting Arms Embargo," *The Washington Times,* June 11, 1995, p. 13.
24. Thomas W. Lippmann, "U.S. Fears Macedonia Flash Point," *The Washington Post,* March 19, 1995, p. A28.
25. The same tool was used against Serbia and Montenegro when they formed the Federal Republic of Yugoslavia in April 1992.
26. The Macedonian government has taken small but critically important steps: the government now includes an Albanian Deputy Prime Minister, and recognizes university degrees from Tirana. "A Balkan Beacon?" *The Economist,* April 6, 1996, p. 56.
27. The UN General Assembly resolved on August 25, 1992 that the UNSC should take further measures to end the war in the former Yugoslavia, including direct military action, but the Security Council never took up such a resolution.
28. George Soros, "This is the Moment of Truth," *The Washington Post,* July 16, 1995, p. C-7.
29. Richard K. Betts, "The Delusion of Impartial Intervention," *Foreign Affairs* 73, no. 6 (November/December 1994), p. 24.
30. The dual key procedure was only modified in July 1994, after the successful Serbian attacks on Srebrenica and Zepa, and the commencement of punitive NATO attacks. See Craig R. Whitney, "NATO Gives UN Officials Veto on Air Strikes in Bosnia," *The New York Times,* July 26, 1995, p. 1.
31. Secretary of State Warren Christopher, Statement at February 10 Press Conference, *The Washington Times,* February 10, 1993.
32. Alan F. Fogelquist, "Turning Points in Bosnia and the Region," in Zalmay M. Khalilzad (Ed.), *Lessons,* p. 14; Susan Woodward, *Balkan Tragedy,* p. 14.
33. The international community may be moving toward this approach: reports of agreements struck with Croatian President Tudjman suggest Croatia would be admitted into NATO's Partnership for Peace in return for Croatia extending the mandate of UNPROFOR in Croatia, and EC Ministers are stalling trade negotiations with Croatia until the UNPROFOR extension is approved. See "Croatia Forms Alliance with Bosnians," *Baltimore Sun,* March 7, 1995, p. 4.

34. Richard Perle, "Will We Finally Recognize the Right to Self Defense?" *The Washington Post*, July 19, 1995, p. 21; Christopher S. Wren "U.N Quagmmire in Bosnia: Perils of Peacekeeping," *The New York Times*, July 14, 1995, p. 14.

35. "Victims of Bosnian Realpolitik," *The Economist*, July 22-28, 1995, p. 47.

36. Ann Devroy, "Clinton Said 'Nothing Improper' in His Stance on Iran Arms for Bosnia," *The Washington Post*, April 10, 1996, p. 24; Ann Devroy, "Internal U.S. Probe Faults Policy on Bosnian Arms," *The Washington Post*, April 16, 1996, p. 1; "Bosnia: An End in Sight, at Last," *The Economist*, September 23, 1995, p. 43-44; and "The Impotence of the West," *The Economist*, July 15-21, 1995, p. 31.

37. Todd S. Purdum, "Clinton Now Tries to Define Role for the U.S. in Bosnia," *The New York Times*, July 23, 1995, p. 8.

38. The difficulty of the UN position came into sharp relief when, during the withdrawal of UN forces from Srebrenica in July of 1995, Bosnian force threatened to kill the UN troops unless NATO airstrikes were undertaken against the Bosnian Serb forces, and Serbs threatened to kill the troops if the airstrikes were undertaken. See Chris Hedges, "Bosnia Threatens U.N. Troops Unless NATO Jets Aid Defense," *The New York Times*, July 19, 1995, p. 1.

39. "The West's Two-Track Mind," *The Economist*, September 9, 1995, p. 49-50; "Ratko Refuses to Leave the Sinking Ship," *The Economist*, September 16, 1995, pp. 57-58.

40. David Owen argues that Milosevic was always the key to an agreement on Bosnia and that the West should have demonized him less and dealt with him sooner using a flexible approach to sanctions; *Balkan Odyssey*, p. 287.

41. David Owen, *Balkan Odyssey*, p. 340; "Ethnic Cleansing: Blood and Earth," *The Economist*, September 23, 1995, p. 16.

42. The Accords were formally signed as the General Framework Agreement for Peace in Bosnia and Herzegovina in Paris on December 14, 1995.

43. U.S. Department of State, "Summary of the Dayton Peace Agreement," (Washington, DC: November 21, 1995). Under the accords, Sarajevo remained united, Gorazde was to be connected by a land corridor to the Bosniac-Croat Federation, and the status of Brco was subject to further arbitration.

44. The Dayton Accords include a constitution establishing the "single state composed of two Entities," outlining responsibilities of the Bosnia and Herzegovina government, creating a 3-member Presidency, and authorizing a bicameral legislature with a 15-member House of Peoples selected from Entity legislatures and a 42- member House of Representatives with direct election for membership. Seats in both houses are apportioned on the basis of power-sharing arrangement in which two-thirds of the representatives come from the Bosniac-Croat Federation and one-third from the Serb Republic. The central government of Bosnia and Herzegovina retained responsibility for foreign policy, trade, customs, immigration, monetary policy, law enforcement, and air traffic control and transportation. U.S. Department of State, "Constitution," (Washington, DC: November 21, 1995).

45. U.S. Department of State, "Elections," (Washington, DC: November 21, 1995).
46. U.S. Department of State, "Military Aspects of Implementing the Peace Agreement," and "The Peace Agreement and Regional Stabilization," both: (Washington, DC: November 21, 1995).
47. The force consists of 55,000 personnel in theater, including forces from all 16 NATO nations (Iceland has no military forces but sent medical technicians), and 16 non-NATO nations. "IFOR Fact Sheet," (Brussels: NATO Integrated Data System) February 16, 1996; "Second Report to the Security Council on the Operations of the Multinational Implementation Force (IFOR)," January 18, 1996.
48. NATO, "Fifth Report to the Security Council on the Operations of the Multinational Implementation Force (IFOR)," April 23, 1996; "Bosnia: Hiccup or Seizure?" *The Economist*, February 10, 1996, pp. 49-50; "Soldiers in Bosnia Won't Be Able to Meet Deadline for Pullback," *The Washington Times*, April 19, 1996, p. 15. For exceptions, see Carlos Bongioanni, "Lagging Arms Turn-In Angers IFOR," *European Stars and Stripes*, April 10, 1996, p. 1.
49. Mike O'Connor, "Opposition Party in Bosnian Elections Being Terrorized," *The New York Times*, August 17, 1996, p. 1.
50. Edith M. Lederer, "Bosnian Serbs Free 3 Before Aid Conference," *Philadelphia Inquirer*, April 10, 1996, p. 13; Daniel Williams, "War Crimes Experts Endure Dig of Death," *The Washington Post*, April 10, 1996, p. 21; Daniel Williams, "Probers Close Search for Evidence of Bosnia Killings," *The Washington Post*, April 14, 1996, p. 23.
51. The United States pledged $100 million in equipment, Turkey offered $2 million in training, but all other countries—including 16 European and Islamic countries—have so far declined to participate. Jonathan S. Landay, "U.S. Plan for a Balance of Power in Bosnia is Left Out of Kilter," *Christian Science Monitor*, April 15, 1996, p. 6; "McLarty-led Group Visits Gulf States for Bosnia Aid," *The Washington Times*, April 16, 1996, p. 14.
52. NATO "Fifth Report," para. 4; "Bosnia: Hiccup or Seizure, *The Economist*, February 10, 1996, pp. 49-50.
53. Daniel Williams, "Administration Backs Extension of Bosnia Cease Fire," *The Washington Post*, March 17, 1995, p. 36.
54. The United States has provided $30 million for these activities, a fraction of what is being spent for military aspects of the Dayton accords. Steven Greenhouse, "Clinton Meets with Bosnian and Croatian Chiefs," *The New York Times*, March 17, 1994, p. 9.
55. David Owen, *Balkan Odyssey*, p. 353; Javier Solana, NATO Secretary General, "Letter to UN Secretary General Boutros-Ghali," January 23, 1996; "Bosnia: Europe Versus America, Again," *The Economist*, April 13, 1996, pp. 40-41.
56. Chris Hedges, "Swiss Diplomat Resists U.S. On Certifying Bosnian Vote," *The New York Times*, June 8, 1996, pp. 1, 4; "Darkness Visible," *The Economist*, March 16, 1996, pp. 52-53; "Serb Accused of Hurting Prospects for Free Vote," *Baltimore Sun*, April 16, 1996, p. 9.
57. Susan Woodward, *Balkan Tragedy*, p. 18.

58. During NATO airstrikes in July of 1995, Radovan Karadzik said, "NATO threats don't mean anything to us," quoted in "The Impotence of the West," *The Economist*, July 15-21, 1995, p. 31.

59. National Security Advisor Anthony Lake acknowledged this relationship in an on-the-record speech to the Council on Foreign Relations on September 12, 1994, saying, "The progress we have made in Bosnia, for example, came when power was tied to our diplomatic ends. The Sarajevo ultimatum largely succeeded because the threat of NATO air power was judged real." The same point has been made by former Secretary of State James Baker in a speech to the Republican National Committee Foreign Policy Forum, on "The World Today—the Imperative of American Leadership," July 27, 1994, p. 6.

60. David Owen argues that the Bosnian government would have been better off accepting any of the peace plans prior to Dayton: the March 1992 Carrington-Cutiliero plan, the May 1993 Vance-Owen Peace Plan, the December 1993 European Union Action Plan, or the July 1994 Contact Group Plan. The Bosnian government would have received more territory (because it would have had to share less with the Croats) and had considerably less suffering for its population. David Owen, *Balkan Odyssey*, pp. 364-365.

61. This point is made forcefully by both Susan Woodward and Charles Boyd.

62. For example, U.S. Secretary of State Warren Christopher, in May 1993 meetings with NATO allies said "this problem is at the heart of Europe's future." Russia was not consulted on this trip, or routinely involved in the deliberations about the former Yugoslavia until the creation of the Contact Group in April 1994, although their support was crucial in order to influence the behavior of Serbia and critical for action of the UN Security Council. State Department "Consultation Trip Talking Points for Secretary Christopher," May 1, 1993. Statement of Secretary Christopher from meeting with Russian Foreign Minister Kozyrev in Geneva, April 26, 1994.

CHAPTER 4

The Somalia Syndrome

April Oliver

"We should have done something about Somalia earlier. But just how do you get busy people to stop and pay attention to a country like Somalia?"

FORMER U.S. SECRETARY OF STATE LAWRENCE EAGLEBURGER

I. INTRODUCTION

Somalia today is displayed as the poster child for isolationists in Congress. They point and say "never again." How did such a well-intentioned mission go astray? Some argue that the death knell came when the United Nations took over the operation in the spring of 1993, shifting from mere humanitarian intervention to an ambitious agenda of restoring civil order. This transition, done with the support of many senior officials in Washington, is now widely regarded as an overreach.

The Intervention Cycle suggests, however, that the tale of the international community's misadventures in Somalia started much earlier. The pattern of failed intervention—humanitarian, diplomatic and military—is profound. It sets the stage for the later, more spectacular, failure of the UN in 1993. Because of the total breakdown of nearly all Somali institutions, the UN stepped in as an authority of last resort. By then, the burden was simply too great.

April Oliver is a producer with the weekly news magazine IMPACT, CNN and TIME on Special Assignment. She was previously a foreign affairs reporter for the MacNeil/Lehrer NewsHour; while there, she produced numerous programs on the Somalia crisis. Oliver is a 1983 honors graduate of Princeton University's Woodrow Wilson School of Public and International Affairs.

Examined through the Intervention Cycle, the case of Somalia highlights several types of intervention, all differing in goals and levels of success. Through the prism of the Intervention Cycle, this chapter examines several phases of international attempts to alleviate the Somali crisis. It asks:

- Could the muscular U.S. and subsequent UN intervention in Somalia have been prevented?
- As the crisis built over several years, when and how could preventive measures been undertaken?
- While the massive infusion of U.S. troops may have seemed a compassionate response to apocalyptic famine, was it the correct one?
- What led to those conditions of widespread famine and chaos, with so-called technicals ruling the streets?

One dead U.S. soldier dragged by vengeful mobs stains the memory of much good achieved in Somalia. But the debacle of October 3, 1993, with the toll of 18 dead Americans and 75 wounded, is only one of several tragic consequences that may ultimately have been avoidable. "If the international community had intervened earlier and more effectively in Somalia, much of the catastrophe that has unfolded could have been avoided," claimed a central player in the drama, Algerian diplomat Mohamed Sahnoun.[1]

The legacy affects more than the tiny country of Somalia. The experience directly contributed to U.S. and UN lethargy during the next massive crisis: Rwanda. Hundreds of thousands of people died during the spring and summer of 1994. The laggard world response to stamp Rwanda "genocide," and act accordingly, can be traced in part to the vexing experience of Somalia.

A report released in 1995 by Human Rights Watch/Africa concludes that "the international community risks misreading the Somalia experience as a blunt warning against all engagement in the crises that generate complex emergencies, from war-driven famine to genocide."[2] Even years after the interventions, with UN troops withdrawn, Somalia's legacy mounted. In Washington, Somalia so tarnished the image of UN peacekeeping, it encouraged a policy reversal within the Clinton administration to restrict U.S. participation. A more severe bill to curtail U.S. peacekeeping became an integral component of the 1994 Republican "Contract with America." The bill savagely slashed contributions to the UN and many other organizations in the UN system. According to former Secretary of State Lawrence Eagleburger, "Congress has drawn all the wrong lessons out of Somalia, including not wanting to put U.S. troops under a foreign general. It's just crazy."[3]

With hindsight, some analysts sum up the whole Somalia venture as painfully naive. "An intervention that can be stopped in its tracks by a few dozen fatalities, like the U.S. operation in Somalia was, is one that should never have begun," suggests one critic.[4] Is this so? Or could the operation have been prevented altogether?

Traditional analysis depicts Somalia as the forgotten stepchild of the cold war. Failed states are on the rise in the post-cold war world, and Somalia would seem to be a textbook case. With no central government and few resources, these rogue states lurch along, without a big brother, to provide economic succor and political support.

Chaos, environmental degradation, and famine are inevitable in such a state of flux, some suggest. Somalia is but a casualty of a greater peace. In such an unruly world, some say we must restrain our compassion, rein in our heart strings, and not rush to the rescue of every child whose eyes flutter and fall away on live television, a half a world away. Les Gelb of the Council on Foreign Relations dubs this dictum for post-cold war restraint "a doctrine of limited tears."[5]

But conditions in Somalia are not merely the byproduct of vast, sweeping economic and political trends. The famine and its aftermath are also the result of power plays by individuals. Human psychology—and vanity—played a powerful role in the privation of Somalia. The personalization of the conflict, including long-standing animosity between UN Secretary General Boutros Boutros-Ghali and the warlord General Mohamed Farah Aideed, marred mediation. The power of individual action cannot be overlooked in the case of Somalia. This chapter suggests that carefully laid intervention plans, with clear aims and the force necessary to accomplish the tasks, can help ameliorate the potential for lone players to decide the destiny of such countries.

The following chapter is written after conversations with dozens of players in the Somali crisis. Through the prism of the Intervention Cycle, it outlines the historical roots of the crisis, identifies several missed windows for action, briefly traces the work of UNOSOM I, UNITAF, and UNOSOM II, and finally suggests whether any action is possible today. While the world may want to forget Somalia and move on, it is vital that those interested in the prevention of such humanitarian disasters stop, look, and listen again, to see that past mistakes are not repeated.

II. HISTORICAL BACKDROP: SEEDS OF FAMINE

Poised at the tip of the Horn of Africa, Somalia has, for centuries, been a land inhabited by itinerant herders. The dusty, dry earth did not nurture a settled lifestyle. The constant search for water, food, and shade bred instead a loosely connected web of nomads. With their camels, cattle, and sheep, Somalis wandered the land, from campsite to watering hole, perhaps since the dawn of humankind. Such a harsh heritage of wanderlust makes Somalis, by nature, fiercely independent.

Though all one ethnic tribe, Somalis are divided by clans, and those cleavages are deep. It boasts a unique heritage that few outsiders know intimately. One veteran of UN peacekeeping suggests that Somalia's culture itself jeopardized effective intervention from the start. "I don't think the UN understood Somalia very well. It is a nomadic society with very odd institutions. Power is spread in peculiar ways, through strongmen, tribal institutions and village elders," says former senior UN official Brian Urquhart. "Somalia possesses just about the worst set of conditions for a UN peacekeeping operation that you can imagine. It is a very difficult society to penetrate."[6] Somalis concur. Somali historian Said Samatar of Rutgers University says that "extreme individualism is the political culture, so that it is practically impossible for one Somali to command the allegiance of another Somali. Everyone is a king unto himself."[7]

This proud heritage, as well as a lineage system which immediately pits all kin against intruders, are keys to understanding the pattern of failed international interventions in Somalia. From the outset, cultural values suggest that the only solution to the crisis is one that involves Somalis intimately.

A. Colonial Experience

Somalia's cohesiveness as a nation, always fragile, was broken in part by its colonial experience. Colonized by England in the north, and Italy in the south in the early 1900s, the power of village elders and clan chiefs was sharply undermined. In its place, European authority reigned with centralized government, foreign customs, and institutions. When the Europeans later withdrew, it left Somalis bereft, without a historical memory of the old way of life, nor a complete command of European government.

Somalia emerged fleetingly as a democracy from 1960 to 1969. But as with many other African nations, a strongman quickly filled the colonial vacuum. The central figure in Somalia's decline had a violent imprint on Somalia from the beginning. Grabbing power in a military coup in 1969 was dictator Mohammed Siad Barré.

When Siad Barré took over in 1969, he quickly moved to populate his inner echelons of government with members of his clan, the Marehan.[8] While his government achieved some reforms, such as granting women the vote and a massive literacy campaign, he also ruled despotically. Siad Barré undercut his own reforms by creating increasing political and economic disparities between clans, by favoring his own. Increasingly Somalis throughout the country felt disenfranchised, without a voice in their own future, and without representation.

Siad Barré was also territorially ambitious. With aid and arms from the Soviet Union, he supported secessionist guerrillas in the Ogaden. He longed to create a greater Somalia, carved from portions of northern Kenya and eastern Ethiopia. In October 1977, he launched a full-fledged war against Ethiopia.

As the border war heated with Ethiopia, the Soviet Union changed its support from Somalia to the other side. The Soviets left behind huge caches of weapons, as well as a modern airstrip and port in the northern city of Berbera. This switch of client states occurred just as the Carter administration had decided—in the wake of an oil crisis, the overthrow of the Shah of Iran, and the Soviet invasion of Afghanistan—that a bulwark in the Persian Gulf might prove prudent. The United States obliged where the Soviets left off, funneling arms and economic aid into Somalia, as a potential forward position in the Persian Gulf to protect oil reserves. Even today, former U.S. diplomats and military officials admit that a more volatile environment was created in Somalia by such aid. One clear lesson from Somalia is that if a despot rules, and political and economic disparities are on the rise, foreign military and economic aid will not ensure stability, but may rather encourage its descent.

Over the next ten years, the United States poured nearly $250 million in lethal and nonlethal arms into Somalia. U.S. military aid included not merely guns and grenades, but also armored personnel carriers with Tactically Operated Wire-guided (TOW) missiles attached. The combined stockpiles of Soviet and U.S. weaponry turned Somalia into an arsenal, with more machine guns, automatic rifles, mines, tanks, and mortars than almost any other country in Africa.[9] Much of the weaponry would be used not against a Soviet threat, however, but against the Somali people by their own leader.

The large stockpiles of lethal weaponry would later contribute to a huge rift between the United States and UN over whether and how to disarm. Clearly, in retrospect, keeping a check on military assistance in countries prone to violence, despotism, and instability is one clear lesson for prevention. The sheer quantities of weapons in Somalia greatly increased the warlords' ability to loot and terrorize later. The arming of Somalia was a central factor in its demise and a key obstacle in the international community's subsequent ability to intervene effectively. But weapons alone do not make a civil war. The brewing sense of social and political disenfranchisement, spawned initially by Siad Barré's cruelty, created a climate of lawlessness and fear in which people were more apt to use such weapons.

B. Missed Opportunities for Mediation

In May and June of 1988, Siad Barré's government was hit with an organized internal uprising in the north. The insurgency spread, and ultimately led to the end of his rule, famine, and civil war.

The northerners' dissatisfaction was rooted in economic frustration, caused by a lack of development, as well as clan rivalry. Northerners resented the dominance of Siad Barré's clan and the lack of equitable distribution of resources in their region.[10] They clearly wanted better representation in Mogadishu. But their plea for enfranchisement, despite a worldwide move towards democracy, went unheeded. With the growing culture of disenfranchisement, and a citizenry seething with anger and armed with guns, the Somali crisis had begun.

Unable to seek redress through democratic institutions, a group dubbing itself the Somali National Movement (SNM) rose against the government. It was severely punished by Siad Barré. Aircraft and heavy weapons were used to bombard the northern cities of Hargeisa and Burao. Over the course of several months, as many as 50,000 Somalis may have been killed, a half-million were forced across the Ethiopian border as refugees. While human rights reports decried the repression, the international community barely blinked.[11]

In retrospect, civil unrest on this scale should have been a clarion call to the international community. One diplomat calls the atrocities of this period the first "missed opportunity" for mediation.[12] The United States suspended military assistance in July 1988, but economic aid to Siad Barré's regime continued. As the Intervention Cycle suggests, such forceful repression by a dictator will only encourage the culture of disenfranchisement. Predictably, the rebellion spread.

As the rebellion escalated beyond the north, other groups took up arms. Several prominent opposition groups fought, but never formally united against Siad Barré in a government-in-exile. Joining the Somali National Movement were the Somali Salvation Democratic Front, the United Somali Congress, and the Somali Patriotic Movement. While joined by their hatred of Siad Barré, the groups were divided by clan and ideology as well as geography. The ascent of the warlords had begun.

Somalia began to fragment. The culture of disenfranchisement became more pervasive. On a national level, no one had a legitimate claim to leadership. On the local level, not only did the political institutions begin to fray, but so did the social institutions. A climate of fear and lawlessness began to grip villages and towns caught in the middle of civil war.

The late 1980s represent an essential early missed opportunity in Somalia. No real international effort was made to mitigate the crisis at this early stage in the Intervention Cycle. "If the international community could have intervened by helping to unify the opposition, it might have prevented the gradual slide towards chaos," says historian Said Samatar.[13]

C. 1990–1991

The trauma of the growing civil war was compounded by drought. Harvests of 1991-1992 were as little as ten percent of normal levels. According to Office of Foreign Disaster Assistance reports, food prices began to rise sharply in the cities, as much as 1,000 percent. This encouraged hijacking and looting of relief supplies by ruthless profiteers. Somalis began the long trek to starvation.

As conditions deteriorated throughout the country, Somalis themselves attempted solutions. At grave risk, in May 1990, 144 well-known Somali leaders signed a manifesto calling for a national reconciliation conference. But the manifesto was mostly ignored by the outside world. There was no response from the UN, the United States or the USSR. The effort collapsed, and the insurgency against Siad Barré spread. According to veteran diplomat Mohamed Sahnoun, this manifesto was the second great "missed opportunity" in Somali history for preventive diplomacy.[14]

With the retreat of the superpowers from cold war clients, global preoccupation with the Gulf War and the indifference of the United Nations, neighboring states in Africa were left to act alone. In July 1991, a conference was held by the Djibouti government. Former Assistant Secretary of State Hank Cohen acknowledges that the United States didn't really lend much support: "We blessed the new agreement, even though we knew it was a mere fig leaf. We should have given the mediation effort more support. We should have been more interventionist."[15]

Those three junctures in time—Hargeisa in 1988, the Manifesto of 1990, and the Djibouti conference of 1991—are historical windows that begged for diplomatic action. But action by whom? Veteran diplomats Robert Oakley and John Hirsch admit the problem is thorny: "Neither the United Nations nor the United States was ready to do so. The UN Secretariat and Security Council was already engaged in more issues than they could handle . . . The Organization of African Unity (OAU) lacked the capacity, will, and focus, as did the Arab League and the Organization of Islamic Countries. None of these regional organizations had given much thought to or undertaken serious efforts at preventive diplomacy."[16]

And others also debunk Sahnoun's notion that mediation through regional organizations, even if money and political will had existed, could have worked. Andrew Natsios, who headed the U.S. Office of Foreign Disaster Assistance, suggests that "we overestimate the use of preventive diplomacy. Diplomacy is not

terribly useful in a place such as Somalia, where traditional diplomatic institutions do not even exist."[17] Still, mediation efforts, focused on unifying the
opposition groups and enfranchising the public, as well as actively engaging traditional leaders, might have given Somalia an important psychological lifeline.
The effort would have suggested that the outside world cared enough to act. It
might have served as a relatively cheap deterrent to the descent into chaos.

The lack of a unified political opposition escalated the violence. This in
turn encouraged the further erosion of civic and social institutions to the
point of no return. This raised the ante, by causing an ever growing power vacuum. The flood of relief supplies and international attention to come enlarged
the pot even further, by creating more food, jobs, and power to fight over. At
a point when the costs were relatively low, a concerted effort to unify the
opposition might have worked.

But in the early phase of the Somalia crisis, the international community
never really marched beyond two o'clock on the Intervention Cycle. Nothing
was done to keep Somalia from self-destructing. The lack of real efforts to mitigate or prevent conflict only widened it. This ultimately caused much more
expensive international interventions later, which neglected to include Somali
institutions, because few viable Somali institutions remained. The
Intervention Cycle suggests that one key to viable intervention is timing. The
time to intervene at lowest cost with potentially greatest effectiveness is when
the commitment to violence is smallest, and local institutions of power (i.e.,
enfranchising organizations—police, churches, schools, civic organizations,
intellectual groups) remain intact.

III. THE BATTLE FOR MOGADISHU

Siad Barré was ousted in January 1991, creating a gaping leadership hole. As
the vacuum increased, chaos filled it. Anarchy reigned throughout the rest of
the year. In late 1991, intraclan rivalry erupted in Mogadishu, as warlords Ali
Mahdi and Aideed, former allies, fought for control of the capital. The gun
battles and rocket fire transformed one of the older cities of Africa into a
wasteland. Hundreds of thousands of people subsisted in the rubble, without
plumbing, water, or electricity. Many fled the city into a countryside bereft of
crops or livestock and riddled with drought. The appalling conditions and
lack of viable infrastructure even caused UN humanitarian agencies to retreat
from Somalia, making their base of operations in Nairobi. At the end of 1991,
Mogadishu was a hell on earth.

The civil war reached the height of violence in early 1992. It was exacerbated
by as many as 40,000 weapons, left when the Somali Army disbanded at the

end of Siad Barré's rule.[18] The departure of Siad Barré represents another key juncture and another missed opportunity. A handful of military leaders or warlords had emerged as key in the overthrow of Barré. Many were divided by clan, a far deeper division in Somalia than religion, race, or village. They included Aideed, Ali Mahdi, Colonel Jess, General Hersi Morgan, and Abdulla Hi Yusuf. While it would certainly have been an extremely difficult diplomatic challenge, if these five could have been prompted into a power-sharing formula, the escalation of violence might have been avoided. But no international effort was undertaken during 1991 to achieve such a last ditch diplomatic solution.

A dictator had fled and a country that had held the attention of superpowers for two decades waited to be noticed. The spiral downward was not yet over. And there was to be little assistance from abroad. The United States at this moment was just rebounding from the stressful but jubilant victory of the Persian Gulf War and was also preoccupied by the collapse of the Soviet Union. Despite the pressing problems in Somalia, and the intimate historical relationship of the U.S. and Somalia, according to one former diplomat, the problems of Somalia "just didn't make the cut."[19]

A. Sahnoun and UNOSOM I

If a lesson about prevention is to be drawn from Somalia, it might be told through the experiences of one man: Mohamed Sahnoun. If Somalia posed an ultimate challenge for preventive diplomacy, Mohamed Sahnoun would seem to be an envoy with the cultural background, temperament, and skills for the job. A quiet, serious diplomat of deep resolve and moral purpose, Mohamed Sahnoun was dispatched on a fact-finding mission to Somalia in March 1992, at the request of UN Secretary General Boutros Boutros-Ghali. On April 24, 1992 the United Nations Security Council passed Resolution 751, establishing the United Nations Operation in Somalia (UNOSOM I), with Sahnoun as point person on the ground. The UN Secretary General seemingly could not have chosen a more qualified envoy.[20]

Sahnoun had lived in the Horn of Africa for nearly a decade, and had been deeply involved in conflict resolution as a deputy secretary general of the OAU. He was familiar with the turf and subculture of the region, as well as with many of the players. Most importantly, Boutros-Ghali considered Sahnoun a good friend. This would seem to bode well for clear communication, from the field back to UN headquarters.

What Sahnoun found on that fact-finding mission troubled him enormously. Already, hundreds of thousands had died, the result of both drought and civil war. As many as 3,000 were dying every day. "What I was seeing now was total disaster . . . here I was, alone, without support staff, and I was being asked to undertake the task of working out a plan whereby the United Nations could facilitate the cessation of hostilities between the Somali factions, promote reconciliation, and provide urgently needed humanitarian assistance."[21]

It was overwhelming. Sahnoun proceeded, undaunted, for weeks alone, without support staff. During the course of his seven month tenure as the secretary general's special envoy, he helped enforce a cease-fire through diplomatic meetings with all the warlords. His style was one of intimate contact, seeking to win the personal confidence of individuals, from faction chiefs to local grassroots leaders. U.S. negotiator Robert Oakley would later assume a similar approach to this important task. Sahnoun had plenty of problems with the prickly Somalis, but his greatest frustration was the lack of support he received from his own boss back at the UN.

In an urgent report back to the UN in June 1992 Sahnoun wrote: "Some 4,500,000 people are in urgent need of food . . . An absence of food breeds insecurity which, in turn, causes instability leading to starvation, suffering and disease. Breaking this diabolical and vicious cycle may be the key to resolving the intricate social and political problems in Somalia."[22]

Sahnoun felt his efforts at mediation would be more effective with more food. Dividing the country into four regions, he was making progress with the elders and local leaders. But he felt that adequate food distribution was necessary to bring warlords, elders, and local leaders to the table with good will. Instead of the food he urgently requested, some 50,000 metric tons per month, what did he receive? Another technical team dispatched from UN headquarters to assess the situation. The delay infuriated Sahnoun.[23] According to Andrew Natsios, formerly head of the U.S. Office of Foreign Disaster Assistance, "Sahnoun was not at all familiar with UN bureaucracy, and how it can eat you alive."[24]

Sahnoun was also burdened with the legacy of the UN in Somalia. The departure of UN relief agencies in 1991, and their absence of nearly one year, had created intense anger among Somalis. They felt abandoned, and saw no reason to trust the UN now. The UN Secretary General's personal history as a former Egyptian diplomat in the region didn't help. "When Boutros-Ghali gave a speech about UN ambitions in Somalia, heard on short-wave radio, Somalis thought he was trying to recolonize the country," says one relief activist.[25]

Another of Sahnoun's frustrations, beyond food and bureaucratic delays, was the looting and banditry that engulfed the country. The violence was reaching epidemic levels. Sahnoun recognized that the situation in Somalia was not only a food crisis, but also a security crisis. Yet he proposed the hiring of local Somalis, who would later become an embryonic national police force, rather than a massive outside force.[26]

Sahnoun did want a small peacekeeping mission sent, based on a fragile cease-fire agreement which seemed to be holding. One State Department diplomat suggests that during Sahnoun's tenure "if only a small amount of UN troops, perhaps 3000, could have been deployed, they might have handled it. It would have been worth the money at that point."[27] Andrew Natsios, now with the relief group World Vision, concurs: "If three to four thousand UN troops could have been dispatched in the spring and summer of 1992, it would have had a profound effect. It could have put the whole situation under control."[28]

But the Secretary General could initially muster only 500 men from Pakistan. Even that frugal number took enormous haggling with member states. The United States, fatigued from the Gulf War, stonewalled the effort completely, according to sources inside the State Department at the time. Voices inside the administration felt strongly that peacekeepers should not be sent where there was no clear peace to keep. In addition, the United States felt that the UN was already overcommitted, and therefore could not do a good job in Somalia. Finally, the United States was concerned about possible American involvement. Says former Assistant Secretary Hank Cohen, "The Pentagon was very worried about the slippery slope syndrome. If Americans get into trouble on the ground, the DOD [Department of Defense] was very concerned that more and more Americans would be called upon to help them." [29]

Not surprisingly, one of the main players in Mogadishu, the warlord General Aideed, also objected strongly to the UN force. Sahnoun carried out protracted negotiations with Aideed to ensure the safe landing of the 500 peacekeepers.[30] But he did this on the presumption that only 500 were coming. As the deal was being sealed for their landing, both Sahnoun and Aideed heard over the BBC that the Security Council was authorizing an additional nearly 3,000 men. The force was to be composed of well-armed Canadians, Belgians, and Egyptians, in order to make an impressive showing in south Mogadishu.

Some analysts suggest that such a showing might have been the only thing to deter someone as power-hungry as Aideed. "It's impossible to negotiate with a warlord like Aideed. The only thing he understands is force," claims Andrew Natsios. "Aideed had no incentive to negotiate. That said, he wasn't even in control of his own militia. Those kids had never had it so good. They had their own rooms, cars, bathrooms, food. Under Aideed, they had a much better life. Would mediation alone have been enough to get them to give this up? I don't think so."[31]

Robert Oakley agrees. "If strong, well-equipped NATO forces had come in, it might have made an impression on Aideed. He is smart enough not to be suicidal."[32] But on the ground, diplomat Sahnoun and warlord Aideed were both infuriated by the authorization of more UN troops. Sahnoun felt blind-sided by the UN, and maintains he heard not a word from Boutros-Ghali of the impending deployment. Aideed felt betrayed by Sahnoun. Those thousands of UN peacekeepers were never dispatched, ultimately thwarting the one possible crucial preventive measure that could have been taken.[33]

The 500 Pakistanis who composed the UNOSOM I force did not arrive until September, four months after their authorization. In the interim, the security situation deteriorated. When they finally arrived, by several accounts, they were ill-equipped for the job. They made a poor impression.

In addition, the UNOSOM I peacekeepers were nearly paralyzed by restrictive rules of engagement. Their mission? To secure the food supply from the airport to several key feeding stations. But because of the UN's narrow rules of engagement that restricted them to shooting only if fired at directly first, their mission was stymied. They remained sequestered at the airport for two and one-half months, the butt of ridicule of both the looters they were supposed to deter and the people they were supposed to protect. [34]

So despite the presence of UNOSOM I on the ground, with Sahnoun tirelessly working the back huts and formal halls of mediation, no real effort was exerted to secure the food supply. The peacekeepers who arrived did not command the respect of the Somalis, and failed at their task. They were not sent in large enough numbers, nor with a mandate or training to achieve their goal. They were outmanned and outgunned. It was a miserable start to United Nations peacekeeping in Somalia.

The lesson for intervention? Match the intervention mission with the tools selected for deployment. If the decision has been reached to conduct peace enforcement, peacekeepers should be deployed with more than enough manpower and firepower to succeed in that mission. In the case study of Somalia, the Intervention Cycle suggests that efforts to prevent or mitigate violence should not be half-measures. An inadequate peacekeeping force can backfire, triggering more violence and social decay.

In analyzing missed opportunities in Somalia, the tale of the Pakistanis is key. The episode highlights several miscalculations: a lack of clear communication between the UN mediator Sahnoun and his home office over how many peacekeepers were needed, a lack of concern over first impressions of that UN force upon arrival, a lack of resolve by the international community and finally, perhaps an overconfidence on the part of Sahnoun that his meticulous mediation could solve the problem, without a larger, better-equipped peacekeeping mission.

B. In the United States: "We were tired of it."

Just what were the motives of the U.S. intervention? And how did that define the mission? Between January and November 1992, frustration multiplied not just for Sahnoun, but for those stateside interested in Somalia. "We could not get much action going to do with Somalia," claims former Assistant Secretary of State Hank Cohen, who says he tried.[35] But just how hard did he try? Chaos inside Somalia was building, just at the same time that it was falling off the map of vital United States national interests. U.S. Central Command had for years identified Somalia as a strategic asset because the United States had sunk nearly $50 million into the naval base, the associated airfield, and the fuel storage at Berbera. During the nearby Persian Gulf War, the base had not proven vital. It had barely been used. "Desert Storm proved we didn't need it, we hadn't used it, so therefore the attitude was 'let's just get rid of it'," says former Assistant Secretary of State Hank Cohen. He candidly admits that "we just forgot about Somalia. We didn't need it. We were tired of it. We were only too happy to leave Somalia alone."[36]

At the same time, the United States and the UN were experiencing an early case of peacekeeping burnout. Over the previous three years, the United States had supported over 12 major UN peacekeeping operations, including successes in Namibia and Cambodia. The United States had underwritten 30 percent of all UN peacekeeping expenditures. But Somalia immediately followed the Cambodia operation, UNTAC, which had cost a whopping $2 billion, making it the most expensive in UN history. "My view is that Cambodia was the straw that broke the camel's back," says Cohen. "The immediate reaction in the administration was that we just [couldn't] go on indefinitely [using] the UN to solve every emergency. Let's draw the line."[37]

According to Cohen, a directive was issued by the State Department that Somalia was not to be called a "security problem" but a "food problem". The attitude was "if people are in danger of starvation, just send in more food."[38] The Intervention Cycle illustrates that humanitarian intervention, in crises where violence is high and people feel disenfranchised, will be difficult and perhaps even cause more violence. Predictably, the more food that was sent in, the more was stolen. The more that was stolen, the more the warlords' political capital increased. During the final months before U.S. military intervention, as much as 80 percent of UN relief may have been looted, or blocked in the warehouses and harbor, while Somalis starved.

Since Mogadishu was General Aideed's main base of operations, his power was directly enhanced. Relief officials claim that when food was seized, it was sold for guns. It bought the support of the Somali people for that clan leader, thereby intensifying the rivalry. Seated in South Mogadishu, the warlord

Aideed was the greatest beneficiary. As food mounted in the harbor, Robert Oakley states unequivocally that "the NGOs [non-governmental organizations] paid rent to Aideed, and hired Aideed's men as armed guards to protect them against Aideed. It was your classic protection racket."[39]

Stamping Somalia as a food problem, instead of a food *and* security problem, encouraged an inadequate and inappropriate response. The problem was not merely famine, but lawlessness, banditry and looting in a spiraling civil war. The withholding of food was being used as a weapon by several sides to the conflict. Increasing the supply of food would increase the political capital of the warlords, including General Aideed. By increasing their power, it worked against resolution of the conflict.

In retrospect, making Mogadishu the hub of most relief and diplomatic activity may have given Aideed too much power, at the expense of the rest of the country. A greater effort should have been made outside of Mogadishu to rebuild the hope and confidence of the Somali populace in the early stages of intervention.

(1) Operation Provide Relief. In August 1992 the White House ordered an airlift of food by the Defense Department, consistent with U.S. analysis that Somalia was merely a food problem. The action totally surprised the Africa bureau at the State Department. Then Assistant Secretary of State Cohen says "I would have said 'hire a civilian contractor, they can do it cheaper and better.'"[40]

According to retired Pentagon official Jim Woods, however, a light forces expedition was explored by Pentagon staffers over the summer. Relief expert Fred Cuny submitted a paper to the Pentagon, detailing how several thousand specially equipped forces could fan into the countryside outside of Mogadishu, securing relief lines. A special operations team was even dispatched to research its feasibility. But the plan fizzled over the summer, because Pentagon commanders thought it too risky. It was inconsistent with the doctrine of decisive force, and made them nervous.[41]

But security remained a problem. Food prices had risen so sharply that the deliveries became extremely attractive targets for bandits. The airlift operation could not even provide its own perimeter security. It proved so insecure that planes were often forced to airdrop the food as opposed to landing. Planes would occasionally return to Mombassa, their base of operation, with bullet holes.[42] The airlift was clearly not sufficient, neither to feed the nation nor to satisfy President Bush. By late fall, Bush may have already reached the personal conclusion that only military intervention with the willingness to use force could quickly resolve the crisis. But action would have to wait until after the U.S. elections.[43]

(2) The Moment of Decision. Just when did President Bush decide to send 28,000 U.S. troops en masse? Would he have ordered the deployment if he had not lost the election? According to then Secretary of State Lawrence Eagleburger, the decision was Bush's and Bush's alone. And the president's advisers are convinced he would have deployed U.S. troops in Somalia regardless of the election's outcome.[44] Those who know Bush say his visit to the Sudan in 1985 was pivotal. Somalia was the culmination of his convictions.

In anticipation of action in Somalia, the president started soliciting plans. Those presented by the State Department and the Pentagon contrasted sharply. According to Assistant Secretary Hank Cohen, the State Department's official recommendation was that it be a UN operation, using American aircraft. "We in State thought it would be politically unacceptable to send U.S. forces in. We advocated a UN force, with U.S. airlift."[45]

But the Pentagon had a different approach. In early November at a White House Deputies' meeting, a Pentagon representative presented several plans to address the Somalia crisis. Among them was a plan for the use of overwhelming U.S. force to secure the food supply. Some in the Pentagon believe the plan was presented as a "throwaway" to provide a complete list of options to the president. Insiders say that, at the time of presentation, the Pentagon leadership thought the president clearly would not choose it, and did not want him to choose it, because of its vast scope.

In that option for decisive force, the Pentagon argued that a UN operation would take three to six months to deploy and too many more would die, and that the UN was not up to the task of securing relief. It needed help, and the United States was the only power with the logistical capacity, command and control, and lift to do the job quickly. But the Pentagon was adamant there should be no action beyond securing humanitarian relief. To Pentagon planners, Somalia was just not a vital interest. Beyond that, military planners knew the muck of quagmires and worried about a quick, uncontrollable slide into one. "We were all surprised by the Joint Chiefs' analysis indicating what it wanted to do. But it turned out to be a fine analysis," says Cohen.[46]

Just why were so many troops sent in to intervene? The Pentagon had clearly studied the bungled deployment of the Pakistanis earlier in the year. But the action was also consistent with U.S. doctrine to approach possible conflict with decisive force. And then, too, there was Bosnia. Somalia might prove to be an inoculation against a much bloodier Bosnia conflict. Says retired diplomat Hank Cohen simply, "Somalia just looked easier."[47]

That certainly was the thinking in the State Department. Former Secretary of State Eagleburger recalls that 1992 was a busy year, and Somalia simply had not been high on his agenda. What galvanized his attention were two memos sent to him on the same day in November, both written by Assistant Secretary of State for Political/Military Affairs, Robert Gallucci. Both memos called for U.S. intervention. One dealt with Somalia, the other with Bosnia. Says Eagleburger, "I was then and am now staunchly and firmly opposed to U.S. action in the former Yugoslavia. But I looked at the Somalia memo, stared out the window, and decided that this was one we could probably deal with without great cost."[48]

After Eagleburger decided a Somalia intervention might be "manageable," he gave his recommendation to the White House. The president's final decision was made after he received two things: the recommendation from Eagleburger, and, secondly, the Pentagon plan to intervene with minimal loss of American life. In the end, even though many Pentagon planners were skeptical of the mission, no one opposed President Bush's decision to intervene for humanitarian purposes only. The Intervention Cycle suggests, however, that there is no such thing as a purely humanitarian intervention. Such an intervention may seem easier, and therefore more achievable; but as shown earlier, the problem in Somalia was far greater than a humanitarian crisis.

(3) Fissures in the Relief Community. In the final analysis, opportunities for prevention of the massive crisis in Somalia were not just diplomatic or military; the failure was humanitarian as well. Perhaps foremost, the crisis deepened in Somalia as the result of a humanitarian community that, for understandable reasons, pulled out when it became too dangerous. If a larger humanitarian presence had persisted in 1991, there is a chance that the implosion would not have occurred. Except for the International Committee for the Red Cross (ICRC) and a few NGOs, most relief groups fled Somalia during the crucial year of 1991, after Siad Barré's departure. The UN itself was totally absent during the crucial year of 1991. Those who stayed risked their lives.

As conditions deteriorated inside Somalia, so did security for the NGOs. As a result, the ICRC hired armed protection for the first time in their history. They hired as many as 20,000 Somalis at one point, labeling them (and their armed vehicles) "technical assistance."[49] Some "technicals" turned on the agencies themselves. Many relief workers lost their lives; others were severely injured while trying to deliver or protect supplies.

The picture of young men riding on a rampage in their armed vehicles became a symbol for growing chaos in Somalia. Even though the armed vehicles were of little military value, they had a powerful political impact on Somalis as well as on the outside world. Inside Somalia, they killed enough civilians and destroyed enough property to create a climate of pervasive fear. Outside of Somalia, the technicals presented such a vivid picture of lawlessness that the image only reinforced the international community's postponement of action.

As the crisis deepened, the relief community became deeply divided about what to do. Not all wanted military intervention. Some worried that military intervention might hinder their work, making themselves vulnerable pawns in a war. Others worried about the possible obstruction of the fragile political reconciliation process started by Sahnoun. Nevertheless, many prominent agencies decided to act. Eleven agencies, through the auspices of an umbrella organization called InterAction, signed a letter calling for a stronger UN presence and mandate. Several of them—including Oxfam America, the International Rescue Committee, and CARE—held a highly publicized press conference on November 24, 1992 in Washington to underscore the need for the international community to help protect their convoys. By so doing, they helped build broad public support for the decision on military intervention about to be taken by President Bush.

Relief officials were actively engaged as the logistics, goals, and speed of the invasion were decided. With input from relief officials, the military planners also gave consideration to how to ensure the safety of private voluntary organizations. Ultimately, no evacuation was mandated. Regular meetings were conducted, for the duration of the operation, between senior government officials and relief agencies at the State Department.

But some relief workers and human-rights advocates maintain that their vision of the U.S. and UN roles in Somalia was a limited one. Keenly sensitive to the delicate issue of sovereignty, they say they never called for more comprehensive action. Says Holly Burkhalter of Human Rights Watch, "What we called for was not full-scale nation building. My own vision was of a more minimal strategic intervention—to protect the ports and airports, and protect the truck convoys so food could be distributed. We didn't want American soldiers involved in all aspects of Somali society. We knew that would have a bad effect."[50]

Ultimately the goals developed by the partnership between the U.S. military commanders, State Department, and relief community were limited and clear-cut:

- stop the starvation through secure delivery of food;
- disarm only to the extent that armed militia interfered with food delivery;
- stop the epidemics by the restoration of basic public health system; and
- create enough security to hand off the operation to the UN.

By assessing those goals through the prism of the Intervention Cycle, the outcome of the UNITAF mission would have been predictable. Muscular intervention would be enough to mitigate the crisis, but not to resolve the underlying causes of conflict—the power vacuum, social and political disenfranchisement, and messy clan rivalry. Despite good intentions, and clearcut results in creating a better humanitarian climate, UNITAF set the stage for yet more violent conflict, particularly in southern Mogadishu.

C. Operation RESTORE HOPE

The UN Security Council passed Resolution 794 in December 1992, authorizing U.S.-led force to "use all necessary means to establish as soon as possible a secure environment for humanitarian relief operations." The mission was dubbed Operation Restore Hope. While not a formal Chapter VII operation under the United Nations Charter, the Somalia effort is often considered a Chapter Six-and-a-half, that is, a U.S.-led operation with the ability to use decisive force, similar to Korea and Desert Storm. The United Nations International Task Force, or UNITAF, was the most successful of all international attempts to intervene in Somalia.

UNITAF marked a clear departure for U.S. foreign policy, as well as for the UN. The Pentagon had been involved in humanitarian action before, as with Operation "Provide Comfort" in northern Iraq. But in Somalia, for the first time, America was willing to intervene far from its shores, in an area of marginal strategic influence, where no discernible national interest was at stake. The U.S. goal for intervention was clear and precise: stopping starvation. This was the largest purely humanitarian intervention in human history. It succeeded in saving the lives of hundreds of thousands of people. But, despite its clear successes, UNITAF was far from perfect. Just what went right? What went wrong? And what does the Intervention Cycle suggest could be executed better?

American and other international forces landed with strength and speed, and moved quickly throughout the country. In contrast to the initial UNOSOM I Pakistani force, the U.S.-led force made a great impression on Somali citizens and the armed factions. They met with little resistance.

In addition to deploying decisive American force, President Bush appointed his own personal envoy, diplomat Robert Oakley. Oakley had previously served as a U.S. ambassador to Somalia, and like Sahnoun, knew the terrain. He arrived in early December 1992, in advance of U.S. troops, with the delicate mission of explaining to proud Somalis just why American troops were going to flood into their country. He served as political adviser to the heads of the U.S. military mission. But his most immediate mission was to warn Aideed and Ali Mahdi not to interfere with the United States—or else. The American force underscored this with an impressive show of force. When the Amphibious Ready Group and its carrier air cover showed up off the coast and in the air over Mogadishu, the warlords understood that Oakley and company meant serious business.

Oakley was also charged with the more far-reaching mandate of helping the UN to encourage political reconciliation, a process started by Sahnoun. Oakley now declares that, in retrospect, that diplomatic mandate was perhaps too ambitious. By creating the political goal of national reconciliation, the position of supreme national leader existed in the minds of feuding political leaders. Instead of providing an incentive to reconcile, it created tension. "Maybe we all pushed too hard on the idea of getting an agreement for a national government. It just provoked antagonism between Ali Mahdi and Aideed. When the UN left in March 1995, and there was no national leadership position to fight over, they stopped fighting," says Oakley retrospectively.[51]

The well-intentioned goal of national reconciliation raised the stakes. Instead of spending so much time at the top of the pyramid, Oakley now suggests the focus should perhaps have remained on the grassroots. Somalis, who had never had a history of strong national government, perhaps could have survived more peaceably without one altogether.

Human rights analysts argue that the diplomatic effort and repeated meetings with Ali Mahdi and Aideed only increased the warlords' power and prestige by lending them the legitimacy of a position in the international community. "The UN dealt with the war leaders as if with national leaders, but without holding these claimants to authority and legitimacy accountable for their actions against any consistent standard," stated a Human Rights Watch document.[52] Given the deep rivalry fracturing Mogadishu, the mission of lasting political reconciliation may have been unachievable, as Oakley now admits. But upon arrival, he met immediately with both Ali Mahdi and Aideed, the two main warlords in Mogadishu. He then arranged for a rare meeting of the two leaders, face-to-face, and pursued reconciliation between these two archenemies and other leaders throughout his tenure.

But beyond the task of placating the warlords' egos, Oakley had another more immediate problem. U.S. leaders, in the middle of a transfer of power, gave him little guidance. The Bush team, as a lame duck administration handing off to a new party and president, did not have a long-term vision. Congress was not in session. The Clinton team was not yet assembled. And the UN, inexperienced at massive humanitarian operations, didn't have a clear vision either. "Nobody had a plan for Somalia. There was no systematic plan to demobilize the militia, disarm the population and put them to work. We had to try and cobble one together on the spot," Oakley says.[53]

Oakley and the U.S. military leaders drafted an operational plan to divide Somalia into eight humanitarian relief sectors in the south, where suffering and starvation was worst.[54] They hoped to be fully deployed by late January; they moved with such efficiency and dispatch, however, that that goal was achieved by December 28th, almost a month ahead of schedule.[55] In addition, a Civilian-Military Operations Center was established at UNOSOM headquarters to coordinate the work of the military and nongovernmental organizations. At these daily sessions, information and intelligence were freely exchanged, establishing a new relationship between players who had previously been suspicious of each other.

With a total force of 40,000 soldiers, UNITAF commanders felt it vital to limit the scope of their mission. They concentrated on the central and southern regions where famine had hit hardest. The UN was not happy with the de facto plan, arguing that force should have been deployed throughout the country. U.S. commanders felt this would constitute mission creep, and stayed south. Oakley and UNITAF commanders developed a formula for penetrating the southern countryside, to secure relief distribution. Oakley and General Johnston painstakingly coordinated their approach. Their method was to dispatch Oakley or his personal representative in advance of U.S. soldiers in order to explain the troops' mission, just as Oakley had done in Mogadishu. The diplomats encouraged input of local leaders, and listened patiently to their concerns. Usually, the troops were greeted with enthusiasm and relief upon arrival.[56]

Mogadishu had quieted down by mid-January, in part because of the strong show of decisive force. But Oakley still pursued political reconciliation. He felt strongly that one key to political stability was the establishment of a credible national police force, to help rebuild Somalis' faith in government. When the United States exited, the interim police force—though they were unarmed and had marginal authority—numbered more then 3,000 men in Mogadishu alone.[57]

On January 15, under UN sponsorship, warring parties signed an initial agreement in Ethiopia. The Addis Ababa Accords called for a national ceasefire, disarmament, confiscation of heavy weapons, and the demobilization of militias. Just who should enforce the agreement was unclear. The United States, preparing to exit, did not want the job, and the UN did not have the staff in place. The embryonic national police force was barely more than an idea on paper. In retrospect, Oakley criticizes the lack of support for the Addis Accords from both Washington and the UN. "There was no response from Washington (the fledgling Clinton team) or from the UN headquarters. So we (the military commanders and I) did what we could locally with no resources and no mandate and no serious support."[58]

Oakley and General Johnston felt disarmament should be limited to cantonment of heavy weapons, and eliminating "technicals" and light weapons from the streets of cities. They also feared that widespread disarmament would have dire political and military consequences. They argued it could lead to major confrontations with key Somali leaders, whom Oakley was still trying to woo into reconciliation. Disarmament also could tie up UNITAF forces, so they would be unable to continue to protect relief deliveries. Finally, the scope of national disarmament was simply daunting. Since UNITAF deployment was confined mostly to the south, disarmament throughout the country seemed beyond their capacity.

The Secretary General of the UN, however, had a far more ambitious vision, one that Oakley, General Johnston, and the Bush administration felt was unachievable.[59] Eagleburger today insists that the U.S. definition of disarmament in Somalia had always been clear and precise. "I told the Secretary General in November that we would disarm only to ensure the secure delivery of food, or to protect our own forces. No further!" says Eagleburger adamantly.[60] Boutros-Ghali disagreed about the word "disarmament". He argued for a far more invasive definition, including more coercive house-to-house searches for buried weapons. But Boutros-Ghali did not address, to the satisfaction of UNITAF leaders, who should protect Somalis from banditry and looting, if they were to be disarmed. Again, UNITAF leaders worried about a pernicious mission creep, that Americans would suddenly be responsible for the safety of all Somali civilians, instead of merely for delivery of relief. For intervention to be effective, they felt it had to stay precise.

So the scope of disarming by U.S.-led forces stayed limited. Working guidelines were called the "Four No's". The United States would permit: no technicals, no banditry, no roadblocks, and no visible weapons.

Not satisfied with the policy of "Four No's", the UN Secretary General began to drag his feet on the deployment of a second UN force, claiming that UNITAF had not completed its mandate. The issue of disarmament was central in the messy hand-off from the United States to the UN. Trust eroded between the two, because the scope of disarmament was not clearly decided prior to the mission. Ultimately, the Secretary General's vision of a Somalia stripped of weapons may have addressed a central root problem—insecurity. But it was overly ambitious, given the limited U.S. commitment.

A third tension between the United States and UN was how to help the large refugee population, numbering about one-third the population. Approximately two million people were internally or externally displaced. UNHCR leaders queried whether it might be possible for the United States to escort hundreds of thousands of refugees home. Some relief officials felt this vital to normalize the country, to rebuild the social fabric, and to end famine by tilling of fields. But the U.S. military argued resettlement was beyond their mandate and capacity. They felt they did not have the personnel or equipment to move such a wave of humanity. They kept their objectives narrow—to secure humanitarian relief, rather than address underlying causes of famine.

Today, former OFDA head Andrew Natsios claims UNITAF missed an opportunity in Somalia. "If the military had focused on resettling those two million people, providing them seeds and tools, the entire country could have been normalized in six months instead of two years," says Natsios. Instead, 1.3 million refugees stayed in camps, and in 1995 hundreds of thousands still had not returned home.[61]

Andrew Natsios believes the problem was broader. "The American military is designed and trained to fight and win wars," he says.[62] Stopping starvation, not analyzing the root causes of this crisis, was the mission.

During late March another collision occurred between U.S. and UN plans. This conflict was over whether and how to the establish a formal national government. By March 1993, the handoff to the UN by the U.S.-led force was in progress. Secretary General Boutros-Ghali wanted national reconciliation between the warlords, and called another large conference in Addis to achieve just that. In Addis, Somalis agreed to a National Reconciliation Council. The net result was another round of power struggle between Aideed and Ali Mahdi. Ali Mahdi even formally proclaimed himself to be interim president, infuriating Aideed. But UNITAF strived to remain impartial. Says Oakley, "I ducked this rivalry by explaining the U.S. was not involved in their rivalry, and would not take sides."[63]

At this point, Oakley was no longer serving in an official capacity, but was still a powerful player behind the scenes. He says that "[he] hoped that the bottom-up strategy they had begun during UNITAF with local councils would result in choosing regional councils, and then . . . a National Council. In fact, Addis touched off a battle to dominate the National Council, aggravating the old Aideed–Ali Mahdi rivalry for national leadership. The UN was seen by Aideed as against him, and for Ali Mahdi, and things went downhill from there."[64]

Although UNITAF failed to quell this political rivalry, the U.S. military achieved a stunning success in fighting off starvation. It achieved its stated goal convincingly. It also provided a measure of security where it was deployed. But the Intervention Cycle suggests that in several other areas the effort was less impressive. For one, the well-intentioned mediation aimed at reconciliation may have raised political stakes and prolonged conflict. While the U.S. military moved quickly to create security, even grooming a budding police force, its disarmament effort was modest. Finally, in failing to support refugee resettlement aggressively, the United States failed to solve a central underlying source of starvation, empty fields without hoes or seeds or people to work them.

D. UNOSOM II

In May 1993 the original UNOSOM and the UNITAF forces were formally replaced by a new UN mission, with a broad geographical reach, and more ambitious mandate. Somalia, recovering from drought and famine, was to be the showcase of new UN power. It proved the opposite.

For the UN, UNOSOM II was the first formal application of Chapter VII of the UN Charter, utilizing force not to peace keep, but to secure the peace. A bold attempt to use the UN in a new way, it sought to revive a failing nation-state, where no clear national government existed. Its scope was sweeping.

Specifically the nations composing UNOSOM II were charged with the mission to:

> provide humanitarian and other assistance to the people of Somalia in rehabilitating their political institutions and economy and promoting political settlement and national reconciliation. Such assistance should include economic relief and rehabilitation of Somalia, the repatriation of refugees and displaced persons within Somalia, the reestablishment of national and regional institutions and civil administration in the entire country, the reestablishment of Somali police, mine-clearance and public information activities in support of the United Nations activities in Somalia.[65]

The new UN goal of nation building may have been impossible. The mission was also not well received in southern Mogadishu, Aideed's base of operations. Whereas the American-led intervention was applauded by Somalis, the UN already boasted a long, controversial track record in the country. Some Somalis, including supporters of General Aideed in the Somali National Alliance, assumed the new expanded mandate implied a UN takeover. They were not reassured that the new UN special representative was an American, Admiral Jonathan Howe. The perceived challenge to Somali sovereignty was buttressed by a more coercive approach to disarmament by UNOSOM II forces.

In addition, Howe did not meet with faction leaders face-to-face, unlike diplomats Oakley and Sahnoun. His approach to Aideed and the other warlords was a military "us versus them" mindset.[66] From the outset, Aideed was seen as the problem, instead of part of the solution. The diplomatic courtship of Aideed had ended. He was dealt with as a warlord, instead of a future leader. In addition, Howe shunned contact with the Somali intelligentsia. "He felt that Somalis wouldn't give him good advice because of their ethnic allegiances," says one Somali intellectual.[67] Howe insulated himself from Somali culture, reinforcing the notion that the UN was a colonizing force.

Shortly after UNOSOM II's arrival, on June 5, 1993, 24 soldiers from Pakistan were killed, with scores wounded. They were ambushed after carrying out a weapons inspection with prior notification. The attacks were quickly attributed to General Aideed. The decision to retaliate was not Admiral Howe's alone, though he advocated a strong response. In the face of such a lethal challenge to UN authority, the Security Council and President Clinton's fledgling national security staff agreed a forceful reply was needed. UNOSOM retaliated later in the week, when the U.S. Rapid Deployment Force attacked Aideed's headquarters, radio station, and weapon depots. In addition, Admiral Howe initiated a national manhunt for Aideed, placing a price of $25,000 for his arrest.

The targeting of Aideed marked a key shift in emphasis of the UN intervention. The UN was no longer an impartial peacemaker; it had taken sides, and taken sides decisively, in the conflict. Aideed was publicly proclaimed the enemy, a criminal, and a fugitive from justice. This offended the deep-rooted pride of some Somalis. The UN, in their mind, had become not savior, but occupier and oppressor. As UNOSOM commanders focused more exclusively on waging battle against Aideed's Somali National Alliance, he achieved greater stature in the eyes of his supporters. It even caused a measure of unity that had eluded Somalis for years before. Some of Aideed's enemies, those countrymen who were not even members of his Habr Gidr clan, filtered into Mogadishu to fight on his behalf.

According to historian Said Samatar, the cherished lineage system came clearly into play, "my brother and I against my father, our household against the uncle's . . . my nation and I against the world, that's the Somali way. Outside interventions cause Somalis to unify; by targeting Aideed, the UN fell into a trap."[68] Beyond strengthening Aideed, one immediate result of the manhunt was a neglect of humanitarian work. OFDA estimates show relief efforts were reduced by half[69]

UNOSOM II's work was complicated by growing antagonisms among participating countries. "The Italians were angry about being shut out by Americans, the Africans felt the Europeans had taken over, and the Americans looked down on everyone else, because they had the muscle and firepower," sums up historian Samatar.[70]

The conflict between Aideed and the UN escalated during the summer of 1993. After considering for days whether to step up military action, UN commander Howe decided to target Aideed's command and control centers. In the most controversial clash, in July, the UN targeted a civilian house in Mogadishu, where it believed hard-line Aideed commandos had gathered. The 17-minute attack largely destroyed the building. The International Committee of the Red Cross estimates nearly 60 people were killed, and almost 200 wounded.[71] SNA supporters claimed that women and children were killed. They also said that within the house a political reconciliation meeting had been taking place, with dozens of important local leaders present.

The attack was a crucial miscalculation, militarily and politically. Immediately, the mood in Mogadishu turned sour. A group of journalists covering the story was attacked, and four were killed. In a 1995 report, Human Rights Watch/Africa says,

> Widely regarded as having claimed overwhelmingly civilian victims, among them advocates of reconciliation, the Abdi house attack became a symbol of the UN's loss of direction in Somalia. From humanitarian champion, the UN was itself in the dock for what to the casual observer looked like mass murder. The United Nations, and in particular its American forces, lost much of what remained of its moral high ground.[72]

As the UN's credibility eroded, the fruitless search for Aideed intensified, political and military goals became entirely out of synch. If the goal was to rebuild the country politically and socially, the militarization of the conflict seemed to do the opposite. Clashes continued throughout the fall; civilian casualties mounted. As tensions escalated in Mogadishu, the United States decided to deploy elite American Army Rangers to bring the manhunt for Aideed to a close. Four hundred Rangers were dispatched in late August; 18 came home in body bags.

The drama of October 3-4, when 18 Army Rangers were killed, 75 injured and 1 taken prisoner, has been graphically described by Human Rights Watch.[73] Television images of an American body dragged through streets, while Somalis cheered, took its toll on the American people. They wanted their troops to come home. Although President Clinton ordered an initial increase in forces by some 10,000 men, soon thereafter came the deadline for withdrawal. U.S. troops would depart Somalia by March 1994. According to reports at the time, General Aideed, once the implacable enemy, "emerged even more powerful than he was before the operation began."[74]

The U.S. decision to exit Somalia in a hurry was not welcomed by the UN. According to one senior UN official, Kofi Annan, "The impression [was] created that the easiest way to disrupt a peacekeeping operation is to kill Americans."[75]

That skirmish is widely portrayed today as a parable of UN incompetence. The Rangers, however, were at all times under American command. But the deadly clash was perhaps the inevitable outcome of the broader policy of targeting Aideed, instilling visceral hatred of the UN throughout Mogadishu. It turned the streets of Mogadishu into enemy territory. One member of Aideed's Somali National Alliance summed up the mood toward the UN, just after the October clash, "Boutros-Ghali used the United Nations as an instrument against the Somalis . . . He has ruined Somalia."[76]

The Secretary General thought differently. In a speech in October 1993, he implied that the UN had saved Somalia. "We, the United Nations, are rebuilding Somalia. We must show that collective action can be an active force for good, not merely a defensive shield against evil."[77] But the world was tired of Somalia, and of Boutros-Ghali's grand vision of Somalia as a laboratory for UN action. As other nations followed the U.S. retreat, a cease-fire was reached with General Aideed, whose Somali National Alliance had been largely decimated in the Ranger attack. The manhunt was called off. Just by eluding capture, Aideed had won. It appeared to his followers that he had conquered the colonizers. Ironically, the UN withdrawal would mean that Aideed's main source of capital, both financial and political, would dwindle. Aideed's control of relief supplies would be curtailed, as would be his cuts from paychecks from thousands of UN-related jobs.

The UNOSOM II concentration of aid and might in Mogadishu, where Aideed maintained his base, may have been the apex of a slippery slope. By virtue of the terrain, it created an almost inevitable power struggle between Aideed and the UN. While the UN retaliation to the attack on the Pakistani peacekeepers may have been necessary, escalating the conflict wider, as well as starting a manhunt for Aideed, were not. Pentagon and UN planners now admit the manhunt was a mistake, which will not be repeated again soon. While UNOSOM II won the war against starvation in the rest of Somalia, it lost the battle of southern Mogadishu. Given Aideed's strength and popularity there, it was perhaps a battle the UN should never have waged on the warlord's home turf.

Though the UN spent nearly two billion dollars in Somalia, it ultimately failed to bring Aideed to justice, anoint a new president, find a lasting peace, or create a working national government. But perhaps these should never have been its goals. It should have focused instead on the root causes of the violence: the social, political, and economic disenfranchisement of millions of Somalis, especially the clearly disenfranchised members of the militias. A bottom-up approach may have, over time, more effectively solved the Somalia syndrome.

III. LOOKING TO THE FUTURE

UN troops departed Somalia in March 1995 quietly, without the flood of camera lights or stampede of journalists. Somalia has not yet slid back into total anarchy. Crops are harvested, cattle herds graze, peasants plant, and bananas are exported. No central government exists, but local authority, through elders and clan leaders, has been resurrected. Critical for recovery, much of the refugee population has returned home.

After all the interventions are over, even the best intentioned and most successful, the responsibility for rebuilding a country must rest with its own citizens. This is the most lasting lesson of the Intervention Cycle in the case study of Somalia. A will to rebuild must be born from within. Resolution requires the active participation of the population, or an end to the culture of disenfranchisement. Outside intervention may help in rebirth, by providing finances, force, and diplomatic frameworks. But it can also complicate the process. As suggested by diplomat Robert Oakley, the world community may have been, in retrospect, too intrusive in Somalia, creating ever greater stakes that prolonged the violence and conflict.

The following is a list of some lessons learned from Somalia, based on the application of the Intervention Cycle:

- early prevention has the greatest chance of success;
- to succeed in intervention, figure out what is in tune with local realities, based on existing power structures—in other words, enfranchise all parties to the conflict by making them feel they have a stake in the outcome;
- don't be too intrusive; the more intrusive, the bigger the potential for backlash—in other words, political settlements (resolution) cannot be imposed from outside;
- realize that any intervention, even purely humanitarian, helps some parties to the conflict and impairs the actions of others;
- peace enforcement needs a strong mandate, sufficient will and the right training and equipment for the job;
- if peacekeepers are only deployed in areas of unmitigated conflict, prepare the public for casualties;
- develop a systematic plan for putting warring parties back to work;
- consider whether and how disarmament is possible;
- if a transition from one intervention force to another is planned, make sure that hand-off is smooth, and that planners work in concert from the beginning; and
- overall, keep the goals achievable—any intervention needs a clear concept of what is to be achieved and how.

Somalia imploded because prevention failed, mediation lacked a clear focus, peacekeeping was piecemeal, and the humanitarian presence had almost vanished by 1991. Only a massive, expensive intervention could mitigate one of the worst crises in recorded human history.

UNITAF was the most successful of the Somalia interventions because its goals were specific and U.S. commanders did not over-promise. The intervention force was impartial and well-armed; diplomats worked intimately with the military relief effort, reaching out to both warlords and lower levels of society; communication was clear and precise; and sufficient level of force was committed to deter violence. However, the crisis was only mitigated, and not resolved, in part, because root causes of the conflict were not addressed. Central to this conflict was the near total disenfranchisement of the wild, young militia members who fought for their chosen warlords.

UNOSOM II was less successful than UNITAF because its goals were too vast. Despite ambitious blueprints for the reconstruction of civil society, there was no follow-through on rehabilitating the courts, the police, or the political institutions. Diplomacy was abandoned in favor of militarism. UNOSOM II's troops were not as well-equipped, coordinated, or prepared as the U.S.-led force. But UNOSOM II also failed because of a political miscalculation by the UN. The decision to make General Aideed public enemy number one changed the political and military landscape of Mogadishu. It tore asunder the earlier successful strategy of linking political and military action.

One lesson of UNOSOM II is that interventions are inherently political acts. Stakes are raised when the international community takes sides, and taking sides can be dangerous. If a military decision is reached to enforce action against one or more sides, the force level committed must be sufficient to achieve quick, convincing results. A simultaneous diplomatic investment must be made. Further, targeting individuals may only turn them into local heroes and the terrain into hostile territory for the intervention force. Disenfranchising individuals and groups only further compounds the root causes of the conflict.

Finally, interventions that leave the perception of failure, despite any good achieved, have repercussions well beyond that country's borders. Despite the success of UNITAF, Somalia today stands as a metaphor for failure of American power in the post–cold war world, and the raison d'être not to tread upon distant sands again.

NOTES

1. Mohamed Sahnoun, *Somalia: The Missed Opportunities.* Washington, DC: United States Institute of Peace Press, 1994, p. xiii.

2. Human Rights Watch/Africa, "Somalia Faces the Future: Human Rights in a Fragmented Society," (April 1995), p. 1.
3. Lawrence Eagleburger, telephone interview with author, May 10, 1995.
4. Richard Betts, "The Delusion of Impartial Intervention," *Foreign Affairs* 73, no. 6, (November/December 1994), p. 30.
5. Les Gelb, in General Bernard Trainor, (Ed.), *Military Perspectives on Humanitarian Intervention and Military-Media Relations*, Berkeley, CA: University of California Press, 1995, p. 4.
6. Brian Urquhart, telephone interview with author, May 4, 1995.
7. Said Samatar, "Anatomy of a Tragedy," The MacNeil/Lehrer NewsHour, Public Broadcasting System, December 2, 1992, transcript p. 9.
8. Sahnoun, *Somalia*, p. 5.
9. MacNeil/Lehrer NewsHour, p. 10.
10. Sahnoun, *Somalia*, pp. 5-6.
11. Ibid., p. 6.
12. Ibid., p. 6.
13. Said Samatar, telephone interview with author, May 31, 1995.
14. Sahnoun, *Somalia*, p. 8.
15. Hank Cohen, telephone interview with author, May 2, 1995.
16. John L. Hirsch and Robert B. Oakley, *Somalia and Operation Restore Hope*. Washington, DC: U.S. Institute of Peace Press, 1995, p. 170.
17. Andrew Natsios, telephone interview with author, May, 9, 1995.
18. Sahnoun, *Somalia*, p. 17.
19. Chet Crocker, telephone interview with author, May 8, 1995.
20. Hirsch and Oakley, *Somalia and Operation Restore Hope*, p. 21.
21. Sahnoun, *Somalia*, p. vii.
22. Ibid., p. 18.
23. Ibid., p. 21.
24. Natsios, telephone interview with author, May 9, 1995.
25. Ibid.
26. Sahnoun, *Somalia*, p. 29.
27. Cohen, telephone interview with author, May 2, 1995.
28. Natsios, telephone interview with author, May 9, 1995.
29. Cohen, telephone interview with author, May 2, 1995.
30. Hirsch and Oakley, *Somalia and Operation Restore Hope*, p. 26.
31. Natsios, telephone interview with author, May 9, 1995.
32. Robert Oakley, telephone interview with author, May 15, 1995.
33. Hirsch and Oakley, *Somalia and Operation Restore Hope*, p. 26.
34. Ibid., p. 27.
35. Cohen, telephone interview with author, May 2, 1995.
36. Ibid.
37. Ibid.
38. Cohen, telephone interview with author, May 2, 1995.
39. Oakley, telephone interview with author, May 15, 1995.

40. Cohen, telephone interview with author, May 2, 1995.
41. Jim Woods, telephone interview with author, April 17, 1996.
42. Andrew Natsios, "Learning from Operation RESTORE HOPE: Somalia Revisited," paper delivered at Princeton University, April 21, 1995, p. 6.
43. Hirsch and Oakley, *Somalia and Operation Restore Hope*, p. 24.
44. Eagleburger, telephone interview with author, May 10, 1995.
45. Crocker, telephone interview with author, May 8, 1995.
46. Cohen, telephone interview with author, May 2, 1995.
47. Ibid.
48. Eagleburger, telephone interview with author, May 10, 1995.
49. Natsios, "Learning from Operation RESTORE HOPE: Somalia Revisited," p. 7.
50. Holly Burkhalter, telephone interview with author, May 4, 1995.
51. Oakley, telephone interview with author, May 15, 1995.
52. Human Rights Watch, "Somalia Faces the Future," p. 1
53. Oakley, telephone interview with author, May 15, 1995.
54. Hirsch and Oakley, *Somalia and Operation Restore Hope*, p. 65.
55. Ibid., p. 67.
56. Ibid., p. 71.
57. Ibid., pp. 88-89.
58. Oakley, note to author, June 1, 1995.
59. Eagleburger, telephone interview with author, May 10, 1995.
60. Ibid.
61. Natsios, telephone interview with author, May 9, 1995.
62. Ibid.
63. Oakley, note to author, June 1, 1995.
64. Ibid.
65. United Nations Department of Public Information, Information Notes: United Nations Peacekeeping, Update: May 1994, DPI/1306/Rev. 3/Reprint-July 18 1994, p. 106.
66. Oakley, note to author, June 1, 1995.
67. Samatar, telephone interview with author, May 31, 1995.
68. Ibid.
69. Hirsch and Oakley, *Somalia and Operation Restore Hope*, p. 123.
70. Samatar, telephone interview with author, May 31, 1995.
71. Human Rights Watch, "Somalia Faces the Future," pp. 62, 63.
72. Ibid., p. 63.
73. Ibid., p. 66.
74. Donatella Lorch, "As U.S. Exits, Somali Clan Chief Stands Strong," *The New York Times*, March 2, 1994, p. A3.
75. Human Rights Watch, "Somalia Faces the Future," p. 67.
76. Donatella Lorch, "From Aidid's Supporters, Three Main Demands," *The New York Times*, October 21, 1993, p. A8.
77. Julia Preston, "Boutros-Ghali Sees Somalia as Key To Establishing New Role for UN," *The Washington Post*, October 9, 1993, p. A16.

CHAPTER 5

Rwanda: Never Again?

Deborah Kobak

Rwanda's intergroup conflict first attracted the world's attention in the days immediately following the mysterious April 6, 1994 plane crash that killed Rwandan president Juvenal Habyarimana and Burundian president Melchior Ndadye. It was an event that triggered a genocidal campaign that surpassed the horrors of Cambodia's killing fields during the Khmer Rouge's reign of terror. CNN television coverage flashed images around the globe of machete-mangled corpses laying along distant roadsides and clumps of lifeless bodies clogging the waterways that separated Rwanda from its central African neighbors Burundi, Zaire, Uganda, and Tanzania. As the toll of bleak statistics from this spasm of Hutu-Tutsi violence mounted—an estimated 500,000 people killed and another 750,000 permanently displaced over three months—the international community of nations watched, seemingly unable or unwilling to commit an intervention force capable of ending the bloodshed.

Rwanda's agony became the source of a major policy struggle among the member states of the United Nations Security Council; and as the tragedy unfolded before the eyes of the entire world, the international community vacillated. To intervene in a genocide orchestrated by members of the former Rwandan government against fellow compatriots required more political

Deborah Kobak is a Project Associate/Research Analyst at the Joint Center for Political and Economic Studies, a Washington, DC, policy research institution. She has written several articles on African politics and has worked on projects designed to build technical, financial, and administrative capabilities of African civil society institutions to better link them with the policymaking processes of newly emerged democratic governments. Kobak has an M.A. in International Development from American University.

and economic will than the United Nations was able to muster, and no individual nation was willing to spearhead a UN peace enforcement intervention. The United States, for example, was reluctant to take the lead in yet another African mercy mission following its protracted and ultimately unsuccessful experience in Somalia. However, the magnitude of the Rwandan crisis demanded a response, and UN Secretary General Boutros Boutros-Ghali pleaded with the world community to provide relief.

Critics of the international efforts to mitigate the impact of the 1994 genocide often focus on the inability of the UN peacekeeping mission deployed in Rwanda to enforce the negotiated settlement of the four-year civil war between the Rwandan government forces and the Tutsi-dominated rebel army. However, interventions that preceded the UN effort also warrant deeper examination for their relevance to the Rwandan tragedy. Specifically, the implementation of a macroeconomic structural adjustment program funded by the World Bank and the International Monetary Fund (IMF) in 1990, during the early stages of the civil war, seems in retrospect to have contributed to the country's internal destabilization. Rwanda thus raises some critical questions for policymakers: what was the cumulative impact of separate yet concurrent international intervention efforts to contain the vicious cycle of economic decline and political tension that ultimately led to the genocide, and how could the international community have better crafted a response to the spiraling cycle of violence that ultimately killed or uprooted two-thirds of the country's total population and created a regional refugee crisis of massive proportions?

The events leading up to the Rwandan genocide underscore the degree to which various actors and institutions within the international community failed to coordinate their intervention efforts. Indeed, the potentially destabilizing influence of aggregate activities by international actors upon conflict-torn societies has been ignored in most scholarly analyses of international interventions to date. Consequently, the lack of coordination and communication of critical information between the various institutions and governments engaged in intervention activities in Rwanda, has not figured prominently into many accounts as a factor in this country's descent into chaos.

Rwanda is a heartbreaking example of the complicated and often disjointed policymaking process that dictates the timing, scope, and effectiveness of international intervention efforts. And although no single policy option is appropriate for all situations, the Intervention Cycle framework suggests that international efforts to mitigate the 1994 eruption of violence in Rwanda did nothing to alleviate the root cause of the genocide: the long-term political conflict between Hutu and Tutsi elites.

I. HISTORICAL BACKGROUND

Prior to colonization by the Germans (pre–World War I) and then the Belgians (post–World War I through 1962), Rwanda was dominated by the Tutsi, a tribe of tall, nomadic herders who migrated to the area southwest of Lake Victoria in search of land. The Tutsi (now approximately 15 percent of the total Rwandan population) established a monarchy in the sixteenth century that lasted for eighteen generations, ruling over the more numerous Hutu cultivators (roughly 85 percent of the current population) until the Germans arrived. Historically, Rwanda's nobility, military commanders, government officials, and cattle owners were predominantly Tutsi, while most Hutu were subsistence farmers. Over time, Tutsi and Hutu identities blurred until the distinctions between the two were more economic than ethnic: the two groups spoke the same language, Kinyarwanda, and essentially represented different classes of the same society where, as one writer observed, "the distinction had much to do with status: a rich Hutu who owned cattle could become a recognizable Tutsi, while a Tutsi who lost cattle could wind up being labeled a Hutu."[1]

The integration of Tutsi elites into their governing institutions by both the German and Belgian colonial authorities served to further exacerbate Hutu resentment of Tutsi domination in Rwanda. Catholic missionaries similarly favored the Tutsi over the Hutu, deepening the ethnic division between the two groups. Some of the more overtly invidious Belgian colonial policies included issuing identity cards that categorized the card bearer as Hutu or Tutsi and excluded Hutu men from the colonial education system.[2] Scholar Catherine Newbury has noted that colonization fundamentally altered the traditional patron-client relationship between Tutsi and Hutu, upsetting a delicate balance of powers that had largely contained intergroup hostilities. As the central state authority introduced by the colonial powers (with the help of Tutsi elites) gained control of the country's economic resources, the Hutu population grew increasingly disenfranchised from the emerging political order. This resulted in a hardening of the ethnic distinctions between the two groups during the period when Rwanda began to integrate itself into the world economy prior to independence in 1962.[3] In 1959, Hutu insurgents organized a bloody rebellion that killed an estimated 20,000 Tutsi and forced another 150,000 into exile, mostly to neighboring Uganda and Burundi. During the ensuing five-year conflict, the Belgian government quickly switched sides and supported the Hutu rebellion prior to its formal withdrawal from Rwanda in 1962. However, the viciousness with which the Hutu rebel forces attacked their former Tutsi masters spawned the cycle of violence that has plagued Rwanda since its independence.

A. Introduction of Key International Actors

Before delving into the specific details of events leading to the 1994 geno-cide, it is first useful to identify the key actors engaged in significant intervention activities in Rwanda to properly frame the reaction and response of the international community. In November 1990, the World Bank and the International Monetary Fund (IMF) agreed to fund a macroeconomic structural adjustment program (SAP) in Rwanda. The economic crisis that precipitated the IMF and the World Bank's decision to implement the SAP was triggered by plunging world prices for coffee throughout the 1980s. Although coffee (and, to lesser extent, tea) accounted for approximately 45 percent of GDP and 80 percent of exports, the Rwandan government was unable to make the economic policy adjustments necessary to offset the devastating impact of declining terms of trade for the products of its single most important industry:

> In response to emerging financial imbalances, the Government adopted restrictive fiscal and monetary policies . . . At the same time, it increased its level of intervention in the economy. Beginning in 1983, for instance, price controls were applied to prevent prices of imported goods from rising excessively as a result of tightened import licensing. Moreover, inefficient industrial enterprises were protected through the imposition of "temporary" import prohibi-tions on competing exports.[4]

Between 1988 and 1993, however, Rwanda's external payments greatly exceeded the revenue generated by exports earnings (which had decreased by roughly 43 percent), while import spending increased.[5] Thus the immediate focus of the SAP was to correct Rwanda's balance-of-payments deficit. Furthermore, World Bank and IMF assessments determined that while the decline in world prices for coffee was the primary cause of Rwanda's balance-of-payments difficulties, the over-valued exchange rate of the Rwandan franc, low productivity, and excessive use of regulatory mechanisms also contributed to the country's economic deterioration.[6]

Between 1940 and 1991, Rwanda's population swelled from 2 million to 7.15 million, with an annual population growth rate of 3.1 percent.[7] This made Rwanda Africa's most densely populated country, a fact that greatly con-tributed to the country's declining food production capability and accelerated rate of environmental degradation throughout the 1980s. Lastly, the Rwandan economy was further weakened by the commencement of a civil war in October 1990. According to World Bank data, the combined effect of all these factors was a GDP per capita decline from plus 0.4 percent in 1981-86 to a negative 5.5 percent in 1987-91.[8]

For its part, the Rwandan government was desperate for foreign assistance to help finance the budget deficit created by the general economic decline and increased defense spending—which reached seven percent of GDP by 1993.[9] Fearing the dual prospect of soaring inflation (a potential consequence of the government's decision to increase the money supply as a means of financing its military expenditures) and impending military defeat, it is reasonable to conclude that President Habyarimana agreed to accept the SAP with the hope that the short-term stabilization of the country's economic crisis would buy his regime enough time to reverse its war losses.

The primary objective of the SAP was to "restore economic growth to about four percent and to contain the annual inflation rate to five percent by 1993, while at the same time reaching a sustainable budgetary and balance-of-payments situation."[10] Towards this end, the SAP required two immediate economic reform measures: a civil service wage freeze and currency devaluation. Furthermore, the SAP stipulated the removal of regulatory obstacles that inhibited the liberalization of trade and the development of the private sector in Rwanda. The SAP therefore stressed greater reliance on market forces and the private sector to guide the economy, as well as an increased role for export-oriented industry to generate growth. All of these measures entailed significant economic disruption and thus would require broad-based political support and managerial competence to be achieved. These measures would have been difficult to achieve in a state with a high degree of political enfranchisement, much less Rwanda's environment of deep political and social cleavages between Hutu and Tutsi.

The UN also played a significant role in orchestrating international intervention activities in Rwanda. In August 1993 the UN, with the assistance of the Organization of African Unity (OAU), assembled representatives of the Rwandan government and the Rwandan Patriotic Front (RPF) rebel forces in Arusha, Tanzania to forge a negotiated settlement of the civil war. Although the RPF had made significant gains in its pursuit of a military settlement and was by this time close to victory, both sides agreed to negotiate the terms required to resolve the fundamental point of contention between the parties to the conflict: the repatriation of approximately 500,000 exiled Rwandan Tutsi. The UN was not only instrumental in crafting a peace agreement, it also deployed an international peacekeeping force to enforce the cease-fire and to monitor the implementation of the Arusha Accords.

Lastly, the governments of France and the United States had a substantial impact on the international response to the genocide. France was deeply engaged in the conflict, having provided the Rwandan government with military hardware, defense training, and troop support throughout the civil war.

France considered the outcome of Rwanda's civil war to be of vital importance to its national interests because of Rwanda's status as a francophone country and a French trading partner. Due to France's historical relationship with the Habyarimana regime, the French government's eventual decision to undertake a unilateral military intervention to "protect" the victims of the genocide in the summer of 1994 was viewed suspiciously by many analysts and human rights activists concerned by a renewed French presence in Rwanda following the genocide.

For its part, the United States was largely disinterested in becoming engaged in an international intervention effort in Rwanda following its disastrous experience in Somalia. As one of the most influential nations within the UN Security Council, the United States' lack of resolve to stop the genocide was arguably a critical factor in the UN's slow and ultimately ineffective response to the crisis.

B. Rwanda's Structural Adjustment Program

The implementation of the World Bank and IMF-funded structural adjustment program in 1990 had a dramatic and immediate impact in Rwanda. The SAP's emphasis on the role of the market rather than the state in generating economic growth required a fundamental restructuring of the economy, where the government was expected to downsize, balance the budget, slash spending, promote free enterprise and export-led growth, eliminate subsidies and relax tariffs and other trade barriers, and implement a currency devaluation. Rwanda was similar to many other African nations whose postindependence governments heavily subsidized vital sectors of the domestic economy such as food production, the construction and maintenance of transportation systems, and the provision of health and education services. Consequently, the abrupt application of a blueprint World Bank/IMF structural adjustment policy prescription sent the Rwandan economy into a tailspin:

> Touted as a way to increase coffee exports and rehabilitate the war-ravaged economy, the measures had exactly the opposite effect. From a situation of relative stability, inflation soared, real earnings declined, state enterprises went into bankruptcy, child malnutrition rose, and health and education collapsed under the austerity measures.[11]

While Rwandans were deeply troubled by the loss of public sector jobs, the severe reduction in basic services provided by the government, and the currency devaluation that the terms of the SAP dictated, the poor timing of the reform effort was perhaps the most devastating aspect of all. Incredibly, the first of the reforms included in the SAP, an IMF-sponsored $125 million balance of payments credit that recommended a 40 percent currency devaluation, went into effect just six weeks after the resumption of hostilities between Hutu government forces and exiled Tutsi rebels in October 1990.[12] Although the World Bank itself, through its soft-lending affiliate, the International Development Association (IDA), did not approve a structural adjustment credit of $95 million until June 1991 (the first tranche for $55 million was released in November 1991), neither international institution can legitimately assert that the Rwandan government's decision to accept the SAP was merely a simple and convenient way to obtain international financing. By 1990 the country's economic situation was desperate and getting worse by the day, and the government had no choice but to go to the lenders of last resort—the IMF and the World Bank. Nevertheless, throughout the period following the genocide, the World Bank and IMF have rather disingenuously attempted to shift primary responsibility for the decision to implement the structural adjustment program during the civil war onto the Rwandan government.

As noted previously, the SAP implemented in Rwanda included two particularly unpopular reform measures: the civil service wage freeze and a monetary devaluation. In addition, the terms of the SAP also stipulated that the government introduce a multiparty political system. However, the austerity of the economic reform package seemed to fuel dissent within a general population already chafing against the authoritarian, one-party rule of President Habyarimana. Eventually, increased domestic dissatisfaction with the economic reforms, as well as with the civil war, compounded the international pressure applied by the World Bank and the IMF and, later, the UN, to compel Habyarimana to further liberalize the Rwandan political system. Thus in 1993, Habyarimana agreed to appoint members of opposition political parties to ministerial posts.[13]

Habyarimana's decision to accept the political conditions attached to the SAP set in motion a nearly concurrent process of political and economic liberalization in Rwanda. However, because Habyarimana's own government was deeply opposed to political liberalization of any kind, the two-pronged reform effort ultimately served to undermine the president's authority with the hard-line Hutu members of his inner circle. Moreover, when peace negotiations between the Hutu regime and the Tutsi rebel forces reached a stalemate in early 1993 and the government was unable to continue scheduled budgetary, civil service, and labor market reform measures, the World Bank did not release the second tranche of the approved structural adjustment credit ($40 million), thereby canceling SAP financing and ending the economic reform effort.

C. Civil War: 1990–1994

The four-year civil war that preceded the Rwandan genocide was largely fought over the practice of ethnically based political and economic discrimination. When former defense minister Habyarimana, a hard-line Hutu, seized the Rwandan presidency in 1973 during a coup d'etat deposing another Hutu-dominated regime, he promised to fairly serve the interests of both ethnic groups. Nonetheless, key government appointments and state resources were distributed to Hutu friends and relatives who hailed from Habyarimana's home region in northwestern Rwanda. Thus under the Habyarimana regime, the long-established, colonial practice of government-sanctioned political and economic disenfranchisement based on ethnic origin continued, only this time the marginalized population group was Tutsi rather than Hutu.

Prior to the 1994 genocide, Rwanda had a total population estimated at 7.5 million people, of which 1 to 1.5 million were Tutsi and 6 to 6.5 million were Hutu. Another 500,000 Rwandan Tutsi were believed to be living outside of Rwanda as refugees or in refugee-like circumstances.[14] The RPF troops that invaded Rwanda in 1990 were primarily comprised of Tutsi refugees and their families who had been living in Uganda since Rwanda's independence from Belgium. This particular Tutsi population is English speaking, a fact that further complicates the demographic composition of postgenocide Rwanda.[15]

Habyarimana established around himself an inner circle of advisors called the *Akazu* or "Little House." Little House cabinet members were known to be Hutu extremists who actively supported political and economic policies that reinforced Hutu domination within the country. Little House members were adamantly opposed to the reintegration of exiled Tutsi into Rwandan society. The Habyarimana regime's reluctance to permit the return of exiled Rwandan Tutsi combined with the Ugandan government's refusal to grant the Tutsi refugees citizenship precipitated the 1990 RPF military invasion of northern Rwanda. The exiled Tutsi population was under great pressure to return to Rwanda because the UN High Commission on Refugees (UNHCR) mandate granting them refugee status was due to expire.[16]

According to a report prepared jointly by Africa Watch, the International Federation of Human Rights (Paris), the Inter-African Union of Human Rights (Ouagadougou), and the International Center for Human Rights and Democratic Development (Montreal) in March 1993, both the RPF and Rwandan government troops committed gross abuses of civilian rights during the 1990-94 civil war. Members of Habyarimana's regime distributed small arms, including AK-47s and machetes, to government-sponsored militias who ravaged local Tutsi villages, raping women, slaughtering animals, and burning huts and crops. Approximately 2,000 civilians were killed and another 8,000 were detained. For its part, the RPF executed hundreds of people suspected to be collaborating with the government and forcibly moved hundreds and perhaps thousands.[17] However, the impact of the civil war on Rwanda's civilian population was relatively minor when measured against the devastation wrought by the orchestrated campaign of violence in 1994 that specifically targeted Hutu political moderates and the Tutsi population still living within Rwanda's borders.[18]

The 1990 RPF invasion of Rwanda marked the official entry of France as a key player in the Rwandan intergroup political conflict. Prior to the invasion, Belgium was Rwanda's main trading partner and provided the Rwandan government with the bulk of its military equipment and training. But shortly after the beginning of the RPF campaign, all military aid to Rwanda was cut off due to a Belgian law that explicitly prohibits Belgium from supplying arms to a country at war. Furthermore, the Belgian ambassador to Rwanda was recalled in 1991 following the release of the International Human Rights Commission report.[19] Thus Belgium's refusal to assist the Rwandan government in its war against the RPF resulted in the strengthening of what was to become a critically important alliance between the Habyarimana regime and the French government.

The bonds between France and the political regimes of francophone Africa are stronger than those shared by other Western powers with their former colonies, as exhibited by the high degree of coordinated policymaking within la francophonie, a commonwealth-like association of French speaking countries around the world, and the presence of two francophone African nations on the UN Security Council.[20] Thus the twin objectives of French policy in Rwanda were to shore up the Habyarimana regime, a loyal French trading partner, and to maintain the country's French linguistic tradition. In so doing, the French government signaled its loyalty to other francophone African leaders: "If we fail to fulfill our promises . . . our credibility towards other African states with which we have similar accords (Central African Republic, Cameroon, Djibouti, Gabon, Ivory Coast, Senegal, and Togo) would be seriously damaged, and we would see those countries turning to other supporters."[21]

Since the establishment of a defense agreement between France and Rwanda in 1975, the French government lent assistance to the Habyarimana regime through the direct and indirect supply of military hardware, equipment, training, and financial backing. In 1990, France spent nearly four million francs in military assistance to Rwanda. By 1992, however, that number had swollen to 14 million francs, an increase of 250 percent. Furthermore,

France provided the Rwandan government with clandestine shipments of military hardware (artillery, Alouette and Gazelle helicopters, Guerrier and Noratlas aircraft) and deployed elite commandos to Rwanda to help the government fight the English speaking RPF between 1990 and 1994. Most analysts agree that the RPF would have won the civil war much earlier had it not been for the presence of French combat troops in Rwanda throughout this period.[22] Indeed, French troops intervened in the civil war on a number of occasions: a notable example being the 450 French paratroopers who actively defended Kigali against the encroaching RPF in 1990.[23]

The neocolonial orientation of French policy towards Rwanda was intended to reinforce the alliance between the governments of the two countries. Consequently, French policy did not address the equity issues created by the Habyarimana regime's practice of Hutu partisanship that favored the political and economic development of one ethnic group at the expense of the other. The Intervention Cycle suggests that stable societies require an equitable distribution of social, political, and economic opportunity amongst all citizens, regardless of ethnic origin. Thus, the political, economic, and military support lent by France to the Rwandan government ultimately contributed to the destabilization of the country because France provided the Habyarimana regime with the tools it needed to impede the development potential of a single ethnic group.

D. Arusha Accords: Failed Resolution

By the early 1990s, the Habyarimana regime was besieged by political, social, and economic problems including the civil war against the RPF, a non-sustainable annual population growth rate of 3.1 percent, the AIDS pandemic, and collapsing world prices for coffee, Rwanda's primary export product.[24] Despite French efforts to prop up the Rwandan government, Habyarimana agreed to a negotiated peace settlement with the RPF in August 1993.

The international community played a large role in bringing the two sides together to sign the Arusha Peace Accords, which were brokered by the UN and the Organization of Africa Unity (OAU) in Arusha, Tanzania. However, at the same time that the international community was applauding Habyarimana and the RPF for reaching agreement on the implementation of peace in Rwanda, Hutu extremists in the Rwandan government were plotting a scheme to derail reforms forged by the accords. Tragically, the very process of negotiation carried out in Arusha with the approval and support of the international community hardened the opposition of Little House ministers to the accords.

The Arusha Accords stipulated that both sides demobilize and disarm their troops (in 1993 the Rwandan army had a force of approximately 30,000 soldiers, while the RPF had roughly 15,000 members). Furthermore, the terms of the accords called for the Rwandan army to be reconstituted into a unified Hutu-Tutsi force, that the Rwandan Tutsi refugees scattered throughout the region be repatriated, and that a transitional government (with Habyarimana still serving as president) assume power by mid-September 1993. Lastly, the transitional government was mandated to hold multiparty elections within 22 months.[25]

As stated previously, Habyarimana implemented some limited political reforms under pressure from the World Bank, the IMF, and an increasingly antagonistic domestic population several months before he signed the Arusha Accords. This included the appointment of several opposition party members (both Hutu moderates and Tutsi) to government posts. These individuals had little real authority, however, as the Little House cabinet members surrounding the president retained tight control of the government and remained hostile to the political liberalization process supposedly underway.

The fragile peace forged in Arusha and the tentative steps taken by Habyarimana to establish a more open political system in Rwanda ultimately proved to be his undoing. Almost all accounts of the events leading to the April 6 plane crash indicate that Little House Hutu extremists, unwilling to share power with Tutsi and Hutu moderates, engineered the assassination of the president with the intent of reengaging the RPF in armed combat and thus preventing the peace process from moving forward.

The first indication that the hard-line cabinet members would not accept a negotiated settlement with the RPF was the formation of an Hutu extremist group, the Coalition pour la Défense de la République (CDR). Both the CDR and the President's main political party, Mouvement Républicain National pour la Démocratie (MRND), subsequently founded militias known respectively as the Interahamwe (Those Who Attack Together) and the Impuzamugambi (Those Who Have the Same Goal).[26] By April 1994, 10,000 Hutu militia members had been armed by the presidential guard and the Rwandan army.[27] It is still unknown who fired the two rockets that brought the President's plane down as he and Ndadye returned to Kigali from another round of peace talks; however, within minutes of the crash members of the presidential guard and the army had sealed off the site and given the command for the militias to begin the search and destroy mission that specifically targeted Tutsi and moderate Hutu throughout the country.

II. GENOCIDE AND THE INTERNATIONAL RESPONSE

A vitally important element of the agreements reached in Arusha was the provision of international peacekeepers to enforce the cease-fire agreement and to monitor the implementation of the accords. As noted previously, the international community was actively engaged in the negotiation process that led to the cessation of the civil war. The deployment of OAU and UN peacekeeping forces to Kigali built up the expectations of Rwandans anxious for a peaceful resolution of the protracted political conflict. Thus, the failure of the international community, and the UN in particular, to respond to the numerous indications that Hutu hardliners were systematically preparing to derail the peace process was seen as abandonment of the peace process by many Rwandans:

> We have been very, very disappointed with the United Nations in Rwanda. The conduct of the UN with regard to the setting up of the broad-based Government of Transition, particularly the role of [the UN Special Representative], was terrible. If [the UN Special Representative] had really wanted to push along the implementation of the agreements, he could have done so much more. But I think he was afraid of Habyarimana and his entourage. Faced with the slightest obstacle created by the government, aware of the least worry that the President had, and [the UN Special Representative] was paralyzed.[28]

The initial deployment of an international peacekeeping force actually predated the signing of the accords; in July 1992 fifty soldiers from Senegal, Congo, and Tunisia sponsored by the OAU arrived in Kigali to secure a cease-fire prior to the beginning of the negotiations in Arusha. Although the first deployment of the OAU's "Neutral Military Observer Group" (NMOG) failed to secure a lasting cease-fire, a second NMOG contingent of 132 soldiers was credited for establishing a demilitarized zone between the Rwandan army and the RPF long enough for the Arusha talks to get underway.[29]

In October 1993, the NMOG mission was relieved by 2,500 UN peacekeeping troops led by Canadian general Romeo Dallaire. The mandate of the United Nations Assistance Mission for Rwanda (UNAMIR) was to enforce the cease-fire and to assist the Rwandan government and the RPF in the implementation of the Arusha Accords.[30] However, UNAMIR was fraught with serious problems from its inception. The mission was rendered virtually ineffective by its UN Charter Chapter VI mandate, which did not permit UN troops to forcibly address the occasional violations of the cease-fire agreement that took place during the period between the signing of the Arusha Accords and the April 6, 1994, plane crash. In addition, UNAMIR was hindered by lengthy delays in the deployment of troops and the acquisition of equipment needed to outfit the mission.

UN troops could not use force to protect civilians from the campaign of violence, nor could it carry out critical intelligence gathering operations needed to determine precisely who was orchestrating the genocide.[31] Since leaving Rwanda, General Dallaire has been outspoken in his criticism of the UNAMIR operation:

> If the international community does not take the necessary steps to mandate the UN to manage crises, genocide will occur again. . . . Arusha called for the UN security force to be deployed within five weeks, but we didn't get the mandate for two months, and we didn't get the equipment for another five months.[32]

UNAMIR's inability to stem the slaughter was further compromised by the withdrawal of Belgium's 440 troops from the UN peacekeeping force in mid-April 1994. This was prompted by the murder of ten Belgian soldiers as they tried to protect interim prime minister Agathe Uwilingiyimana from the militias. Without a Chapter VII mandate to use force to protect his own troops, Dallaire had little choice but to order UN soldiers to withdraw to their barracks.

The withdrawal of Belgian troops from the UNAMIR force prompted UN Secretary General Boutros-Ghali to present the Security Council with three policy options for UN peacekeeping troops in Rwanda: 1) to change the UNAMIR mandate so that adequate troops and equipment would be provided "to coerce the opposing forces into a cease-fire, and to attempt to restore law and order and put an end to the killings. [Such a] scenario would [have required] several thousand additional troops and UNAMIR . . . to be given enforcement powers under Chapter VII of the Charter of the United Nations;" 2) to reduce the UNAMIR force from 2500 troops to 270, leaving a small force to act as an intermediary between the Rwandan government forces and the RPF to broker a cease-fire agreement; or 3) a complete withdrawal of all UNAMIR troops.[33]

In the end, Security Council members determined that the complete withdrawal of UNAMIR forces would be too great an admission of the UN's limitations, thus the second option proposed by Boutros-Ghali was eventually adopted. Simply put, the Security Council was unable to reach sufficient consensus on the terms of a UN peace enforcement mission to Rwanda because no UN member state was willing to shoulder the costs of such an effort.

The United States in particular took a firm position within the Security Council against the immediate deployment of additional UN peacekeeping troops. The timing of the Rwandan crisis was a significant factor in the U.S. reaction to the tragedy: the Clinton administration had issued Presidential Decision Directive 25 (PDD-25) in May 1994, a document drafted in response to the American experience in Somalia that stipulated sixteen specific considerations used to determine whether the United States would engage in international peacekeeping missions. Rwanda was the first test of PDD-25; consequently the United States would only agree to participate in an expanded UN peacekeeping mission to Rwanda after the stringent conditions set forth by the document had been satisfied.[34]

Another factor that dictated the slow pace of the U.S. policy response to the situation in Rwanda was the Clinton administration's insistence on securing a cease-fire agreement between the RPF and the government forces as a precondition for an expanded international intervention.[35] President Clinton articulated this concern in his weekly radio address:

> On behalf of the American people, I call on the Rwandan army and the Rwandan Patriotic Front to agree to an immediate cease-fire and return to negotiations aimed at a lasting peace in their country. The pain and suffering of the Rwandan people have touched the hearts of all Americans. It is time for the leaders of Rwanda to recognize their common bond of humanity and to reject the senseless and criminal violence that continues to plague their country.[36]

Given the intractable nature of the intergroup political conflict in Rwanda, the Clinton administration and the UN's preoccupation with securing a new cease-fire agreement suggests an incomplete understanding of the dynamics of coercion, deterrence, and disenfranchisement that precipitated the country's implosion in 1994. The Hutu-Tutsi conflict reached its zenith when President Habyarimana's plane was shot down: surely the international community should have recognized that diplomatic efforts alone could not prevent Rwanda from descending into a spiraling cycle of violence.

Senior RPF commanders had clearly and repeatedly stated to UN diplomats, members of the press, and representatives of nongovernmental organizations that they would not agree to a new cease-fire until the government-orchestrated attack on the civilian population had subsided. Thus the fixation on crafting a cease-fire agreement in the days and weeks following the April 6 plane crash clearly illustrates the fundamental flaw in the initial approach to the crisis. The international community failed to address the genocide of Rwandan civilians as an issue separate from but related to the political conflict between Hutu and Tutsi elites, and therefore did not take the measures necessary to stop the senseless slaughter.

Although U.S. reluctance to support an expanded UN peacekeeping force to Rwanda was a contributing factor in the international community's disjointed response to the crisis, other UN member states were surprisingly apathetic in their support of the proposed intervention. Notably, several African countries (Ghana, Senegal, Ethiopia, Zimbabwe, Congo, Mali, and Nigeria) only offered to send (unequipped) troop contingents to Rwanda in June, two months after the genocide began.[37]

The OAU did make strong statements condemning the international community's indifferent response to the situation in Rwanda, and ultimately helped Boutros-Ghali piece together the troops needed for the second UN intervention effort.[38] The UN finally agreed to adopt Security Council Resolution 918 in May 1994, a plan authorizing the deployment of 5,500 UN peacekeeping troops (UNAMIR II) that was once again only given a Chapter VI mandate to provide humanitarian assistance. However, bureaucratic maneuvering further delayed the troops' arrival in Rwanda. The UN and the United States continued to quarrel over both the cost of the intervention (America would have to absorb one-third of the total cost of the operation as well as assume the logistics and equipment expenses) and the strategic placement of UN troops.[39]

Against this backdrop, the French again intervened, unilaterally launching a military operation code-named *Opération Turquoise*. The French deployed 2,500 Marines and Foreign Legion troops in Rwanda, ostensibly to secure a safe zone for civilians in the southwestern portion of the country.[40] The UN Security Council reluctantly approved the mission, despite the RPF's strong opposition to a renewed French presence in Rwanda. Given the degree of suffering endured by the civilian population and the lack of sufficient international resolve to commit military forces to stop the genocide, the Intervention Cycle discussion does not preclude the implementation of a short-term intervention effort such as the French plan. While the UN-sanctioned French military operation was clearly neither impartial nor a step towards resolution, it was the only viable mitigation option to emerge in the weeks following Habyarimana's death.

The Security Council resolution authorizing *Turquoise* called for the French to remain in Rwanda for two months, after which time the UNAMIR II peacekeeping force would be assembled, equipped, and ready to take over. Given the historical repercussions of French military operations in Rwanda, the UN resolution authorizing *Turquoise* permitted a Chapter VII mandate to use "all necessary means" to protect civilians, but stipulated that the operation remain "strictly humanitarian . . . impartial and neutral."[41] French neutrality was certainly suspect given the relationship between the Habyarimana regime and Paris, but the French effectively portrayed the safe zone as an area in which critically needed humanitarian assistance could be provided to Rwandan civilians who survived the genocide. However, new evidence suggests that the very same Hutu extremists who perpetuated the genocide fled to the French safe zone to await evacuation out of Rwanda to either Zaire or France.

Government troops and militia members also retreated to the safe zone following the RPF victory, from which they were able to blend into the larger stream of Rwandan refugees seeking humanitarian assistance in camps located across the border in Zaire.[42]

III. CONCLUSIONS

Clearly there was inadequate UN Security Council support for either a complete withdrawal of UN peacekeeping forces from Rwanda or for the deployment of a sizable peace enforcement mission that could forcibly stop the militias and thus save thousands of civilians from genocide. But even before the events of April 1994, the political and economic reforms imposed by a number of international actors failed to recognize the growing opposition of Hutu hardliners to a peaceful resolution of the intergroup conflict. This failure to enfranchise broad-based political and economic reform among Hutus and Tutsis set in motion the chain of events that led to the genocide of an estimated 500,000 people. This analysis suggests that, to a certain extent, the international community bears some responsibility for the genocide. It failed to fully recognize the potential for serious internal destabilization caused by the implementation of massive economic reforms funded by the World Bank and the IMF without the requisite political support of the Rwandan population. Additionally, the international community lacked the will to commit to the UNAMIR peacekeeping mission the resources necessary to stop the massive and wholesale slaughter of innocent civilians.

Blame for the Rwandan tragedy cannot be laid solely on the shoulders of international financial institutions and the UN, but the impact of the austere structural adjustment package and the IMF devaluation surely contributed to the country's internal destabilization at a time when it was already rocked by the outbreak of civil war. The Intervention Cycle notes the importance of sequencing intervention in accordance with internal progress. Furthermore, the sad reality of the Rwandan situation is that the international community was both unable and unwilling to make the investment necessary to enforce the terms of the Arusha Accords and potentially break the cycle of violent conflict in Rwanda.

Given that the entire Central Africa region is still teetering on the brink of renewed violence, one must consider whether precious political capital and economic resources should have been expended in Rwanda at all. However, if the international policymaking community accepts the premise that the vicious slaughter of scores of innocent Rwandan civilians violates international standards of acceptable behavior, the key issue becomes how the international community should best coordinate an intervention strategy.

A middle ground policy option was eventually adopted by the UN for UNAMIR II. It involved the deployment of a humanitarian assistance mission with a Chapter VI mandate and had, at best, a limited impact on the conflict. The report issued in May 1995 by Human Rights Watch confirms that the former government troops and militia members responsible for carrying out the genocide were rearming in the very same refugee camps that were sponsored and supported by the UN and international relief organizations.[43] The humanitarian relief efforts in refugee camps, while effective in saving the lives and mitigating the further suffering of innocent Rwandan citizens caught up in the violence, also facilitated the rearming of forces openly opposed to a political settlement of the Rwandan conflict.

This unfortunate consequence underscores the reality that international interventions have a great impact on all involved parties. Furthermore, reports filed by Human Rights Watch in late 1994 confirmed that the openly belligerent actions of the former Rwandan government armed forces living in the refugee camps were, at the very least, condoned by France and Zaire.[44] Moreover, France's continued engagement in the Rwandan civil war was a direct violation of UN Security Council Resolutions 918 and 925.[45] The assistance lent by assorted members of the international community to known perpetrators of genocide has seriously compromised the capability of ongoing humanitarian and development intervention efforts in Rwanda.

The presence of so many Rwandan refugees in neighboring countries has greatly destabilized a region already struggling to generate economic growth and to foster political enfranchisement. The situation in neighboring Burundi, which has hosted Rwandan refugees, continues to rapidly deteriorate. Amnesty International reports that the country is deeply divided along ethnic lines, and ethnic violence is a daily occurrence. The government is unable to control its own security forces as well as armed opposition groups, resulting in an average death rate of 1,500 people per month throughout 1995 due to ethnic violence.[46]

The Intervention Cycle framework suggests that perhaps a more appropriate focus of intervention efforts during the postgenocide phase of the Rwandan conflict would be the provision of critically needed funding and technical assistance for developing judicial and political systems towards reconciliation and reconstruction. The Rwandan government formed following the RPF victory in July 1994 waited for months for international donors to send desperately needed funds to support basic reconstruction and reconciliation services and finance a War Crimes Tribunal to prosecute those individuals implicated in the 1994 genocide. In fact, one of the primary obstacles preventing the voluntary return of Rwandan refugees is the absence of a functioning judicial system.

Another option suggested by the Intervention Cycle model, while clearly limited in scope, is perhaps the most viable long-term policy alternative: limiting international intervention efforts to the periphery of conflict unless the security organization involved receives a Chapter VII mandate, or the parties to the conflict are ready to engage in cease-fire negotiations. This policy option is premised on the assumption that a lightly armed peacekeeping force with a Chapter VI mandate will be of little assistance unless the majority of parties involved want the violence to end.[47] International resources could then be channeled where they will be most useful, for example, providing humanitarian assistance to civilians located in safe zones and refugee camps where police or constabulary forces are able to provide for their security.

Critics will argue that limiting the international presence to the periphery of a major conflict such as Rwanda will still result in massive and unnecessary loss of life, environmental degradation, and economic ruin. Given that the optimal international response was not forthcoming in the Rwandan case, intervention efforts should have attempted to contain rather than to perpetuate the Hutu-Tutsi political conflict. It is unfortunate that the collective intervention efforts of the international community failed to achieve even these limited objectives.

Rwanda is perhaps the most glaring contemporary example of the international community's practice of intervention politics without responsibility. Policymakers should take heed of the lesson contained in the Rwandan tragedy and remember that once the international community makes the commitment to intervene in the settlement of an intractable and violent intergroup conflict, it must stay the course of conflict resolution. The Intervention Cycle is a useful tool for identifying intervention policy alternatives to indifference that are less than full-blown peace enforcement operations. Efforts must also be made to gauge carefully the impact and viability of sweeping economic and political reforms in countries already struggling with intergroup conflict. The international community must enforce its own commitment to the intervention process and make the tough policy decisions that will best ensure sustainable conflict resolution and, ultimately, break the cycle of underdevelopment that so often breeds violence. Otherwise, the promise of "never again" will resonate against the chilling silence of another lost generation.

NOTES

1. Frank Smyth, "The Horror," *The New Republic*, 4, No. 144, June 20, 1994, p. 19.
2. Smyth, p. 19. Ethnic identity cards played a large role in the genocide because physical and linguistic differences between the Hutu and Tutsi have blurred over

time. The victims of genocide were often killed at roadside check points where they were forced to show their identity papers. Those who refused to hand over their papers were presumed to be Tutsi and killed regardless.

3. In her book, *The Cohesion of Oppression: Clientship and Ethnicity in Rwanda, 1860-1960* (New York: Columbia University Press, 1988), Newbury shows how the traditional patron-client relationship *umuheto* (Hutu clients give a cow to their Tutsi patrons in exchange for protection) gave way under colonialism to *ubuhake* (an individual Hutu receives a cow from his Tutsi patron in exchange for client loyalty). Newbury argues that the individualization of the patron-client relationship disturbed the delicate balance of power in preindependence Rwanda, ultimately weakening the ability of the Tutsi to control the Hutu and providing Hutu elites with the space to mobilize and organize an opposition movement just as Rwanda was moving toward independence.

4. "Rwanda Financial Sector Review," *World Bank Report* 8934-RW, p. 2.

5. "Programme of National Reconciliation and Socio-Economic Recovery of the Government of Rwanda," roundtable conference report, Geneva, Switzerland, 1995, p. 6.

6. "Rwanda Financial Sector Review," *World Bank Report* 8934-RW, p. 2.

7. "Under the Volcanoes: Rwanda's Refugee Crisis," *World Disasters Report Special Focus.* International Federation of Red Cross and Red Crescent Societies, 1994, p. 6.

8. Michel Chossudovsky, "IMF-World Bank Policies and the Rwandan Holocaust," *Third World Network Features,* (Penang, Malaysia: Third World Network), January 26, 1995, p. 6.

9. "Programme of National Reconciliation and Socio-Economic Recovery of the Government of Rwanda" roundtable conference report, p. 10.

10. "Rwanda Financial Sector Review," *World Bank Report* 8934-RW, p. 3.

11. Michel Chossudovsky. "IMF and World Bank Set the Stage," *Covert Action,* 52, (May 1995), p. 11.

12. According to Dr. Michael Chossudovsky, Professor of Economics at the University of Ottawa, Ontario, and author of several articles on the IMF and World Bank policy in Rwanda, the decision to implement a currency devaluation was reached on September 17, 1990 during meetings held in Washington, DC, between the IMF and the Rwandan mission headed by former Minister of Finance Ntigurirwa, approximately three weeks before the civil war began.

13. "Peace Accord in Rwanda May Be the Real Thing," *Africa Report,* 38, No. 5, (New York, NY: The African-American Institute, September/October 1993), p. 10.

14. Jeff Drumtra, "Site Visit to Rwanda, Zaire, and Burundi, October 20–November 17, 1994," report to U.S. Committee for Refugees (USCR), p. 2. Demographic data based on USCR estimates collected before and after the genocide.

15. The USCR site visit report conducted in October-November 1994 identified six key Rwandan population groups: (1) the 100,000 to 500,000 Tutsi living in Rwanda who survived the 1994 genocide; (2) the 400,000 exiled Tutsi who have returned to Rwanda since the RPF ousted the former government in July 1994; (3) the approximately 1.5 million internally displaced Hutu; (4) the approximately

1.7 million Hutu refugees located in Zaire, Tanzania, Burundi, and Uganda; (5) the approximately 2.5 to 3.5 million Hutu who were not displaced by the genocide; and (6) the 500,000 to 1 million estimated Tutsi victims of the genocide whose "absence is apparent and is an important element in the political and social dynamics of current-day Rwanda." Jeff Drumtra, "Site Visit to Rwanda, Zaire, and Burundi, October 20–November 17, 1994," report to U.S. Committee for Refugees (USCR), pp. 4-5.

16. Author's interview with Kathi L. Austin, Director of the Africa project at the Institute for Policy Studies and consultant to the Human Rights Watch Arms Project, June 22, 1995, Washington, DC.

17. Frank Smyth, "Blood Money and Geopolitics," *The Nation*, 258, No. 17, May 2, 1994, p. 585.

18. Author's interview with Kathi L. Austin, May 29, 1995, Washington, DC.

19. Frank Smyth, "The Horror," *The New Republic*, 4, No. 144, June 20, 1994, p. 20.

20. *Rwanda: Death, Despair, Defiance.* (London: African Rights Press, September 1994), p. 679. France's two loyal francophone African allies on the UN Security Council seats are Djibouti, "a country totally economically dependent on France," and Rwanda itself. Ironically, the very government accused of orchestrating the genocide was represented at the Security Council until July 16, 1994, that is, throughout the period that the genocide was taking place.

21. Ibid., pp. 669-70.

22. France sent 300 troops to Rwanda after the October 1990 RPF invasion, but subsequently reduced the force to 170 soldiers (military training exercises continued). After another RPF offensive surge in 1993, French troop strength increased to 680. Uniformed French soldiers left Rwanda after the signing of the Arusha Accords in August 1993, although military training of the government militias continued. Kathi L. Austin, "Rearming with Impunity: International Support for the Perpetrators of the Rwandan Genocide," *Human Rights Watch Arms Project Report*, 7, no. 4, (May 1995), p. 5.

23. Hervé Gattegno, "L'Armée française dans le piége Rwandais," *Le Monde*, September 22, 1994, p. 3.

24. "Under the Volcanoes: Rwanda's Refugee Crisis," *World Disasters Report Special Focus*. International Federation of Red Cross and Red Crescent Societies, 1994, p. 6. By 1991 Rwanda was Africa's most densely populated country, which greatly contributed to the country's environmental degradation and declining food production capability. These factors combined with the precipitous drop in coffee prices on the world market to force Habyarimana's acceptance of an austere structural adjustment package offered by the IMF. Thus Habyarimana was feeling both domestic and international pressure to liberalize his regime when he agreed to negotiate with the RPF and end the civil war.

25. "Peace Accord in Rwanda May Be the Real Thing," *Africa Report*, 8, no. 5, (September/October 1993), p. 10.

26. Lindsey Hilsum, "Settling Scores," *Africa Report*, 39, no. 3, (May/June 1994), p. 14.

27. Milton Leitenberg, "Rwanda 1994: International Incompetence Produces Genocide," *Peacekeeping and International Relations*, 23, no. 6, (Canadian Institute of Strategic Studies, November/December 1994), p. 6.

28. *Rwanda: Death, Despair, Defiance*, (London: African Rights Press, September 1994), p. 665. Marc Rugenera was formerly Minister of Finance in Rwanda. The former Special Representative to the UN Secretary General referred to is Jacques Roger Booh-Booh. Booh-Booh was roundly criticized for his failure to address the numerous indicators that Hutu government hardliners openly violated the Arusha Accords during the months preceding the genocide. He then stubbornly insisted that the UN should negotiate a new cease-fire agreement between the government and the RPF after the government-orchestrated campaign of terror began. Booh-Booh was eventually recalled and replaced by Shaharyar Khan Mohammed, a Pakistani diplomat.

29. Scott Stearns, "An Uneasy Peace," *Africa Report*, 39, no. 1, (January/February 1994), p. 35.

30. UNAMIR was created on October 5, 1993 by UN Security Council Resolution 872, evolving from the United Nations Observer Mission to Uganda-Rwanda (UNOMUR). The full UNAMIR mandate was the following: (1) to mitigate the military conflict between Rwandan government forces and the RPF; (2) to maintain subsequent cease-fire agreements; (3) to provide humanitarian assistance to refugees; and (4) to support the process of political reconciliation.

31. Hilsum, "Settling Scores," p. 17. UNAMIR troops were not given permission to use force as stipulated in Article 42, Chapter VII of the UN Charter. Since World War II, the UN has permitted the use of force only four times, including Somalia.

32. Romeo Dallaire, "Lessons Learned in Peacekeeping: What Worked, What Didn't, and Why." (Washington, DC: Council on Foreign Relations), 8 May 1995.

33. Leitenberg, "Rwanda 1994," p. 7.

34. The rationale behind PDD-25 is as follows: "When deciding whether to support a particular UN peace operation, the United States will insist that fundamental questions be asked before new obligations are undertaken. These include an assessment of the threat to international peace and security, a determination that the peace operation serves U.S. interests as well as assurance of an international community of interests for dealing with that threat on a multilateral basis, identification of clear objectives, availability of the necessary resources, and identification of an operation's endpoint or criteria for completion." A National Security Strategy of Engagement and Enlargement, The White House, Washington, DC. July 1994, p. 13. These criteria are significant in that they reflect the incorporation of military and strategic concerns into political policy objectives.

35. The cease-fire agreement between the RPF and the government collapsed when the genocide began. UN Special Representatives Booh-Booh and then Shaharyar Khan pressed for cease-fire negotiations up until the RPF captured Kigali on July 4, 1994. The RPF defeated the government forces by mid-July, thereby ending the genocide.

36. The White House, Office of the Press Secretary, "Radio Message by the President on the Situation in Rwanda," April 30, 1994, as quoted in *Rwanda: Death, Despair, Defiance*, pp. 688-89.

37. Leitenberg, "Rwanda 1994," p. 8.
38. The regional split between francophone and anglophone Africa was probably a factor in the African response to the Rwandan crisis. Zaire was a long-time supporter of the Habyarimana regime as well as a close ally of France, while Uganda's links to the RPF were well-known and documented. Burundi did not take an active diplomatic stance given the internal turmoil that followed the death of its president in the same plane crash. Tanzania had been actively engaged in the political resolution of the Rwandan political conflict, but withdrew from the situation as the political crisis gave way to genocide. Tanzania's spring 1995 closure of refugee camps is a more current example of that country's increasingly distant diplomatic stance towards the Rwandan conflict.
39. Paul Lewis, "U.S. Forces UN to Put Off Plan to Send 5,500 Troops to Rwanda," *The New York Times*, May 12, 1994, p. A9; and Michael Gordon, "UN's Rwanda Deployment Slowed by Lack of Vehicles," *The New York Times*, June 9, 1994, p. A10.
40. Significantly, the French plan to create safe zones in southwestern Rwanda, a defensive action wherein the French command stated it would authorize the use of force against any encroaching RPF forces, did not receive prior authorization from the UN. The original, stated intention of *Turquoise* was saving surviving Tutsi civilians from militia attacks. See *Rwanda: Death, Despair, Defiance*, p. 706.
41. Julia Preston, "UN Backs French Move into Rwanda," *The Washington Post*, June 23, 1994, p. A24. Five member states abstained when the Security Council voted on Resolution 929 to approve the French plan: China, Nigeria, New Zealand, Brazil, and Pakistan.
42. Kathi L. Austin, "Rearming with Impunity: International Support for the Perpetrators of the Rwandan Genocide," *Human Rights Watch Arms Project Report*, May 1995, p. 7. The French Radio *Trois Milles Collines* transmitter was also relocated to the safe zone, where broadcasts encouraging Hutu to kill Tutsi continued to be aired. The militarization of refugee camps both within and outside of Rwanda has been widely documented in the months following the end of the genocide. This is directly attributed to the fact that (former) Rwandan government troops and militia members who sought protection from the RPF in the refugee camps have been able to regroup and rearm with the assistance of France, Zaire, and to a lesser extent, South Africa and China.
43. Human Rights Watch estimates former government troop strength to be about 50,000 soldiers, most of whom are scattered throughout refugee camps in Zaire. Significantly, Hutu commanders have been able to tighten control over militia members, who have now allied themselves with Hutu militias from Burundi.
44. Austin, "Rearming with Impunity." The Human Rights Watch report also alleges that South Africa and China violated the terms of the UN embargo to Rwanda.
45. Respectively, these resolutions prohibit the sale of arms and related material to Rwanda—and by extension, to the former Rwandan government—as well as require states and organizations to report information related to the transport of arms to Rwanda's neighbors to the UN. Austin, "Rearming with Impunity:

International Support for the Perpetrators of the Rwandan Genocide," *Human Rights Watch Arms Project Report,* May 1995, p. 4.

46. Amnesty International, press release on the report "Rwanda and Burundi—The Return Home; Rumors and Reality," issued February 20, 1996, Geneva.

47. Ironically, a U.S. government official interviewed for this study stated that the United States presented the UN with a safe zone scenario prior to the authorization of the UNAMIR II mission. The UN chose not to adopt this strategy because it believed the safe zone option would not receive the full support of the Security Council.

CHAPTER 6

Third Time Right: Haiti

Esther Brimmer

I. INTRODUCTION

In June 1995, the democratically elected president of Haiti, Jean-Bertrand Aristide welcomed his fellow members of the Organization of American States (OAS) to the annual hemispheric foreign ministers meeting. Whether he would ever return to Haitian soil had been a matter of international debate barely a year before; that he would be hosting such a gathering would have been virtually unthinkable. However, this gathering, and many other events like it, were part of the process of binding Haiti back to the international community that had served to restore his government to the country.

Although its lasting impact will only become evident over time, international intervention is being hailed as a success in Haiti. While the introduction of the U.S.-led Multinational Force (MNF) into Haiti to restore President Aristide in September 1994 in many ways was a classic case of intervention, over three years the international community used a range of tools from economic sanctions to military force. Some tools were more effective than others, and the combination of tools and timing were important too. The Intervention Cycle can help clarify which tools were effective and why.

A. Elements

The Haiti case has both elements of a classic intervention, and several elements that make it unique. Most advocates of intervention have a conception

---

Esther Brimmer is a Senior Associate of the Carnegie Commission on Preventing Deadly Conflict. From 1993-1995, she served as Special Assistant to the Under Secretary of State for Political Affairs where she handled international organizations, peace-keeping, human rights, refugee, and other issues. Prior to that she was the Foreign Affairs and Defense Analyst with the Congressional Democratic Study Group. She received her Ph.D. in International Relations from Oxford University in 1989.

that if an egregious wrong is committed against international norms or basic human rights within a country, outsiders have a claim, and indeed a duty, to try to remedy the situation. Furthermore such advocates argue that appropriate action by outsiders can do more good than harm. When deciding when to act, even policymakers who might believe that positive intervention is possible must weigh how close a situation comes to ideal conditions, and whether the deviations are enough to undermine the objective. Haiti would seem to have elements that bring it close to the "ideal" conception.

At first glance the Haiti case has several key elements that made intervention more likely to succeed, including the nature of the conflict, the position of international institutions, and the interests of a superpower. Inside and outside the country the conflict was seen as a political one (who should run the country), rather than an interethnic one (who is the nation). Interethnic conflict can give policymakers greater pause as they may be concerned that the international community cannot solve longstanding social grievances.

Thus, Haiti differs from many of the other cases in this book. The violence in Haiti is not the manifestation of intergroup conflict between different ethnic contingents, nor a battle between two or more large groups as in Rwanda or the former Yugoslavia. Instead violence in Haiti emerges from the tension between a small oligarchy and a large poorly educated populace. The people can speak the same language (Creole) and eat the same food; the differences in Haitian society are economic and cultural, not ethnic.[1]

If the problem was political, the political choices were clearer than in many situations. A president who had been selected in internationally sanctioned elections was available to be restored (though there was a question of how to work with him to develop a political center). There were formal structures of the international community, the United Nations and the OAS, in place that were competent legally and politically to handle the situation once the member states' political wills had been engaged. Changes in both institutions wrought by the end of cold war ideological rivalries meant that both institutions were better positioned to be useful than previously.

Furthermore, the outflow of refugees to U.S. shores meant that a power, a country that was able—and eventually willing—to mobilize international resources, was directly affected by the crisis. Haiti was already in a distinct category vis-à-vis the United States. In 1981 Haitian President Jean-Claude "Baby Doc" Duvalier and President Reagan signed an agreement that permitted U.S. ships to interdict fleeing Haitians on the high seas and return them to Haiti. From 1981 to 1991 over 20,000 people fled. In the months after the coup the numbers shot up to over 30,000. The refugee outflow called into question the implementation of U.S. obligations toward refugees, as well as engaging high profile domestic political concerns ranging from the 1992 presidential election to the 1994 hunger strike by Randall Robinson.

Nevertheless, it took three years for the elected president to be restored. The tools may be available, the national interest may be present, but political will is required to use them. Once political will results in the decision to intervene, then the right tools can—and must—be selected to do it effectively.

B. The Framework

The end of the Cold War occasioned a rethinking of the use of force and humanitarian intervention. From the vantage point of spring 1995, Haiti is a policy success. It is even more so after the peaceful presidential transition in February 1996. However, since the coup in September 1991, many tools were tried. Why was the MNF able to achieve its objectives? Why was this form of international action effective at that time? The Intervention Cycle suggests some answers that can help policymakers understand their choices in complex situations where international action may be appropriate.

This chapter will explore how the Intervention Cycle can be applied to events in Haiti since the 1991 coup that deposed President Jean-Bertrand Aristide. As with all policy, an evaluation of success depends on the criteria. This chapter assumes the objective to be the restoration of democratically elected government to Haiti. Other related long-term goals could be discerned, such as achieving stability or developing a political consensus to sustain democracy.

As applied to Haiti the Intervention Cycle points out the differences between conflict mitigation and conflict resolution, and suggests why application of a mechanism inappropriate to the extant stage of the cycle will not be successful. The model also presents a way to evaluate different types of coercive mechanisms, including sanctions and the use of force. Moreover, Haiti's underlying situation reinforces the importance of political, economic, and social enfranchisement to resolving conflict.

The model is particularly helpful in considering conflict mitigation and conflict resolution. The international community in the form of the OAS and the UN, as well as national governments were quick to impose sanctions. Key countries and international organizations engaged in diplomatic action to try to overcome the 1991 coup. Analysis based on the Intervention Cycle shows that much of the initial international effort was focused on mitigating the conflict and trying to improve political enfranchisement, before the violence was stopped. The model indicates that violence must be curbed before mitigative measures are effective. This chapter examines this idea against the experience in Haiti and concludes that one of the reasons the MNF was successful was that it could contain violence, thus allowing space for mitigation.

The model also suggests where the international community can play a role. Activities such as peacekeeping and peacemaking that involve international action are clustered on the right hand side of the chart. These are mitigative responses. Those that entail levels of enfranchisement are grouped on the left hand side. Thus the model would suggest that the international community can play a role in mitigation, but that the people of the country have to take the lead in long-term enfranchisement.

Peace operations can provide a breathing space for the parties to move beyond violence. If they are backing down from their spiral toward violence, they can begin to address the enfranchisement questions. Haiti poses interesting questions about whether peace operations can stop the violence. From the vantage point of 1995 the answer seems to be yes. The MNF was able to establish, in the words of UN Security Council Resolution 940 that authorized it, "a safe and secure environment." Over time we will see how well the parties use the breathing space.

II. THE FIRST ITERATION: LIMITED ECONOMIC SANCTIONS

Four days after delivering his first speech as the Haitian head of state at the annual opening ceremonies for the UN General Assembly, Aristide was deposed in a coup led by Lt. Gen. Raoul Cédras. General Cédras had been made provisional commander-in-chief only a few months before in June 1991. In the period immediately following the coup as many as 3,000 Haitians may have been killed by the military and their supporters. The violence pushed Haiti from seven o'clock on the Intervention Cycle to twelve midnight.

Haiti has suffered multiple coups since its independence from France in 1804. In less than two centuries there had been 41 heads of state, of whom 29 had been assassinated in office.[2] This time, however, the international community became engaged. There were several reasons for stronger international involvement in the fall of 1991 than in some past Haitian crises. One was that earlier that year the OAS had made a commitment to counter threats to democracy in the region. In the "Resolution on Representative Democracy" the OAS members agreed to call for an automatic meeting of the OAS Permanent Council, "in the event of any occurrences giving rise to the sudden or irregular interruption of . . . the legitimate exercise of power by the democratically elected government in any of the Organization's member states."[3] The Santiago agreement was a milestone in a hemisphere traditionally very sensitive to national sovereignty. The coup in Haiti was the first challenge to that commitment. Although Haitian politics evolved *sui generis*, Haiti had been part of the recent process of political change in the region, which made it a little harder for outsiders to ignore the coup. By the early 1990s, democratically elected governments led all the countries in the region except Cuba and Haiti (after the coup). Baby Doc Duvalier had left power and left Haiti in 1986. Elections were scheduled for 1987 but had been sabotaged. However, on December 16, 1990, Haiti had conducted a free and fair election watched by international observers. Jean-Bertrand Aristide had been elected with over 67 percent of the vote.

The international community's response to the coup was one of classic deterrence. It contained three key elements: enforcement of sanctions, containment of refugee and migrant outflow, and attempts to establish human rights monitoring, all conducted within a diplomatic framework in which military force was not seen as a leading option.

A. Sanctions

The imposition of sanctions was swift, but the initial round was not extensive enough to force a change in behavior by the military regime. Acting in the context of the Santiago agreement, the OAS was quick to impose sanctions. On October 3, 1991, the OAS called for the "full restoration of the rule of law of the constitutional regime" through the reinstatement of Aristide, the diplomatic isolation of the junta, and the request that member states to suspend nonhumanitarian assistance and commercial contacts.[4] Moreover the OAS followed up on October 8 with a condemnation of the regime's decision to replace Aristide as president.

The Bush administration, too, stated its interest in the restoration of the government. On October 2, at the OAS meeting of foreign ministers, U.S. Secretary of State James A. Baker said, "it is imperative that we agree—for the sake of Haitian democracy and the cause of democracy throughout the hemisphere—to act collectively to defend the legitimate government of President Aristide."[5] Within four days of the coup the President Bush had frozen the assets of the coup government, stopped payments by U.S. companies to that government and suspended U.S. assistance. The United States halted its $50 million aid program.

However, sanctions, while affecting the poor, had little impact on the very wealthy who could afford to travel to obtain goods outside the country. According to von Lipsey's Intervention Cycle discussion, sanctions should have (1) a target group, (2) targeted behavior, (3) a clear understanding of the desired effect, and (4) clear conditions for removal. The initial round of sanctions imposed in late 1991 did not have all of these characteristics and were criticized for not really impeding the activities of those who carried out or supported the coup. The sanctions did not specify what behavior the supposed target subjects were supposed to undertake. Were they to leave government, leave Haiti, permit the return of President Aristide?

Although the sanctions were supposed to affect those in a position to change the government, they affected the poorest most. While most Haitians had to deal with even greater deprivation at home, the families of the coup leaders were able to leave the country to get what they needed. The personal assets of those close to the regime were not frozen. Thus the de facto leaders and their supporters could, with effort, continue their lives as normal and hope for an erosion of international commitment to enforcing sanctions. Life in Haiti has always been hard; sanctions made it a bit more difficult, but not unbearable, for the elite. Indeed the sight of Mme. Cédras and others shopping in Miami angered many critics of the regime and the U.S. government. Although the initial sanctions were not enough to effect change, they were tightened over time. Indeed the ratcheting up of sanctions pressure is a sign of the increased dedication to bringing about political change and could signal a transition into a new iteration on the Intervention Cycle.

The conditions for sanction removal, as pointed out earlier, have to be clear and doable. In this first phase of international engagement, it was not as clear what the regime should do for the lifting of sanctions. The message of the international community was further clouded by not staying the course. As early as February 1992, the Bush administration permitted U.S. companies to be exempted from the sanctions, enabling them to resume business in Haiti and sending mixed messages about the U.S. view of the coup.

B. Refugees and Migration

Sanctions may be seen as one effort the contain the Haitian problem, but the most dramatic and controversial was the maritime operation to keep Haitians from fleeing Haiti to the United States. Fleeing to the United States from Haiti was not a new phenomenon. From 1791 to 1809, during the upheavals of the French and Haitian revolutions, thousands of black Haitians had fled to the United States.[6]

The Bush and Clinton administrations both argued that *economic* migrants were being returned, while the rights of *refugees* were being respected. Many Haitian advocates in the United States disagreed and brought a law suit against the U.S. government that ultimately went to the Supreme Court. The case of the treatment of migrants can be seen both as an important case in refugee law, but also as an example of an effort to contain the problem of the coup in Haiti.

According to Harold Hongju Koh, a Yale professor and one of the lawyers who argued the case, the crux of the legal case was whether the United States was violating its treaty commitments under the UN Convention Relating to the Status of Refugees.[7] The United States became a party to the convention in 1967 when it acceded to the UN Protocol on the Status of Refugees. Article 33 of the 1951 convention says that "no Contracting State shall expel or return *("refouler")* a refugee in any manner whatsoever to the frontiers of territories where his life or freedom would be threatened on account of his . . . political opinion."[8]

Migrants from Haiti were in a unique position. In 1981, under President Reagan, the United States signed an agreement with the government of Baby Doc Duvalier that created a "cooperative program of interdiction and selective return to Haiti of certain Haitian migrant vessels involved in illegal transport of persons coming from Haiti."[9] The resulting Alien Migration Interdiction Operation (AMIO) allowed the United States to intercept Haitians leaving Haiti by sea and return them to their country. At the time this was an arrangement unique to Haitians.[10]

The objective was to separate those migrants who were refugees with a legitimate fear of prosecution from economic migrants toward whom the United States would have no obligations under the refugee convention. Those who were screened in could apply for refugee status. After the September 1991 coup, the outflow of Haitians increased. The Bush administration began detaining those *screened in* as refugees at the Guantanamo naval base in Cuba. While there they were not permitted to meet with lawyers from the United States. Therefore, in November 1991, the Haitian Refugee Center sued James Baker as Secretary of State charging that the refugees were being denied due process. The Eleventh Circuit Court twice ruled against the plaintiffs. In February 1992, the U.S. Supreme Court denied the Haitian Refugee Center's petition for *certiorari*, with only Justice Blackmun dissenting.

The refugee numbers continued to mount. In that same month, February 1992, there were over 3,000 Haitians being held at the base. The plaintiffs had requested a temporary restraining order that was pending with the Second Circuit court in the late spring of 1992 when the Bush administration changed policy. While in Maine before the Memorial Day holiday, President Bush issued the "Kennebunkport order," which said that all Haitians fleeing Haiti would be returned to Haiti without interviews. Whereas before Haitians with a credible fear of prosecution if returned were screened in and taken to Guantanamo, now they would be returned directly without questions. The Second Circuit first denied the pending temporary restraining order, but then said that the new policy was illegal.

Those Haitians who were then at Guantanamo had already been screened in. With the circuit court's decision they were permitted into the United States, except for approximately 300 found to be HIV positive. Those screened in were cleared to enter the United States on June 21, 1993—ironically the same day that the Supreme Court issued a decision that the overall migration policy did not violate Article 33, the *nonrefoulement* clause, of the Refugee Convention.[11]

The premise of the AMIO was that fleeing Haitians were economic migrants rather than political ones. However, a case can be made that many of the people fleeing Haiti after the coup were political refugees. From 1981 to 1990, 22,940 Haitians were intercepted under the AMIO program. Of these, 11 were determined to qualify for asylum.[12] However, in the eight months after the coup, the number intercepted surged to 38,000. The rate of screening people in increased such that before the policy change in May 1992, 11,000 had been screened in and 27,000 returned.[13]

When the Second Circuit declared the Bush policy of returning people without questioning to be illegal, presidential candidate Bill Clinton commended the court's decision. His campaign statements had led both Americans and Haitians to expect him to change U.S. policy toward Haitian migrants upon entering office. During the campaign he had said, "If I were president, I would—in the absence of clear and compelling evidence that they weren't political refugees—give them temporary asylum until we returned the elected government of Haiti."[14]

However, the incoming administration became very concerned about a flood of people trying to come to the United States after inauguration day. As an administration official noted in early January 1993, "the main goal is to keep Haitians in Haiti."[15] Even with the policy of direct return intended to discourage people from leaving, 5,000 people had been returned between May 1992 and January 1993; over the year (1992), 31,000 people had fled.[16] There were widespread reports of intensified boat building suggesting that Haitians were just waiting for the change in the White House to head for the United States. Many Haitians expected the new U.S. president either to welcome the migrants, or to be determined to return Aristide and help rebuild the country.[17] If the legitimate government was not restored then people would continue to flee oppression. As one potential migrant put it, "If they can't bring us Aristide, the moment Guantanamo opens, I'll be on the first boat I can climb aboard."[18] As a boat builder told *The New York Times*, "All this time they have been unable to settle our crisis, people have only gotten more desperate."[19]

These sorts of preparations spurred the incoming Clinton administration to announce that it would continue the Bush administration policy. In a radio message to Haiti, president-elect Clinton said that people fleeing the country would be returned.[20] President Aristide cooperated with the policy and over the Voice of America appealed to his compatriots in Creole, "Until constitutional order is returned to Haiti, I ask all of you to stay home and help reestablish democracy. It hurts me a lot to think about people preparing to risk their lives in flimsy boats. That's not the road to freedom."[21] The administration also decided to look at in-country processing to give potential migrants an alternative to taking to the seas.[22]

At this stage, in terms of refugee and migration policy, both administrations were trying to contain the problem of the outflow of Haitians fleeing the regime. According to the Intervention Cycle analysis, U.S. policy focused on trying to mitigate the effects of people wanting to leave the country rather than deal with the cause of their desire to depart. One of the reasons for this was a perception that most of these people were economic migrants, not political refugees. However, compared with the 1980s, and the level after the coup, the number of people leaving Haiti by sea dropped dramatically during the eight months Aristide was president. With the end of the exploitative Baby Doc regime, and hope for the future, people seemed to have not felt the need to flee.

However, the widespread violence that was driving people to flee between 1991 and 1993 continued. The policy of returning migrants did not get at the root cause of their departure. The Intervention Cycle points out that as the policy did not stop the violence, it could not contain the problem. Thus the Intervention Cycle helps illuminate the underlying problem with Haitian migration policy during the first phase of the crisis. From the point of view of outsiders, the international community was acting to try to resolve the conflict. Sanctions had been imposed by both by OAS member states, and by the UN. However, from the point of view of the "Haitian-in-the-street," or Haitian advocates outside, the focus of the international community from 1991 to 1993 seemed to be on containing the problem, not on solving the immediate cause—the de facto regime's seizure of power from the democratically elected government. In the language of the Intervention Cycle the international community was *preventing* a wider spread of the conflict by imposing coercive sanctions, while from the point of view of Aristide supporters, the international community should have been *mitigating* the violence by using force against the Cédras regime. These actions focus on entirely different phases of the Intervention Cycle. Fortunately, the situation was about to change. Although the new administration did not immediately change U.S. migration policy, it did undertake new efforts.

III. SECOND ITERATION: DIPLOMATIC ENGAGEMENT AND GOVERNORS ISLAND

In 1993, the Clinton administration began efforts aimed at resolving the crisis through diplomatic means. This second phase of intervention spans from the spring 1993 appointment of Lawrence Pezzullo as the special envoy to Haiti until the spring of 1994 when policy shifted more directly to the restoration of Aristide. In this second phase, the administration looked for a political solution that could restore an internationally acceptable, politically moderate, government to Haiti. However, as highlighted by the Intervention Cycle, not enough elements were in place to stop the violence. Although the Governors Island Agreement, the diplomatic achievement of this phase, was signed, the violence continued in the form of high-profile assassinations and human rights abuses. The continued violence was an important factor in the subsequent Harlan County incident.

The diplomatic lead was undertaken by the United States and the international community as represented by the UN and the OAS. In December 1992, the UN Secretary General named Dante Caputo, an Argentinean diplomat, as the UN representative. Caputo served as the joint representative of both institutions. Basic questions included: Would Aristide return and when? Who would serve as prime minister and how should he or she be chosen? And, what would be the fate of Cédras? These questions would persist as key diplomatic choices. Also, should Aristide return immediately or after the political and economic institutions stabilized?[23] Just before the inauguration of the new American administration in January 1993, the United States sent LtGen John Sheehan from the Joint Staff to talk to the Haitian generals. In this first visit by a high level officer since the coup, he told them that the Haitian military leaders would not "be able to look to their American counterparts for any kind of assistance."[24]

However, during 1993 there were dissonant voices from within the executive and legislative branches that doubted that the U.S. government should align itself closely with Aristide. CIA analyst Bruce Latrell's critical view of Aristide was widely cited.[25] Rumors of drug use and psychiatric care circulated making the democratically elected leader appear an unstable partner for the United States. Moreover, there was always the question of whether Aristide would behave differently if he were returned to office. His infamous comment about "necklacing," the practice of killing opponents by placing a burning tire around them, and the accusation that he ordered the killing of Roger La Fontant, created uncertainties about his commitment to the rule of law.[26] The United States had often supported unsavory right-wing leaders in the region. Supporting a left-wing leader was a larger leap for some in Washington.

During the first half of 1993, the crux of diplomatic efforts were to get the military to the negotiating table and to get guarantees for Aristide's safe return.[27] Concurrent with the diplomatic efforts was a Defense Department plan to try to give the Haitian military incentives to change their behavior. The idea was to give the Haitian military an alternative purpose by focusing them on civic action and disaster assistance, and by providing training.[28] The new administration did signal that it was closer to Aristide and was more serious about trying to use nonmilitary means to remove the de facto regime. Aristide was invited to the White House. The Treasury Department froze the assets of the coup leaders themselves, and the United States pushed for an UN embargo on oil and arms.

A. The Governors Island Accord

The imposition of the oil embargo spurred the de facto regime to the negotiating table. President Clinton announced targeted economic sanctions against the Haitian military leaders and their associates on June 4, 1993. On June 16, the UN Security Council passed Resolution 841, which imposed an oil and arms embargo on Haiti and directed member states to freeze Haitian government assets. The July 3 Governors Island accord, signed on that island in New York harbor, and the July 16 New York Pact establishing procedures for implementing the accord, were diplomatic milestones laying out the basic political framework for ending the crisis.

The Governors Island agreement had several key provisions:

- political dialogue under the auspices of the UN and the OAS, including the procedure for enabling the parliament to function;
- the return of Aristide, on October 30, 1993, and the retirement of Cédras as commander-in-chief;
- selection of the new prime minister by President Aristide, with confirmation by the parliament;
- suspension of the UN sanctions under UNSC Resolution 841, and those imposed by the OAS once the prime minister had been confirmed and had taken office;
- amnesty granted by the president under Article 147 of the Haitian constitution; and
- technical assistance for administration and judicial reform, and modernizing the armed forces and creating a police force (separate from the military).[29]

France and Canada would provide the training for the new police force, and the military training would be provided by the United States (under a U.S. commander).[30] On September 23, 1993, the Security Council passed Resolution 867 authorizing the deployment of United Nations Mission in Haiti (UNMIH) for six months to implement the promise of training in Paragraph 5 of the Governors Island agreement. The resolution authorized 567 UN police monitors and a 700-person military construction unit, which included 60 military trainers.

The agreement seemed to include the features needed to end the crisis. Aristide would return, the head of the de facto government would leave, and the sanctions would be lifted. Countries such as the United States, France, and Canada with long-standing ties to Haiti were to be involved in helping reform the armed forces and implement the peace. The international community was attempting to reenter the Intervention Cycle at three o'clock, in the peacekeeping phase of mitigation. The agreement was an improvement over earlier efforts because it recognized that the departure of the de facto military leaders was required to resolve the crisis. It also tried to provide a way for the international community to remain engaged in the transition back to the legitimate government. It both got the military to the negotiating table and seemed to set the stage for Aristide's safe return. President Aristide did nominate Robert Malval as prime minister, and the Haitian legislature ratified Malval and his cabinet.

However, the agreement was not fully realized in 1993. The agreement, and the related New York Pact, had no enforcement mechanism. There were no penalties for the military if they did not abide by the accord.[31] Nor did it include measures for the reimposition of sanctions if the agreement were broken. Furthermore, the sanctions were to be lifted not on the return of Aristide, but on the confirmation of a new prime minister. Perhaps Cédras seemed to have no alternatives,[32] but the agreement was not enough to tie the de factos to an internationally acceptable course of action. The agreements did not require the coup leaders to leave Haiti, even though the United States had insisted that other dictators, such as Jean-Claude Duvalier and Prosper Avril in Haiti and Ferdinand Marcos in the Philippines, depart their countries.[33]

The violence continued despite the accord. The dreaded attachés abounded, and it was not only the poor, anonymous Aristide supporters who were targeted. In September 1993, the pro-Aristide mayor of Port-au-Prince, Evans Paul, was attacked as he tried to go to his offices. However, the most blatant attack was the assassination of Antoine Izméry who was pulled out of mass and murdered outside the church.[34]

Meanwhile, the international community was trying to decide how to configure UNMIH. The U.S. administration could not agree internally on exactly how the UNMIH participants should be equipped. Cobbling together the elements of a peacekeeping mission is usually difficult. However, the policy environment in which decisions were being made was becoming more complex. Haiti decisions, like almost all complex policies, were not taking place in a vacuum. Choices about Haiti were profoundly affected by perceptions of peacekeeping policy and the U.S. experience in Somalia.

B. Peacekeeping Policy

Upon entering office, the Clinton Administration had launched a review of peacekeeping policy known as Presidential Review Document-13.[35] During the cold war neither the United States nor the Soviet Union had contributed troops to peacekeeping operations. The end of the cold war had freed both countries to participate. Understanding that participation in such operations was having and would continue to have a profound affect on the U.S. foreign and defense policy, the Administration began the review in February 1993.

The final Presidential Decision Directive (PDD-25) was signed in May 1994 having been honed by the experience of the U.S. participation in UN peacekeeping operations in 1993.[36] In a short period of time the American experience of peacekeeping had included the extremes of Operation Desert Shield/Storm in Iraq, the United Nations International Task Force in Somalia, the U.S.-led humanitarian assistance operation in Somalia, and UNOSOM II, the UN's first attempt at a UN-led Chapter VII operation. As has been discussed elsewhere in this book, the international effort in Somalia had important lessons for the Intervention Cycle. The summer of 1993 had seen the expansion of the activities UNOSOM II to include hunting for Somali leader Aideed in his home base of Mogadishu. Although UNOSOM II helped establish stability and provide food in the rest of the country, international media and hence policy-makers' attention was focused on the action in the Somali capital.

On October 3, an operation by the Rangers, who were under U.S. command and operational control, went wrong. Eighteen U.S. soldiers were killed and their bodies dragged through the streets. This was not what the American public expected from a humanitarian operation. Calls went up in Congress and the press to end American involvement in UNOSOM II and in peacekeeping in general. The tragedy in Somalia brought the issue of American casualties in a peacekeeping operation into the living rooms of millions of citizens. Even before the incident in Somalia there had been a debate about exactly how to equip the U.S. participants in UNMIH,[37] with President Aristide worried about heavily armed foreign troops in his country, while the Pentagon was concerned about sending underarmed personnel into a volatile situation, even though they were not serving in a combat capacity.

C. The USS Harlan County and the Intervention Cycle

Over Columbus Day weekend of 1993 many of the administration's foreign policy officials were dealing with the production of the report to Congress on Somalia due Friday, October 15. Meanwhile the USS *Harlan County* was sailing to Haiti carrying 200 U.S. and Canadian soldiers. On the docks at Port-au-Prince a demonstration led by civilian thugs at the behest of the military was under way and a another ship had been docked to block the landing of the U.S. vessel. There appeared to be domestic resistance to the deployment of peacekeepers. The UN Security Council had authorized UNMIH to operate under Chapter VI of the Charter, in permissive conditions. The U.S. Defense Department was worried about deploying personnel equipped as peacekeepers in a contested situation.[38] The Defense Department recommended that the ship turn around and leave, and the president agreed.[39]

The *Harlan County* incident had many repercussions, including reinforcing the arguments of those who would a year later advocate using overwhelming force when the decision was made finally to use military force. While many factors led to the decision to turn the *Harlan County* around, the Intervention Cycle helps explain the overall context and that there was a mismatch of action and situation. In this incident the overall problem can be seen: the international community wanted to act to mitigate the crisis without having first dealt with the continuing violence. Irrespective of whether that ship needed to turn back on that day, the Intervention Cycle suggests that the international community would have had to reconsider its approach to the Haiti situation. The basic violence wreaked by the de facto military regime on the fragile Haitian polity needed to be curbed before efforts could be made to refocus the armed forces or train a police force.

The Governors Island agreement and the attempt at deploying UNMIH were the centerpieces of the hub of the second iteration of the cycle. As in the first iteration, the international community was trying to enter the cycle at around three o'clock while the ongoing violence, especially the murder of Izméry, put the situation closer to midnight. In this iteration, some of the elements were in place for a resolution of the crisis, but not all. Among the factors required were a mechanism for getting the military to the negotiating table, a schedule for getting Aristide back in office, and programs that demonstrated the commitment of the international community to the restoration of democracy in Haiti. The imposition of a UN oil embargo helped get General Cédras to the negotiating table to sign the Governors Island agreement. However, the agreement did not contain penalties if the date for President Aristide's return was not honored, nor did the implementation of UNMIH allow for an adequate demonstration of an international military commitment. The international community, in particular the United States, was not ready to make a military commitment in the face of local opposition.

Violence continued after the departure of the Harlan County. Desperation in the country rose. In mid-November and December 1993, migrants left Haiti at a rate of approximately 600-700 a day.[40] Meanwhile, in December, France, Canada, and the United States said that they would support tougher economic sanctions. Tighter sanctions could include cutting all commercial traffic, a naval blockade, improved enforcement of sanctions along Haiti's border with the Dominican Republic, or the cessation of unscheduled flights.[41] The situation continued to deteriorate, and the international community, led by the United States, had to decide whether to take a different course.

D. Human Rights Abuses

One of the most telling signs that violence was a key factor in the crisis was the mounting numbers of human rights abuses. The conflict in Haiti was not ethnic but class based, with a small elite preying on a larger very poor population. In such an environment, civil violence was manifested as human rights abuses by the regime and atrocities committed by paramilitary groups affiliated with the regime. Therefore, the abuse of the human rights of the population can serve as a barometer of conditions.

Violence has always been a part of the Haitian polity. The dreaded Tontons Macoutes of the Duvalier era were an example of quasi-official paramilitary elements that helped a given regime maintain its power. After the 1991 coup, there had been another round of killing; this time directed at Aristide supporters. Sending human rights monitors is a classic tool of deterrence. They can be used in anticipation of a deterioration in the human rights situation, but they may also be deployed once abuses occur to remind a regime that the international community is watching.

In January 1993, Aristide formally requested a large observer team. However, those deployed in early 1993 had been confined to Port-au-Prince. The OAS had 16 human rights observers on the scene, but the government of then prime minister Marc Bazin had restricted them to the capital. According to the UN Special Rapporteur on Haiti's February 1994 report, as many as 3,000 people, mostly Aristide supporters had been killed by the regime in 1993.[42] In addition to the killing of Izméry, there were other prominent crimes, most notably the murder of the justice minister, Guy Mallary, on October 14, 1993. Recognizing the importance of human rights, the OAS backed an International Civilian Mission (ICM) led by Colin Granderson. Indeed it was the de facto regime's expulsion of the ICM in July 1994 that was an important factor in convincing other members of the

Security Council that the military regime was not trying to solve the situation. It was too late for deterrence.

E. Renewed Refugee Outflows

The violence led many to try to flee. In two months in the summer of 1994, 21,000 people were rescued at sea. The outpouring prompted the administration to shift policy and seek safe havens for the those escaping the country. Prominent political activist Randall Robinson, president of TransAfrica, went on a hunger strike to protest the treatment of the Haitians. Several members of the Black Caucus in the U.S. House of Representatives protested and were arrested in front of the White House. Journalists, as well as lawyers who acted on the Haitians' behalf, pointed out the discrepancy between the treatment of Haitians and Cubans. While Haitians were being repatriated when their crafts were intercepted, Cubans were taken to the United States where the 1966 Cuban Adjustment Act permitted them to be paroled into the United States. Over the past two decades, the U.S. had accepted around 900,000 Cubans.[43] The contrast was exacerbated by the separate outflow of Cubans in the summer of 1994. The United States was faced with a major refugee and migration problem as thousands of Haitians and Cubans were housed at Guantanamo (after the United States decided to grant Haitians safe haven in July 1995). Although the granting of safe haven was a morally defensible choice, and a fulfillment of Clinton's campaign promise, it was a temporary measure until the basic political problem in Haiti could be solved.

IV. THIRD ITERATION: USE OF FORCE

A. Spring 1994: Policy in Transition

The first iteration of international involvement had brought about UN and OAS sanctions, the second had sketched out the diplomatic framework of Governors Island, but neither had resulted in the end of the crisis—the departure of the de facto regime and the restoration of legitimate government in Haiti. Through the winter of 1994, the administration continued diplomatic efforts. However, there was a growing sense that more dramatic steps would have to be taken. Aristide was still not back in office and the refugee flow was continuing. Some argued that not only did the United States have a responsibility to help restore a democratically elected government so close to home, but that the only way to stop the refugee outpouring was to solve the underlying problem of the existence of the illegitimate regime.[44]

In the spring of 1994 the administration decided to stand more closely with the democratically elected president of Haiti rather than to continue to try to broker an agreement between Aristide and other political elements in the country. The administration moved to make maximum use of the international tools available including intensified sanctions and better sanctions enforcement. Most importantly the administration began to countenance the use of force. In its statements the administration began to say that the use of force had neither been ruled in or out.

The vice president's national security advisor, Leon Fuerth, led the coordinated interagency effort to bolster international sanctions and to improve sanctions enforcement. The United States led the effort to get key countries to agree to specific actions. On May 4, 1994, the Security Council adopted Resolution 917, which imposed even tighter sanctions, including a comprehensive trade embargo and a ban on commercial air service, but also set conditions for their removal. The resolution required a stable environment for the deployment of UNMIH, the retirement of Cédras as the commander-in-chief of the armed forces, and the resignation and departure from Haiti of two other coup leaders, Lieutenant Colonel Michel François, chief of staff of the armed forces, and Brigadier General Philippe Biamby, chief of the metropolitan zone of Port-au-Prince.[45] The ban on commercial air service made it harder for coup leaders to leave the country to obtain goods made expensive or denied by the international sanctions. The United States took unilateral measures too. On June 21 the United States revoked almost all nonimmigrant visas held by Haitians that had been issued before May 11. The administration also worked with the Dominican Republic and other states to improve sanctions enforcement along the porous land border between Haiti and the Dominican Republic.

B. Building the Coalition

If the sanctions provided the economic stick, the UN Security Council Resolutions 933 and 940 provided the diplomatic framework for international action including the use of force. As signatories of the UN Charter, member states agree to use force under certain circumstances; the self defense provision of Article 51 has been stretched broadly to fit many situations. However, as part of its peacekeeping policy the administration thought long and seriously about U.S. participation in peace operations. At times acting in concert with others could add greater legitimacy to an effort and help share the burden. Gaining the support of countries in the region and the blessing of the UN Security Council could legitimate the use or threat of the use of force. However, Latin and Central American countries' historic wariness of U.S. military activity in the region had made them particularly sensitive to the use of force and to the question of sovereignty. Thus in order to support, or at least not oppose UN action, countries in the region had to be convinced of the uniqueness of the situation and the need for decisive international action.[46]

The June expulsion of the International Civilian Mission, and the August 28 killing of Father Jean-Marie Vincent, a prominent pro-Aristide cleric, persuaded many in the region that the de facto Haitian government was not trying to resolve the situation. International military action might be required. Yet, there was still concern about intervening in a conflictual situation. Were the situation already stabilized, then peacekeepers could be deployed to maintain the condition. Furthermore, humanitarian assistance could be also provided.

The problem was how to stabilize the situation. The answer was a two-stage process as outlined in the Secretary General's July 15, 1994, report to the Security Council.[47] In phase one a multinational force would be deployed under Chapter VII to secure the departure of the de facto regime. Then that force could hand over the operation to peacekeepers operating under Chapter VI. UNSC Resolution 940 laid out the terms. Under Resolution 940, member states were authorized to form a multinational force and to use "all necessary means,"[48]—the same language as in the Desert Shield/Storm resolutions for the Gulf War—which implied a use of force. Resolution 940 was a milestone not only for the UN, but for the United States. For the first time, the United States was willing to go to the UN for authorization to intervene in its home region, and one in which it is the dominant power.

Haiti had the elements of a test case. A combination of factors helped make this prominent: The Clinton administration had made the promotion of democracy one of the tenets of its foreign policy. Moreover, along with Cuba, Haiti was the only country in the hemisphere without a democratically elected government. Whereas in 1990-1991 Haiti seemed part of the regional trend toward democracy, the coup made it a symbol of backsliding. Thus, there was greater regional support for taking action, despite the historic and persistent wariness of U.S. intervention in regional affairs. The revitalized OAS was able to play a key role, and the United States was willing to go to the Security Council to gain international legitimacy. Furthermore, the 1992 election brought Democrats into the White House, many of whom believed in humanitarian intervention and intervention to promote democracy, and felt that Haiti merited another chance at change. The end of the cold war, which had been waged in so many countries in the region, made it possible for the administration to ally itself with a leftist leader against a military regime.

C. Carter/Nunn/Powell, the MNF, and the Restoration of Aristide

According to UNSC Resolution 940, the international community was ready to intervene at one o'clock on the Intervention Cycle, forcibly imposing conflict mitigation. However, the extraordinary mission by former President Jimmy Carter, former chairman of the Joint Chiefs of Staff General Colin Powell, and Senator Sam Nunn shifted the situation to a more permissive one. Over the weekend of September 17-18 the team negotiated with the coup leaders. As the planes bearing the first wave of thousands of American troops were in the air, Cédras agreed to go. Indeed it was the knowledge that the planes were in the air—and that the United States was initiating forcible intervention—that made it clear to Cédras that the United States and the international community were serious.[49]

V. CONCLUSION

Swooping down into Port-au-Prince in a U.S. Air Force jet, President Aristide was returned to his country on October 15, 1994. Jubilant crowds thronged around the city to welcome him home. Also there to ensure his safe return were over 20,000 troops from the United States and the rest of the multinational force. By the standard of returning the democratically elected leader to office, the third iteration of intervention in Haiti was a success. The MNF did create a "safe and secure environment." On March 31, 1995, the U.S.-led coalition turned over the operation to UNMIH with an authorized strength of 6,000, of which half were Americans.[50] In the third iteration, the international community finally committed itself to acting to deal with the violence. A purely diplomatic arrangement had not worked, but diplomacy backed by the threat, and finally the use of force, was able to end the de facto regime and restore the democratically elected government. Haiti was returned to seven o'clock on the Intervention Cycle.

Political enfranchisement is ongoing, but the path is not necessarily smooth. The June 25, 1995, parliamentary elections were held, but with instances of serious mismanagement.[51] Still, there are signs of progress. Presidential elections were held in December 1995. The new democratically elected president, René Preval, took office on February 6, 1996, in a peaceful succession to Aristide. According to the Intervention Cycle, after political enfranchisement, the next steps (which may run concurrently) are to undertake the complex long-term task of economic and social enfranchisement. Economic and social development will be an important part of solving the deeper problems in the poorest country in the hemisphere. This was understood in the second and third iterations of Haitian intervention. During the height of the crisis the U.S. Agency for International Development was feeding nearly one million people, and programs to build and rebuild the economy were part of the U.S. commitment to help Haiti. However, lack of progress caused the United States to suspend certain assistance programs in earlier attempts at conflict resolution. Whether this third attempt at intervention continues to succeed will be borne out in the long-term stability of the Haitian state.

NOTES

1. Sidney W. Mintz, "Can Haiti Change?" *Foreign Affairs*, 74, no. 1 (January/February, 1995), p. 83.
2. "U.S. Policy Toward Haiti: Pros and Cons," *Congressional Digest*, 73, no. 8-9, (August-September, 1994), p. 194.
3. Harold Hongju Koh, "The Haiti Paradigm in United States Human Rights Policy," *Yale Law Journal*, 103, no. 8, (June 1994), p. 2393.
4. Ibid., p. 2394.
5. Ibid., p. 2393.
6. Melissa Lennox, "Refugees, Racism, and Reparations: A Critique of the United States' Haitian Immigration Policy," *Stanford Law Review*, 45, no. 3, (February 1993), p. 692.
7. Koh, "Paradigm," p. 2392.
8. Ibid., p. 2393.
9. Ibid., p. 2392.
10. In 1995, additional AMIO agreements were signed with other Caribbean countries as part of an effort to reduce the illegal flow of migrants in the region. However, the other countries are democratic states, reducing the likelihood that people returned under the new AMIOs would be sent back to very oppressive regimes.
11. Koh, "Paradigm," p. 2397.
12. House Committee on the Judiciary, "Report of Haitian Refugees Protection Act of 1992," House Report Number 437, 102nd Congress, 2nd Session, 1992, cited in David E. Ralph, "Haitian Interdiction on the High Seas: The Continuing Saga of the Rights of Aliens Outside United States Territory," *Maryland Journal of International Law and Trade*, 17, no. 2 (Fall 1993), p. 237.
13. Ibid.
14. Elaine Sciolino, "Clinton Says U.S. Will Continue Ban on Haitian Exodus," *The New York Times*, January 15, 1993, p. A1.
15. Elaine Sciolino, "Clinton Aides Urge Freer Haiti Policy," *The New York Times*, January 6, 1993, p. A1.
16. Howard W. French, "352 Haitians Reach Miami Where U.S. Detains Them," *The New York Times*, January 6, 1993, p. A5.
17. Howard W. French, "Haitians Hope for January 20: A Fair Wind for Florida," *The New York Times*, January 12, 1993, p. A4.
18. Ibid.
19. Calypso Marks quoted in French, "Haitians Hope," p. A4.
20. Sciolino, "Clinton Says . . . ," p. A1.

21. Howard W. French, "Aristide Urges Big Observer Team for Haiti," *The New York Times*, January 14, 1993, p. A3.
22. Kate Doyle, "Hollow Diplomacy in Haiti," *World Policy Journal*, XI, no. 1 (Spring 1994), p. 52.
23. Howard W. French, "Visiting U.S. General Warns Haiti's Military Chiefs," *The New York Times*, January 9, 1993, p. A5.
24. Ibid.
25. Kate Doyle, "Hollow Diplomacy . . . ," p. 52.
26. French, "Visiting U.S. General . . . ," p. A5.
27. Ibid.
28. Doyle, "Hollow Diplomacy . . . ," p. 53.
29. United Nations, "Agreement of Governors Island," July 3, 1993.
30. Ibid.
31. Doyle, "Hollow Diplomacy . . . ," p. 53.
32. Ibid., p. 54.
33. Koh, "Paradigm," p. 2432.
34. Doyle, "Hollow Diplomacy . . . ," p. 54.
35. The "13" denoted that it was the 13th subject reviewed. When the document was signed by the president in May 1994, it was then called Presidential Decision Directive-25 (PDD-25), simply denoting that it was the 25th directive signed. Some analysts have argued inaccurately that the two different numbers had policy significance.
36. See "The Clinton Administration's Policy on Reforming Multilateral Peace Operations," unclassified white paper, May 1994.
37. Elaine Sciolino, "State–Defense Department Tensions," *The New York Times*, October 8, 1993, p. A1.
38. Doyle, "Hollow Diplomacy . . . ," p. 56.
39. Ibid.
40. Ibid., p. 57.
41. Ibid.
42. United Nations, Report of the Special Rapporteur on Haiti, February 1994.
43. Harold Hongju Koh, "Reflections on *Refoulement* and *Haitian Centers Council*," *Harvard International Law Journal*, 35, no. 1 (Winter 1994), p. 19.
44. While there was a policy review at the senior most levels, others were also rethinking options. In a private March 23, 1994, memo to the Under Secretary for Political Affairs, the author argued against then-current policy making a case that the outflow of refugees was linked to perceptions in Haiti of the prospect for a political resolution and the end of the military regime, rather than to economic factors.
45. United Nations Security Council, "Report of the Secretary General on the United Nations Mission in Haiti," S/1994/828, July 15, 1994, para. 1-3.
46. United Nations Security Council, Resolution 940, S/Res/940, July 31, 1994, para. 2.
47. UNSC, S/1994/828, para. 12.

48. UNSC, Res. 940, operative para. 4.
49. Robert Pastor, David Gergen, personal communication, April 20, 1995.
50. As of June 30, 1995, the operational military component of UNMIH numbered 4,864, with 1,746 from the U.S. Joint Task Force. The military support element of UNMIH was 1,201, and there were 847 civilian police. The excess, over 6,000, can be attributed to overlapping troop rotational schedules. Numbers cited in the UNMIH Progress Report, United Nations, S/1995/614, July 24, 1995.
51. *The Washington Post*, June 26, 1995.

CHAPTER 7

Implied Resolution? West Bank and Gaza

James B. Seaton III

Political, social, economic, demographic, and other circumstances combined in the Middle East to produce one of the twentieth century's most
enduring and volatile intergroup clashes—the Arab-Israeli conflict.
During the decade of the 1980s and into the 1990s, regional tensions diminished considerably as, at the state level, major Middle East protagonists began
nibbling at the more hostile edges of their relationship and tacit acceptance
replaced historical hostility. But, largely ignored in the shadow of the broader
Arab-Israeli conflict was the unsettled relationship at the subregional level
between Israelis and Palestinians.

On September 13, 1993, Israeli and PLO representatives in Washington,
D.C., signed a Declaration of Principles (DOP). Implicit in this agreement
was recognition that a solution was possible and, indeed, imminent. Israel
recognized the PLO as the legitimate representative of the Palestinian people
and agreed to grant limited autonomy in the Gaza Strip and Jericho. Sealed
with a symbolic handshake between Israeli Prime Minister Yitzhak Rabin and
Palestinian Liberation Organization Chairman Yasir Arafat, the event was
heralded worldwide as a sign of hope, peace, and reconciliation—a major
breakthrough in Palestinian-Israeli relations. The historical 1993 tableau
was replayed two years later when Rabin and Arafat signed a second set of
accords at the White House. The September 1995 agreement extended

James Seaton is a Marine Corps officer currently serving as Director for Defense Policy
at the National Security Council. He previously served as a Council on Foreign
Relations International Affairs Fellow, taught political science at the U.S. Naval
Academy, and served in Grenada and Lebanon in 1983-1984. He has previously written on civil-military relations and nontraditional conflict. He has an M.A. in political
science from Duke University.

restricted self-rule and called for a withdrawal of Israeli security forces from much of the West Bank. While more complex and detailed than the earlier agreement, the 1995 accord was still but an "interim agreement" set to expire in May 1999.

The handshake held unlimited promise; yet, in the first few years following the 1993 White House ceremony minimal maturation occurred in Palestinian-Israeli relations. For Israelis, the internal security situation worsened as Muslim fundamentalist groups launched a bombing campaign that killed and injured hundreds of Israelis. For Palestinians, little changed in their day-to-day existence as Gaza and West Bank residents remained victims of economic neglect, failed political promises, and deteriorating social conditions. Absent still was a viable vision of the future or a genuine ability for Palestinians to control their destiny.

THE INTERVENTION CYCLE

In response to unremitting Palestinian-Jewish conflict during the last century, numerous countries and organizations have repeatedly intervened in some capacity or another. This recurrent requirement to intervene presupposes some combination of the following: (1) failed earlier involvement; (2) incomplete involvement because conditions precipitating the outbreak of intergroup violence were never ameliorated; or (3) deliberate or benign neglect during the overt violence interregnum. Recognition of the need to "jump start" the process agreed to in the September 1993 DOP has led to increased involvement by states and organizations (interveners) in an effort to facilitate Palestinian autonomy efforts. Von Lipsey's Intervention Cycle provides a conceptual model to assist potential interveners as they work toward a viable, lasting peace settlement amidst the historical complexities grounding contemporary Palestinian-Israeli relations.

The Intervention Cycle refers to measures taken by an intervening party to conflict as it (1) attempts to mitigate actual acts of violence; (2) achieves a state of resolution whereby the actual triggers of violence are quieted and a stable relationship resumes; and (3) takes preventative actions intended permanently to address historical conditions, which, if left unresolved, perpetuate a cycle of violence. By successfully integrating mitigatory and preventative measures, the intervening party can prevent future outbreaks of intergroup violence. As explained in an earlier chapter, however, intervening parties too often focus their efforts on mitigating violence and minimize efforts at preventing future violent outbreaks. This has been the history of Israeli-Palestinian relations.

This chapter examines the Palestinian-Israeli relationship through the prism of the Intervention Cycle. While highlighting contemporary conditions, it also examines the era of Jordanian and Egyptian control over the Palestinians and the approaches of consecutive Israeli governments as they sought to suppress Palestinian nationalism and violence. A look at the Jordanian/Egyptian-era provides necessary context to current problems, but the actions of Israeli governments have the greatest impact on contemporary developments; for, subsequent to abating actual acts of violence, Israelis did little to address societal and cultural insecurities or the underlying impulse to do violence. Instead, mitigation resulted from subduing outbreaks of violence and exacting punishment on the Palestinian community. Putting down acts of violence achieved, from the Israeli perspective, a tolerable state of existence (an implied resolution). Mitigation provided a satisfactory, albeit tempo-rary, alternative to conflict for the dominant party, although it failed to lead to a permanent resolution of intergroup differences.

As the history of repeated violence and acts of forcible mitigation demon-strates, however, this view is shared by only one of the conflict parties and ignores the conditions that precipitated subsequent outbreaks. Whereas repeated Israeli governments viewed the resolution of violent conflict as an end-state of sorts, Palestinians viewed the state of abated violence as a mid-point in their struggle. Implied resolution to the Israeli was, to the Palestinian, merely a state of calm before the next storm.

I. INTERVENTION IN GAZA AND THE WEST BANK: 1947–1987

A. The First 20 Years: 1947–1967

Over a five-month period from the end of 1947 and into 1948, the Palestinian Arab community systematically dissolved, ceasing to exist as a stable social and political entity.[1] From the passage of the November 29, 1947, UN Partition Resolution through April 1948, approximately 75,000 Palestinians became refugees. The majority of these were the local Arab elite—teachers, civil servants, public officials, landowners, merchants, doctors, lawyers, and other profession-als. The departure of this leadership class, explains Mark Tessler, "sapped morale, rent the fabric of Palestinian society, and set the scene for an expanding exodus in the months ahead."[2] Though each side blamed the other, both Jews and Arabs shared culpability in the exodus of between 600,000 and 760,000 Palestinians from late-1947 through 1949, as each side at times nudged and cajoled Palestinians to leave or even forcibly evicted the local Arab inhabitants.[3]

The 1948 refugees anticipated returning to their homes in short order. Most had lost nearly everything and were highly dependent on international

assistance. Various organizations established temporary camps and provided food and medical services for the widespread refugee population. In
1950 the UN created the UN Relief and Works Agency (UNRWA) to consolidate and eventually take over all relief efforts. In time, the UNRWA touched
virtually all aspects of Palestinian refugee life as it provided water and sanitation services, and education and social services assistance, in addition to
food and medical support.[4]

The Palestinian diaspora resulted in Palestinian Arabs living throughout
the world. The vast majority, however, fled to areas contiguous to Israel, primarily to Lebanon and Syria and those parts of Palestine held by Jordan and
Egypt. The 140-square mile Gaza Strip was an artificial creation that fell under
Egyptian military control after the 1948 war. Its population more than tripled
as 200,000 refugees joined the 80,000 indigenous inhabitants. Similarly,
Jordan retained control over the 2,100 square mile West Bank after the war and
eventually annexed it in 1950. By the early 1950s, the West Bank's prewar population of approximately 380,000 Palestinians had swollen to over 700,000.
A large percentage of these refugees were absorbed into the West Bank's population or later emigrated from the West Bank to the East Bank. Even so, significant numbers remained in refugee camps constructed in both the East and
West Bank regions.[5] (There were eventually more than 50 camps spread
throughout Lebanon, Syria, Gaza, and the East and West Banks of Jordan.)

In Gaza the Palestinians experienced Egyptian neglect; in the West Bank,
Jordanian discrimination and inattention. Between 1948 and 1967, the primary aim of the Gaza Strip's Egyptian administrators was to limit institution
building or political development, and Gaza's borders were virtually sealed.
Migration was greatly restricted, and the majority of those who did leave were
remnants of the professional class—those with money and resources, education, or skills. Egypt denied the Palestinians citizenship, provided little assistance, and permitted Gaza's economic stagnation. By 1967, eight of ten
Palestinians resided in camps and towns, Gaza's agricultural development
lagged far behind its pre-1948 level, primarily because 90 percent of the
Gaza district's citrus and grain production lands now fell within Israel's borders, and Gaza's per capita GNP was one of the world's lowest, at 80 dollars.[6]
Baruch Kimmerling and Joel Migdal describe how the near-universal poverty
and associated social ills, economic crippling, and heavy dependence on
outside support begun during the era of Egyptian administration—in essence,
the political, economic, and social disfranchisement of the Gaza
Palestinians—created a situation where Gaza represented a new refugee society whose dismal existence portrayed a "permanence of temporariness"—a
condition to which there was no foreseeable end.[7]

Conditions on the West Bank differed somewhat from that of Gaza society. Jordan extended citizenship to Palestinians and viewed itself as the "inheritor of Arab Palestine." It created an educational system that embraced both the East and West Banks, encouraged Palestinian settlement on the East Bank, and provided assistance to Palestinians affected by the 1948 war. At the same time, however, it actively suppressed any hint of a separate Palestinian national identity and discriminated against West Bank residents and refugee camp inhabitants on both banks. The aim was to absorb the most educated, skilled and productive Palestinian elements into Jordanian society and to hold or contain the poorer, less educated and productive Palestinian refugees.

In light of the recurrent risk of war, a policy of Jordanian East Bank economic favoritism was prudent. Thus, Amman applied pressure, or negative incentives, to invest in the East by transferring existing industries, and limiting proposed West Bank ventures. Accordingly, Palestinian capital and manpower migrated to the more favored East Bank. When Jordan annexed the West Bank in 1950, West Bank residents comprised approximately two-thirds of Jordan's total population. Roughly 600,000 Palestinians were added to the 300,000 original Bedouin inhabitants. By 1967, however, the West Bank population made up only 40 percent of Jordan's overall population. Similarly, in 1967 the West Bank accounted for only 35 percent of Jordan's agricultural production and just 20 percent of its industry.[8] While Jordan provided beneficial and lasting direct assistance to the Palestinians from 1948 until 1967, the "inheritor of Arab Palestine" also benefited greatly at the expense of its West Bank cousins.

B. The Second 20 Years: 1967–1987

From an Israeli perspective, defeat of the Arab armies in June 1967 and the concomitant capture of geopolitically and psychologically significant real estate strengthened the security of Israeli citizens and provided promise of international respect and domestic normalcy. The overwhelming victory expanded the security buffer by pushing the borders of Israeli-controlled territory outward. Moreover, the victory reinforced Israel's right to exist, for psychologically and spiritually it forged historical and religious links with its Jewish past.

Prior to June 1967, Arabs and Jews alike commonly viewed the issue of a Palestinian homeland as peripheral to the much larger Arab-Israeli conflict. Six days of warfare changed that. Not only did Israel now occupy new lands, it also controlled over one million Palestinian Arabs who resided in the Gaza Strip, the West Bank, and East Jerusalem. (Israel also captured the Golan Heights from Syria and the Sinai from Egypt.) To some Israelis, control over these new lands, particularly East Jerusalem and the biblical lands of Judea and Samaria (the West Bank), presented the possibility of a geographically larger Israel—an Israel of biblical dimensions. Yet, occupation of these lands also potentially threatened the identity and well—being of the Jewish state. The "Palestinian problem," an external Arab issue during the first 19 years of Israeli statehood, was transformed literally overnight into an internal Israeli concern.[9]

Palestinians experienced conflicting feelings about the results of Israel's 1967 victory. The most obvious were those of catastrophe and loss. The Arab armies, behind which had rest Palestinian hopes for a return to their pre-1948 homes, were in ruins. And Israel now controlled all the territory allocated for Jewish and Palestinian states by the UN in 1947. Yet, there was also a growing realization that the Palestinian future lay in their own hands, not in those of Arab neighbors who had lost another war and had done little to advance Palestinian interests during the previous 20-year period and this led to increased support for the numerous military and political organizations that fell under the PLO umbrella.[10]

In the war's immediate aftermath, the Israeli government annexed East Jerusalem, thereby removing Jerusalem from the pale of any future negotiated settlement. Simultaneously, they implemented a series of policies that continued Jordanian rule over the Palestinians but ensured Israeli physical control over the territories. These policies provided open borders across the Green Line (the border between Israel and the territories) and for movement between Gaza and the West Bank, ease of travel between the East and West Banks, and minimal official Israeli involvement in administering the territories.[11] The Israelis oversaw the establishment of the first Palestinian universities, granted a fair degree of self-governing authority to local leaders, expanded suffrage to women, and oversaw two municipal elections in the 1970s. But the early years of Israeli occupation were not without violence nor were the occupiers as benevolent as the foregoing might suggest. Avenues of protest were virtually nonexistent and armed resistance was brutally crushed. General strikes, demonstrations, violence, and widespread social upheaval in the territories, such as occurred throughout the 1967-1971 period and again in 1973, 1976, and 1982 were forcibly contained. Nationalist sentiments were stifled and the more overt displays met with arrests, deportations, land seizures, and collective punishment, such as business and school closures, curfews, and censorship. Government councils were periodically disbanded and local leaders were arrested or kept under close surveillance by Israeli security forces. Families of suspected Palestinian fighters (or terrorists) were detained or relocated and their homes bulldozed or dynamited.

During this period, most Israeli policies in the occupied territories, many with tacit Jordanian backing, were influenced by political and economic factors designed to prevent the creation of a Palestinian state structure and culture. The logic behind this was twofold. First, Israel's security interests, the dominant reason for the occupation, centered on the territories, not the territories' inhabitants. And second, the Israeli-Palestinian relationship was deliberately a limited one because it was envisioned that any potential solution to the Palestinian problem would operate under a Jordanian framework. So, rather than create economic and social programs to aid the Palestinian population, these considerations underlay policies designed to inhibit nationalist tendencies (a practice that Jordan, whose population was half Palestinian, supported) and to create a better working relationship with Jordan.[12] In the mid-1970s Larry Fabian summarized this largely unstructured economic and political approach:

> Every Israeli cabinet since 1967, while insisting that there will be no return to the June 1967 borders, has decided not to decide the political future of the West Bank and the Gaza Strip. But government policy, including economic policy, was grounded in three understandings. Israel would not formally annex the territories. Israel would not withdraw from them. And Israel would not allow them to become a net budget burden.[13]

The migratory labor situation; the integration of road, electricity, water, and communications networks intended to support Israeli settlements in the territories, but that also benefited the Palestinian inhabitants; the requirement for Palestinian products to arrive or depart through Israeli ports; government subsidies and benefits to Israeli businesses; and Israeli policies prohibiting Palestinian industrial and agricultural developments that competed with Israeli products assured Palestinian dependency on Israel.[14] Gaza and the West Bank were outlets for Israeli products and sources of cheap labor. Israel provided 88 percent of the West Bank's imports in 1980 and received over half of its exports. Five years later, 92 percent of Gaza's imports were from Israel and 82 percent of its exports went to Israel.[15] And by the outbreak of the *Intifada* in 1987, between 107,000 and 120,000 West Bank and Gaza inhabitants—over 40 percent of the territories' work force—was employed in Israel.[16] The natural result of these migratory labor practices, wages from diaspora Palestinians and an expanded power grid, was a considerable rearrangement in the Palestinian standard of living, although interpretations of the overall effect vary. While some observers emphasize the purchase of more consumer goods, access to the electric grid, and improved education and health systems as indicative of a higher living standard,[17] others argue that the Palestinians' deepening dependency on Israel, declining production capacity, lack of infrastructure investment, and overreliance on labor exports displayed critical economic weakness.[18] This was the context for the *Intifada*, the largest and most comprehensive Palestinian uprising to date.

II. THE INTERVENTION CYCLE AND THE *INTIFADA*

A vertical line through the center of the Intervention Cycle divides it into two halves with distinctly different foci. The right half focuses on violence reduction and elimination—the mitigation of conflict. Its outlook is commonly short or near term and is guided by the immediacy of violence, threats, or disorder. The left half emphasizes security and confidence building—the prevention of conflict. Its orientation is long term and seeks to resolve societal differences and prevent future eruptions of violent intergroup conflict. Over the years, many interveners in the Israeli-Palestinian conflict have paid generous lip service to elements contained within the left or prevention half of the cycle, but their actions have largely aligned with the cycle's mitigation half.

Israel is the most obvious protagonist in this right half fixation, but other interveners are similarly narrow in their approaches to intervention. While administering Gaza and the West Bank, neither Egypt nor Jordan actively sought to empower or enfranchise the Palestinians and improve their lot. Remember, the Egyptians sealed off the Gaza Strip for much of the period of Egyptian administration and Jordan stymied Palestinian efforts at nation building—a practice it continued into the Israeli occupation. Similarly, the UNRWA, in providing food, housing, and services, prolonged the dependent, refugee identity by encouraging Palestinians to retain their refugee status. This continued even after many of the camps essentially developed into urban neighborhoods that were fully integrated into the region's economy.[19]

A viable peace process employs a dynamic building approach that involves moving beyond mitigation and into the prevention phase. The resolution arrow (diagrammed on Figure 1) provides the avenue for this transformation from violence to lasting peace. Resolution requires a significant alteration of the status quo—a structural change in the intergroup relationship and an acceptable methodology to resolve the dysfunctional nature of the relationship. It is a complete process requiring uninhibited and equal involvement by the conflict parties. True resolution cannot be imposed. In the context of intergroup conflict intervention in Israel and the territories, resolution typically meant only mitigation. Resolution was not viewed as an ongoing, dynamic process; rather, it was a static endpoint located at about four o'clock on the Intervention Cycle.

The dynamics of resolution were absent for various reasons, but two clearly stand out. First, the Palestinians did not bring anything of real value to the negotiation table. Israel and the other conflict interveners were largely satisfied with their state of affairs; thus, they saw little need to enter fully into negotiations aimed at permanent resolution. The second reason is closely related to the first, as it too pertains to equal negotiating positions. Throughout much of the post-1948 period, the Palestinians lacked a credible negotiator who could command a respected seat at the table. Even after the PLO was recognized at the 1974 Rabat summit as the sole legitimate representative of the Palestinian peoples and Yasir Arafat was accorded special status at the United Nations, much of the world continued to view the PLO as simply a terrorist organization. In the PLO's dual capacity as "sole legitimate representative" and "terrorist organization," the latter was naturally the dominant label; thus, the Palestinians' legitimate representative lacked wider acceptability and credibility. (In the United States, the terrorist label dominated until Arafat denounced terrorism in 1988; in Israel until the 1993 Declaration of Principles.) To the Egyptians, Jordanians, Israelis, and much of the international community, resolution was a tolerable, though unsettled, state of minimal violence where quiescent Palestinians apparently accepted their stateless and nationless status. Though recognizably temporary, resolution—implied resolution—sufficed for the short term, as it kept the Palestinian problem in the background.

Intifada. In February 1988, Yitzhak Rabin admitted to a gathering of Labor Party members that since the start of the *Intifada* three months earlier he had learned "that you can't rule by force over one and a half million Palestinians."[20] Besides serving as a tacit admission that there could never be a Greater Israel that included the West Bank and Gaza, Rabin's statement also emphasized the new visibility of the Palestinian people. For nearly 20 years, the occupied territories of the West Bank and Gaza were viewed in a somewhat paradoxical fashion. On the one hand they were seen as a remote and unpopulated land, and, on the other, almost as if they were an extension of Israel. The Green Line demarcation between the territories and Israel proper was rooted in the older generations' memories as a distant memory and a distant place, but a whole generation of youths and immigrants had grown up viewing the Green Line as a historical concept, not a barrier between two peoples. Consequently, Israelis routinely traversed the territories to reach Jewish settlements or other parts of Israel, to take their automobiles to Palestinian mechanics in the territories, to train at military camps in the West Bank, or to go on group outings.

But just as the Green Line took on an air of invisibility because of the Israelis' regular traversal of the occupied territories and the territories' economic links with Israel, so too did the corporate Israeli outlook toward the Palestinian people. Over the 20-year period leading up to the *Intifada*, the Palestinians had receded from the radar screen of the Israeli political conscience. The Palestinians, to a large extent, became invisible to the Israelis and were far removed from larger Arab-Israeli issues.[21]

While the Israelis may have lost sight of the Green Line, the Palestinians were reminded daily of its presence or status as a psychological, if not a physical, barrier. The tens of thousands of Palestinians who worked in Israel were continually bombarded by the economic, social, and political disparities between the Palestinian and Israeli cultures. Likewise, a generation of Palestinians, the vast majority of the Palestinian population, was born in the period following the 1967 war. They knew firsthand of the indissoluble economic linkages between Palestinians and Israelis—the mutual, but really more one-sided dependency inherent in this relationship—and the proximity of Jews and Arabs in the postwar era. Unknown, and unnecessary in the context of contemporary life, were memories of the harshness of life in the prewar period of Egyptian and Jordanian territorial administration. Through their general historical compliance—an apparent acceptance of their situation—the Palestinians fed into this culture and climate of invisibility. The *Intifada*, however, brought the Green Line back into the Israeli political conscience, and, as a consequence, the Palestinians achieved greater visibility in their own collective eyes.[22]

On December 9, 1987, a series of confrontations spontaneously erupted between Israeli soldiers and Gaza Strip Palestinians. In what became the most protracted incidence of mass militant Palestinian resistance, the popular uprising spread rapidly throughout Gaza and to most of the West Bank and East Jerusalem. The Israeli Defense Force (IDF) was overwhelmed by the scope and intensity of resistance. Curfews, border closures, increased patrols, riot control agents, equipment and weapons, live ammunition, deportations, house demolitions, and school closures—military security tactics and punitive civil measures successfully employed to enforce peace, to achieve implied resolution during the previous 20 years—were ineffectual. Eighteen months into the *Intifada*, even Israel's defense minister was forced to admit that the IDF was unable to depreciate the levels of violence significantly nor to provide an environment that permitted normal governmental functions in the territories.[23]

As noted, the Israeli government focused its efforts on enforcing an unequal peaceful coexistence in the territories during the 20-year occupation leading up to the *Intifada*. Peace making and its attendant nation building efforts, as defined in the lexicon of the Intervention Cycle, were deliberately ignored; in fact, they were illegal. Israeli policies in the territories were primarily designed to maintain a stable Israeli-centered economic, political, and social environment—to advance Israel's national sense of security. In the process, however, these policies minimized the Palestinian sense of security. The *Intifada* was a prolonged overt manifestation of this sense of Palestinian insecurity.

Explanations for the *Intifada* abound, although most center on feelings of deprivation and helplessness. Over 40 years of virtual invisibility and an inability to control or positively influence the Palestinian future exploded in a popular uprising of rage and frustration. The widespread harshness of living conditions in the refugee camps, an overwhelming desire for divestiture of Israeli control, a clear awareness that other Arab countries and the PLO could not solve the Palestinian problem, a downturn in the Gulf Arab oil economy that limited repatriated income to the territories—these and more fueled the fires of rage. In essence, the *Intifada* was a collective protest against Palestinian economic, political, and social disenfranchisement.

The *Intifada* was a political act with far-reaching political and psychological shifts in the territories' resident Palestinian psyche. Two of these shifts stand out. First, residents of the occupied territories had traditionally looked to external actors (Arab states, diaspora Palestinians, or the PLO) to achieve their goals. Erika Alin points out that the uprising occasioned "a shift in the political [center of] gravity" within the Palestinian national movement from the exile community to the West Bank and Gaza resident community. And second, the uprising exemplified a shift in the Palestinian national movement's political position from one focused on "preserving the option of military struggle and liberating all of historic Palestine to a commitment to political negotiations as the exclusive means" of achieving a West Bank and Gaza Palestinian state.[24] These shifts are particularly significant for long term Palestinian developments: the latter as a foundation for Israeli-Palestinian negotiations, and the former for its civil society characteristics.

The *Intifada* exemplified a new social and political empowerment of the resident Palestinian community and a stunning capacity for mass mobilization in the territories. Through its diverse forms, the civil disobedience campaign was a vehicle to support the uprising's more violent aspects. Some elements, particularly the general and commercial sector strikes and Civil Administration employee resignations, were intended to diminish Israel's hold on the territories. The widespread acts of civil disobedience and the spontaneous grass-roots nature of the *Intifada* caught the exile community (especially the PLO leadership) by surprise and permanently changed the relationship between the Palestinians in the territories and the national movement's exile leadership. In order to remain relevant as the unified representative of all Palestinians, the PLO had to respond to resident Palestinian concerns. In Gaza and the West Bank, Palestinians sought an immediate end to the occupation and many implicitly understood that this meant recognizing the state of Israel. The *Intifada*-generated dynamic, where resident Palestinians lead the traditional exile Palestinian leadership, eventually forced the PLO to conform to the residents' goals and ultimately enter into negotiations with Israel.[25]

A key distinction between earlier protest periods and the *Intifada* is the latter's unique political and social character and its unifying tendencies amongst Palestinians of all ages and backgrounds. Participants included virtually the whole of resident Palestinian society and demonstrated a capacity for social cohesion and political mobilization that was absent during the previous years of occupation.[26] The grassroots nature of the "popular committees" that coordinated diverse services and needs for the Palestinian community brought on by both Israeli closures and Palestinian strikes greatly assisted Palestinians in their efforts to disengage from Israel—to reduce their reliance and dependence on Israel for goods and services.

This and other homegrown Palestinian efforts fed into the larger political processes. Erika Alin notes that "it was the uprising's early social cohesion and the political realism of its leadership that enabled the initially spontaneous street demonstrations to be transformed into a coordinated mass movement" of demonstrations and civil disobedience.[27] This is true, but it is also worth noting that the *Intifada's* rapid spread throughout the territories was due in large part to Israel's "iron fist" policies and methods that collectively punished all Palestinians. One author states that "Israel's political establishment declared war against everyone—young and old, rich and poor, women and children," and that the Israeli leadership's decision "to crush the *Intifada* was the crucial factor behind its spread to all sectors of the Palestinian population," thus contributing to the uprising's broad support base.[28] Rabin was correct: the *Intifada* clearly demonstrated that Israel could not rule by force over the Palestinians. Furthermore, the uprising showcased a new generation of Palestinians—one less reticent about provoking change—a generation that aggressively sought empowerment and fundamental change from within the resident Palestinian community and not from without.

III. MOVING THE PEACE PROCESS FORWARD

The September 1993 Declaration of Principles (DOP) is not a peace agreement; rather, it is an agreed framework for negotiating disputed issues in the Israeli-Palestinian conflict. In the DOP, Israel and the PLO agreed that it was time to end the many decades of confrontation and conflict, to "recognize their mutual legitimate and political rights," to "strive to live in peaceful coexistence and mutual dignity and security," and "to achieve a just, lasting and comprehensive peace settlement and historic reconciliation." The DOP laid out a timetable and goals for progressive stages of Palestinian self-rule. The first stage provided limited autonomy in Gaza and Jericho. In the next stage Israel would withdraw and redeploy forces from Palestinian population centers; Palestinians would conduct "direct, free and general political elections" that "constitute a significant interim preparatory step toward the realization of the legitimate rights of the Palestinian people and their just requirements;" and Israel would turn over greater control over civil matters in the occupied territories. Finally, both parties would begin discussions leading to final settlement of the most contentious issues, such as refugees, Jewish settlements, borders, and so on. In line with the 1995 accord (after building additional roads to bypass Palestinian cities and link settlements), Israel did withdraw from portions of the West Bank, and in January 1996 Palestinians held their first ever elections for an executive council and council chairman. However, the subsequent election of Prime Minister Benjamin Netanyahu and the renewed construction of Israeli settlements raised new questions for the resolution timetable.

A. Sliding Along the Resolution Arrow

Von Lipsey's Intervention Cycle provides a template for intergroup conflict resolution and prevention by laying out essential tasks and intermediate objectives for actual or would-be interveners to conflict. In theory, the DOP process partially conformed to this interventionary template by bringing both parties to the table where they agreed to continue talking. In reality, however, both sides continued negotiating during the first few years of the post-DOP period, although only minimal and incremental progress was made toward achieving the euphoric expectations generated by the DOP. The dynamics of resolution were quickly infected with a stasis of sorts, as Palestinians saw their tantalizing journey toward enfranchisement jeopardized by a lack of consensus within the Palestinian and Israeli camps and delays in implementing the DOP's most basic provisions.

This situation largely resulted from the two sides' conflicting goals. Palestinians generally viewed the DOP as simply the first step in achieving statehood. Limited autonomy, to the Palestinian, was limited on two counts. It was limited in the sense that the Israeli government was partially disengaging from the territories, but also in that the disengagement period was limited too. The Palestinian leadership (and many in Israel) believe that implicit in the

Declaration of Principles is eventual independence and a Palestinian state of negotiable dimensions—the details to be worked out in the final stage of the accords when the most conflictual issues are broached. Limited autonomy for Gaza and Jericho was a start point for the Palestinians, but not the endpoint.

On the other hand, many Israelis saw the DOP as "more of the same" with at least two competing, yet related visions of the current peace process. In one vision, the DOP framework was a useful mechanism for disengaging from the most troublesome territory (Gaza) and placating larger Palestinian demands for autonomy. It was a way to grant the Palestinians limited government and some determinative control over their future without creating a separate Palestinian state. In a second vision, Israelis recognized that eventual settlement requires a separate Palestinian state, but there is no requirement to rush into it. While one vision rejects a Palestinian state and the other apparently accepts ultimate Palestinian statehood, they both share a common view of the DOP framework as a means to temporize indefinitely. Though the Declaration of Principles moved the resolution process along somewhat (from four to possibly five o'clock along the resolution arrow), the DOP negotiating framework was more realistically viewed, from the Israeli perspective, as a placatory construct to delay true resolution until some distant future date. In many sectors of Israeli society there existed a form of group denial and a rejection of the imperatives for true resolution to the conflict. Resolution is yet again implied.

B. An Insecurity Dilemma

Violence by Palestinian and Israeli extremists sours the peace process, though to date Palestinian extremist violence has been more planned and orchestrated. Where some viewed the *Intifada*-associated violence as the most likely incentive to move Israel toward seeking real resolution, more recent acts of violence have deliberately targeted the peace process itself. This extremist violence has invited traditional Israeli mitigatory responses and has the potential to affect Israeli outlook on any future Palestinian entity adversely. This was clearly reflected in Israel's initial reaction to the spate of suicide bombings that killed more than 60 people during a nine-day period in February and March 1996. Prime Minister Shimon Peres sealed off the Palestinian West Bank and Gaza, and launched attacks against Hezbollah guerrillas in southern Lebanon as Israelis clamored for increased security from Palestinian terrorism and violence.

At the heart of intergroup conflict lies a sense of group insecurity. Because the concept of "security" is subjective, it is possible that what makes one individual or group feel secure may be insufficient to engender the same sense in another. In fact, it is quite possible that policies that intended to promote security can actually precipitate insecurity.[29] This has been the case in the Israeli-Palestinian conflict.

In some places, the West Bank is only eight miles from the Mediterranean Sea. In the pre-1967 era, this was genuinely seen as a geographical outcropping potentially poised to split the state of Israeli. Similarly, during the 20 years prior to the 1967 war, Israel was repeatedly attacked by Palestinian guerrillas from Jordanian-controlled territory and the Gaza Strip; thus, legitimate national security issues were at stake when Israel captured and retained control over the West Bank and Gaza Strip. Retention of the occupied territories was, in the context of the time, quite properly viewed as a security buffer to protect Israel. Over time, however, national security became less and less a factor for retaining these territories as economic and hegemonic rationales predominated. As explained previously, Israeli policies created such a feeling of security that many Israelis "forgot" the pre-1967 Green Line and looked on the territories as part of Israel.

From the Palestinian perspective, these same Israeli policies exacerbated a long-standing sense of insecurity and anxiety. While conditions did not worsen during the first 20 years of Israeli occupation (in most cases the Palestinian lifestyle was markedly improved over the pre-1967 situation), there was a collective Palestinian perception that others controlled all the Palestinian cards—that they had no way of influencing their environment, either now or in the foreseeable future. As Israel's de facto position of implied resolution took firm root, Palestinian perceived insecurity grew until it exploded in the violence and demonstrations of the *Intifada,* where violence was seen as a legitimate form of protest by many Palestinians.[30] More than a year after the DOP, a significant percentage of Palestinians—in some polls even a majority—still viewed armed violence against Israelis as an appropriate response to the contemporary situation.[31]

These Palestinian attacks understandably increased Israel's sense of insecurity, particularly the randomness associated with car and bus bombings that targeted everyone from Israeli soldiers to Jewish settlers, to Tel Aviv shoppers. Widespread Palestinian cheering and celebration in the wake of deadly attacks against Israeli targets fed into existent negative Israeli perceptions of Palestinians and further bred a sense of insecurity. As a result, many Israelis renewed calls for further Palestinian isolation, which in turn increased the collective Palestinian sense of insecurity; thus, a cycle of violence—and insecurity—was perpetuated. This is the paradoxical mindset that pervaded both Palestinian calls for increased armed attacks against Israelis, and Israeli calls for border fences creating a new Green Line between Israel and the territories.

Other issues feed into the mutual dilemma of insecurity, but two clearly stand out above the rest: the issue of Jewish settlements in Gaza and the West Bank, and Palestinian demographics. Since the 1970s successive Israeli governments supported the creation of Jewish settlements within the 1967 Green Line. Over 120,000 Israelis, or two percent of Israel's population, reside in settlements within the borders of the occupied territories. To Palestinians, this is a continuing manifestation of Israeli dominance and signifies the long-term intention to delay final and fair resolution of the Palestinian problem. To many Israelis, these settlements are rightful extensions of Israel proper—islands within a Greater Israel granted to them by biblical prophets and sanctioned by contemporary Israeli policies. As islands within the occupied territories, settlements are natural targets for armed Palestinians and are thorns in the side of current and future peace processes.

Palestinian demographics also feed into the cycle of insecurity and are a virtual time bomb waiting to explode. Currently, nearly 50 percent of West Bank and Gaza Palestinians are under 14 years old. In 1987, 20 percent of the Palestinian residents of the occupied territories were under five; they will reach adulthood in 2000 or shortly thereafter.[32] These youths, children of the *Intifada* and beyond, will have been raised in a climate that overwhelmingly sanctioned anti-Israeli violence and thrived under the perceived unfulfilled promises contained within the Declaration of Principles. Raised in this environment and facing fewer employment opportunities within the territories and Israel, these children of violence confront an even bleaker adulthood than their parents and the two generations preceding. We see then, that Palestinian insecurity feeds into Israeli insecurity, which feeds back into Palestinian insecurity, and so on. This is the near-term (i.e., years 2000-2003) climate facing Palestinians and Israelis—a breeding ground for maximum intergroup violence such as outlined at the Intervention Cycle's 12 o'clock position.

IV. CONCLUSION

As intervener states and organizations attempt to move the peace process forward, they seek to ensure Israel's security and improve the Palestinians' lot. Central to the latter is the necessity to aid in developing a Palestinian voice and a vision of the future where Palestinians are truly enfranchised socially, economically, and politically. On January 21, 1996, Palestinian elections legitimized a representative leadership and served as a basis and mandate for a future democratic-style Palestinian government. And economically, outside donors are pledging hundreds of millions of dollars for Palestinian development and strong arguments are made for creating a form of free market economic cooperation between Israel, the Palestinians, and Jordan.[33] Yet, in pushing for these reforms, intervening parties overlook one of the key characteristics of the Intervention Cycle.

As explained in an earlier chapter, resolution is a prerequisite step in the path to intergroup violence prevention. This suggests that those elements central to violence prevention (i.e., confidence building, enfranchisement measures, etc.) are mitigated, or even for naught, if true resolution is not first achieved—if there is not a convergence of goals between parties to conflict. So, until and unless agreement is reached on Palestinian autonomy or independence there will not be a true convergence of Palestinian and Israeli goals, and the dissimilar ends sought through the DOP negotiating framework are likely to produce continued frustration and, on some levels, failure. In the interim, the DOP and subsequent implementing agreements will inevitably fall short of the expectations of "success" envisioned by many who witnessed the historic 1993 handshake.

NOTES

1. For a description of the Palestinian displacement and dispersion of this period, see Baruch Kimmerling and Joel S. Migdal, *Palestinians: The Making of a People.* Cambridge, MA: Harvard University Press, 1994, pp. 127-156.
2. Mark Tessler, *A History of the Israeli-Palestinian Conflict.* Bloomington: Indiana University Press, 1994, p. 303.
3. Benny Morris, "The Causes and Character of the Arab Exodus from Palestine: The Israeli Defence Forces Intelligence Branch Analysis of June 1948," *Middle Eastern Studies,* 22, no. 1 (January 1986), pp. 5-19; and Shabtai Teveth, "The Palestinian Refugee Problem and Its Origins," *Middle Eastern Studies,* 26, no. 2 (April 1990), pp. 214-250.
4. For an understanding of the development and continuation of Palestinian refugee camp culture, see Emanuel Marx, "Palestinian Refugee Camps in the West Bank and the Gaza Strip," *Middle Eastern Studies,* 28, no. 2 (April 1992), pp. 281-294.
5. Tessler, *A History . . . ,* p. 465. See also Ann Mosely Lesch and Mark Tessler, *Israel, Egypt and the Palestinians: From Camp David to Intifada.* Bloomington: Indiana University Press, 1989, pp. 225-228.
6. Meron Benvenisti, *The West Bank Data Project.* Washington: American Enterprise Institute, 1984, p. 9.
7. Kimmerling and Migdal, *Palestinians,* pp. 197-201. See also Tessler, *A History . . . ,* p. 401.
8. Terrence M. Tehranian, "The Politics of Israeli Policy in the West Bank," *Middle Eastern Studies,* 19, no. 4 (October 1983), pp. 412-413. See also Kimmerling and Migdal, *Palestinians,* pp. 188-195.

9. Aaron David Miller, "The Arab-Israeli Conflict, 1967-1987: A Retrospective," *Middle East Journal*, 41, no. 3 (Summer 1987), p. 351.

10. Edward Said captured the Palestinian mood of the late-1960s when he wrote: "After 1948 most Palestinian refugees had been obliged to take on the identity of the Arab states to which they came as refugees. In Syria, many became Ba'athists, in Egypt they were Nassarists, and so on. For the first time, after 1967 it became possible not only to become Palestinian again but also to choose Fatah, or the Popular Front, or the Democratic Front as one's movement of choice: each was Palestinian, jealously guarding its own vision of a Palestinian future." *The Politics of Dispossession: The Struggle for Palestinian Self-Determination.* New York: Pantheon, 1994, p. xv.

11. See Tehranian, *Politics of Israeli Policy . . .*, pp. 412-425. Meron Benvenisti refers to the period prior to the 1973 war as "the 'self-conscious' years of Israeli administration," when "Israel saw itself as a quasi-trustee of the territories." *The West Bank Data Project*, p. 10.

12. Shmuel Sandler and Hillel Frisch, *Israel, the Palestinians and the West Bank.* Lexington, MA: Lexington Books, 1984, pp. 58-59.

13. Larry L. Fabian, "Prologue: The Political Setting," in Brian Van Arkadie (Ed.), *Benefits and Burdens: A Report on the West Bank and Gaza Strip Economies Since 1967.* New York: Carnegie Endowment for International Peace, 1977, p. 12. Fabian continues: "Each of these imperatives meant something different for economic policy. The first meant that the territories could be neither treated as if they were fully part of the Israeli economy nor tied to that economy in such ways that would amount to overt 'economic annexation.' The second meant that Israel had to deal somehow with the economic needs of the people in the territories; as long as Israel was holding them, it could not simply be indifferent to their welfare. The third meant that the extent of Israeli economic activities was limited by the finite revenues provided directly or indirectly by the territories themselves, and that this ledger of resources and expenditures—not some overall economic plan—determined the level of Israeli public investment in the territories' economic development."

14. Meron Benvenisti, the former deputy mayor of Jerusalem, summarized Israeli economic policy toward the Palestinians: "We should not develop the economy of the territories, but we should not object to the improvement of the standard of living there. Development would cause competition with Israeli products. By gaining economic independence, subversive elements would achieve political power that would enable them to further their objective: the creation of a Palestinian state—a political and security risk for Israel. A reasonable standard of living can be achieved by employment in Israel, which, on the one hand will increase dependence on Israel and, on the other hand, will diminish national aspirations." *The West Bank Data Project*, p. 12.

15. Tessler, *A History . . .*, p. 523; Sarah Roy, "The Gaza Strip: A Case of Economic De-Development," *Journal of Palestine Studies*, 17, no. 1 (Autumn 1987), p. 75.

16. Kimmerling and Migdal, *Palestinians*, p. 250. See also Joshua Teitelbaum and Joseph Kostiner, "The West Bank and Gaza: The PLO and the *Intifada*," in Jack A.

Goldstone, Ted Robert Gurr, and Farrokh Moshiri (Eds.), *Revolutions of the Late Twentieth Century.* Boulder, CO: Westview Press, 1991, p. 303.

17. See Tessler, *A History* . . . , pp. 524-25; and Benvenisti, *West Bank Data Project,* p. 9.

18. See Tessler, *A History* . . . , pp. 526-27. One author even claims that the Gaza economy is an auxiliary of the larger Israeli economy and has experienced economic *de-development*: "a process which undermines or weakens the ability of an economy to grow and expand by preventing it from accessing and utilizing critical inputs needed to promote internal growth beyond a specific structural level. In Gaza, the de-development of the economic sector, has, over two decades of Israeli rule, transformed that economy into an auxiliary of the state of Israel." Roy, "The Gaza Strip . . . ," p. 56.

19. Marx, "Palestinian Refugee Camps . . . ," pp. 281-94.

20. Quoted in Mark Perry, *A Fire in Zion: The Israeli-Palestinian Search for Peace.* New York: William Morrow, 1994, p. 46.

21. Tessler, *A History* . . . , p.708. See also Ze'ev Schiff and Ehud Ya'ari, *Intifada: The Palestinian Uprising-y-Israel's Third Front.* New York: Simon and Schuster, 1990, pp. 40-41.

22. Palestinian spokesperson Hanan Ashrawi once commented: "I do not think that people believe that we even have a point of view. We have been invisible for so long that that is what we have become: 'the invisible Palestinians.' So because no one would listen to us, the Israelis assumed that we would just disappear. But we have not." Quoted in Perry, *A Fire in Zion,* p. 131.

23. Aryeh Shalev, *The Intifada: Causes and Effects.* Boulder, CO: Westview Press, 1991, pp. 99-122.

24. Erika G. Alin, "Dynamics of the Palestinian Uprising," *Comparative Politics* 26, no. 4 (July 1994), pp. 479-80. See also F. Robert Hunter, *The Palestinian Uprising: A War By Other Means.* Berkeley: University of California Press, 1991, pp. 3-4.

25. Teitelbaum and Kostiner, "The West Bank and Gaza," p. 315.

26. One author groups the uprising's leadership into three categories: (1) the thousands of teenagers and young adults who organized protest activities and self-help "popular committees" to confront specific issues (many of which were exacerbated by the Israeli crackdown) such as food, medical care, education, agriculture, and security; (2) representatives of the four main PLO factions operating in the territories who, two months into the *Intifada,* formed the underground Unified National Leadership of the Uprising (UNLU), which centrally coordinated the uprising and issued communiques and instructions to West Bank and Gaza residents; and (3) Palestinian intelligentsia (journalists, academics, professionals) who mediated between the resident and exile communities, and the international and Israeli media. Ian S. Lustick, "Writing the *Intifada*: Collective Action in the Occupied Territories," *World Politics,* 45 (July 1993), p. 565.

27. Alin, "Dynamics of the Palestinian Uprising," p. 488.

28. Hunter, *The Palestinian Uprising,* p. 88. See also Alin, "Dynamics . . . ," p. 486; and Shalev, *The* Intifada, pp. 100-106.

29. In international relations theory, this situation is viewed within the context of a "security dilemma," where State A takes certain actions to assure its own security (such as building more missiles or tanks) but in the process tends to threaten the security of State B. State B's natural response it to build/deploy more of its own missiles or tanks, but this in turn threatens State A. One state feels compelled to arm itself because of actual or perceived security threats, but in doing so it does not necessarily increase its own security, for its neighbors or rivals also arm. Ultimately, a climate of greater insecurity is bred by the attempt of one party to increase its own security.

30. In one survey Palestinians were asked to identify the primary cause of Palestinian violence. In response, 83 percent stated that violence resulted from the struggle for self-determination. Less than nine percent attributed Palestinian violence to poor conditions and harsh measures taken against them. Mohammed Shadid and Rick Seltzer, "Political Attitudes of Palestinians in the West Bank and Gaza Strip," *Middle East Journal*, 42, no. 1 (Winter 1988), p. 21.

31. In an October 1994 poll conducted by the Center for Palestinian Research and Studies in Nablus, 28.6 percent of West Bank respondents, and 38.8 percent of Gaza respondents supported "the continuing resort of some Palestinian factions to armed operations against Israeli targets in Gaza and Jericho." See excerpts in *Journal of Palestine Studies*, 24, no. 2 (Winter 1995), pp. 147-148. A January 1995 Palestinian Center for Public Opinion poll suggested that increasing percentages of West Bank Palestinians support armed violence against Israelis. In the survey, 57 percent of respondents said that they approved of the Beit Lid suicide bombing. Cited in Barton Gellman, "As Violence Grows, Palestinians and Israelis Lose Enthusiasm for Peace Accord," *The Washington Post*, January 31, 1995, p. A17.

32. See Alon Ben-Meir, "Israelis and Palestinians: Harsh Demographic Reality and Peace," *Middle East Policy*, 2, no. 2 (1993), pp. 74-86, and also Michael C. Hudson (Ed.), *The Palestinians: New Directions*. Washington, DC: Georgetown University, 1990, p. 261.

33. See, for instance, Stanley Fischer, Leonard J. Hausman, Anna D. Karasik, and Thomas C. Schelling (Eds.), *Securing Peace in the Middle East: Project on Economic Transition*. Cambridge, MA: MIT Press, 1994.

CHAPTER 8

At the Crossroads: Nagorno-Karabakh

Susan Ellingwood

> *"The U.S. government doesn't have a clue how to solve most of the world's ethnic conflicts, and never will. The expertise, leverage, and political will simply doesn't exist . . . "*
> PETER W. RODMAN[1]

While this pessimistic view of ethnic conflict may contain an element of truth, it should not be the guiding premise in determining U.S. foreign policy. When opportunities for intervention engage our strategic, humanitarian, economic, or political interests—and when a framework for conflict intervention such as the Intervention Cycle presents itself as a plausible guide by which to shape that intervention—those opportunities should not be squandered.

Far away, on the periphery of U.S. interests, a violent, bloody war has raged for nearly eight years in the former Soviet republics of Armenia and Azerbaijan. This war over possession of the tiny enclave of Nagorno-Karabakh has transformed a potentially prosperous, oil-rich region into perhaps one of the greatest tragedies of present-day Eurasia. Nagorno-Karabakh lay in the Caucasus region, the strategic crossroads between Islam and Christianity. Lacking high levels of international attention and partisan willingness to resolve the situation peacefully, the region has been locked in a brutal stand-off with a history of deep-rooted animosity among the players.

Susan Ellingwood is an Assistant Editor at *The New Republic*. Previously Ms. Ellingwood worked in the Washington bureau of *The New Yorker*, served as a Consultant to the Special Assistant to the President and the Secretary of State, and worked for the Council on Foreign Relations in Washington, D.C. and New York. She was educated at Dickinson College and Oxford University and has written on foreign and domestic policy, including U.S. policy toward Russia and the former Soviet Union.

The conflict over Nagorno-Karabakh is representative of many highly charged, emotional struggles of nationality, ethnicity, and territory. It is an interesting case study within which to examine the Intervention Cycle for a variety of reasons:

- Nagorno-Karabakh highlights the dangers of a false political, economic, and social enfranchisement in a state where inter-group conflict was kept in check with physical and ideological deterrence and coercion by the Soviets;
- it demonstrates that violence can erupt when those pressures are released in the absence of enfranchising mechanisms;
- it underscores the premise that early intervention, though not often exercised, is most cost effective, both in financial and in human terms;
- it reveals the inefficacy of peacekeeping attempts when violent conflict has not been mitigated;
- it shows that in the absence of a forcible mitigation mechanism, stalemate—or *battle fatigue*—may be the only impetus for bringing conflicting parties to the negotiating table;
- and finally, it highlights the point that in order to resolve the conflict in Nagorno-Karabakh, the previously existing status quo must be changed.

Nagorno-Karabakh provides a test case for hope in effective intervention. While the conflict is far from being resolved, the path toward breaking the cycle might be found by examining the situation through the lens of the Intervention Cycle.

I. BACKGROUND

The primary players in the conflict over Nagorno-Karabakh are the Armenians and the Azeris. It has been the home of Armenian and Turkic communities for almost 1000 years. A mountainous region, Nagorno-Karabakh is an agriculturally dependent economy and was at one time a renowned producer of wine. The headwaters of the river that flows through Baku, the capital of Azerbaijan, are located in Nagorno-Karabakh. Therefore, control of this region is very important to the Azeris.[2]

Armenia is an ancient nation formed nearly 2,300 years ago. The Armenians, a largely urban and service-oriented population, are predominately Christians and are closely tied to their western neighbors, particularly the Russians. In contrast, Azerbaijan did not exist as a separate people until the twentieth century. The Azeris, a primarily rural and peasant population, are Muslim with close ties to Iran and Turkey.

Both Armenians and Azeris have strong memories of slights and attacks against one another. The defining event for the Armenians was the 1915 genocide of Armenians by the Turks, creating a diaspora community not dissimilar to that of the Jewish diaspora, with deep animosity toward the Turks. The Armenians refer to this massacre as their holocaust and feel slighted because their suffering has not received the same public attention as the Jewish holocaust. In contrast, the defining moment for the Azeris was their assumption of control over their own territory and legitimization as a people by the Soviet Union—and the international community.

II. ALONG THE PATH TO VIOLENCE

A. Deterrence

The Soviets, under Joseph Stalin, manipulated the borders of Armenia and Azerbaijan to territorialize and politicize nationality. Stalin purposefully created minority pockets within borders to insure that these minority groups would be dependent on Moscow for protection. In the case of Armenia and Azerbaijan, Stalin created a largely Armenian (70 percent of the population were Christian Armenians) Nagorno-Karabakh Autonomous Oblast within and under Azerbaijan control, and an Azerbaijan Nakhichevan Autonomous Soviet Socialist Republic surrounded by, but not under, Armenian rule.[3] Soviet communism created a false atmosphere of political, economic, and social enfranchisement bound together under one roof for the greater good of communism. For years, the Soviets were able to deter violence by keeping the hostilities between Armenians and Azeris in check through various laws, secret police, and communist policies.

B. Coercion

During the waning days of the Soviet Union, Mikhail Gorbachev's policies toward the Soviet republics exacerbated the roots of the historical animosities between Armenians and Azeris. First, Gorbachev's anti-alcohol campaign led to the destruction of vineyards in Nagorno-Karabakh and threw thousands of ethnic Armenians out of work. This prompted the government of Armenia to extend protection to their brethren living in Nagorno-Karabakh.[4] Second, Gorbachev, without a considerable amount of thought but desperate to prevent ethnic tensions from exploding, strongly hinted that he would give the

Nagorno-Karabakh Autonomous Oblast (NKAO) to Armenia. This naturally angered the Azeris. They responded in February 1988, by killing and torturing more than 100 Armenians living in Azerbaijan. This forced Gorbachev to renege on any consideration of giving the NKAO to Armenia, which in turn upset the Armenians and led the Armenian Radical Karabakh Movement to demand control over the NKAO. These events led to the forced migration of nearly 170,000 Azeris from Armenia and an equal number of Armenians from Azerbaijan.

Gorbachev, dealing with his own problems at home, refused to use force against the Azeris who were reportedly carrying out pogroms in major cities, blockading rail lines from Baku to Yerevan, and threatening to use violence if the Russians attempted to intervene in their blockade. Gorbachev's reluctance to intervene forcibly sent a message that violent resistance could bring about the desired results.

In terms of the Intervention Cycle discussion, there was no enfranchising mechanism among the minority groups within Armenia and Azerbaijan; therefore, deterrence was not an effective, long-term tool in preventing violence. Furthermore, as the parties to the conflict came closer and closer to the outbreak of widespread violence, there was no Russian commitment forcibly to coerce the parties into some kind of stability.

By the time the Soviet Union collapsed, there was no stopping the conflict. Violence among the Armenians, Azeris, and Karabakhis erupted. Russia was dealing with so many internal problems that it did not have time to concern itself with the situation in all of the former Soviet republics; further, the international community failed to realize the degree of volatility within the former Soviet republics. In their excitement over the demise of Soviet communism, the international community did not recognize the need for intervention mechanisms, by way of political development and economic support, nor even the magnitude of the conflict in time to prevent bloodshed.

C. Violence

The Soviet-imposed structure of this region has always contributed to the hostility between the Armenians and Azeris. The region was waiting to break out into full conflict as soon as the lid of communism was lifted. Violence is generally thought to have begun with the massacre in Sumgait, Azerbaijan, in February 1988, when the Azeris killed and tortured more than 100 ethnic Armenians. In the military confrontation that ensued, the Azeri forces succeeded in encircling and capturing 40 percent of Nagorno-Karabakh before being stopped seven miles from Stepanakert, the capital of Nagorno-Karabakh.[5] The resulting Karabakh War—to which the conflict is often referred—escalated with little attention from the West and virtually no serious attempts at outside mediation. The dynamics of the fighting shifted over the years with each side taking turns in holding the lead over the other.

At this writing, the war has left over 20,000 Azeris, Armenians, and Karabakhis dead, as heavily armed forces on both sides have waged war with tanks, artillery, rockets, and combat aircraft.[6] It is interesting to note that previous violence in the region had been restricted to localized feuds. Violence was generally limited by the high financial cost of war, the absence of modern weaponry, and a lack of coordinated command structure. In the waning days of the Soviet Union, however, Gorbachev unintentionally armed the Armenians and Azeris through a policy of training military preinductees in their hometowns; this provided them weapons for training and gave them an identity and esprit de corps.[7] In no place was this more evident than among the Karabakh forces.

In mid-1992, Karabakh forces broke through Azeri lines at Lachin and established a partial land corridor between Armenia and Nagorno-Karabakh. This corridor allowed the transfer of weapons and ammunitions from Armenia to Nagorno-Karabakh with the support of the Armenian diaspora.[8] Following a Karabakh offensive in the spring of 1993, a full-length corridor (commonly referred to as the Lachin Corridor) was established. Since that time, the Karabakhis, with support from Armenia, have pressed the offensive, routed the Azeri military, and pushed their forces deep into Azeri territory. As a result, the Karabakh forces have secured full control over Nagorno-Karabakh and currently occupy nearly one-quarter of what was previously Azerbaijan.[9] Although Armenia has undoubtedly provided significant support to these forces, it has generally avoided direct involvement in the fighting. Rather, the war is primarily controlled by Karabakh leaders who have become increasingly independent of their Armenian brethren.

In mid-1993, the Azeri army took advantage of a three-month cease-fire to rebuild and regroup; it planned a major offensive aimed at retaking lost ground and preventing Karabakh forces from completing a southward drive to the Iranian border. Despite the commitment of enormous numbers of ground troops and renewed aerial bombardment of Stepanakert and other Karabakh cities, the December, 1993, offensive quickly stalled, returning the situation to an uneasy status quo.

Military offenses in Nagorno-Karabakh led to the displacement of over 500,000 Azeri, Karabakhi, and Armenian civilians. These refugees—plus more than half a million homeless Armenians displaced by a 1988 earthquake in Armenia—have created a major political, economic, and humanitarian disaster in the region.[10] The capture of Azeri energy resources by Karabakh forces have eased the conditions inside Nagorno-Karabakh while contributing to economic and political turmoil in Azerbaijan. Despite an Azeri blockade of humanitarian supplies and heating oil shipments to Armenia, Armenia was one of the few members of the Commonwealth of Independent States (CIS) to experience economic growth in 1995. This was largely achieved by considerable budget tightening and support from the Armenian diaspora.

It is interesting to note that the devastating earthquake in Armenia demonstrates how, as pointed out in the Intervention Cycle discussion in Chapter 1, natural disasters can contribute to or heighten intergroup conflict. In the case of Armenia, the international community tried to respond with humanitarian aid for the earthquake victims, but due to the Azeri blockade, little aid was able to get through to the victims. This further contributed to the social upheaval in the region, ratcheted up Armenian anger with the Azeris, and heightened Armenia's frustration with the lack of international support.

III. EFFORTS TOWARD MITIGATION

The international community seems to have opted out of the peace enforcement option—the first phase of the mitigation process on the Intervention Cycle. In order to avoid this phase and move directly into an environment suitable for peacekeeping, consent among all parties to the conflict is required. Until the summer of 1994, attempts at peacekeeping failed; the parties to the conflict were not yet prepared to pursue their political objectives through means other than the use of force.

One of the early attempts at intervention in Nagorno-Karabakh was made by the Minsk Group, created by the Conference on Security and Cooperation in Europe (CSCE) in the early 1990s. The CSCE was then seen as the ideal group to attempt intervention because it posed no military threat; included all the states of Europe, North America, and the former Soviet Union on an equal basis; and utilized consensus procedures to assure credibility.[11] The CSCE hosted a peace conference in Minsk in order to discuss the Karabakh War; that conference led to the creation of a standing Minsk Group. The purpose of the Minsk Group was to bring all the parties to the conflict to the table for face-to-face negotiations; to agree on a cease-fire with CSCE-sponsored international monitoring; to provide for stabilizing measures such as humanitarian assistance, refugee aid, and blockade removal; and to reach a negotiated agreement on the political status for Nagorno-Karabakh.

The well-intentioned CSCE mission has been mostly unsuccessful for a variety of reasons:

- First, there has been a lack of sustained high-level Western interest in resolving the conflict. It thus lacked military power, economic capital, and political suasion with which to influence the partisans.
- Second, the Minsk Group/CSCE process tended to be disorganized and cumbersome.
- Third, when Sweden took over the chairmanship of the Minsk Group from Italy in the fall of 1993, the U.S. role was marginalized. U.S. participation in the formal CSCE negotiations lent legitimacy to the process. Italy's adoption of a shuttle-diplomacy concept for Minsk Group activities resulted in the elimination of many of the meetings in which the United States and Russia had been actively engaged.
- Finally, a heated debate within the United States on the entire issue of peacekeeping muted enthusiasm for deeper involvement in this far-away conflict.

Most importantly, however, the Minsk Group failed because the Armenians, Azeris, and Karabakhis still found objectives (mainly territorial) to pursue by force and were not prepared to begin the negotiation process in earnest until recently.

A parallel attempt at mitigation occurred through the Black Sea Consortium. The Consortium was designed with the hope that economic cooperation alone would lead to a peaceful settlement. As a leader in the Black Sea Consortium, Turkey (a state with close ties to the Azeri community) decided to establish a regular forum for Armenian-Turkish consultation by including Armenia in its Consortium. In late 1991, Turkey reached a tentative agreement with Armenia on building port facilities in the Black Sea port of Trabzon that were linked by road into Armenia.[12] This agreement would have improved Turkish relations with Armenia and opened up a dialogue that may have helped foster discussion of past disputes. It would also have opened a back channel for dialogue between Armenia and Azerbaijan through Turkey.

There was so much hope for the efforts of the Black Sea Consortium that Armenian President Ter Petrosyan reportedly requested that the American-Armenian community moderate its anti-Turkish rhetoric.[13] All of this hopeful cooperation fell through in late 1991 and early 1992 as Armenian-Azeri military action intensified.

As prospects for CSCE success through the Minsk Group dwindled, Russia began to engage in unilateral efforts to mitigate the conflict over Nagorno-Karabakh. These activities were able to broker a cease-fire that has remained in place since May 1994. While other cease-fires have failed, this one seems to be holding with only occasional outbreaks of violence—and these appeared to be highly localized.

One reason for this apparent cease-fire success may be battle fatigue. There is a sense of weariness among the Karabakhis; they seem to have reached a limit to the amount of territory that they can physically control—or deem necessary. Likewise, the Azeris appear unable to mount a potent offensive and are additionally burdened by an internal refugee crisis. The impact of battle fatigue is not to be taken lightly: in this case it may be the single factor enabling the establishment of a peacekeeping force in the region. Battle fatigue, and a sense that continued violence lacks fruitful gain, has served as a mechanism for peace enforcement and allowed the possibility of movement into the peacemaking phase and conflict resolution.

The increasingly prominent role that Russia has played in the region, absent the international community, while commendable is also a cause for alarm. The Russians have offered to send CIS peacekeeping forces to the region. However, in light of the Russian attack on Chechnya, the Armenians, Azeris, and Karabakhis are naturally concerned about Russia's long-term intentions. Many experts believe that Russia is primarily interested in Azerbaijan's agreement with a consortium of western oil companies that projects a total investment of $8 billion in Baku oil fields, and may be trying to reestablish control over what it sees as its sphere of influence.[14] Furthermore, Russia is regarded as harboring an anti-Azeri (read, Muslim) bias and has been accused of selling arms to Armenia. There is reason to believe that Russia was behind an attempt to overthrow the government of Azeri President Gaidar Aliyev and the assassination of two high government officials in Baku while President Aliyev was in the United States celebrating the signing of the oil deal in the fall of 1994.[15] Many believe that the Russians were upset with President Aliyev, a former KGB general and Communist Party boss, for signing the contract against their wishes.

Russia's role in Nagorno-Karabakh's conflict demonstrates that intervention is not always benign. Since Russian intervention may not necessarily be for purely humanitarian reasons, Turkey's role as an ally to the Azeris becomes ever more important. Turkish support acts as a counterbalance to any harmful or bias tendencies that Russian troops may have toward Azeris. Further, as major international powers and neighbors to both Armenia and Azerbaijan, Russia and Turkey play important roles in assuring and legitimizing the facilitation of mitigative and resolutionary mechanisms.

At the CSCE Summit in Hungary in December 1994, with support of both Washington and Moscow, members decided to strengthen the CSCE. In order to give the institution more permanence and weight, the name was changed to the Organization on Security and Cooperation in Europe (OSCE). Further, the OSCE agreed to send its own peacekeeping mission to Nagorno-Karabakh. In Washington, the Clinton administration subsequently supported the proposal to send a 3,000-member multinational peacekeeping force to the region.[16] Moscow, who was responsible for brokering the unofficial cease-fire, was unhappy with the prospect of forces other than its own dominating the mission. The apparent willingness, however, of the international community to commit to a multilateral peacekeeping force was diminished by subsequent events in Bosnia and Chechnya.

The OSCE decision to send a multinational force will be a key test of the viability of an internationally controlled peacekeeping force, and could give the OSCE a meaningful post–cold war conflict resolution role. Naturally, the mission of the multinational forces depends on whether the cease-fire remains in effect. Further, the composition of the force needs to be ironed out not only between OSCE members and Russia, but also with Turkey, since Armenia has objected to Turkey's participation in the peacekeeping mission. At the time of this writing, OSCE-sponsored peace talks, while continuing, have been temporarily stalled by the Azeri government, which is willing to offer autonomy but not the independence upon which the Karabakhis insist.

Due to the ethnic, territorial, political, and economic components of the conflict in Nagorno-Karabakh, resolution requires the support of all regional players, to include Armenia, Azerbaijan, Turkey, Iran, Russia, and the United States. However, actual resolution can only be achieved by the parties directly affected by the conflict: the Armenians, Azeris, and the Karabakhis. Yet, neither Armenia nor Azerbaijan, at this stage, has the necessary political, judicial, and economic mechanisms fully in place to run their own governments effectively. The 1995 elections in Armenia and Azerbaijan give hope that democracy will prevail, as both were deemed generally free—but not necessarily fair—by outside observers. Both countries are still defining their own sense of nationhood and mechanisms of enfranchisement.

That said, it is also difficult to imagine Nagorno-Karabakh standing on its own as a viable state. Yet, Robert Kocharyan, the president of the self-declared Republic of Nagorno-Karabakh is playing an increasingly prominent role in OSCE negotiations. The Karabakhis have clearly defined themselves as an independent force in this conflict.

The Outside Players. The equity of the outside players in this conflict appears to have developed as follows:

(1) Turkey. Turkey wants a swift and enduring peace; yet despite their Muslim ties, Turkey is unlikely to support Azerbaijan unconditionally because

it fears being cut off from the West.[17] Turkey has made some effort to show
Armenia that it can be a trusted ally, however it is unlikely that Armenia will
ever fully trust Turkey because of its long history of distrust. In the spring of
1995, Turkey made overtures toward opening a border crossing with Armenia;
however, heavy pressure from the Azeri government forced Turkey to postpone those plans indefinitely. It is even more unlikely that the Armenian diaspora, Armenia's major source of support outside the region, will ever allow
Armenia to develop close ties with Turkey. However, the drain of nearly six
years of fighting has fragmented the Armenian diaspora between those willing to accept compromise and those supporting continued war as a means to
regain lost Armenian territory.

Further, Turkey appears unwilling to accept the mantle of mediator
because the inherent compromises could undercut their influence in other
Muslim former Soviet republics. Turkey also has political problems within the
international community. Within the OSCE membership, Turkey has been
criticized on issues of human rights—particularly on the Kurdish minority
issue.[18] Turkey has expressed interest in participating in an OSCE multinational force; however, in light of Armenia's reservations the weight of their participation remains tentative.

(2) Iran. Iran, though an important player in this region, has been marginalized by the Western players. On one hand, Iran is afraid that an
Azerbaijan separatist movement could develop within their own borders
should Baku achieve significant gains in the resolution of this conflict. On the
other hand, Iran knows that a defeat of Azerbaijan by Armenia would undercut its ability to influence Central Asia.[19] Iran will likely be reluctant to work
with the OSCE because it is a Western institution. Moreover, it is unlikely that
the OSCE—or, more specifically, the United States—will allow Iran to play a
highly significant role. However, Iran's geostrategic role in the region makes
it an important participant in regional solutions to this conflict.

(3) Russia. Russia also wants a quick and peaceful settlement in the
region. Russia's principle concern has been that the violence in the region
could spread north. Initially, Russia's domestic problems made it hesitant to
intervene in the conflict. With the failure of the Minsk Group, however,
Russia has not only taken the lead by brokering a cease-fire in Nagorno-
Karabakh, it has been one of the leading proponents of sending a multinational (albeit Russian-dominated) OSCE peacekeeping force into the region.

There are lingering doubts of Russia's neutrality. Regional history shows
that Russia would tend to intervene on the side of the Armenians. The
Armenians would naturally welcome Russian involvement in the region;
however, the Azeris would be rightfully hesitant. Further, the December 1994

Russian attack on Chechnya has made it difficult for the international community to trust Russia's intentions. One cannot help but question whether Russia can fill the leadership position in a peacekeeping force for Nagorno-Karabakh after the disaster in Chechnya. In the spring of 1996, however, President Yeltsin called for a peace agreement for Nagorno-Karabakh with the hope of improving his image and chances for reelection.

(4) United States. The United States would like to see the region reach a peaceful settlement but is reluctant to invest in efforts to ensure a settlement. While the Clinton administration supported an OSCE-led multinational peacekeeping force, the U.S. government remains engaged in an introspective review of multinational peacekeeping efforts. Furthermore, deficit-reduction measures, defense spending reviews and election-year politics, at the time of this writing, make it doubtful that the conflict over Nagorno-Karabakh will receive a high priority in the American security debate.

In March of 1996, the Clinton administration, even while preoccupied with other international events, particularly the enforcement of the Dayton Peace Accords in Bosnia, sent Deputy Secretary of State Strobe Talbott and Deputy National Security Adviser Sandy Berger to Azerbaijan and Armenia to discuss a peaceful resolution to the conflict. As a result of a subsequent summit in Moscow during April 1996, a communiqué was issued from Luxembourg by the presidents of Azerbaijan and Armenia calling for a continuation of the cease-fire, the release of POWs and hostages, and the intensification of direct dialogue between the parties. The time remains ripe for successfully breaking the cycle of conflict in Nagorno-Karabakh while the parties appear willing to seek resolution at the negotiating table rather than on the battlefield.

IV. THE PATH TO RESOLUTION

Even with a cease-fire in place, resolution in Nagorno-Karabakh will take time to develop because of deep-seated animosity and distrust, both inside and outside the region. The international community and the parties to the conflict will have to remain committed to the process. Presently, few appear willing to do so. In fact, it may be the case that several members of the international community have an interest in excluding, or diminishing the influence of some other.

With the cease-fire in place, battle fatigue on both sides, an OSCE-led multinational force being formed, and the economic interests of Western oil companies keeping Nagorno-Karabakh in the glow of Western interest, there is some hope that peace can be kept and humanitarian relief efforts can begin. The time for peaceful resolution, however, may not be unlimited. As of this writing, some of the internal players are under pressure from their own people to move in a direction that does not make resolution possible. The Karabakhis want full independence and the Azeris are only willing to grant them autonomy. Neither side seems willing to negotiate on this issue. While mitigation can be imposed by external forces, the resolution process must include and engage the interests of the Armenians, Azeris and Karabakhis. Thus, for the cycle of Nagorno-Karabakh's violence to be broken, strong, cooperative, leadership must be exercised by those who choose to intervene. At this point in time, it appears that Russia and the United States are best positioned to take the lead in keeping the parties on the path toward resolution.

The Intervention Cycle discussion indicates that for the conflict to be truly resolved, it is likely that the current status quo will have to change. The Armenians, the Karabakhis, and the Azeris must draw up an agreement that is generally inclusive, rather than exclusive, of each other's needs. The current system of ethnic enclaves has proven itself untenable; thus efforts toward resolution must include politically and economically enfranchising mechanisms as a basis. Some of these may include minority and religious rights protection, proportional representation architectures, a common legal system, land distribution and use agreements, transit rights, revenue sharing, and free trade areas.

The United States has proposed a plan by which Azerbaijan would grant Nagorno-Karabakh the status of an "autonomous state" with its own executive, parliament, armed forces, and legal authority. The Karabakhis and Armenians would in turn agree to withdraw from 20 percent of the Azerbaijan territory that they now occupy. Under this proposed plan, the Lachin Corridor would be placed under the control of an international peacekeeping force. However, the problem with this proposed plan, in light of the Intervention Cycle discussion, is that it does not fundamentally change Nagorno-Karabakh's status as an ethnic enclave disenfranchised from its parent state. Therefore, it is unlikely to ensure an end to the conflict in the long run.

Each one of these states has shown itself worthy of independence during the Karabakh War. The Karabakh forces, have been able to conquer significant parts of what was formerly Azerbaijan. While it seems that perhaps some of the Azeri territory that the Karabakhis have conquered should be returned, the Karabakhis have certainly proven their determination to keep the Lachin Corridor. Issues of land possession, however, are always the most wrenching and difficult.

Most importantly then, regional stability requires Armenia, Nagorno-Karabakh, and Azerbaijan to establish some formal mechanism of political engagement. Perhaps, the three separate states will eventually reach an accord under a loose Armenian-Azerbaijan federation agreement. This may seem far-fetched, and may indeed be impossible in light of the animosity that currently exists between the states. However, if the cycle of regional ethnic and religious conflict is truly to be broken, there must be a fundamental and politically enfranchising change to the status quo.

While the concept of an Armenian-Azerbaijan federation may seem surprising, the Intervention Cycle leads us to consider methods by which to maximize the political, economic, and social enfranchisement of groups and individuals who are parties to the conflict. With the sticking points of territorial borders and free movement eliminated, the Karabakh, Azerbaijan, and Armenian governments could gradually begin to consider and adopt policies that would help politically, economically, and eventually socially enfranchise the people of each state within a viable Armenian-Azerbaijan nation. Only a change in the equities of ethnic and religious affiliation versus membership in an enfranchising polity can completely break the cycle of violent conflict. "We have a tremendous opportunity that unfortunately *remains* an opportunity," remarked a Western diplomat in Baku recently.[20] Many worry that this deadlock will be broken only by resumed fighting.[21]

NOTES

1. Peter W. Rodman, "Points of Order," *National Review,* May 1, 1995, p. 36.
2. Paul A. Goble, "Coping with the Nagorno-Karabakh Crisis," *The Fletcher Forum,* 16, no. 2, (Summer 1992), p. 19.
3. Michael Specter, "Armenians Suffer Painfully in War, but with Pride and Determination," *The New York Times,* July 15, 1994, p. A3.
4. Paul A. Goble, "Coping . . . ," p. 21.
5. Caroline Cox and John Eibner, "Leverage Beneath the Caspian," *International Herald Tribune,* November 21, 1994, p. 7.
6. Carey Goldberg, "Hopes Rise in Hapless Azerbaijan," *Los Angeles Times,* September 13, 1994, p. A1.
7. Paul A. Goble, "Coping . . . ," p. 22.
8. Kate Alderson, "Upsurge of Fighting Puts End to Hopes of Karabakh Peace Deal," *The London Times,* October 27, 1993, p. 12.
9. Lally Weymouth, "The Azerbaijan Question," *International Herald Tribune,* November 21, 1994, p. 7.
10. Florence Avakian, "The Armenian Quake: Still Much To Do," *The Christian Science Monitor,* July 26, 1989, p. 18.
11. John J. Maresca, "An Important Role for the Evolving CSCE: Preventative Diplomacy," *International Herald Tribune,* August 23, 1994, p. 6.
12. Graham E. Fuller and Ian O. Lesser with Paul B. Henze and J. F. Brown, *Turkey's New Geopolitics: From the Balkans to Western China.* Boulder: Westview Press, 1993, p. 79.

13. Ibid., p. 79. American-Armenian lobbyists in the United States had been a vocal group and had been effective in destroying previous attempts at negotiations. It is interesting to note the influence of the American-Armenian community that shows that external effects on negotiations and not necessarily benign actors can play a destructive role in conflict intervention and destroy prospects for peace and, perhaps, what is best for the region.

14. Jim Hoagland, "Russia Still Playing the Great Game," *The Washington Post,* September 27, 1994, p. A21.

15. Lally Weymouth, "The Azerbaijan Question," p. 7

16. Jane Perlez, "Unease at European Security Parley," *The New York Times,* December 5, 1994, p. A13.

17. Paul A. Goble, "Coping . . . ," p. 23.

18. Ibid., p. 24.

19. Ibid.

20. Daniel Sneider, "Ethnic Conflict in Ex-Soviet Region Keeps Riches Out of Reach," *The Christian Science Monitor,* June 1, 1995, p. 7.

21. Ibid., p. 7.

CHAPTER 9

El Salvador and the Intervention Cycle

Kirk Kraeutler

The defining event in the history of El Salvador this century was a communist insurrection. A band of intellectuals, for the most part artisans who were hardly better off than the peasants who worked the fields, devised a naive plan to seize weapons from military garrisons and distribute them to "the masses." The military caught wind of the plot and brutally put it down even before it had begun. Between 10,000 and 30,000 Salvadorans were killed in a matter of days. One communist who survived those days later recalled, "The vultures were the best fed creatures of the year in El Salvador, they were fat with shiny feathers like never before and, fortunately, never since." [1] That was 1932.

Nearly 50 years later, the country was again convulsed by violence between the military and a communist "liberation front" named for the very revolutionary, Farabundo Marti, who had led the same fight a half-century before. The civil war of the 1980s killed another 75,000 Salvadorans—in a country the size of Massachusetts and with a population of about 4.5 million. That war was the second act of a conflict that had simmered since 1932, and one that had its roots in a colonial history that long preceded even that year. How then, in 1992, did the sides stop fighting? Will that peace, brokered by the United Nations in a series of accords, succeed in finally breaking El Salvador's cycle of violence? Or is it but a pause in the life of a country that has a chronically sad history.

Using the Intervention Cycle, El Salvador makes for an important study in why some international efforts may succeed in breaking persistent cycles of

Kirk Kraeutler is a staff editor at the foreign desk of *The New York Times*. He was previously Associate Editor of Foreign Affairs, where he is a member of the Board of Advisors. He is a graduate of Columbia University's School for International and Public Affairs and has written occasional articles on international affairs.

violence and why others may fail. Having straddled the end of the cold war, El Salvador's civil war represents both a cold war conflict and an early post–cold war peace. The Intervention Cycle is helpful in understanding why the change that occurred in the international environment after 1989 made such a difference in finally ending El Salvador's war. It reveals much about the climate in which international peace efforts will take root and when the parties to a conflict may finally be willing to stop fighting and negotiate a peace.

The Intervention Cycle also helps illuminate the various types of intervention that El Salvador both suffered and benefited from during its 12 years of war. Some of those who intervened acted almost as distant parties to the war. Others provided the kind of benign, neutral intervention that the Intervention Cycle presumes. The model helps demonstrate that difference. Moreover, those outside parties, especially the United Nations, used an array of tools—from aid to peacemaking and then peacekeeping—to penetrate Salvadoran society at various times and to varying degrees. The model also helps make distinct these types and levels of intervention and when they occurred.

Most important, the Intervention Cycle helps in assessing the success of the UN accords. Those accords are routinely cited as one of the great success stories of international intervention. El Salvador's war wound down in the cold war's last gasp, one that helped resuscitate the UN and that breathed such overreaching ambition into many of its future missions. It is thus important to understand precisely at what and why the UN succeeded in El Salvador. While the fighting in El Salvador is undoubtedly ended, the real measure of success will only be witnessed over the long term. The ruler the Intervention Cycle uses—the same used by the UN itself—is nothing less than the degree to which the accords have guaranteed the political and economic enfranchisement of the determined majority of Salvadorans who are committed to peace. The true test is whether the accords helped build the institutions of a civil society to perpetuate that peace.

I. HOT WAR, COLD WAR

In Latin America, especially, the guiding precept of U.S. policy has been order. Instability, it was feared, would be exploited to the advantage of outsiders—whether British, Spanish, German, or Soviet, depending on the historical period—and used by them to gain unwanted influence in the American hemisphere. Of course, it was all for the better if order could be achieved through democracy. But, until quite recently, the two interests rarely coincided. The default, then, was often to support governments that at least had a lacquer of legitimacy—who held elections, no matter how rigged—but who at the same time held a tight grip on any aspiration for the kind of revolutionary change that, ostensibly at least, promised greater political, economic, and social enfranchisement.

El Salvador in many ways fit this history. Even the carnage of 1932 had the effect of drawing some support from the United States for the man whose army carried out the massacres, General Maximiliano Hernández Martínez. The killings at least demonstrated that the general could, however brutally, control his country. Within two years of the massacres, Washington had granted the Martínez government full diplomatic recognition.[2] In the context of the cold war, this historical predilection for stability and for sealing off the hemisphere from the sway of outside powers was only magnified.

The cold war had three general effects on local conflicts, not only El Salvador's, but most others that fell within its scope. Each effect tended to reinforce the others. First, policymakers often viewed local conflicts through a kind of distorting prism. This policy view exaggerated the stakes and threats of otherwise limited conflicts, as well as the power of the smaller actors who were now playing out their struggles on a stage elevated to a global height. This view tended to be self-fulfilling, as the local actors indeed gained leverage in manipulating superpower interests to their own advantage.

Second, in the eyes of policymakers, the cold war left little room for compromise. They came to see each conflict as a zero-sum contest in which one superpower could only gain at the expense of the other. In a losing conflict, then, a stalemate was not only preferable but often all that was possible given the enormous resources available to each superpower and the relatively modest level of money and commitment needed to fuel a distant conflict by proxies. El Salvador surely fell into this category. The other alternatives— attrition or power sharing (in which theoretically both sides could win)— were for the most part excluded. Moreover, once compromise was excluded by U.S. policymakers, it was also less appetizing to the local parties themselves, who were often already arch rivals divided over ancestral disputes.

Finally, there was the issue of credibility. The arms race aside, the cold war was fought as a series of hot, microwars on which policymakers staked America's commitment to the larger cause of containing Soviet power. Any backsliding or anything less than total victory, they believed, would not only signal a weakening of American resolve but also leave America vulnerable to further Soviet provocation, and in regions far more central to American interests.

Until 1989, this cold war environment probably eliminated any real prospect of ending El Salvador's civil war. Far from pursuing the kind of neutral intervention to settle a dispute that is presumed by the Intervention

Cycle, the United States pursued what it believed to be its security interests. The American "intervention"—defined by its rhetorical support for and military and economic assistance to the Salvadoran government—was not disinterested, but rather prejudicial. Policymakers saw El Salvador's war as part of the global struggle to contain Soviet aggression. Reluctant to jettison the Salvadoran regime, they alternated between trying to moderate it gradually or steel it as a bulwark against communist expansion. In any case, given the overriding influence of American preferences in the hemisphere, without active U.S. leadership to pursue a peaceful solution to the war, a peaceful solution was unlikely to be found.

It was in this atmosphere that Salvadorans renewed their warring over the scarce land resources of one of the hemisphere's most densely populated countries. El Salvador was a society with an extraordinarily high degree of economic disfranchisement. In the early 1980s, about 2 percent of El Salvador's population (notably, the "Fourteen Families") owned some 57 percent of the land. In a country where 60 percent of land was used for agriculture, and where nearly 60 percent of people lived on the land, this amounted to a kind of feudalism.[3] Through the 1970s, global recession, inflation, and the oil shocks placed added strains on an economy that had already seen its number of landless families triple in the decade before 1971.[4]

But the war was not fought over land rights alone. It also concerned greater political enfranchisement—that is, opening the political system to the safe participation of the entire population. Through low-level violence the military had managed for decades to ensure public compliance with a political order that guaranteed the suzerainty of the oligarchy. Public dissatisfaction with this system grew through the 1970s. For instance, blatant fraud in the 1972 presidential election reinforced both a sense of exclusion and frustration in much of the country. Protests after that thwarted vote left more than 300 Salvadorans dead or wounded.

Thus alongside the increasing economic hardship came the military's continued efforts to cut off avenues to peaceful political participation. As violent expressions of public dissatisfaction grew, so did the levels of repression used by the military to tamp them down. By 1979, a communist insurgency was initiated, the Farabundo Marti National Liberation Front (FMLN), which was inspired and influenced by the success of the communist Sandinista revolution that took power in nearby Nicaragua that same year.

That Sandinista victory did more than buoy El Salvador's own revolutionaries. The overthrow of Anastacio Debayle Somoza in Nicaragua in July 1979 also helped invigorate American support for the Salvadoran regime. The Carter administration, which came to office emphasizing human rights, had initially tried to split the difference between the forces of repression and progression in the Salvadoran military. It supported a coup by a "progressive" group of Salvadoran army officers in 1979 in the hope of moderating the abuses of the regime. With an eye toward Nicaragua and in an effort to buttress the Salvadoran regime, President Carter in 1980 requested $5.7 million in military supplies for the Salvadoran government.[5]

It was not long, however, before the Salvadoran army's limited talents for reforming itself became painfully clear. Even after the 1979 coup, the Salvadoran regime persisted in a long-established pattern of coercion. By the early 1980s right-wing death squads had killed thousands, including the highly publicized murders of three American nuns and the Archbishop of San Salvador, Oscar Arnulfo Romero. Thus the contradictions of the Carter policy were lost on hardly anyone, least of all the Salvadoran military or Mr. Carter's political opponent in the 1980 presidential elections, a conservative California governor named Ronald Reagan.

President Reagan came to office with avowedly anti-communist views. He himself had made the point early in his administration that he considered the Soviets unworthy negotiating partners. They reserved for themselves, the new president said, "the right to commit any crime, to lie, to cheat" to pursue their ends as what he would later describe as "the focus of evil in the modern world."[6] The president was good for his word. In fact, he did not meet with the Soviet leader, Mikhail Gorbachev, until November 1985, already President Reagan's second term.

The Reagan administration's early outlook where the cold war was concerned—and the administration held no doubt that the cold war did indeed concern El Salvador—precluded the pursuit of compromise. Quite to the contrary, the Reagan Doctrine—a policy of supporting and arming surrogates against perceived communist aggression—actively fueled war in countries as far-ranging and far-flung as Afghanistan, Angola, and Nicaragua. From the outset the Reagan administration pursued a policy that, for all intents, favored a military solution to the conflict in El Salvador as well.

These policies were not without opponents, and as political tensions rose, President Reagan took the unusual step of addressing a joint session of Congress on a foreign policy issue, one of the few times in the country's history that a president had done so. He also made a televised appeal to the nation in 1984 in which he laid out in stark terms what his administration perceived as the stakes in Central America in general and El Salvador in particular:

> What we see in El Salvador is an attempt to destabilize the entire region and eventually to move chaos and anarchy toward the American border. . . . If we do nothing or if we provide too little

help, our choice will be a communist Central America with additional communist military bases on the mainland of this hemisphere and communist subversion spreading southward and
northward. This communist subversion poses the threat that 100
million people from Panama to the open border on our south
could come under the control of pro-Soviet regimes.[7]

Thus, by the mid-1980s, El Salvador's conflict had become as much a part
of the cold war as the ritual East-West summits themselves. El Salvador's
insurgency indeed received outside support from Cuba, Nicaragua, and the
Soviet Union in the form of arms, training, and money. But that support
hardly seemed decisive, especially given the mounting levels of U.S. assistance
going to the other side. Between 1980 and 1984, U.S. military aid to El
Salvador increased more than tenfold, jumping from $6 million to $65 million.[8] While the support of either side was never entirely unfettered, for a
decade it helped fan the flames of the conflict. As long as both El Salvador's
rebels and the regime believed they would be supported in their efforts to gain
advantage through violence, they would do just that. And, in the international
context of the time, neither side had any reason to believe differently.

The Reagan administration tried to forge some variety of democracy in the
heat of the Salvadoran conflict. It supported the drafting of a new Salvadoran
constitution in 1983 and promoted elections in 1984, which brought to power
a moderate government under the leadership of José Napoleón Duarte. At the
same time, it also tried to steal some thunder from the rebels by supporting certain reforms, however modest, to help alleviate some sources of the conflict.

But to many observers those policies seemed less a sincere attempt to open
El Salvador's political process than an effort to salvage the old regime. The evidence was that the Reagan policies largely failed in increasing political and economic enfranchisement within Salvadoran society. In many ways, those policies
may even have contributed to achieving the opposite. They served in effect to
buttress the exclusion of the left, increase the rigidity of the political system, and
help inflate the compromises needed for a negotiated solution.

For instance, after 1983 it could be said that the new constitution had
addressed the problem of land reform. But the statement overlooked the fact
that the constitution blocked the reforms after only 17 percent of the population had benefited.[9] The 1983 constitution also made passing more far-
reaching reforms on land and other issues more difficult, creating in effect
another obstacle to be negotiated away, which is indeed what eventually
happened. Eight years later, the UN-brokered peace accords would come to
hinge on a vote by the Salvadoran Assembly to amend 35 of the constitution's
274 articles.[10]

Elections are often pursued by American policymakers as an absolute good; they are equated directly with democracy. However, in an atmosphere of unmitigated violence, elections may still leave large swaths of the population disenfranchised. In fact, the 1984 election did little to ease El Salvador's core disputes. Not only did the Salvadoran rebels boycott a political process that had never guaranteed their safe participation, but they also sought to sabotage it. Not all eligible voters were registered, and all those who were registered suffered intimidation at the hands of both sides. Even as late as 1989, only 25 percent of eligible voters took part in the elections that brought to power Alfredo Cristiani.[11] Thus while it was indeed possible to point to a "democratically elected government" in El Salvador through much of the 1980s, the quality of that democracy was depressingly poor. Elections in effect had reinforced the will of only a small part of the population.

Taken together, the elections and the new constitution provided a lacquer of legitimacy that perhaps made it harder to get at the real problems that continued to divide much of Salvadoran society from the political system itself. After 1983, for instance, the Salvadoran government could insist that negotiations be based on the existing constitutional framework. But for the left to agree to the demand would have meant its capitulation to a political order in which it had never been allowed to participate, had never accepted, and, as yet, had no stake in preserving.

The Reagan policies, however, did have the positive effect of creating an elected, civilian political leadership, no matter how small the minority that chose it. This was an important step for El Salvador. It marked the beginning of a process of wresting some political levers from the military. Ever since General Martínez, the dictator who carried out the massacres in 1932, had seized power in a coup in December 1931, the military had become more than just El Salvador's main coercive force for ensuring public order. It was also the nation's prevailing political force. Creating a viable, civilian political leadership, then, was the beginning of reasserting some civilian control over the army. That civilian leadership would struggle through the 1980s to become more autonomous and to assert its authority. Eventually, after 1989 under President Cristiani, the civilian political leadership's commitment to peace talks, its critical role in those talks, and its ability to exert some influence over the army would be important in finally "delivering" the army's acceptance of a negotiated peace.

Through the 1980s the efforts of concerned outside parties to help settle the conflict consistently failed. Those efforts had little chance of succeeding given the countervailing preferences of the superpowers, especially the United States. Washington possessed the greatest leverage to persuade the sides in El

Salvador to pursue peace, but it was reluctant because of cold war considerations to bring that leverage to bear. As a result, outside meditation efforts were manipulated over time to further strategic ends rather than to pursue peace. This was true, for instance, of the efforts of the Contadora Group, a concerned clutch of Latin American nations made up of Colombia, Mexico, Panama, and Venezuela.

As James Chace, a keen observer of the conflict at the time, noted, "The Reagan Administration soon found Contadora useful as a way of avoiding negotiations; Washington could simply put aside any serious consideration of bilateral approaches that it did not want to consider by insisting that they be submitted to Contadora."[12] For many years, then, duplicity on both sides and a disconnection between stated policies and actual intentions poisoned the climate for fruitful negotiations.

By the end of the 1980s, what eventually broke the Salvadoran deadlock was the strength of the deadlock itself. It took a decade, but eventually both sides came to see that neither could win by killing. Terry Lynn Karl, a political scientist at Stanford, observed that this deadlock "consisted of a set of mutually reinforcing vetoes," which she explained this way:

> The Reagan administration was committed to the defeat of a communist revolution on its watch, which ruled out a military victory for the FMLN. Congress, however, refused to condone either an open alliance with the violent ultra-right or intervention by U.S. troops, which ruled out the full restoration of the old Salvadoran regime and the FMLN's total defeat. Finally, the FMLN demonstrated that it was too strong to be defeated militarily alone or excluded from the consolidation of a new order. In sum El Salvador faced gridlock in a set of domestic and international circumstances that prevented either an authoritarian or a revolutionary outcome.[13]

After the autumn of 1989, a series of four events finally combined to tip that deadlock toward negotiation. The first was the rebels' November 1989 offensive, an event that became known as El Salvador's "Tet." Like the Tet Offensive that helped precipitate the winding down of America's involvement in Vietnam, the attack—in which the rebels entered even exclusive neighborhoods of the capital, San Salvador—came so late in the conflict and with enough coordination that it made clear that the rebels, after already a decade of war, were not about to be wiped off the battlefield. Yet the offensive's ultimate failure to rally a popular uprising also demonstrated that the rebels could not win outright. They could merely persist in antagonizing indefinitely.

The second event occurred on the fourth night of the rebel offensive, when members of the Salvadoran army's U.S.-trained Atlacatl battalion killed six Jesuit priests, their housekeeper, and her daughter at the Central American University. The killings aroused strong criticism in the United States and reignited the debate in Congress over continuing military and economic assistance to the Salvadoran government. The killings also seemed to expose the failures of American policy in El Salvador. After nearly a decade of support and more than $4 billion in aid, the United States was still unable to moderate the abuses of the Salvadoran army or to build a civilian government that could exert full control over its own military.

The third event occurred half a world away and had nothing to do with El Salvador, per se, but was nonetheless as important to concluding the war there as it was to ending the long, cold war division of Europe. It was the fall of the Berlin Wall in December 1989. Alongside the revolutions against the communist regimes that swept though Eastern Europe that winter, that German celebration signaled in a very visible way that communism as an ideology was itself collapsing. The writing was on the wall, and the wall had just been toppled. The cold war was rapidly closing, and it was clear that outside support for the parties to El Salvador's conflict would soon end as well.

Finally, events in nearby Nicaragua played a decisive part in helping to wind down El Salvador's conflict. In many ways the war in El Salvador, despite having unique features of its own, was a function of the war of its larger neighbor. The success of the Sandinista takeover in 1979 had helped inspire El Salvador's rebels. Its consolidated leadership had helped supply and train the Salvadoran rebels throughout the 1980s. And now its eroding position and ultimate defeat in elections to Violetta Chamorro in February 1990 would help signal that an era of revolution inspired by communist ideals was drawing to a close.

These events, in particular the end of the cold war, also changed the political calculus in Washington. For a decade, a Democratic Congress and successive Republican administrations wrestled over U.S. policy in Central America, especially where it concerned human rights. In 1982 and 1983, before Congress could approve military aid, the Reagan administration had been required every six months to certify before a congressional committee that the Salvadoran government was making substantial progress in improving its human rights record. Even afterward, both the Reagan and Bush administrations had chronic problems justifying military aid in the face of continuing rights abuses. With the cold war quickly unraveling, parties in both Washington and El Salvador knew that Congress now had a far freer hand in carrying out its threats to cut or eliminate military aid to the Salvadoran government, and that the Bush administration had far less justification to turn a blind eye toward the atrocities.

It was no accident, then, that within six months of these events the parties to El Salvador's conflict began negotiating in earnest to resolve their dispute. This is not to say that the subsequent course of negotiations was in any way predetermined. It was a hard-fought process. But it was only then, in the changed international context, that the positive leverage of outside parties could finally be brought to bear and the parties to the conflict could be influenced to pursue peace because peace was suddenly in their own interests. Mitigation of violent conflict suited the best interests of all sides.

II. WINDING A PATH TO PEACE

After 1989 the way was opened for the kind of benign intervention presumed by the Intervention Cycle. The rebels approached the UN even during their November offensive, and the following month asked for the UN to play an enhanced role in peace talks. This overture helped clear a path for the serious participation of UN officials, especially the outgoing Secretary General, Javier Pérez de Cuéllar, who would personally oversee the peace process after the spring of 1990.

The most important issues to be negotiated and later agreed upon concerned judicial, agricultural and military reform. (In El Salvador's system, military reform was in a sense the equivalent of political reform.) To get there, however, the UN used a gradual accumulation of negotiations, deadlines, and lesser agreements in a catch-as-catch-can approach that slowly increased the pressures on the participants, their stake in the peace process, and their interest in finally reaching an overarching accord. This process was not entirely by design, but it holds valuable lessons for similar kinds of negotiations.

The talks lasted 20 months. This extended timetable gave the parties time to adjust themselves to the new rules of the game. It allowed them to build confidence in one another. Importantly, it also gave each side the opportunity to bring along all of its factions and prepare them for the compromises ahead. The negotiated enfranchisement had to be as inclusive as possible. Stragglers or those left outside the emerging political order could undertake to sabotage it. The gradual nature of the process also provided the time for Salvadoran society, weakened by decades of corrosive animosities, to prepare itself for the eventual peace. Small breakthroughs were used to maintain a sense of momentum as the peace process slogged along. Moreover, as the negotiations advanced and agreements were reached on lesser issues, the sense of isolation increased around those factions, especially the military hierarchy, who became the holdouts blocking the success of a final accord.[14]

Just to begin the first round of negotiations in April 1990 in Geneva, both sides had substantially altered long-standing positions about the conditions under which they would enter into talks. The rebels had previously insisted on a power-sharing formula in a provisional government that would oversee new elections; the government had never before agreed to outside mediation and previously insisted on a cease-fire before negotiations could begin. Both those positions were now set aside.

From the very start it was clear that the most difficult issue would be reforming the military. After talks had bogged down repeatedly over the issue, despite minor concessions by the military, it was for the most part set aside and the focus of the negotiations was placed elsewhere. In July 1990 in San José, Costa Rica, the sides reached an agreement that allowed the UN to send a mission to El Salvador to monitor human rights violations. Although fighting continued, this agreement helped foster a more secure environment in the country, which in turn added confidence to the continuing negotiations. Most important, it was unprecedented for the UN to send human rights observers into a country in the midst of civil war. Because these monitors were not military peacekeepers, however, there was little risk of them being caught in the middle of the fighting. Instead, their entry into the country was an important step in each side accepting a neutral outside authority and relinquishing a measure of autonomy or sovereignty.

Importantly, for the peace process to begin at all, each side had to perceive the UN as a trusted and neutral arbiter. Moreover, as the negotiations progressed, the UN conducted itself in a way that reinforced those perceptions. A slowly mounting confidence in the UN eventually led both sides to agree to give the UN mediator enhanced powers. After six months of the talks alternating between slowly grinding progress or gridlock, the UN was allowed to do more than merely arbitrate between the parties but also to present proposals to both sides. This enhanced role gave the UN greater leverage over each side and helped keep the negotiations moving. But had the UN presumed such a position from the start, without the consent of both sides, it could have jeopardized its neutral status in the talks.

A year after the negotiations had begun, the sides were finally forced to come up against the tougher issues that they had deadlocked over or delayed addressing for so long—electoral, judicial, and military reform. They agreed to write constitutional amendments in an effort to enact those reforms. But this formula left the negotiating process at the mercy of the El Salvador's National Assembly, which had to approve any amendments, creating a potentially disastrous obstacle to the peace process. After intensive lobbying, by both international and domestic forces, the amendments were ultimately approved on April 29, 1991.

Those amendments were the first steps toward restraining El Salvador's armed forces. They limited the army's duties to border defense, circumscribed the jurisdiction of military courts, and allowed for the creation of a national police force under civilian control, which would take over responsibility for domestic order from the armed forces. They also reformed the electoral and judicial systems, including changes in the selection of Supreme Court judges and in voter registration. In April 1991, the sides agreed to set up a "Truth Commission," an outside panel sponsored by the UN that would look into the war's most egregious atrocities.

The next eight months would be given to negotiating the cease-fire, the purging of the officer corps, the reintegration of FMLN guerrillas into Salvadoran society and even into its new police force. Breakthroughs on these issues came finally in New York in September 1991, where the sides also agreed to set up two national committees, one to assess the human rights records of army soldiers and a second to draft legislation on the negotiated agreements and then to make sure that those laws were carried out after a cease-fire had begun. Those issues settled, the sides signed a preliminary peace accord on December 31, 1991, and a formal end to the war in a ceremony in Mexico City on January 16, 1992.

III. THE INTERVENTION CYCLE

In terms of the Intervention Cycle, the UN was successful in ending the war in El Salvador largely because it allowed itself to be used, in a kind of therapeutic way, to facilitate peace between parties who were interested in peace but who knew they did not have the ability to achieve it by themselves. Its primary role, then, was as a peacemaker and later as an invited peacekeeper and institution builder. By contrast, it was not seeking to impose peace on two parties to a civil war who did not want peace. In conflicts beyond El Salvador's, such a role as a neutral party seeking to enforce peace has consistently proved more difficult, dangerous, and ultimately unsuccessful.

In El Salvador's case peace enforcement was impossible for three reasons. First, the UN Security Council remained divided between the two superpowers, who were supporting opposing sides in the conflict. Second, the United States (even today) would be unlikely to allow such an enforcement action in the hemisphere by any combination of outside powers, except perhaps under its leadership, like the U.S. intervention in Haiti in 1994, which was later turned over to the UN. Finally, the UN has never successfully imposed peace on the parties to a civil conflict.

The Intervention Cycle, in fact, discourages attempts by outside parties to impose peace by picking a side in a given dispute. In the case of El Salvador, it would theoretically have meant siding with the Salvadoran regime because that was the preference of the United States. But any effort by the United States or the UN to combat a guerrilla movement in El Salvador would have faced the same lengthy, dangerous, and costly prospect as that faced by the Salvadoran government in its attempt violently to eliminate the FMLN. And at the end of the enforcement action, the problem of enfranchisement for the FMLN and its constituents would still persist.

The UN's greatest contribution, then, was certainly not in peace enforcement. Rather, its first and perhaps most important role was in peacemaking— that is, in helping to resolve the disputes at the root of El Salvador's violence. Such a peacemaking role means using arbitration skills to nurture a difficult negotiation, which the UN successfully did. Successful arbitration often requires applying outside leverage in the form of carrots (say, promising aid or to guarantee any future accord) and sticks (perhaps trade sanctions or withholding aid) to reach an accord that is something more than a mere cease-fire but instead seeks to resolve a conflict's core disputes.

In El Salvador's case, this was no easy task. As an often cumbersome multinational organization, the UN has certain institutional handicaps when it comes to a role as mediator.[15] The leverage of the UN, for instance, depends mostly on the political and economic weight that its most powerful member states will lend to its efforts. Nearly a year into the negotiations, doubts about the political commitment of the United States to the UN-led peace process at times created an awkward stumbling block. Once the extent of the U.S. and Soviet commitments was made clear—in an explicit statement by Secretary of State James Baker and Soviet Foreign Minister Eduard Shevardnadze—then the negotiations continued in a far more secure environment.

The UN, moreover, does not have the ability to commit the resources of its member states (beyond those already paid and allocated in UN budgets) or those of international lending institutions like the World Bank and International Monetary Fund. A more coordinated effort on the part of UN officials, concerned UN member states, and outside lending institutions might have increased the UN's ability to negotiate the accords by giving it more leverage in the form of promises of future benefits to the new Salvadoran state.[16] Once the accords were negotiated, moreover, it might also have helped the UN carry them out more effectively.

The Intervention Cycle makes an important distinction between mitigating violence and resolving core disputes. It sees violence as a symptom of disputes that revolve around the problems of disfranchisement. Only by addressing those disputes that underlie the fighting—a process of resolution that is intended to open the political and economic systems to greater participation— can a neutral intervening party hope to prevent the cyclical return of bloodshed.

The distinction is important in the case of El Salvador. The UN played little role in mitigating El Salvador's bloodletting, and in fact it would probably have failed in any attempt at peacekeeping in El Salvador prior to the signing of the official cease-fire in January 1992. In a civil war where the opposing "sides" are mixed in one population and fighting each other in guerrilla and terror campaigns, peacekeeping troops have no clear battle lines to monitor, no identifiable armies to interpose themselves between, and may become easily victimized or drawn into the dispute.

The UN was careful to increase the commitment of its prestige and resources only in step with the commitment to peace of the Salvadoran parties themselves. The UN Observer Mission in El Salvador was created by a Security Council mandate in 1990 to oversee the accord on human rights signed in San José. At the request of the parties, the Security Council agreed to introduce human rights monitors into El Salvador before the fighting had ceased. While even the initial mandate can rightly be described as giving the monitors "wide-ranging powers unprecedented in UN history," those powers did not include separating the parties or enforcing peace.[17]

The Security Council then unanimously enlarged the monitors' mandate, along with the UN forces in El Salvador, in January 1992. That new mandate allowed the UN to oversee the comprehensive, final accords signed in Mexico City. Specifically, it allowed the UN to introduce into El Salvador a military division to verify the cease-fire arrangement and a police division to maintain pubic order while a new national civil police was being formed. Importantly, however, UN peacekeepers were brought into the country only once there was indeed a peace to keep.

Rather than first negotiating a cease-fire, the UN instead immediately began talks aimed at resolving the disputes at the root of El Salvador's violence. Absent a cease-fire, confidence among the parties was built in other ways, primarily by reaching agreement on lesser issues of common interest, like the San José accord on human rights. This was done by necessity, as neither side would commit to quitting the fighting entirely. Nonetheless, after 1989, once they had entered into talks, the sides had for the most part chosen to mitigate the violence themselves. By 1990, for instance, only 62 political killings were recorded.[18]

The UN was thus able to facilitate peace through negotiations only after the parties themselves had come to understand that killing was less useful than talking in gaining their ends. This calculation of self-interest on each side was vital. Despite the absence of a cease-fire, the sides in El Salvador were for the most part negotiating in good faith. While the FMLN did pursue a strategy of launching attacks before new rounds of negotiations, those attacks on the battlefield were made in an effort, however wrong-minded, to increase its leverage at the bargaining table. But the bargaining table was not being used merely to increase the FMLN leverage on the battlefield.

It is important, then, to consider whether a conflict is indeed ripe for negotiations. In the case of El Salvador, the exhaustion of the parties after 12 years of war meant that they were not only more disposed to talks but also that a kind of equilibrium had been reached, a miniature balance of power. Under such a circumstance, compromise is eventually far more likely to be achieved than if one side has, or believes it has, a decisive military advantage.

Premature diplomatic efforts to arrange a cease-fire can turn out to be more of a distraction than an asset. The terms of an even momentary truce can sometimes be negotiated nearly interminably. Even if a cease-fire can be put into place, without outside monitoring or enforcement it is easily susceptible to sabotage. It may prove to be a hollow accord if arranged only at a political level among deal makers who cannot guarantee military command and control of the factions on all sides. In such a case, a cease-fire may only help elevate the leverage and profile of factions not committed to stopping the fighting, as the significance of even relatively minor levels of violence becomes magnified as violations of the "peace." And instead of building trust, the repeated collapse of cease-fire accords can corrode confidence on all sides.

The importance of the proper climate for and commitment to peace talks cannot be overestimated. Negotiations under the opposite circumstance, like those that prevailed in El Salvador in the 1980s, had consistently proved counterproductive. The Reagan administration, for example (and to a lesser measure, the Carter administration before it), pursued a kind of two-pronged policy that tried to combine what was called "low-intensity" warfare with what can be called low-intensity enfranchisement. That policy ended up largely failing on both scores.

Part of the problem was that such a two-pronged policy was simply unsuited to a civil war. In other spheres of its foreign policy (specifically, with the Soviets) the Reagan administration had often expressed its commitment to negotiating from a position of strength. Such strength may prove fruitful in negotiating conflicts with a rival state or when it is attached to active diplomacy that intends to reach a settlement. But in El Salvador's civil war the concerns of the "adversary" centered in large part around its inability to safely participate in the political process. Achieving a position of "strength" thus ended up looking too much like complicity in the Salvadoran regime's long history of coercion. It heightened the insecurity of the left, drove it farther from the political process and ultimately proved counterproductive.

Importantly, the Intervention Cycle presumes a benign, if not disinterested, intervention on the part of an outside party. But one unfortunate paradox is that countries closest to a conflict—and hence those with the greatest selfish interest in its outcome—are precisely the same countries most likely to be motivated to intervene and to have some measure of influence over the warring sides. Distant countries and organizations are less likely either to be interested in or to possess the kinds of leverage needed for brokering a settlement. Thus, given its proximity and power, the United States was seemingly in a perfect position to mediate El Salvador's conflict, but its own strategic concerns made a neutral role impossible.

That neutral role, for better and worse, was left to the UN. The UN's deep participation in mediating the accords made it easier after they were signed to carry out the oversight roles it had in large measure defined for itself.[19] At the same time, the various hats it wore after 1992 as investigator, verifier, chastiser, and enforcer often clashed and placed UN officials in a precarious position. That position proved tenable only because the UN skillfully made the most of its limited leverage. It kept itself vital to both sides by continuing to interpret the accords, mediating lingering disagreements, and requiring its imprimatur before Salvadorans could receive foreign assistance.

Problems in effectively implementing and overseeing the accords in a timely manner nonetheless jeopardized the postsettlement peace process. The accords, for example, were carried out over a long timetable that was revised backward several times. Such delays certainly made it harder for the UN to meet the important challenge of walking Salvadorans through the agreements at just the right pace. That pace had to be gradual enough to shepherd along all parts of the society and leave no stragglers. And yet it had to be fast enough for Salvadorans, especially those who were direct parties to the conflict, to see a manifest difference in their lives and not be tempted to opt out of the process or to exploit opportunities to backslide on previously agreed commitments. The UN hit repeated problems in registering all voters before the country's landmark 1994 elections and in efficiently transferring land and demobilizing combatants. But not enough for the sides to return to violence.

Clearly it is wrong to measure success in El Salvador by the absence of violence alone. For nearly 50 years after 1932, Salvadorans were spared large-scale political violence. But the conflicts that divided the country were merely dormant, not dead. That is why the years of peace since 1992 provide some ruler of success, but not the definitive one. The real test is if the Salvadoran accords gradually change the country's economy, society, and polity enough to perpetuate that peace. The Salvadoran accords, and the peace itself, depend nearly entirely on that process, which is one of enfranchisement.

IV. ASSESSING SUCCESS AND LOOKING TO THE FUTURE

Then UN Secretary General, Boutros Boutros-Ghali, called El Salvador's accords "a prescription for revolution achieved by negotiation." Indeed, the agreements intended vast change in El Salvador: to disarm the guerrillas and weave them back into the country's political, economic, and social fabric; to lift the military's oppressive hand from social and political life; to open the political system by increasing the electoral participation and representation of those previously excluded; to create a justice system that deserves the name; to create a more equitable balance of economic power by redistributing land.

Nonetheless, a far narrower reading of the accords is possible. The agreements could also be seen as, in a sense, an attempt to buy off the conflict's most ardent participants—the combatants—who were after all only a minority of the population.[20] Such an interpretation would not change the assessment of the UN success in mediating an end to the war. It does, however, take a different view of what was indeed negotiated. Rather than transforming El Salvador, all that may have been done was to bring the country's most extreme elements back into the fold of the state. That in itself is no minor achievement. But it is not a revolution. And perhaps, too, it does not guarantee a broad enfranchisement.

Events since the signing of the final accord may have in fact born out such a view. Many Salvadorans have taken an increasingly negative view of the accords. By February 1995 only 33 percent of Salvadorans viewed the accords positively, down from 54.5 percent in October 1992. In the same period, the percentage of those who viewed the accords indifferently rose from 1 percent to 20 percent.[21] Moreover, other polls taken in December 1993 and February 1994 indicated that 52 percent of Salvadorans believed that "death squads" still existed within the country.[22]

As late as October 1995, the Secretary General reported that the implementation of many parts of the accords faced "significant delays" or remained incomplete.[23] This was true of the screening and vetting of judges as well as other work toward judicial reform. More than four years after the signing of the peace accords, some of those eligible to receive titles to land still had not gotten them, and many who had received them did not have those titles filed with the land registry so that they could sell them if they chose, which was considered an important measure of the ultimate success of the program. Relocating most people still settled on lands belonging to others also posed a lingering and potentially volatile problem that lent itself to no simple solution.

The slow pace of judicial reforms allowed human rights violations and impunity for crimes including murder and rape to persist. Although the country's old security forces were successfully abolished, serious problems hindered the consolidation of a national civil police in which Salvadorans could have confidence. Problems related to the proper screening and training of officers led to the excessive use of force and increasing incidents of police brutality. This was especially true in responses to public demonstrations and labor strikes. Moreover, there were reports that criminal elements, including some from old security forces, had entered the new civilian police force. By February 1995, only 33 percent of Salvadorans polled nationwide considered the conduct of the new police to be "good."[24]

That fledgling force faced a surging tide of common crime. An extraordinary 473 officers were killed between March 1993 and November 1995 alone.[25] The inability of the national police combined with a dramatic rise in crime prompted the government to rely increasingly on the armed forces, a move that the peace accords and the Salvadoran constitution limit to extraordinary circumstances. The rise in general public insecurity also led to calls for measures that would clearly violate the spirit, if not the letter of the accords. The problems within the national police, the rise in crime, the high number of weapons that remained in country, the reemergence of "parallel" security forces, and the heightened public insecurity combined to lead careful observers to warn that the government might be increasingly tempted to tilt toward undemocratic solutions.

None of these difficulties and weaknesses should obscure the tremendous achievements of the UN in El Salvador, especially in carrying out the 1994 vote. Fragile as they might be, the UN accords have persevered. Yet both the accords and, more generally, the Salvadoran political system itself may remain vulnerable to the country's extremes, and hence might yet be susceptible to sabotage by a minority of relatively minor actors. But the success in overcoming past challenges is heartening, as was a second landmark vote held in March 1997 that saw the former rebels greatly increase their representation in the Assembly, and hence, the political process. These steps indicate that a critical mass of Salvadorans is finally committed to pursuing the country's enduring struggles peacefully, within the confines of a new political process rather than attacking that system from the outside.

Only time will tell exactly what was negotiated in El Salvador, a merely temporary end to the war or a permanent peace. The difference will come in whether the accords were able to lay the foundation for building durable political institutions that can help perpetuate peace. Even if El Salvador's accords were not the revolution that they are so often billed to be, to succeed over the long term they must at least keep happy the country's political extremes. That will require some kind of enfranchisement, although perhaps not the sweeping one that would match the expectations that so many had harbored for the accords when they were first signed.

Thus, it is difficult even today to claim that El Salvador's peace is irreversible. This is so even after the UN peace accords that ended the fighting there, even after the ground-breaking UN mission that placed human rights monitors inside a country still at war with itself, and even after spending millions of dollars over five years on a mission in which hundreds of UN officials including peacekeepers and police, election monitors, and observers carried out land, judicial, and military reforms, penetrating nearly all levels of Salvadoran society.

Beyond the borders of El Salvador, then, the most lasting impact of the UN mission there may be to instruct the international community on the time, patience, and resources needed to ensure a durable peace. In El Salvador that commitment is far from ending. For years ahead the challenge will remain to secure the enfranchisement of a growing number within the society. This process will mean guaranteeing the full political and economic participation of enough Salvadorans that even the country's historically recalcitrant fringes can do nothing else but refuse a return to war.

NOTES

1. Roque Dalton, "Miguel Marmol," Willimantic, CT: Curbstone Press, 1982, pp. 308-309, 304-305.
2. Walter LaFeber, *Inevitable Revolutions*. New York: W.W. Norton, 1984, pp. 73-74.
3. Marvin Gettleman, Patrick Lacefield, Louis Menashe, and David Mermelstein (Eds.), *El Salvador: Central America in the New Cold War*. New York: Grove Press, 1986, p. 4.
4. LaFeber, *Inevitable Revolutions*, p. 243.
5. Ibid., p. 251.
6. Gettleman et al. (Eds.), *El Salvador*, p. 7.
7. Ibid., p. 12.
8. James Chace, *Endless War: How We Got Involved in Central America—and What Can Be Done*. New York: Random House, 1984, p. 70.

9. Terry Lynn Karl, "El Salvador's Negotiated Revolution," Foreign Affairs, 71, no. 2, (Spring 1992), p. 150.

10. Ibid., p. 157.

11. Ibid., p. 154.

12. Chace, *Endless War*, p. 101.

13. Karl, "El Salvador's Negotiated Revolution," pp. 148-49.

14. This section draws much from Karl's excellent summation of the events leading up the Salvadoran accords provided in "El Salvador's Negotiated Revolution."

15. See Saadia Touval, "Why the UN Fails," *Foreign Affairs*, 73, no. 4 (September/October 1994), pp. 44-57.

16. See Alvaro de Soto and Graciana del Castillo, "Obstacles to Peacebuilding," Foreign Policy, 73, no. 2 (Spring 1994), pp. 69-83.

17. UN Chronicle, December 1992, p. 34.

18. Bernard W. Aronson, *U.S. Department of State Dispatch*, 3, no. 29, July 20, 1992, p. 578.

19. This paragraph draws from William Stanley and David Holiday, "Under the Best of Circumstances: ONUSAL and Dilemmas of Verification and Institution Building in El Salvador," paper presented at a conference of the North-South Center, the United States Institute of Peace, and the Ford Foundation, April 11-13, 1996.

20. This interpretation of the accords was pointed out by Peter Hakim, the Director of Inter-American Dialogue, whose critique of this chapter is appreciated.

21. Processo 651, March 1, 1995, cited in Jack Spence, George Vickers, and David Dye, *The Salvadoran Accords and Democratization: A Three Year Progress Report and Recommendations.* Cambridge, MA: Hemisphere Initiatives, 1995.

22. Institute of Public Opinion at the Central American University, San Salvador, cited in Spence et al., *The Salvadoran Accords.*

23. "Report of the Secretary General," The Situation in Central America: Procedures for the Establishment of a Firm and Lasting Peace and Progress in Fashioning a Region of Peace, Freedom, Democracy and Development, A/50/517, October 6, 1995.

24. Estudios Centroamericanos, April 1995, 360, cited in "Protectors or Predators? The Institutional Crisis of the Salvadoran Civil Police," written by William Stanley and edited by Jack Spence, a joint report of the Washington Office on Latin America and Hemisphere Initiatives, January 1996.

25. Ibid.

CHAPTER 10

Enfranchisement Wanted: Tajikistan

Katherine K. Tucker

WHY DO WE CARE?

The case of Tajikistan provides an example of the difficulties of postcolonial transition to independence for an economically and politically underdeveloped multigroup state. It provides ample examples of a variety of interventions: regional powers, superpowers, international organizations, and nongovernmental and unofficial delegations—some of which are benign, others perhaps less so. Continued instability in Tajikistan, located at a confluence of Russian, Turkic, Persian, and Asian cultures, could have a major impact on a variety of other potential conflicts. It is a conflict not so much between ethnic or religious groups (despite the Islamic fundamentalist label often applied to the opposition); rather, one between those who benefited from the communist system and wish to maintain it and those who did not benefit from the old system and want change.

Tajikistan's geographic obscurity has caused this tragedy to be largely neglected in the West, although "more people were killed in Tajikistan in the six months of fighting between October 1992 and March 1993 than in any other conflict in the former Soviet Union, including the ongoing war in Nagorno-Karabakh."[1] Therefore, the conflict itself is of concern from a humanitarian standpoint. Moreover, due to its strategic location, it is tremendously important that a stable state be created in Tajikistan.

Katherine Tucker is a U.S. Air Force Intelligence Officer with experience in the field and at headquarters levels in the United States and Europe. She received an M.A. in International Relations from Boston University and writes on Central Asia and the Former Soviet Union. This chapter was written while an International Affairs Fellow sponsored by the Council on Foreign Relations at the Center for Science and International Affairs, Kennedy School of Government, Harvard University.

The crisis in Tajikistan highlights a key question: As the authoritarian power of the former Soviet Union fades away, what happens when the artificial enfranchisement and stability the communist system provided disappears suddenly? Without appropriate outside assistance to help smooth the transition, independence is thrust on a state unprepared for the responsibility and political development required of independence. This appears to have two possible results: the return of highly authoritarian forms of government or civil war. Authoritarianism may vary from extreme repression to a relatively free state of existence, depending, in part, on the bureaucratic power of the state. In the case of Tajikistan, where there was a minimally developed state structure from the start, independence yielded a struggle for power and national identity that resulted in both civil war, complete with massive refugee flows and extensive human rights abuses, *and* an authoritarian regime.

While several different organizations and groups are now attempting to intervene to help resolve the conflict, these efforts strike at different portions of the Intervention Cycle and are thus unlikely to bring about true resolution. The case history suggests not only efforts that have failed in bringing resolution of the conflict, but also efforts that should be tried in similar situations as former republics transition from authoritarian states to independent democracies.

I. BACKGROUND

As the Soviet Union broke apart in the wake of the failed coup in August 1991, Tajikistan declared independence. It was, however, a state wholly unprepared for independence. Even members of the opposition party readily admit that most were not seeking political independence; rather, they sought a spiritual and national revival of Tajikistan.[2] Not only was Tajikistan unprepared in terms of a common sense of nationhood, but it was also economically and politically unprepared to separate from its Soviet central authority in Moscow.

Like many regions of the former Soviet Union, Central Asian boundaries created under Soviet rule were artificial and not built on a historic sense of nationhood. In fact, scholars generally agree there is no such thing as a Tajik national identity. There are no tribes in Tajikistan that serve as a basis for group identification; the settled peoples have tended to derive group identity based on their region, a force Olivier Roy refers to as "localism."[3]

The geographic area that today is the independent state of Tajikistan has no historical basis as a state prior to the creation of the USSR. While this general area was populated with peoples speaking Persian-based languages and had distinct cultures for centuries, there was no single unified "Tajik" identity. Since the movement of Turkic tribes into the region, the Persian-speaking peoples of this area were ruled by the Turkic-speaking, but the Persian-based culture retained a dominance in government and the arts.[4] As a result, many people in the region spoke both Persian-based Tajik and Uzbek (a Turkic-based language), allowing for cultural intermixing and a muted sense of ethnic identity. Indeed, the traditional cultural centers of Persian-speaking peoples in this area are the cities of Bukhara and Samarkand—both of these are located in Uzbekistan. Particularly in the intermixed areas, group identity came to be tied to the region rather than to a sense of ethnic identity.[5]

When the Soviet leaders first created republics within the Russian empire, the republic of Uzbekistan covered the entire Uzbekistan/Tajikistan area. At that time, Tajikistan was an autonomous region within Uzbekistan. In 1929, an independent republic of Tajikistan was created, leaving the important cities of Samarkand and Bukhara in Uzbekistan, but incorporating the predominately Uzbek Fergana Valley area in the north (later called the Leninabad or Khojand region) into Tajikistan. In an effort to define a Tajik nationality close to the Russian culture, and prevent identification with a (then) pro-Western Iran, the written language of Tajikistan was changed from Arabic script to a Latin script and then subsequently to a modified Cyrillic script in 1941.

Stalin's nationality and collectivization policies led to the resettlement of thousands of Persian-speaking mountain Tajiks from the Gharm area into the cotton producing area of Kurgan Teppe. These resettlers contrasted with the Turkic-speaking indigenous peoples; thus, they adapted and took on an identity based on their location rather than tribe, clan, or ethnic history. All of these factors contributed to the lack of a Tajik nationality around which the population might rally.

Economically, Tajikistan had always been the most disadvantaged republic in the former Soviet Union, surviving on subsistence farming, relying heavily on subsidies and producing raw materials, principally cotton, for export. As was typical of ethnic republics under the Soviet system, the limited infrastructure was center-oriented and ethnic Russians played key roles in managing both the government and industry. Access to education as a means to alter this situation was, for the majority of the population, extremely limited.

Politically, the power had long been in the hands of the economic elites from the Khojand region, who figured prominently in the party structure. Khojand was more Russified, industrialized, and closer, both geographically and in terms of ethnic mixing, to Uzbekistan. Starting in the 1970s the party elites began to include members from the southern region of Kulab, as well, some of whom rose within the government structure.[6] The predominance of the Khojandis and Kulabis meant that virtually all economic as well as political power was concentrated into these two groups, leaving the rest of the Tajiks disenfranchised.

These party cadres contrasted with the intelligentsia, who, on the other hand, were generally from the southern areas of Tajikistan, mostly Gharmis or Pamiris. They emerged as intellectual leaders as education spread throughout the countryside, eventually gathering in the capital, Dushanbe. The intelligentsia thought power should be shared and entertained notions of democratic development, seriously threatening the power base of the traditional political elites and setting the stage for burgeoning democratic and Islamic movements. The Soviet policy of *Perestroika* resulted in some of these intellectuals forming the Rastakhiz (Resurrection) group to campaign for social and cultural liberalization. They sought the establishment of more traditional, non-Soviet or Russian language and religious patterns; they did not seek significant political reform.

Both sides described and continue to describe, their conflict as an ideological one; hence some refer to the conflict as one between "old communists" and "Islamic fundamentalists." This is, however, mostly a convenient, propaganda description. In fact the conflict is a basic struggle for political and economic power among the regions, resulting directly from independence having loosed the bonds of the old system. Simply put, it is a struggle between those wanting to maintain the old balance of power and those wanting to change it.

II. THE PATH TOWARD VIOLENT CONFLICT

Direct conflict between the old apparatus and those seeking change began in early 1990. The Rastakhiz group was blamed by the government for inciting violent riots that took place in the capital two weeks before parliamentary elections. Although Rastakhiz was subsequently absolved of responsibility by both the government and the independent Helsinki Watch, the government used the opportunity to ban opposition groups from the election and to begin criminal proceedings against its leaders.[7] Consequently, the election produced a largely old-communist parliament that remained intact until the elections in spring of 1995.

The opposition set the stage for new political parties and movements that blossomed in large numbers after the February 1990 elections. These groups varied from democratic movements to the Islamic Renaissance Party, an outgrowth of the Islamic Renaissance Movement. By the November 1991 presidential elections they had gained sufficient momentum and unity to present a single opposition candidate, who was subsequently defeated in a highly suspect election. The defeat was, in some sense, also a victory, because the opposition candidate managed to garner over 30 percent of the popular vote despite government control of news media and other outlets, as well as questionable poll procedures.

The new president, Rahmon Nabiev, and parliament made efforts to control the transition from Soviet to independent state by passing a series of repressive measures.[8] The government's actions specifically discouraged the opposition from feeling that they had a stake, or even a voice, in the government—completely antithetical to the conflict deterrence measures discussed by the Intervention Cycle. One event that played a key role in enervating the opposition was the arrest of the pro-opposition mayor of Dushanbe on trumped-up corruption charges in March 1992. Opposition party protests were countered by pro-government protests. Each side eventually created an encamped group of disenfranchised members in Dushanbe, from which violence exploded in May 1992.[9]

On May 3, 1992, with arms widely distributed among both groups in Dushanbe, violent clashes erupted. Within the Intervention Cycle framework, this event could mark the government's transition from deterrence to coercion. The president, while making conciliatory overtures toward the opposition, announced the establishment of a national guard (later developed into the Popular Front) under his personal command and distributed 1,800 automatic rifles to Kulabis demonstrating in support of the government in Dushanbe. The Russian military was involved in distribution of arms, according to Helsinki Watch.[10]

Pausing to step back from the brink of violence, however, the president made an attempt to form a coalition government that included the opposition. This effort was challenged as hard-liners in Khojand and Kulab refused to go along, claiming that the coalition government was invalid because it had not been approved by parliament—where their absence prevented a quorum. Nonetheless, the coalition retained power over some areas of the country as both sides began fighting in the central regions through the summer of 1992. The opposition drew on weapons from Afghanistan and support from the southern regions; the progovernment forces—the Popular Front—drew on government and Russian stocks of weapons and supporters from Kulab and Khojand.[11]

The continued failure of President Nabiev to achieve recognition from parliament for his coalition government resulted in his resignation at gun point in September 1992. With the support of Tajik democrats and Islamists, Akbarsho Iskandoarov became acting president on September 7, 1992, in a government of "national reconciliation." He announced a policy to tilt Tajikistan's foreign policy priority toward Afghanistan, Iran, and Turkey rather than Russia (although he said Tajikistan would join the CIS).[12] The parliament rejected this government as they had Nabiev's coalition government, and the fighting continued.

It is likely that the Iskandorov government's foreign policy announcement played a key role in spurring the Uzbek and Russian governments into action regarding Tajikistan's conflict. By September 1992, Tajikistan's neighbors, particularly Uzbekistan, began to issue warnings that the conflict was detrimental to CIS security, citing arms flow from Afghanistan as a major threat. The Russian and Uzbek governments decided that their security interests required imposing order on Tajikistan and that the only force capable of establishing political order was that of the excommunists and their supporters.[13] In November 1992, the defense ministers of Russia, Uzbekistan, Kazakhstan, and Kyrgyzstan announced the formation of a CIS peacekeeping force[14] for Tajikistan—a force consisting mainly of Russia's 201st Motorized Rifle Division and a mobile regiment from Uzbekistan.

By December 1992, the coalition government controlled less and less of Tajikistan's territory. Iskandorov resigned and parliament elected a new government dominated by Kulabis and the former old guard from Khojand, with Emomali Rakhmonov as chairman. As the new government fought for control over Dushanbe, the progovernment forces (Popular Front) conducted a campaign of summary executions, looting, and terror throughout regions generally associated with the democratic/Islamist factions, resulting in both large numbers of casualties and a huge displacement of refugees, many of whom fled into Afghanistan. There are conflicting reports as to whether Russian and Uzbek forces actively participated in these atrocities; however, if not conducting operations outright, they at least supported the new government during this period.[15]

In early 1993, one of the first steps of the new government was to ban all opposition groups, forcing their leaders to flee to Afghanistan, Iran, or Moscow. Since that time, sporadic fighting continues in the border regions, involving Russian border guards as well as the CIS peacekeeping force and the Tajik army. The peacekeeping troops, in clearly supporting the incumbent government, are attempting to enforce a peace that does not exist.

III. INTERVENTION EFFORTS

While violence continues, it does so at a reduced level. This reduction in violence can be directly attributed to the efforts of a variety of intervening states and organizations. Foremost among these has been the CIS, particularly Russia and Uzbekistan, but other actors have played prominent roles in reducing the violence, resettling refugees, and building a dialog between the government and the opposition.

A. Regional Players: Actions and Interests

As the political struggle in Tajikistan developed into civil war in 1992 and violence reached new heights, both Russia and Uzbekistan became alarmed. They, under the auspices of the CIS, were the first to intervene, doing so on the side of the old power base with their "peacekeeping force," conducting operations that would be categorized as peace enforcement. They have largely stabilized the country and the government; while by no means impartial, they have supported dialog between the incumbent government and the opposition. Their level of intervention stretches from economics to personnel: the Russian government provides an estimated at 70 percent of the Tajik national budget;[16] Russian and Uzbek officers and officials occupy key positions in the government. This kind of support is a double-edged sword. It may promote some stability, but it does nothing to promote leaders within Tajikistan who can effectively manage the state. Russia also provides border guards to protect the international border of Tajikistan as if it were the border of Russia itself. Both Russia and Uzbekistan have military personnel at risk as long as the conflict continues, although a large number of Tajik soldiers actually comprise the Russian military units in the CIS peacekeeping force.

Russian and Uzbek interests in resolving the civil war are two-fold: they fear the spread of civil conflict as well as a flow of drugs and weapons from Afghanistan into neighboring Tajikistan. Russia and Uzbekistan have long, and somewhat irrationally, feared the rise of Islamic fundamentalism[17] and the influence of Iran. Furthermore, Uzbekistan—where religious-based movements and organizations are banned and a nascent democracy movement has risen against the authoritarian regime—also fears spillover of the democratic/Islamic movement in Tajikistan. For these reasons, both Russia and Uzbekistan have been generally supportive of the incumbent government.

Russia and Uzbekistan recognize, however, the long-term advantages of a resolution to the civil war: especially as a means to reduce economic and military drains. They have become more critical of the government of Tajikistan and applied pressures consistent with moving the situation toward resolution. While maintaining a compliant state may suit the interests of those who seek to restore Russia's empire or to benefit Karimov's Uzbekistan, the strategic objective is to have a stable government in Tajikistan. Accordingly, Russia and Uzbekistan have supported negotiation efforts and, since late 1994, appear to have brought some pressure to bear on the Tajik government resulting in the first stage of a peace accord, signed in September 1995. Furthermore, when the government was intent on holding presidential elections in early fall 1994 and excluding all manner of opposition groups, Russia convinced them to postpone the elections and include additional candidates. While the rescheduled election in November 1994 was certainly not an example of a truly free election, the inclusion of an opposing candidate did represent a compromise on the part of the government.

President Karimov of Uzbekistan has also shown a willingness to apply pressure to the Tajik government; he met with opposition spokesman Qazi Akbar Turajanzade on April 3, 1995. This event is remarkable, given Karimov had outlawed democratic and Islamist parties in Uzbekistan, and was probably meant to show the Tajik government that Uzbekistan's support for their incumbent government was not unshakable. This was reinforced by "intense polemics" between Karimov and Rakhmonov at the CIS summit in late May 1995, where Karimov insisted that Rakhmonov must begin to share power.[18]

Several other neighboring states have supported the opposition party, participated in international mediation efforts and have intervened, although to a much lesser extent than Russia and Uzbekistan. Their actions have had minimal impact. Generally, these states are interested in fostering ties within the new Central Asian governments or encourage a change of regime that will be more liberal in allowing Islamic influences. For example, Iran and Pakistan have been directly involved in facilitating reconciliation; whereas factions in Afghanistan have provided refuge, support, and training for opposition forces and civilians. Other Muslim states have reportedly funded training for opposition fighters.

While Russia and Uzbekistan fear Iran's involvement will encourage Islamic extremism, Iran has been restrained in its support for the opposition,[19] and the opposition has openly and frequently denied that it seeks an Iran-like state. Furthermore, Iran initiated talks on trade with the government of Tajikistan in early 1994, an indication of Iran's economic interests in Central Asia, rather than an interest in fostering the spread of Islamic fundamentalism.

Turkmenistan, another neighbor, has hosted UN-mediated talks between the parties since the fall of 1995. The opposition, however, was reluctant to agree to Turkmenistan's participation, implying that Turkmenistan's involvement may be at the behest of either Tajikistan's ruling elite, Uzbekistan, or Russia. Regardless, any successful talks hosted by a neighbor will strengthen regional ties, even if those ties run through Moscow.

B. International Players: Actions and Interests

"Disinterested" parties have also intervened to foster resolution of the civil war. These efforts include those of nongovernmental organizations, the UN, and the Organization of Security and Cooperation in Europe (OSCE). These activities fall within the mitigation phase of the Intervention Cycle and, if successful, can lead to resolution.

In March 1993, the first of these efforts began with an unofficial effort by the Dartmouth Conference, in which representatives of both the opposition and the government participated. This effort, organized by a group of Americans and Russians, met regularly to initiate and maintain a dialog between the two sides and enable them to identify common ground for official negotiations.

The UN has been involved with the repatriation of refugees and has been the key force behind the peace process. As the CIS peacekeeping force brought some stability to the countryside, refugees began to return to their homelands in early 1993. Some of the resettlement was conducted by the United Nations High Commissioner on Refugees (UNHCR), although a large percentage of the refugees returned on their own.[20] While the government allowed the UNHCR to assist in resettling refugees, they did little to facilitate the process nor to prevent local retaliation against returning people.[21] Returning refugees faced intimidation, harassment, illegal house searches, and arrest.[22] Nonetheless, the government and opposition recognized that successful resettlement was a key element of the peace process and the eventual resolution of the conflict. The only real success of the fourth round of inter-Tajik talks in May 1995 was an agreement on repatriation of the remaining refugees in Afghanistan.

UN agencies responded to the humanitarian crisis stemming from the civil war. The United Nations Children's Fund (UNICEF) and the World Health Organization (WHO) provided food and health care relief and continue to work with the UN Development Program (UNDP) on technical assistance and development programs. Despite their efforts, infant mortality continued to rise and infectious diseases significantly affected children—who constitute roughly one-half the population of Tajikistan.[23] The growing humanitarian crisis sparks factional violence (food riots are frequently reported) and inhibits peaceful resolution of the civil war.

In March 1994, the UN initiated official talks on national reconciliation. The Secretary General appointed a special representative and talks began with the support and assistance of Russia, Pakistan, and Iran. Those talks eventually led to a cease-fire accord in September 1994 (the Teheran Agreement), followed by further rounds of talks (and cease-fire extensions), a limited prisoner exchange, and the creation of a joint commission composed of representatives of both the government and the opposition in order to monitor the cease-fire agreement.[24] This was followed by the establishment of the United Nations Mission of Observers in Tajikistan (UNMOT) in December 1994, which consisted of 55 observers.[25] In September 1995, UN-sponsored talks resulted in both sides signing a protocol on the fundamental principles for establishing peace and national accord. That protocol was a step forward but still did not address the difficult issue of power-sharing and future make-up of the government. Those challenging negotiations are yet to come.

Efforts of the OSCE have been more limited, although they also participated in talks with the faction leaders, assisted in monitoring human rights violations, and made an offer to assist and monitor parliamentary elections in 1995—which was subsequently withdrawn when the Tajik government did not open the elections for broad participation.

C. Tajik Government and Opposition Response

In spite of these various interventions, the Tajik government remained primarily focused on actions best described by the coercion phase of the Intervention Cycle. Despite postponing the September 1994 presidential elections under pressure to allow increased participation by nonincumbent candidates, the president was reelected in November 1994 amid charges of vote rigging. The exiled opposition did not participate in the elections, as they are still illegal parties in Tajikistan; nor was there a prospect for fair elections since the government controlled the media. Nevertheless, the international community accepted the validity of this election, disregarded the lack of impartial observers, and hoped for better results during the parliamentary election in February 1995. However, all of the opposition parties, even those legal in Tajikistan, refused to participate in the February election. The government proceeded. The OSCE refused to send observers and international human rights personnel commented that voting conditions were "seriously flawed."[26]

Pressure has been applied for international recognition of the opposition parties. The spring 1995 meetings between Rakhmonov and the opposition represent a huge step toward high-level recognition and are the direct result of outside intervention efforts. Similarly, recognition of the opposition by President Karimov of Uzbekistan and by Kyrgyz president Akayev's presentation of a statement from the opposition at the May 1995 CIS summit add further credence to the opposition's enhanced position.

Nonetheless, pressures by the international community to proceed with productive steps toward reconciliation seem to be inadequate to bring the government around. At the core of reconciliation is the concept of sharing power, something the government continues to reject.[27] In addition, the government continues to detain political prisoners, allow mistreatment in detention, stifle the press, and has failed to combat or investigate violence against Tajik returnees.[28] The government imposed measures to reduce the number of weapons available to the opposition by outlawing weapons not in the hands of the government.[29] Yet, the movement of many Popular Front thugs into the Tajik national army and the government's inability or disinclination to stem violence against civilians means violence will not be reduced; rather, civilians will be made to feel more vulnerable.

While the UN-negotiated cease-fire has been extended repeatedly, fighting continues. This is due, at least in part, to Russia's insistence that the cease-fire not apply to the Russian border guards or the CIS peacekeeping forces (recall that individuals in these units may be Russian, Tajik, Uzbek, or Kazakh). Russia claims they are simply defending the international border between the CIS and Afghanistan. Moreover, only the Tajik government and opposition signed the Teheran Agreement limiting cross-border military activity; Russia remains unconstrained in defending the border.

However, evidence points to all parties being involved in activities along the border. There have been repeated cross-border incursions by the opposition, prompting counterattacks by the Russian forces both within Tajikistan and in areas of Afghanistan believed to house opposition forces. The Tajik government has also contributed to the border conflict: For example, in April 1995, there was a marked increase in violence in Gorno-Badakhshan, which the government initially labeled a "spring offensive" by the opposition. Eventually, however, the Russian commander of the CIS peacekeeping force acknowledged that the opposition attacks were a direct result of the government's movement of additional military forces into the region, in violation of the Teheran Agreement.[30]

For its part, the opposition artfully used each cease-fire extension as an opportunity to attack and appears routinely to violate the Teheran Agreement strictures against moving forces across the Afghan border. So, they are not without blame in perpetrating violence.[31] Further, there are allegations that the opposition fosters a drug trade to finance their military endeavors. That illicit trade is Russia's rationale for continued, aggressive involvement in border operations. If the opposition is behind the drug trade, they are simply exacerbating the conflict and impeding resolution.

International intervention has, however, resulted in diminished, if still continued, violence compared with that of the 1992 civil war. The reduced violence spurred the return of refugees. The presence of international personnel from UNHCR, OSCE, and the UNMOT has arguably reduced incidents of harassment. Attention by human rights organizations such as Human Rights Watch/Helsinki, Memorial, and Amnesty International have highlighted, and perhaps reduced, human and civil rights abuses committed or condoned by the government of Tajikistan. The participation of the government and opposition representatives in the joint commission that monitored the cease-fire was an excellent first step in building confidence not only among the negotiators, but also among those on the commission and the population they encounter as they investigate issues of Teheran Agreement compliance. Since evidence supporting alleged infractions is often lacking, what little progress the joint commission has made is positive.

Key factors in the eventual resolution of this situation are the recognition by the government of the opposition, its legalization, and efforts on both sides to compromise and work toward developing a concept of a Tajik state that is inclusive in nature. The first step was taken on May 19, 1995, when President Rakhmonov met with opposition leader Sayyid Abdullah Nuri for the first time, in Kabul. While this meeting did not resolve any key issues, it was important for the recognition it gave the opposition, and it was clearly the culmination of efforts from many groups to encourage a peaceful political, rather than military, settlement. In the terms presented by the Intervention Cycle, this was the first step toward resolution-toward political enfranchisement of all parties to the Tajik conflict.

IV. LESSONS LEARNED FROM THE INTERVENTION CYCLE FRAMEWORK

This case shows the unfortunate development of violence from the unraveling of political and social enfranchisement (*Perestroika* and the dissolution of the Soviet Union) beyond stages of meaningful deterrence and coercion to total civil war. There, at the height of violence, is where intervention in the form of the CIS "peacekeeping" was initiated. It is an example of the type of crisis that can occur in a postcolonial state where ideology and coercion falsely enfranchise groups under an authoritarian regime. Such false enfranchisement (specifically a lack of political and social cohesion within the society) sets the stage for conflict rather than preparing the foundation for independence. It is also apparent, with the aid of the Intervention Cycle, that in this case different groups sought to intervene with efforts more appropriate to different stages of the conflict—and to effect a different type of outcome. Few of these interventions reflected the real dynamics of Tajikistan's violence; none were able to succeed in its prevention.

A. False Enfranchisement Prior to Conflict

Under the Soviet system, a patina of enfranchisement made it appear that all elements of society had a political voice through voting, and all had access to economic and social enfranchisement facilitated by broad access to education. In Tajikistan, as with many other republics, the actual opportunities for economic and political advancement were limited. Ethnic Russians held all key positions in the military and industry, severely limiting the spread of those skills and their accompanying economic and social benefits to ethnic Tajiks or Uzbeks. Political power was concentrated within two very narrowly defined groups from Khojand and Kulab: not only was every First Secretary of the Tajik Communist Party from Khojand, they all were from the same street in Khojand City.[32] Similarly, the leaders of the opposition are also a product of false enfranchisement; some scholars question whether the opposition leaders have broad-based support in the countryside, given the key role of "localism" in deciding loyalties. The opposition represents a small group of intelligentsia, mostly now living in Dushanbe, who came from the countryside for access to higher education under the soviet system and who are now competing with the "old guard" leadership for power and influence to correct inequities of the old system.[33]

This lack of true enfranchisement is at the crux of the conflict and is a significant hurdle to its resolution. Since the bulk of the population had no sense of a "stake" in the old system, they never developed the political, social, and economic structures within society that provide outlets to grievances or expand individual or group participation in the society. Thus, when confronted with popular attempts to organize the population—beginning with the Rastakhiz movement during *Perestroika*—the group in power felt immediately threatened. Their status within the old system assured them of political and economic power. When that status was challenged, they became reluctant to encourage efforts at true enfranchisement. As conflict increased within society, they turned their efforts toward deterring violence rather than resolving the underlying causes.

B. Deterrence Phase

The deterrence phase of intervention began in May 1990, when the new political freedom resulting from *Perestroika* was struck down by the government crackdown on Rastakhiz. While the movement was not advocating serious political change, the government clearly saw the Rastakhiz as a challenger and took action to denounce it. This was followed by efforts to contain the growth of any form of opposition; however, each effort at discrediting the emerging movements only seemed to encourage more opposition. As protests erupted, steps taken by the government to maintain its hold on power became increasingly draconian, as predicted by the Intervention Cycle framework.[34]

Starting with the presidential election in November 1991 the government passed up several opportunities to defuse the growing conflict. However, instead of risking the loss of total power, they took actions that only fed the disenfranchisement of the opposition. Rather than attempting to reduce the level of conflict by giving these new movements a stake in the political, economic, and social future of the state, as recommended within the Intervention Cycle discussion, the government instead tried to repress the movements.

C. Coercion Phase

The distribution of weapons to progovernment demonstrators in May 1992 is the point at which the Tajik leadership crossed the line into coercion. This represented a clear escalation of the cost to each side: the government hoped to instill fear into the opposition, forcing them to reconsider their overt resistance to government control. At the same time, the government became committed to pursuing a path of violence against violence from the opposition forces.

While seeming to retreat from confrontation by creating the coalition government in May 1992, President Nabiev at the same time created the Popular Front to take action against the opposition. The Popular Front then set about terrorizing the countryside on what must have been instructions from the central government. As a tool of coercion, the Popular Front was poorly conceived and ineffective. There was collateral damage; violence begot violence and many innocent civilians were killed and forced to flee. Contrary to the recommendations of the Intervention Cycle, there was no effort to identify a desired effect of using coercion as a tool (other than to create terror). There were no conditions for eliminating the use of coercion, nor were there redoubled efforts to resolve the underlying problems of political disenfranchisement. Therefore, there was no prospect that the opposition might positively respond to the Popular Front or any other actions by the old hard-line government.

From May 1992, the government's actions did not significantly stray beyond coercion. For example, while the government supported refugee repatriation, they did little to protect repatriated refugees from the same Popular Front thugs who terrorized them and forced them to flee in the first place. While the government participated in cease-fire talks with the opposition, they relied on the CIS peacekeeping force to continue "protecting" the border area, including attacking opposition fighters. Meanwhile, they violated the Teheran cease-fire accord by repositioning Tajik army (largely composed of former Popular Front fighters) forces into border regions.

Tajikistan has allowed a state of lawlessness to continue in the country, or has simply been unable to prevent it. Kidnapping and gang-style murders are prevalent. The military may not even be under control of the central government: In February 1996, two Tajik brigades (led by Uzbek commanders) mutinied and occupied Kurgan-Tube and Tursunzade until the government met their demands.[35] Thus, the bulk of the evidence suggests that the Tajik government, four years after the violence really began, remained stuck in a pattern of coercion, despite the mediation efforts of outsiders.

D. Peace Enforcement

Of the outside interveners, the CIS peacekeeping force has hardly been impartial. Despite admonitions from the UN,[36] they continue overtly to support the post-Soviet government and its actions. Their insistence that CIS peacekeeping forces are neither subject to the Teheran agreement nor the cease-fire allows them to remain a party to the conflict. They, in reality, protect the border against opposition supporters trying to cross back into Tajikistan from refugee camps in Afghanistan. The special representative of the UN Secretary General is aware of this problem and has been working with Russia to try to resolve the issue. However, until the peacekeeping forces refrain from acting as partisans, they will fail to move this conflict any closer to resolution.

Although the CIS forces have clearly been a party to the conflict and the IC would argue they must be replaced by an impartial force, the opposition has not called for their replacement.[37] This could suggest recognition by the opposition that no other major power would have the staying power or the interest to involve itself in this conflict—as well as a recognition of the importance of Russian aid to the Tajik economy. Further, the presence of the Russian/CIS forces has provided a credible "enforcement" of a partial peace. Unable to defeat these forces, and unable to pursue political objectives through the use of force, the opposition has made tenuous movement toward resolution.

The efforts of the UN, supported by the work of outside groups such as the Dartmouth Conference and other regional states, has assisted that movement. They have provided venues and structures for developing a basis of common understanding and several opportunities for developing of mutual recognition and confidence building measures that will be required to continue the movement toward resolution. However, the road ahead is the most difficult; fractures within each side will become ever more apparent under the pressure of reconciliation.

V. PROSPECTS FOR RESOLUTION

Despite the varied, serious efforts at intervention, the conflict will remain at a standstill until the government of Tajikistan recognizes the need for political enfranchisement to negotiate seriously with the opposition and include them in the power bases and structures of the country. In order to reach that stage, all sides require assistance and encouragement; the conflict is a product of the history of the state, which has lacked the types of political, social, and economic enfranchisement necessary to be able to resolve conflict effectively with anything other than force and coercion. They must, with significant outside support, work to resolve the underlying causes of the civil war and begin steps of empowerment required of a stable, multigroup state. Such enfranchisement will help develop a common stake in Tajikistan's future, contribute to an overarching Tajik identity, and help foster a cohesive, independent state.

Progress rests on both sides knowing that there can be no long-term resolution with a "winner-take-all" approach to a solution. Clearly, this represents a loss of power and prestige for the incumbents and will require serious pressure toward reform from Russia, Uzbekistan, and the supporters of the regime. It will also be a challenge for the leaders of the opposition, who will have to share power with various elements within their own ranks. As the conflict drags on and continues to drain economic and military resources, both Russia and Uzbekistan are more likely to press for resolution. They may fear the specter of a fundamentalist Islamic state, but the reality of continued instability and casualties among peacekeepers and border guards may take precedence.

Russian intervention, however, is no panacea. While the International Community may look to Russia to reign in their client regime directly, it will be a very delicate process. Russians, nationalists and democrats alike, see Tajikistan (and its border with Afghanistan) as a strategic location where they will be disinclined to tolerate much outside intervention. Some aspects of Russia's armed intervention have clearly served more purposes than the long term interests of conflict resolution in Tajikistan. Similarly, the financial and personnel support Russia provides Tajikistan's government may not serve the long-term interests of building a viable, independent state and national bureaucracy. However, given Russian domestic opposition to and outcry against Russian army action in Chechnya, continued conflict in Tajikistan may incline Moscow toward exerting pressure on the Tajik government to resolve their disputes with the opposition peacefully.

If outside intervention is unable to convince the government and opposition to proceed down the path toward resolution, the conflict will continue to build. The opposition is committed to a sustained effort toward recognition and incorporation into the government. Qazi Akbar Turajanzade cited the Irish Republican Army's lengthy struggle with the British government as an example for the Tajik opposition to emulate.[38] While it is inaccurate to portray the Islamic opposition as fundamentalist now, it is probable that continued conflict and disenfranchisement will only serve to factionalize and radicalize both sides and make compromise more difficult over the long run.

Even with serious pressure from outside to accommodate the opposition, it will take some time for the government to reign in its forces of excess and establish productive integration at the grassroots level. Not only are former Popular Front fighters entrenched in the Tajik army, local police forces, and many other areas, the government will also be confronting the challenge of reorienting public priorities and loyalties away from the traditional localism to a national greater good. Doing so will require significant technical assistance and developmental support from the International Community. Beyond political enfranchisement, the geographic–economic divisions within the country must be eliminated through education, development, industrial expansion, and resource management, which will also lay the foundation for economic and, perhaps, eventual social enfranchisement. This—and not more military force—is the assistance Tajikistan needed at the outset of its independence, and will be necessary to develop a true Tajik nation.

NOTES

1. Shahrbanou Tadjbakhsh, "The Bloody Path of Change: The Case of Post-Soviet Tajikistan," *The Harriman Institute Forum*, 6, no. 11 (July 1993), p. 1. The loss of life is significant, especially considering the relatively small population; estimates range from 25,000 (official government account) to 200,000 (claims of the Islamic Renaissance Movement) dead out of a population of five and one-half million.
2. Qazi Akbar Turajanzade, in a speech to the Global Strategy Council in Washington, DC, on February 7, 1995.
3. Olivier Roy, *The Civil War in Tajikistan: Causes and Implications*. Washington, DC: United States Institute of Peace, 1993, p. 10. See also Barnett R. Rubin, "Tajikistan: From Soviet Republic to Russian-Uzbek Protectorate" in Michael Mandelbaum, (Ed.), *Central Asia and the World*. New York: Council on Foreign Relations, 1994, p. 211; and Roland Dannreuther, *Creating New States in Central Asia*, Adelphi Paper, no. 288. London: Brassey's, 1994, p. 11.
4. Olivier Roy, *The Civil War in Tajikistan*, p. 2.
5. For example, in the Gorno-Badakhshan autonomous region in the Pamir Mountains, the "Pamiri" group identification remains one of locale, rather than ethnicity. Most Pamiris speak languages related to eastern Iranian, rather than Persian, and follow the Ismaili sect of Islam (a dissident form of Shi'ism), rather than the Sunni form practiced by most other "Tajiks." Despite these differences in language and religion from the other Tajik areas—and their fairly homogenous culture—their identification remains Pamiri.
6. Roland Dannreuther notes that the Kulabis fulfilled a responsibility under the Soviets that they had also fulfilled under the Bukharan khanate: that of suppressing other southern claimants to power. See Dannreuther, *Creating New States in Central Asia*, p. 27.
7. Shahrbanou Tadjbakhsh, "The Bloody Path of Change," p. 2.

8. Keith Martin, "Tajikistan: Civil War Without End?" *Radio Free Europe/Radio Liberty (RFE/RL) Research Report,* August 20, 1993, p. 20.

9. Barnett R. Rubin, "The Fragmentation of Tajikistan," *Survival,* 35, no. 4 (Winter 1993-1994), p. 77.

10. "War or Peace? Human Rights and Russian Military Involvement in the 'Near Abroad'" *Helsinki Watch,* 5, no. 22 (December 1993), p. 14.

11. Ibid., p. 13

12. Richard K. Herrmann, "Russian Policy in the Middle East: Strategic Change and Tactical Contradictions," *Middle East Journal,* 48, no. 3 (Summer 1994), p. 470.

13. Barnett R. Rubin, "The Fragmentation of Tajikistan," p. 80.

14. The term "peacekeeping" is used here because it is the commonly-used translation. It is important to note, however, that the CIS peacekeeping force does not meet the UN standards; they are clearly partial to the government of Tajikistan and do not hesitate to use force in executing their mission.

15. Roland Dannreuther, *Creating New States in Central Asia,* p. 29.

16. Neela Banerjee, "Russia Combines War and Peace to Reclaim Parts of Its Old Empire," *The Wall Street Journal,* September 2, 1994, p. A5.

17. Many serious scholars note that Islam is more of a cultural rather than religious force in Central Asia, and the Central Asians are not inclined toward extremism. A recent survey of Central Asians substantiated these views. See Nancy Lubin, *Central Asians Take Stock: Reform, Corruption, and Identity,* Peaceworks no. 2, Washington DC: United States Institute of Peace, 1995, pp. 15-19.

18. *Open Media Research Institute (OMRI) Daily Digest,* Part 1, no. 109, June 6, 1995.

19. Shahram Chubin, *Iran's National Security Policy: Intentions, Capabilities, and Impact.* Washington DC: Carnegie Endowment, 1994, pp. 6-8. Chubin points out that Iran's top priority in the region remains its relations with Russia, which is an important source of technology and military hardware.

20. Rachel Denber, *Human Rights in Tajikistan in the Wake of the Civil War.* New York: Human Rights Watch/Helsinki Watch, Memorial, 1993, p. 34.

21. Ibid., pp. 34-45.

22. *Human Rights Watch World Report 1995,* New York, NY: Human Rights Watch 1994, p. 226.

23. "UNICEF [United National International Children's Education Fund] Appeals for US $5.6 Million for Acute Emergency in Tajikistan", PR/GVA/96/11. Almaty/Geneva: United Nations, 1995.

24. "Report of the Secretary General on the Situation in Tajikistan," S/1994/1102. New York: United Nations, 1994, para. 7.

25. UN Security Council Resolution 968, December 16, 1994. See also "Report of the Secretary General on Tajikistan," S/1995/472, June 10, 1995.

26. Reported in ITAR-TASS, quoted in *Open Media Research Institute (OMRI) Daily Digest,* Part I, February 27, 95.

27. *OMRI Daily Digest,* Part I, reported on May 29 1995, the warning from the UN envoy to the Tajik talks, Ramiro Piriz Ballon, that the UN might not extend the mandate of the mission in Tajikistan, citing lack of agreement between the two sides on any constructive steps. This statement came after the fourth round of

talks, when the opposition proposed a power-sharing arrangement for a governing council where 40 percent would go to the incumbent government, 40 percent to the opposition, and the remaining 20 percent to various small ethnic groups.

28. *Human Rights Watch World Report 1995*, p. 225.

29. Anonymous, "Tajikistan: Another Afghan War?" *Bulletin of the Atomic Scientists*, Jan/Feb. 1994, p. 58.

30. *OMRI Daily Digest*, Part I, no. 78, April 20, 1995.

31. "Report of the Secretary General on the Situation in Tajikistan," S/1995/1024. New York, NY: United Nations, 1995, para. 11.

32. Roland Dannreuther, *Creating New States in Central Asia*, p. 27.

33. Olivier Roy, *The Civil War in Tajikistan*, pp. 22-23.

34. Von Lipsey's Intervention Cycle discussion indicates that efforts at deterrence will give way to coercion lacking redoubled efforts of political enfranchisement. Absent enfranchisement, these draconian measures only beget increasing violence, increasing the need for greater coercion and creating a spiraling level of violence in society.

35. *OMRI Daily Digest*, Part I, February 2, 1996.

36. "Report of the Secretary General on the Situation in Tajikistan," S/1994/1102, note to para. 2(a) to Annex 1.

37. Neela Banerjee, "Russia Combines War and Peace," p. A5.

38. *OMRI Daily Digest*, Part I, February 3, 1995, citing *Financial Times*, February 3, 1995.

CHAPTER 11

Anatomy of a Conflict: Chechnya

Maryann Parker

I. INTRODUCTION

The breakaway North Caucasian Republic of Chechnya first seized world attention when Russian troops invaded in December 1994. But just as policy failures in Chechnya long predate that disastrous intervention, so the violence, or its consequences, could continue indefinitely. Terrorist forays beyond the borders of Chechnya keep the conflict in the Russian news but have not prompted earnest peace initiatives. Likewise, Russian Army operations in Chechnya—at the time of this writing—keep the conflict in the Western news; yet the larger questions of Russian-Western political relations dim the prospects for outside intervention. And the April 1996 death of unrepentant Chechen president Dzhokar Dudaev, at once the fiend of war and the key to peace, complicated both Chechen secession and peaceful resolution to the dispute.

Russia went into Chechnya both to make peace between warring parties and to topple the Dudaev regime. As often happens in the pursuit of a dual, contradictory mission, neither goal was achieved. Russia got more than it bargained for—a war that demanded international attention. However, despite widespread concern and frequent outrage, the international community accepted Moscow's claim that the conflict in Chechnya is a Russian affair. International organizations have provided humanitarian assistance and rushed to facilitate negotiations. But for the most part, this is a Russian—or perhaps a regional—headache.

And it's one serious headache. Once billed as a two-hour mission, fighting still raged 18 months after the invasion. Tens of thousands have died, hundreds

---

Maryann Parker was the Assistant Director for Program Coordination in the Moscow Center of the Carnegie Endowment for International Peace. Prior to this, she was a Project Associate with Carnegie's Program on Russian and Eurasian Affairs in Washington, D.C.

of thousands become refugees, cities and an economy have been destroyed, an army humiliated—all bringing Chechnya no closer to settling down within the Russian Federation. For Yeltsin, Chechnya has been a political nightmare; disgust over the war completed the disillusionment with his administration for many Russians.

To invigorate his reelection campaign in April 1996, Boris Yeltsin announced a cease-fire and proposed negotiations with Dudaev, even suggesting Presidents Nursultan Nazerbayev of Kazakhstan and Mintimer Shamiaev of Tatarstan as potential mediators. While the chaos associated with the death of Dudaev days after the announcement stymied the plan, Yeltsin, for one of the first times since Chechnya's independence, seemed committed to seeking a peace acceptable to both sides.

"All happy families resemble one another," Leo Tolstoy opened *Anna Karenina*, "while each unhappy family is unhappy in its own way." So must begin any discussion that attempts to compare dysfunctional parts of the world. Chechnya is unique; the dynamics of the conflict are rooted in the particularly troubled history of the region and the singularly complicated contortions of post-Soviet Kremlin politics. Attention to those dynamics is essential to understanding why violence broke out, how it might have been averted, and what steps hold the most promise for long-term resolution.

Tolstoy's pithy wisdom is not the end of the story. "Unhappy families," psychologist Maggie Scarf writes, "tend to become trapped in fixed patterns of responding and in nonnegotiable positions—get stuck, in other words."[1] Indeed, for all its terribly fascinating uniqueness, Chechnya bears a marked family resemblance to its hot-spot siblings: the root cause of violence there is "an indigenous political failure, a failure to consolidate a regime that has enough legitimacy and capabilities to defend itself and to hold at bay the forces that seek to destroy it."[2] The inability to remedy that failure has dimmed prospects for a vital Chechen republic, in or out of the Russian Federation. And it could have dire consequence for the vitality of the Russian Federation itself.

Chechnya's declaration of independence grew from a profound desire for greater autonomy left unaddressed upon the break-up of the Soviet Union. Like other subjects of the Federation, Chechnya sought more control over its resources and development, politics, and cultural life. Use of force to quell the Chechen drive for independence was counterproductive not only because it lacked both military potency and adequate political will, but also because it was not linked to enfranchisement carrots that could carry the issue beyond violence.

Russian troops entered a country torn both by civil war and between the hope for autonomy and the reality of dependence. Unified through opposition, violence pushed Chechnya further along the fateful path to secession. Thus, only military issues made it to the negotiation table. When root causes of conflict do not enter negotiations, resulting peace agreements are tenuous at best. Interventions of the Chechnya kind breed bitter new generations likely to revisit the same age-old grievances violently.

II. CHECHNYA AND RUSSIA: AUTONOMY AND DEPENDENCE

Chechnya is a small mountain republic located in the North Caucasian region, enclosed by Russia on all sides except its mountainous southern border, which it shares with Georgia. Prior to the outbreak of war, approximately 1.2 million people lived in Chechnya, including some 300,000 ethnic Russians. Ethnic Chechens are predominantly Muslim and have retained their ancient and unique language and culture.

The North Caucasus has been an object of Russian expansion for hundreds of years, and the people of the region have resisted for just as long. The region boasts some mineral wealth, which includes substantial oil deposits. This is also an extremely rich agricultural region. The mountains serve as a vital hedge against strikes at Russia's otherwise vulnerable south, and continue to be of vital strategic importance.

The many violent chapters in Russian-Chechen history live on in the modern Chechen conscience. The Chechen capital city Grozny—which means terrible, fearful—takes its name from an 18th-century Russian fort intended to intimidate unruly Caucasians. The boast did not cow them. Chechen Mansur Ushurma, called *imam* (spiritual guide) of all the Caucasian mountaineers, was captured in 1785 only after years of glorious campaigns against the Russians. In 1859, it took 300,000 Russian soldiers and 30 years to crush the Imamate of Shamil. Things did not improve under Soviet rule; regular rebellions continued into the 20th century. Chechnya, like other Russian peripheries, has long struggled with the tension between autonomy and dependence.

The Chechen crisis both dramatizes the new challenges presented by a multiethnic Russian Federation and evokes strikingly similar actions taken by Moscow in the waning years of the Soviet Union. In January 1991, Boris Yeltsin pleaded with Soviet soldiers on their way to suppress demonstrating Lithuanian nationalists: "You may be told that, with your help, order will be established in society. But is it possible to regard violations of the Constitution and laws as the establishment of peace? Violence . . . will bring about a new crisis in Russia itself . . ."[3]

Four years later in his annual speech to the Federal Assembly of now-independent Russia, President Yeltsin concluded that "The Chechen crisis, just like a drop of water, reflects all the problems of Russian statehood."[4] Indeed, the secession crisis in small Chechnya caricatures Russia's larger problems. The destabilizing forces at work throughout the Russian Federation—crime, ethnically based nationalism, racism, fear of Muslim fundamentalism, the legacies of imperial and Soviet pasts—are distorted and exaggerated in Chechnya, and erupt in garish colors.

When enough of its citizens decided that the Soviet Union provided them neither a political, economic, nor social voice, the state failed. Chechnya, like other autonomous, but not sovereign republics of the USSR, remained a constituent part of the Russian Federation. Every generation of Chechens has nursed a story of Russian oppression; who sits in Moscow—tsar, general secretary, president—has not greatly altered that story.

The 1944 deportation of the Chechens lives in the enraging, humiliating memories of the many Chechens who spent their childhood in Central Asian exile. Toward the end of World War II, Stalin removed the Chechens and several other peoples from their homelands on weak charges of collaboration with Nazi invaders. Without warning or explanation, the Chechens were packed off to Kazakhstan in hideous conditions that killed a large part of their number. The removal was astoundingly ruthless. Locals tell of Soviet troops shooting or burning alive children and the disabled; hunting down those who escaped; mining homes and leaving poisoned food scattered in the forests.[5] Only in 1957 did Khruschev allow Chechens to return to their previous homes.

Many intergroup conflicts spring from one party's sense of political disenfranchisement; one can find few examples of such a complete removal from the political map. Profound disgust with any kind of status under Moscow has helped Chechens endure the mixed results of their attempt at sovereignty. "Listen to me," a Chechen peasant told a journalist on a bus, in defense of the chaotic Chechen republic under defiant President Dzhokhar Dudaev. "We do have our independence, so we can be owners ourselves, so nobody can ever send us off to Kazakhstan like cattle in wagon cars again . . . "[6] They nursed no illusions about their political muscle in the system.

Political estrangement was hardly compensated with economic and social benefits. Chechen education, job opportunities, and living conditions lagged behind those of the ethnic Russians in the mountain republic. Ethnic Chechens were always poorly represented in the universities and among the skilled workers. According to Soviet statistics, social development in the Chechen Republic ranked near the bottom; dismal statistics on infant mortality and environmental health flesh out a grim picture.

By 1991, the genie of freedom had left the bottle. But the nominally autonomous republics and regions—unlike the constituent republics of the

Soviet Union—remained under the thumb of Moscow. Chechnya found the central government increasingly irrelevant and incapable of addressing its immediate concerns. Other constituents of the Russian Federation agreed. In the Republic of Tuva on the Chinese border, only 30.5 percent of voters supported the Constitution of the Russian Federation. In the same election they also approved a Republic constitution granting local authorities the right to suspend the laws of the Russian Federation under certain circumstances.[7]

Though independence-minded, these semiautonomous Russian republics were not doomed to violent confrontation. In the case of Tatarstan, which, like Chechnya, was an early booster for greater local autonomy, the integrity of the Russian Federation was preserved through a deft mix of accommodation and coercion. In February 1994, the government of Tatarstan agreed to a politically enfranchising power-sharing formula with the Russian government. The bilateral treaty represented two years and eight months of negotiations. Significantly, Moscow relied on economic rather than military coercion to draw Tatarstan back into the fold. Though rich in oil, Tatarstan is dependent on neighboring Bashkortostan for refined petroleum products; Moscow's control over pipelines may have been the straw that broke the back of Tatar independence. Russian authorities also brokered an economically enfranchising deal with the diamond-producing region of Sakha/Yakutia, granting it the right to keep tax revenues.[8]

Although the Tatarstan agreement pleased few and angered extremists on both sides, it prevented violent conflict. Russia's pursuit of drawn-out negotiations improved the chances that Tatar interests would be reflected in the settlement. Moscow did depend on coercion to get the agreement signed. However, that pressure was economic, underlining Tatarstan's dependence on pipelines, and it was convincingly backed with the political will to make concessions—such as tolerating the rhetorical discrepancy between Moscow's characterization of the agreement as an internal document and Kazan's assertion that it is a treaty between two sovereign states.

Russia's failure to use a patient and enfranchising strategy in Chechnya reduced the chances for peaceful resolution of that crisis. Of course the Tatarstan analogy can only be taken so far. There, locals were not in armed rebellion; there, an anything-goes free trade zone was not in effect; and there, Moscow had a very clear interest: oil. The resolution process depended on the fact that both sides had something to lose in the demise of the status quo. In Chechnya, digging meaningful channels of communication where precious few had ever existed was a challenge of a different order. So was the creation of enfranchising mechanisms after decades of neglect.

III. HESITANCE, NEGLECT, IMPATIENCE:
RUSSIA BLUNDERS INTO CHECHNYA

Chechnya is economically dependent on Russia. Highly populated but barely industrialized, North Caucasian governments depend heavily on subsidies from Moscow. Before the break-up of the Soviet Union, direct federal subsidies and credits from the Central Bank made up 50-70 percent of budget revenues in those republics—and Chechnya was among the most heavily subsidized.[9] Chafing under that dependence and sharing an national identity that embraces religion, culture, and social structure, Chechens coalesced quickly in the scramble following the break-up of the Soviet Union. As a first act of defiance, the nationalists proposed that Chechnya, reconfigured as a sovereign republic, should be itself a signatory to Gorbachev's new Union Treaty.

The nationalists, led by former Soviet fighter-jet pilot Dzhokhar Dudaev, found their opportunity during the putsch of 1991. The conservative supreme soviet in the Chechen capital, Grozny, supported the putsch; hence the Dudaev forces had a tacit mandate from the victorious Yeltsin camp in Moscow—including prodigal Chechen Ruslan Khasbulatov, chair of the Russian Federation Supreme Soviet—to overthrow the local soviet. To Yeltsin's consternation, Dudaev did not stop there. He took up arms against the reformed soviet and formed his own election committee. On October 27, 1991, he won the presidency. On November 2, he declared the independence of Chechnya.

Moscow hesitated. Yeltsin declared a state of emergency in Chechnya on November 9, 1991. Dudaev countered with martial law; his forces quickly hemmed in some 600 Russian interior ministry troops sent to the scene. Fearing a messy conflict with emboldened Chechen secessionists, the Russian Supreme Soviet voted 177 to 4 to overturn Yeltsin's decree. The Russian troops left sheepishly in tour buses.

That miscalculation wasted an early chance at decisive resolution of Russian and Chechen differences. And Moscow's knee-jerk decision to send down troops signaled to the Chechens that Moscow still considered them children to be slapped for naughtiness rather than co-citizens with serious concerns; there would not be two years and eight months of negotiation with this upstart republic. Also, the reversals in Moscow revealed confusion in circles of power over what to do with restless regions at the fringe of the new Russian Federation. Most importantly, the Russian humiliation emboldened Dudaev. He added a difficult condition to negotiations between Chechnya and Russia: recognition of Chechen sovereignty. Coupled with his decision to raise an army, the prospect of fruitful discussions grew less likely.

Dudaev only gained leverage over the next year, one in which the Russian policy toward Chechnya could best be described as benign neglect. In March 1992, Chechnya (still nominally linked to Ingushetia, although the Ingush were less eager to leave Russia) joined Tatarstan in its refusal to sign the Russian Federation Treaty. Busy enough with peacekeeping on the contested border between Chechnya's North Caucasian neighbors Ingushetia and North Ossetia, Moscow was loathe to involve itself in another politically damaging incident in Chechnya. Dudaev's power increased while Moscow's ability to intervene decisively weakened.

By early 1993, without any sign of interference from Moscow, local opposition to Dudaev's ballooning power began to emerge. In April, the Chechen parliament voted no confidence in the government; Dudaev responded by abolishing the parliament. Civil violence began. In one referendum, Dudaev's leadership was soundly rejected. By mid-June, three regions had declared their intent to secede from the "criminal regime in Grozny."[10]

Inevitably, united by their common distaste for Dudaev, the Chechen opposition and Moscow found each other. Most of the opposition leaders, however, were driven more by hatred for Dudaev than fondness for Russia; sprung from cohesive clan structures and fueled by the Chechen tradition of blood feud, those warlords—such as convicted murderer and former Dudaev partisan Ruslan Labazanov—gained primarily local support. Umar Avturkhanov of the anti-Dudaev Nadterechnyi region in northern Chechnya alone pledged allegiance to Moscow, winning its increasingly open support. Avturkhanov formed the Provisional Council, which Moscow recognized as the sole legitimate organ of power in Chechnya.

Moscow seized on Avturkhanov's Provisional Council as a method of weakening Dudaev from within Chechnya. At first, the levers of influence were primarily economic; but, as on the political score, the strategy was irresolutely implemented. Moscow sent Avturkhanov money to pay pensions, which had been frozen for two years. Heavy economic aid to the three Moscow-friendly districts in the North could topple Dudaev through "peaceful competition between two systems," suggested Emil Pain, a Kremlin advisor on nationality issues.[11] Enriched Nadterechnyi, in contrast to Dudaev's uneasy kingdom of criminal traders in flashy cars and impoverished peasants on mercifully productive farmland, would improve the chances of Russia-friendly forces in 1995 elections.

Moscow's economic pressure on Chechnya was full of holes. Despite an economic blockade, the Republic somehow obtained export licenses for its most precious commodity, oil. The notorious Chechen arms bazaar must owe something to the fact that Defense Minster Grachev inexplicably let half of the Soviet arsenal on Chechen soil fall to Dudaev.[12] In August of 1994, Igor Rotar wrote in *Nezavisimaya Gazeta* that unemployment in Chechnya stood around 70 percent. To make ends meet, he continued, much of the able-bodied population was forced to work outside of the republic—in Russia. Others supported themselves in the shuttle business. Chechnya, flouting Russian custom duties, became something of a free economic zone; low-cost goods arriving from countries to the south cleared through Grozny before being shuttled to cities around Russia. "If Moscow wished to dictate its will to the republic," Rotar suggested, "it would not have to send in tanks—it would be sufficient to seal off the borders."[13]

Moscow's threat to cut the Tatarstan pipeline—lifeline, more accurately, for that republic government—surely played a large role in the Tatar decision to accept accommodation within the Russian Federation. Chechnya is similarly dependent on Russia: wages in the oil fields have gone unpaid, and electricity arrears have run high into the billions of rubles.[14] Control over energy supplies, as part of a strict economic isolation of the republic, may have accelerated the demise of Dudaev without raising the ire occasioned by Russian occupation. However, Russia pursued no parallel course of political engagement during these half-efforts at coercion.

As the year 1994 wore on, it became a kind of open secret that Moscow was not only materially but also militarily supporting Dudaev's opposition, Avturkhanov's Provisional Council. As if making up for lost time, Moscow abandoned patience and began supplying Avturkhanov with covert military support. Paradoxically, Russian support for the opposition undermined the possibility that Dudaev could be toppled. First, the infusion of Russian arms and supplies bolstered the position of local warlords as much as Avturkhanov. More importantly, Dudaev could now claim convincingly that his opposition—and the warlords—were created by Moscow in order to weaken the proud Chechen Republic. And despite Dudaev's declining popularity, public enemy number one in Chechnya had always been Russia. A real Russian threat gave something for Dudaev to fight against, a reason for existence, and a popular rallying point.

By the summer of 1994, still months before the invasion, Moscow's involvement in Chechnya became more intense despite public pronouncements to the contrary and continued calls for negotiation. North Caucasian border troops massed. Although too late to catalyze peaceful capitulation, economic ties were persuasively cut. Reports of a late August meeting at the Kremlin to plan a covert operation in Chechnya appeared in several Russian sources. And, presidential advisors who did not support military action in Chechnya stopped getting feedback from the Kremlin. "Everything that had anything to do with policy in Chechnya was shrouded in secrecy," one reported.[15]

If those in the Kremlin did not, at least the Chechen opposition understood that an impetuously activist Russian role in the crisis could only reduce
the chances of ousting Dudaev. Merely the spectre of a Russian threat strengthened him. "The anti-Chechen campaign in the Russian press will ensure that
Dudaev's position is steadfast for a minimum of another six months," admitted the former chairman of the erstwhile Chechen parliament, Yusup
Soseddin, on August 16.[16] As for Russian military involvement, even its supposed client the Provisional Council was careful to disclaim it.

"Russia does, of course, assist us economically. But otherwise there has
been no Russian intervention in the Chechen issue," declared an aide to
Avturkhanov on October 3.[17] Other regional leaders in Chechnya believed
that Avturkhanov's credibility as an opposition leader would be seriously
undermined if just one Russian soldier surfaced amid his forces. The head of
the Provisional Council headquarters put it most succinctly: "If Russian
troops come to Chechnya, we have lost."[18]

Toward the end of November, Russian forces massed around Chechnya
and bloody clashes within the Republic spelled imminent disaster. However,
Moscow continued to order cease-fires; declare and then ignore moratoriums;
and raise hopes with last-minute high-level negotiations. On November 29,
after a spate of bombing and fighting in Chechnya, Yeltsin threatened to use
"all forces and resources at the disposal of the state" to restore order.[19]

Yet Russian soldiers themselves were a party to that disorder: They were
behind the bullets breaching the cease-fire and the planes flying in the no-fly
zone. On November 26, 1994—reportedly because Chechen soldiers refused
$1,000 apiece to storm Grozny—Russian troops were summoned to take over
the mission.[20] Although several Russian regular army troops were captured by
Dudaev's forces, Moscow continued to call the soldiers mercenaries, acting on
their own free will. Neither the Chechens nor the mothers of the prisoners
were easily convinced. "They are not volunteers for the opposition," demonstrating mothers insisted. "The government and the defense minister refuse to
admit that the Russian army is involved in the conflict in Chechnya."[21] When
interviewed on television, several of the Russian prisoners said that they had
been sent secretly to Chechnya under contract with the Federal
Counterintelligence Service, the successor to the KGB.

The capture of those troops blew the cover off the covert mission of support for the anti-Dudaev forces. A number of damaging reversals ensued.
Russian Deputy Defense Minister Boris Gromov admitted that Russian troops
were in Chechnya on December 4; however, he maintained that they were not
officially ordered to fight the Dudaev forces. On December 5, Defense
Minister Grachev admitted that Russian planes had been involved in deadly

bombing raids the previous week. Yeltsin found himself in a difficult position, stuck between an unpopular war on one side, and another humiliating retreat from puny Chechnya on the other.

While Yeltsin's Security Council prepared plans for an assault, pro forma negotiations continued. Although the productive December 7 meeting between Grachev and Dudaev was taken as a sign of hope in Moscow, Dudaev correctly summed up its results. "Today we have agreed on a peaceful solution to the military aspect," he said over celebratory champagne, "Now we have to solve the political aspect."[22] Unbeknownst to Moscow, by December 1994 the conflict had long since cycled past the stage at which Russia could effect a political solution through coercion.

Much has and will be said of the grave miscalculations that prompted Moscow to send over 40,000 troops to Chechnya on December 11, 1994. Certainly, many of the reasons behind the decision to invade were totally extrinsic to reality in Chechnya; they could be found in Kremlin power politics. Yet while Moscow politics undoubtedly played a role in the timing and rationale for the invasion, Russian intervention no more began on December 11th than Chechen restlessness surfaced with its declaration of independence in 1991. Not as valuable to its economic engine as Tatarstan, Chechnya did not merit the lengthy, difficult combination of negotiation and pressure that has the most success in staving off conflict. Moscow blundered into Chechnya through a policy of hesitance, neglect, and impatience.

Commander Vladimir Mozhaev of the Russian internal border troops boasted in early December: "General Grachev said we could take Grozny in two hours with a battalion of paratroopers. I think it would be quicker."[23] Tens of thousands of dead, a demolished city, and several politically suicidal weeks later, that cocky decision looked fatal. Moscow made the error of assuming that Dudaev could stage no better defense against Russians than he could against his local foes. They discounted the degree of distance from Russia expressed by the peasant on the bus: "If there's a Dudaev, there will be a Chechnya; if there is no Dudaev—there will be no Chechnya."[24] Chechens rallied quite naturally to Dudaev, who had long cultivated himself as the embodiment of Chechen defiance and pride against an oppressive regime in Moscow. The troops backed up his rhetoric.

Militarily, the mission was rushed and done cheaply. The force, a combination of internal and regular troops, was poorly coordinated. Second-year conscripts had just been mustered out, which left combat duty to young and untested soldiers. Second-rate troops and material went up against well-trained and motivated combatants with an excellent arsenal of weapons—no doubt enriched by Russia's military support to the opposition. Russian military analyst Pavel Felgengauer observed, "Yeltsin is a good tactician but not a long-term strategist. . . . Nobody was planning a war until it became a political imperative. Then they started bungling through."[25]

Rhetorically, Moscow never went to war in Chechnya but went to eliminate "illegal armed formations," clean out a nest of bandits, reassert the rule of law and the rights of Russian citizens—among other terms for the action. Yet they were not received as police officers, but as invaders. Moscow continually characterized its presence in Chechnya as limited and even benign, aimed at rebuilding civil society in the wake of Dudaev's harsh regime. "We will strive to reduce the level of force used to resolve the conflict and to switch to primarily political and economic methods for settling the crisis," Yeltsin said just three months into the conflict.[26]

Despite Moscow's spin, the invasion cannot be considered an intervention as von Lipsey strictly defines—that is, an action of benign political or ideological ramifications. Russia has not inserted itself neutrally between combatants; rather, it has allied itself with one party to the conflict. That was demonstrated by its long refusal to involve Dudaev in the peace process. Having chosen a side, Russia could not presume to act as broker between forces in Chechnya.

IV. SECOND GENERATION INTERVENTION: BAILING OUT CHECHNYA

On the way around the Intervention Cycle to conflict, Russia missed many opportunities in Chechnya. By sending token troops in the wake of secession, it failed to enfranchise aggrieved Chechens through negotiation. Inconsistent economic sanctions and weak-willed military commitments doomed Russian efforts to impose order. Last-ditch attempts to make peace—even while acts of violence were going on, if covertly—only strengthened the Chechen conviction that Russia was acting in bad faith. The December invasion established Russia as a party to violence rather than an agent of its resolution.

Despite its uncontested claims that the crisis is an internal affair of the Russian Federation, the back end of the cycle—mitigation and eventual resolution of the conflict—depends on the involvement of a benign, disinterested third party. International organizations play circumscribed roles in Chechnya that mirror the hesitant reaction of the international community at large, and highlights its largely powerless position. In April 1995 the Organization for Security and Cooperation in Europe (OSCE) did set up an official mission in Grozny to lay the groundwork for a democratic transition in postwar Chechnya. Though that transition has hardly begun, the OSCE has

already served a vital function. It has provided a neutral and authoritative setting for periodic attempts at negotiation.

Some reliance on the power of law and legitimately elected politicians is
part of the long-term solution. Both Russians and Chechens looked to the
authoritative elders of the Republic to ameliorate the tensions between bat-
tling local groups. But token officials doing Moscow's dirty work will only
undermine the beneficial role legitimate representatives could play to rebuild
Chechnya, a task that lies ahead.

V. CONCLUSION

In June 1995, Russian prime minister Victor Chernomyrdin struck a deal with
Chechen military commander Shamil Basayev on live television to secure the
release of desperate hostages trapped in the gasoline-soaked hospital of a
sleepy Russian town. Basayev upped the ante of Russia's military involvement
in Chechnya, and Chernomyrdin did not have the cards to see it. Worn from
fighting, both sides came to the table conveniently provided by the waiting
OSCE. The Russian-Chechen peace process through the summer of 1995
gave up on outstanding political questions, including the status of Chechnya,
but did produce a cease-fire. While this seemed to push the conflict down the
mitigation side of the cycle and onto the rocky road toward resolution, that
progress has been uneven.

If it was politics that got Russia into Chechnya, perhaps it would be politics that got it out. His job on the line, Yeltsin put an enormous amount of
political will behind his campaign-inspired peace drive in April 1996. And the
involvement of regional leaders implied that the negotiations, once past the
job of ending bloodshed, could move toward promising political and economic solutions. But the bloodshed only increased once Yeltsin's reelection
was assured.

Peace based merely on a mutual disinclination to fight is inherently
empty. The guns may lay silent for a while, but the attitudes that fed that violence grow more bitter and intractable. To secure the gains of peace,
Russians and Chechen nationalists must resolve the difficult questions that
brought them to violence. The true interveners cannot be Russians enforcing an unwilling peace, international organizations waiting for peace to
come to them, or local puppets proclaiming an empty peace. Any peace that
does not hold the promise of Chechen enfranchisement can revert to violence at any time. If the Chechen remains a subcitizen of his or her own
polity, the Russian soldier in the Caucasus hills will be no safer from guerrilla attacks than in the fabled era of Mansur Ushurma.

NOTES

1. Maggie Scarf, *Intimate Worlds: Life Inside the Family*, (New York: Random House, 1995), p. 23.
2. Sherman Garnett, "The Impact of the New Borderlands on the Russian Military" *Emerging Issues*, Occasional Paper Series of the American Academy of Arts and Sciences, no. 9, August 1995, p. 8.
3. *The Economist*, December 17, 1994, p. 5.
4. "Yeltsin's Annual Message to the Federal Assembly, Februray 16, 1995," *Rossiyskaya Gazeta*, February 17, 1995, p. 3-8 (translation from FBIS-SOV-95-034-5, February 21, 1995, p. 10).
5. Natalya Gorodetskaya, "Chechnya Has Decided to Found a World Islamic Center," *Cegodnya*, May 26, 1994, p. 3.
6. Galina Kovalskaya, "In Russian and Nearby Chechnya: A Conspiracy with No Real Goal" *Novoye Vremya*, September 1994, no. 38, pp. 11-14 (translation from FBIS-USR-94-110, October 11, 1994, p. 18).
7. *Research Report*, Radio Free Europe/Radio Liberty, June 17, 1994, vol. 3, no. 4, p. 8.
8. *Research Report*, Radio Free Europe/Radio Liberty, June 17, 1994, vol. 3, no. 24.
9. Fiona Hill, "Russia's Tinderbox: Conflict in the North Caucasus and Its Implications for The Future of the Russian Federation," Strengthening Democratic Institutions Project, Harvard University, September 1995, p. 3.
10. "Report on Ethnic Conflict in the Russian Federation and Transcaucasia," Strengthening Democratic Institutions Project, Harvard University, July 1993, p. 51.
11. Richard Boudreaux, "Yeltsin's Path to Chechnya Went Step by Bungling Step," *The Los Angeles Times* (Washington Edition), April 3, 1995, p. 3.
12. Ibid.
13. Igor Rotar, "Revenge of a Disgraced Russian Ex-Leader?" *Nezavisimaya Gazeta*, August 31, 1994, p. 3 (translation from FBIS-USR-94-102, September 20, 1994, p. 39).
14. Tatyana Nedashkovskaya, *Novoye Vremya*, no. 20, May 1994, p. 12-13.
15. Boudreaux, "Yeltsin's Path," p. 3.
16. V. Vyzhutovich, "What is Taking Place in Chechnya?" *Izvestia*, August 16, 1994, p. 5, (translation from FBIS-USR, September 22, 1994, p. 25).
17. Margaret Shapiro, "Yeltsin Sets Deadline to End Caucasus War," *The Washington Post*, November 30, 1994, p. 29.
18. Vyzhutovich, *Izvestia*, "What is Taking Place in Chechnya?" p. 5.
19. *Vesti*, Russian Television Company, October 3, 1994.
20. Boudreaux, "Yeltsin's Path," p. 3.
21. Shapiro, "Yeltsin Sets Deadline . . ."
22. Lee Hockstader, "Russia, Breakaway Chechnya Pledge to Seek Peaceful Solution to Conflict," *The Washington Post*, December 7, 1994, p. 31.
23. John Lloyd, *The Financial Times*, December 2, 1994, p. 16.

24. Kovalskaya, "In Russia and Nearby Chechnya," pp. 11-14 (translation from FBIS-USR-94-110, October 11, 1994, p. 18).
25. Boudreaux, "Yeltsin's Path," p. 3.
26. "Yeltsin's Annual Message, February 16, 1995" (translation from FBIS-SOV, February 21, 1995, p. 11).

PART THREE

Breaking the Cycle

■ ■ ■ ■ ■ ■

CHAPTER 12

Lessons Learned

Roderick von Lipsey

Whether viewed from the perspective of a member of the Russian Duma considering future actions in Chechnya or Tajikistan, a representative of Médecins Sans Frontières considering the allocation of humanitarian relief efforts in Central Africa, or a member of the U.S. National Security Council staff considering recommendations for future actions in the Middle East, the Intervention Cycle provides a point of departure with which to assess the appropriate tasks and tools of intervening to mitigate, resolve, or prevent violent intergroup conflict.

The difficulties and complexities of widely differing ideology, sociology, geography, and economy can—and do—present a seemingly impenetrable curtain to the formulation of a comprehensive approach to conflict intervention. This work, however, illustrates that even among cases of profound difference, there exists similarities that may be used to assist in the prescription of remedies and the allocation of precious intervention resources. Identifying these commonalties will not simplify the conflict; rather, it will facilitate our search for appropriate solutions.

Our knowledge of science, for example, can reveal innumerable ways to cause combustion; yet, three simple elements—fuel, air, and a spark—are commonly associated with each occurrence. Then, to mitigate, resolve, or prevent a fire, focusing on methods to remove or isolate one of these elements will go a long way toward achieving success. One would not let the proliferation and complexity of fire hazards thwart one's personal safety and prosperity; why then should one throw up one's hands to the equally threatening complexity of violent intergroup conflict? The Intervention Cycle was born out of a refusal to do just that: to declare the proliferation of violent intergroup conflict too complex and frustrating for us to resolve and prevent from recurring.

I. LESSONS LEARNED

This final chapter returns to the Intervention Cycle with an eye toward applying the lessons learned from the preceding analyses of contemporary interventions to each of its phases. It looks at the three phases of conflict intervention—mitigation, resolution, and prevention—and compares suggestions presented in Part 1 with the lessons learned from the case studies that followed. The result sheds light upon the choices and challenges posed by current and future decisions to intervene.

A. Mitigation

During the mitigation phase of the Intervention Cycle the focus of effort must be on the minimization of violent conflict. Chapter 1 established that in those cases where there exists sufficient will and resources to undertake an intervention at the height of violent conflict, the military forces of security organizations, coalitions, or unilateral states are most capable of performing those missions called for under the lexicon of peace enforcement. Subsequently—or in the presence of a cease-fire agreement between the parties to the conflict, a stalemate, or battle fatigue, or as a decisive victory by one of the parties reduces the level of violent conflict—police/constabulary forces may be introduced to maintain the momentum toward peace and to provide a neutral buffer between previously fighting forces. This follow-on mission is one of traditional peacekeeping.

Recent history shows that the most problematic of these two types of intervention is that of entering conflict during unabated, violent activity between the parties. The Yugoslavia, Somalia, and Rwanda case studies provide very compelling support for the principles discussed in Chapter 1. These cases reflect the importance of intervening with a clear concept of the task at hand, the resources required to perform that task, the hazards of insufficient resolve, and the limitations of neutral, humanitarian interventions.

(1) Bosnia. Kori Schake indicates that in the case of the former Yugoslavia, a peace enforcement mandate was undertaken by UNPROFOR under UN peacekeeping rules of engagement. The resultant mismatch between mission and permission, further complicated by a wavering international commitment to the forcible mitigation of violent acts by all parties, rendered UNPROFOR ineffective at both missions. Schake further points out, as proposed in the Intervention Cycle discussion, that a limited (and possibly premature) focus on humanitarian intervention without the prerequisite mitigation of violence created additional sources of conflict between the belligerents and UNPROFOR, prolonging their will to utilize force in seeking their territorial and political objectives.

These early intervention actions in the former Yugoslavia lacked the clear application of coordinated political and military strategies, to include a distinction between those forces responsible for peace enforcement efforts and those conducting traditional peacekeeping. This reflects the differing perspectives on the reason and purpose of the overall intervention as seen by the various participants: the UN, NATO, Serbs, Croats, Muslims, and the Contact Group. From the vantage point of the Intervention Cycle, one can see that each of these parties sought to influence the situation from a different, and perhaps, nonexistent, phase of the cycle. While NATO wished to enforce, the UN sought to keep peace, the Contact Group wished to coerce, and the diplomats to resolve; meanwhile the parties continued to utilize violence in pursuit of zero sum advantage at every turn.

Part of the flawed logic to the enforcement efforts, as Schake relates, was the mistaken impression that attempts to enforce peace could be done neutrally. As the Bosnian Serbs held the greatest military advantage on the ground, any intervention that sought to preclude the use of force must have been perceived to be decidedly "anti-Serbian"—even if only from the viewpoint of the Serbs. Further, once such a mission is undertaken, those who seek to conduct enforcement must clearly and unequivocally signal the penalty associated with the continued use of force.

On this last point, Schake points out that intervening parties must confront the limits of their interest in solving the problem and commitment to a sustained and robust intervention. Where interests are insufficient to sustain an enforcement action, or even prolonged humanitarian efforts, states and organizations must refrain from creating expectations among their constituencies—and those suffering in the conflict—that cannot be met.

The Intervention Cycle indicates that neither the political process of resolving deep-seated disenfranchisement, nor the humanitarian process of feeding and healing can be effectively conducted without the cessation of violent conflict. The results of the attempt to bypass the mitigation phase of the cycle may also be characterized by some of the more striking lessons learned in Somalia.

(2) Somalia. April Oliver's work underscores that conflict intervention requires a clear conception of what it is that intervention wishes to achieve and how that can be accomplished. UNOSOM I's failed efforts to provide unobstructed food distribution—an humanitarian intervention—came as a result of the international community's failure to assess the real cause of Somalia's "food crisis," determine how to best mitigate that cause, and assess the affect of such an intervention on the Somali society.

UNOSOM I entered a failed state's society at the height of violent conflict with forces sufficient only for peacekeeping and a mandate for limited humanitarian relief. Viewed through the lens of the Intervention Cycle, UNOSOM I was more than a failed humanitarian relief operation, it was a failed attempt at peace enforcement. By introducing insufficiently trained and equipped combat forces into the center a society steeped in violent conflict, UNOSOM I was doomed from the outset. Oliver quite directly states that if the mandate and forces for simple peacekeeping are introduced before a cessation of hostilities, one can, and should, expect disastrous results.

When viewed in the context of the Intervention Cycle, UNITAF's contrasting humanitarian achievement becomes clearly a successful, albeit temporary, peace enforcement mission. The success of the U.S.-led effort to enforce a peace in Somalia allowed the UN, NGOs, and assistance organizations to conduct their humanitarian and developmental relief efforts unmolested. In retrospect, few, if any, parallels exist between the early UN and subsequent U.S. efforts—as they relate to the subject of intervening at the height of violent conflict.

One of the telling lessons of Somalia came as UNITAF's peace enforcement forces withdrew, effecting a hand-over to UNOSOM II. There, a peacekeeping mandate was implemented without a durable cease-fire in place, before all parties had abandoned the violent pursuit of their objectives, and while UNOSOM II leaders sought a political resolution that specifically excluded key parties to the original conflict. This doubly negative approach— premature steps toward resolution and purposeful disenfranchisement of key partisans—resulted in a less than heroic abandonment of the UNOSOM II mission in 1994 and 1995.

(3) Rwanda. It was the painful lesson of Bosnia and Somalia that lent an ironic twist to the UN response to a massive slaughter in the Rwandan capital of Kigali. Deborah Kobak's case study notes, not without regret, the reality of applying the Intervention Cycle's admonishment to refrain from undertaking intervention activities where violent, unabated conflict exists and there is insufficient will to conduct enforcement operations. In the days and weeks after the Rwandan president's fatal airplane crash, the small UNAMIR peacekeeping force was unable of conducting peace enforcement operations; the rest of the world appeared unwilling. As a result, the killing continued until the Tutsi-led Rwandan Patriotic Front (RPF) had taken over the government and most of the country, and Hutu citizens had reached the safety of neighboring states.

Although the Rwanda case study is primarily one of failed resolution and prevention (pre-1994), it horribly depicts what can occur when states and international organizations lack the will, or have sufficient interests at stake, to intervene. An already overextended UN, a hesitant OAU, and a West with few strategic interests at stake in Rwanda, resulted in a decision to allow conflict to mitigate itself (via the natural course of warfare) prior to the initiation of direct intervention. Concurrently, a humanitarian response was coordinated on the periphery of the conflict—where available forces could provide a secure area for purely humanitarian operations.

Kobak points out that, as in the humanitarian operation in Bosnia, the purely humanitarian relief mandate allowed ousted Hutu militia to regain their health and strength, rearm, regroup, and launch sorties across the border into Rwanda against RPF forces and Tutsi civilians. The "troubling question that remains" for Kobak, and the international community, is to what end is a purely humanitarian intervention worthwhile? Continued fighting in Rwanda, Burundi, and to a lesser extent in Somalia, at the completion of huge and costly humanitarian operations illustrate the real drawbacks of "limited," or purely humanitarian interventions.

The Intervention Cycle discussion, while neither arguing in support of nor against a particular form of intervention, clearly illustrates the affect of such an intervention. When choosing to intervene at the height of conflict, efforts peripheral to the direct mitigation of violent activities are not likely to improve the situation that caused the need for intervention. Further, the use of force alone is insufficient for success. James Seaton's case study on conflict in the West Bank and Gaza illustrates how an enforcement-heavy model of limited intervention also falls well short of solving the problem of intergroup conflict. However, the outcome of a limited intervention, when correlated with its point of intersection on the Intervention Cycle framework, can now be better anticipated and more clearly understood by those who contemplate intervening. The reality of the decision made, while possibly unpleasant, is made much more clear to those assigned the task of assessing will, ability, and intention.

B. Resolution

After the mitigation of violent conflict, the process of rebuilding and enfranchisement can begin. It commences, however, in an atmosphere of tenuous opportunity: after the cease-fire is enacted or, perhaps, a peace agreement signed, those who seek to intervene must be wary of renewed conflict. That wariness, according to the earlier discussion, translates into the retention of peace enforcement and peacekeeping capabilities (even if not presence) where these tools were utilized by intervening parties. It further translates into the timely incorporation of all parties to the problem into the solution.

The earlier discussion pointed out that the key to successful resolution is giving each of the parties "a stake" in the resolution process. In other words, the groups in conflict must believe that their interests and objectives are best protected and pursued through other than violent means. They must "buy into" the process.

The extent to which parties to a conflict buy into the process of resolution varies with the method through which mitigation was achieved: some conflicts arrive at this stage of the Intervention Cycle through the forcible denial of violent alternatives (peace enforcement or defeat in combat); some through the physical and psychological exhaustion of all participants; others through moral or diplomatic persuasion of partisan leadership; and most through some combination of the above. In general, however, the less the penalty for reverting to violence, the less these groups will have bought into the resolution process—and the smaller their stake in its success.

The Intervention Cycle discussion in Part 1 urges the use of peacekeeping (police or constabulary) forces for the physical separation of partisans during the later phase of mitigation and early stages of resolution. Moreover, those facilitating the resolutionary process should clearly outline the cost of a reversion to the use of violence. For example, the protracted negotiations in the former Republic of Yugoslavia moved forward only when NATO, then IFOR, exacted tangible penalties upon the military capability of partisan forces. Likewise, despite the Governors Island and New York agreements in Haiti, the process of resolution commenced only after the imminent arrival of U.S. combat forces sent a clear signal to General Cédras and his allies that continued obstinance and acts of political violence would no longer be tolerated by the United States and international community.

Let us look at the lessons learned in Haiti, West Bank/Gaza, Nagorno-Karabakh, and El Salvador and see how they relate to the resolutionary phase of the Intervention Cycle.

(1) Haiti. One of the issues Esther Brimmer tackles in the Haiti case study is that of the role of diplomacy. The Intervention Cycle discussion purposefully avoids defining diplomacy as a discrete intervention task. We feel that diplomacy, in and of itself, rarely succeeds in mitigating conflict or resolving the underlying causes. Diplomacy must work to facilitate the accomplishment of a discrete task or goal. If pursued as an end, it accomplishes little more than dialogue—which is rarely the desired outcome.

To be most effective, diplomatic discussions must proceed hand in hand with some other focus of intervention efforts—mitigation, resolution, or prevention. When linked accordingly, there should exist sufficient will and capability to implement and enforce the terms of agreement. For example, when diplomats arrive at the negotiating table with the ability to articulate clearly the benefits or penalties of each particular course of action—and implement the decisions reached there—they can be most effective.

In the Haiti case, this point is best exemplified by the Carter-Nunn-Powell mission to Haiti in late 1994. That negotiating effort was not one of "continued dialogue." Dialogue most often begets dialogue; however, after nearly three years of dialogue and diplomacy, the United States wanted movement toward resolution. The highly successful Carter-Nunn-Powell mission was a diplomatic engagement with a clear purpose, by credible parties, and with a demonstrated commitment to implement the terms of any agreement or lack thereof. Even though the mission's success relied in great part upon the diplomacy, clarity, and credibility of its participants, the same team would likely not have met with such success had it not been dispatched with the clarity of purpose and resolve of the American administration.

In contrast, protracted negotiations between the UN and parties to the Bosnian conflict between 1992 and 1995 were conducted with tremendous diplomatic aplomb, by skilled negotiators and with great international interest; however, the negotiators were neither in the position to articulate clearly the benefits of ceasing the military confrontation between the parties nor guarantee the penalty to be exacted upon those responsible for continued violence. In short, the various UN, EU, Contact Group, and NATO diplomatic efforts that preceded the Dayton Accords accurately reflected a lack of international (and unilateral) resolve to commit to the conduct of a particular intervention task. The results of these earlier negotiations reflected that disparity. Until linked to Croat-Muslim cooperation, combat reversals for the Serbs, battle fatigue, the bite of sanctions against Serbia, NATO resolve, and unilateral U.S. efforts, diplomatic efforts were seemingly impotent.

In the Haiti case study, Brimmer notes that enforcement provisions were conspicuously absent from the diplomatic effort that resulted in the 1993 Governors Island agreement. This weakness was reinforced by the lack of enforcement action pertaining to earlier and subsequent sanctions regimes as well as the highly symbolic (even if appropriate) withdrawal of the USS Harlan County later that year. The Governors Island accord negotiated away the power of the illegitimate military government without providing them with sufficient disincentives for breaking the pact (or, conversely, incentives to uphold the agreement). Moreover, this lack of enforcement provisions accurately reflected the absence of an international commitment to resolve Haiti's political imbroglio with other than purely diplomatic mechanisms. Without such a commitment, without a linkage between diplomacy and resolve, these early diplomatic efforts were blown about by the political and personal suasion of each interested party. Diplomacy for the sake of diplomacy proved to be ineffectual in determining the course of the conflict between Haiti's legitimate civil government and the Cédras-led junta.

Brimmer further points out that long-term resolution of intergroup conflict requires the participation of all parties to the conflict. One of the contributing factors to the success of the second UN mission in Haiti was that it did not exclude any particular group in the resolution process. Although the coup leaders were removed from the newly restored democratic process, their henchmen and the military were not. To date, former FRAPH, Lavalas, Tonton Macoutes, and members of other paramilitary or extremist groups have been absorbed into the process of political reenfranchisement under the process of Haitian resolution.

The Intervention Cycle discussion suggests that all of the societal elements must be part of the solution; otherwise, they remain part of the problem. That point, and the dilemma it presents, is graphically depicted in the images of the implied resolution between Israel and the Palestinians. That situation remains far from the picture of successful resolution captured in the historic handshake between Israeli prime minister Rabin and PLO leader Arafat on the South Lawn of the White House in September 1993.

(2) West Bank/Gaza. Because resolution requires the participation of all parties, James Seaton notes in his chapter on Gaza and the West Bank that Israel cannot impose resolution upon the Palestinians, nor will physically separating the two parties resolve the conflict. Rather, true resolution will require the blending of Palestinian and Israeli goals into a single commitment to resolve their disputes and conflicts peacefully—a challenging task in the wake of the politically and emotionally charged Israeli elections of May 1996.

Seaton notes that the Intervention Cycle is useful as a descriptive tool for understanding the failures and limits of intervention because it underscores the differences between those things that can be imposed upon parties to a conflict (mitigation) and those that require their cooperation and full participation (resolution and prevention). He points out that Israel's traditional response to Palestinian violence, isolation, and imposed "resolution," begets exactly what the Intervention Cycle suggests to be the result of political, economic, and social disenfranchisement: violence.

Israel is not alone in what Seaton calls "right half fixation." He points out that neither Egypt nor Jordan were able to focus their efforts on anything other than conflict mitigation during their administration of Gaza. Without addressing the need politically to enfranchise Palestinians into a state, a process, or a system of values in which they and the Israelis hold a stake, no set of economic and developmental measures will be sufficient to resolve the "Palestinian question" or prevent the recurrence of violent conflict. Thus, resolution will require a significant change to the status quo—and will require the participation of Israelis and Palestinians.

The situation in Israel is so politically charged and imbued with historic and emotional impediments to progress vis-à-vis Palestine, that such a change is likely to require enormous patience and compromise. However, those who choose to intervene in this process—and seek solutions that continue to disenfranchise Palestinians or isolate parties to the conflict—are likely to be frustrated and perplexed by the accompanying prevalence of violence between these parties. Those interventions that suffer from what Seaton calls "right half fixation," will fail to move Gaza, the West Bank, and Israel itself, forward in their attempt to resolve the deep-seated conflict between these two groups who inhabit the same homeland.

(3) Nagorno-Karabakh. The point that resolution normally requires a change in the status quo is made strikingly clear by Susan Ellingwood's analysis of the Intervention Cycle's implications for resolving the conflict in Nagorno-Karabakh. Ellingwood concludes that resolution in this Soviet-successor state's bloody conflict requires a significant change in the relationship among Armenians, Azerbaijanis, and ethnic Armenians in the autonomous region of Nagorno-Karabakh.

As in the cases of Gaza and the West Bank, simple physical or political isolation is insufficient. Viewed from a strategic resource point of view, Ellingwood points out that Nagorno-Karabakh controls water resources precious to the Azeri state that surrounds it. However, because Nagorno-Karabakh lacks energy and economic resources of its own, it needs Azerbaijan as much as or more than Azerbaijan needs Nagorno-Karabakh. Thus, a belligerent independence between the two is unworkable due to their interdependence. A solution based upon uniting Nagorno-Karabakh with the ethnically related state of Armenia may appear tantalizing to those who favor ethnic national solutions; however, even if Azerbaijan were to agree to some complex land-trade formula, Armenia still lacks a seaport and strategic resources and remains dependent upon access to the Black Sea region for its raw materials and trade. Thus, the long-term stability and viability of Armenia, Nagorno-Karabakh, and Azerbaijan requires mutual cooperation and long-term enfranchisement—a stake—in a system beneficial to all parties to this conflict.

Ellingwood points out that the status quo (which supported the ethnic enclaves of Karabakh Armenians and Nakhichevan Azeris isolated from both the states of Armenia and Azerbaijan) depended upon the overarching ideology of communism—a false enfranchisement—to provide these groups a stake in the political process of Soviet rule. When the topsoil of that ideology and system eroded, the region erupted into violence that revealed the deep rifts between those who were enfranchised into the states of Azerbaijan and Armenian and those residing in the enclaves.

Soviet policies that exploited intergroup conflict as a means of weakening resistance to the center succeeded in controlling violence through its unprecedented system of political, economic, and physical coercion. When the center collapsed the successor states were left with strong ethnic identities that no longer shared a common identity of ideology. The Intervention Cycle suggests that the process of resolution in all of these "non-Russian" republics will likely entail significant changes to the status quo in order to recapture the masses of disenfranchised on the road to long-term stability.

(4) El Salvador. A case study that looks at a relatively successful journey on the road to resolution is that by Kirk Kraeutler on El Salvador. El Salvador is one of the intervention "success stories" that fueled the short-lived euphoria over post-Cold War UN intervention. However, as Kraeutler points out, the success in El Salvador came only after changes to the global balance of power and related changes in the thrust of conflict intervention.

One of the changes in the post–cold war phase of UN intervention in El Salvador was the recognition that all parties to the conflict must be part of the solution. The abject failure of communist ideologies in Latin America and elsewhere changed the concept of intervention in that region to one of creating long-term stability and economic viability (as well as, perhaps, opportunities for American military and political disengagement) from one of reinforcing an ideological bulwark against the westward spread of communism beyond the Eastern bloc and Cuba. These changes allowed the resolution process in El Salvador to incorporate all parties to the conflict into political elections—an essential part of the political enfranchising process.

Kraeutler also notes that when the parties to the conflict in El Salvador wearied of the devastating ideological and civil war, their consent to the introduction of UN peacekeepers signaled their willingness to accept a neutral authority and buy into the process of peaceful resolution. In relinquishing a measure of autonomy and sovereignty over FMLN, military, or political interests, the parties bought into the larger process of Salvadoran interests—an important step toward an enfranchising resolution.

The El Salvador case study also shows the strength of aggregate organizations. The discussion of intervention mechanisms in Part 1 points out that these organizations (the UN being the archetype) are most effective when their efforts are concentrated on facilitating the process of resolution. Aggregate organizations are able to coordinate the diplomatic, developmental, and financial assistance measures required to take full advantage of the reduced state of societal tensions that exists during the resolution phase and coordinate the commencement of a wide array of reconstruction and developmental tasks.

The El Salvador case study supports the Intervention Cycle assertion that the level of violence decreases as stakes in a political process increase. While conflict continues to exist in the economic and politically challenging environment of El Salvador today, and Kraeutler's assessment of its future remains mixed, it is clear that the prospect of true resolution in that state relies on the continued ability of the Salvadoran political process to address the political and economic needs of a struggling population.

Further, Kraeutler and others point out that continued engagement by those interested in El Salvador's success is an essential requirement for continued progress. As the Intervention Cycle warns, a failure to continue the process of engagement through resolution and prevention will result in a renewed increase in conflict and an upward spiral of violence. Premature disengagement in El Salvador, he warns, will fail to break the cycle.

C. Prevention

Conflicts that reach the resolution phase of the Intervention Cycle by virtue of a determined and vigorous intervention are quite understandably hailed as successes. Without wishing to detract from those achievements, Breaking the Cycle cautions that resolution does not obviate the need for continued vigilance and effort.

Almost every case study in Part 2 of this work underscores the importance of preventative measures; unfortunately virtually all point to opportunities lost along the upward spiral toward violent conflict. The benefit of hindsight allows these observations, of course. However, it is our hope that we can apply that benefit to current and future interventions in order to break the cycle of intervention, withdrawal, and the need to reintervene—the legacy of failed interventions of all types.

Part 1 warns that prevention, because it lacks the gripping drama of ongoing conflict, often sits unattended on the "back burner" of international attention. The costly and complex legacy of intervention in those areas that have gone too long unattended, however, brings to the subject of attention a new interest. If we were better able to perform this task, and better understood the dynamics of conflict prevention, our precious intervention resources might be better utilized. By clearly identifying the discrete tasks of each phase of intervention, the Intervention Cycle helps identify which of those limited resources should be the focus of mitigation, which should be conserved for resolution, and how most can be spared through successful prevention.

The discussion of prevention lessons learned may be best suited to two of the case studies from an area of the post–cold war world in which changes to the status quo were thrust upon the society at a pace for which few states could ever be prepared: the region of the former Soviet Union and the case studies on Tajikistan and Chechnya.

(1) Tajikistan. Katherine Tucker's discussion of the relatively unpublicized conflict in Central Asia underscores this book's precept that conflict occurs at a more complex level than that between groups defined in terms of ethnicity. The conflict in Tajikistan is primarily one between local, socioeconomic, or value groups, rather than a traditional ethnoreligious conflict. Further, it is yet another cautionary tale of how the false enfranchisement created by communist ideology and Soviet coercion can result in violent upheaval. Absent the coercive power of authoritarian rule, the "democratic" power newly released in Tajikistan—as in many other post-Soviet states—manifests itself as violent chaos between groups lacking the cohesive bond of political enfranchisement.

To underscore the importance of understanding the stakes of successful prevention, Tucker points out that the danger of continued disenfranchisement in this region, as in others, is that it can foment fundamentalist radicalism by driving individuals and groups to resort to identities—religious, tribal, and so on—other than those that unite them toward the pursuit of shared interests. Chapter 1 discusses the centrifugal power of these other affiliations and how they can lead to increased violence, societal collapse, and ultimately, the spillover of violent conflict into an entire region.

Tajikistan's central location in a region of deep and far-reaching religious, ethnic, ideological, political, and strategic cleavages gives the prospect of a widening conflict a spectre of devastation that should capture the attention of all those parties interested in regional, and perhaps, global stability. Even those uninterested in the particulars of Tajik society can, and should, be compelled by an interest in maintaining stability in this volatile region of Central Asia. Should the region devolve into a wider and more violent conflict, the mitigation and resolution of that conflict will come at a much greater cost, and peril, than that of prevention.

Tucker argues that the Intervention Cycle provides a framework with which to assess the urgency of international efforts to intervene in this conflict, as well as a tool with which to coordinate the range of ongoing efforts that strike at different, and not necessarily extant, phases of this conflict. The Tajik case study infers that preventative measures by aggregate, developmental, and economic organizations may preclude the need for a more costly intervention should this conflict spill into wider areas of Afghanistan or engage the potentially conflicting interests of Russia, China, Iran, India, or Pakistan.

With the application of preventative measures, the level of conflict in Tajikistan may be "backed down" the left side of the Intervention Cycle and allow the redoubling of efforts at political and economic enfranchisement.

This is an opportunity missed in the second case study of this section, Chechnya.

(2) Chechnya. Any hope that the Soviet legacy of brutal repression had passed with the fall of the Berlin Wall in 1989 vanished in late 1994 as the world watched Russian troops and aircraft fire upon the city of Grozny, the capital of the autonomous republic of Chechnya. Maryann Parker points out that these violent acts of coercion by the Russian military have been, and will continue to be, ineffectual absent Chechen political enfranchisement in either a Russian or Chechen government that serves the political and economic interests of its citizens.

While many authors have recently hailed the merits of preventative diplomacy, few have provided an explanation of how, or in what form, these preventative mechanisms should be implemented. More importantly, they have left few clues on how the need for prevention can be readily recognized. In the case of Chechnya, Russian leaders hoped to prevent the rising tide of political and social conflict from breaking into violent conflict with the implementation of economic sanctions and other coercive measures up to and including the use of military force. While the need for prevention, from Moscow's point of view, manifested itself clearly in the autonomous leanings of this "breakaway republic," the measures adopted to fulfill that preventative need lacked an understanding of the root causes of Chechen rebellion.

The Intervention Cycle discussion points out that the use of preventative measures such as deterrence and coercion require careful consideration in their application. It further stresses that these are ultimately ineffective absent enfranchisement. In Chechnya, the Soviet legacy left no semblance of political empowerment for the overwhelmingly non-Russian citizens of this republic. Ethnic Chechens, Parker explains, are predominantly Muslim, have retained their traditional culture and language, and share a legacy of disenfranchisement from the Russian center.

Chechnya's disenfranchisement from a Russian political, economic, and social system stems from a long history of Russian dominance and coercion. Historic Russian oppression forged the Chechen ethnic identity into a symbol of rebellion against Russia and Soviet rule. With such a precedent, Parker finds little surprising about the Chechen rebellion and the bloody clashes that thrust it upon the world's consciousness in late 1994.

For Parker, and for Breaking the Cycle, the case of Chechnya is a cautionary tale for those who seek to find ways to prevent ethnic, cultural, or religious conflicts from recurring and spreading as the area of the former Soviet Union yields to a changing world order. Under the scrutiny allowed by democratic freedoms, the extent of political and economic disenfranchisement throughout the region is staggering. In Chechnya, Russia sought to apply preventative measures right out of the old Soviet playbook. Their failure to prevent Chechnya from exploding into massive violence came not only because of a sloppy and inept application of coercive measures, but because the chimera of a Chechen stake in Russia's political future had long passed from the Chechen society's outlook for the future. Nor was a glimmer of such a hope proffered by the Yeltsin government.

Parker indicates that, ironically, Moscow may have had a solution to the Chechen problem at hand. Had Russian leaders recognized that key elements of their successful application of deterrent and coercive measures in Tatarstan, the catastrophic events that occurred in Grozny may have been avoided. The elements of Russia's successful prevention of a Tatar break from the republic, as outlined by Parker, were economic deterrence coupled with power-sharing (politically enfranchising) and tax-revenue sharing agreements (economically enfranchising). These elements resulted in Russian efforts to achieve what the Intervention Cycle presents as two of the key elements to conflict resolution.

The discussion presented in Part 1 suggests that, rather than the efficacy of Russia's economic coercion, it was the promise of Tatar political and economic relevance that led to Russian success in Tatarstan. Unfortunately, neither Moscow's intervention in Tatarstan nor Chechnya were conducted with a concept such as that presented in this book. Yet, through the framework of the Intervention Cycle and this discussion, the correlation between Russian success in Tatarstan and failure in Chechnya need not be lost upon us.

An earlier discussion on the preventative phase of the Intervention Cycle notes that sanctions and other coercive measures require close consideration of several factors—target group, targeted behavior, desired effect, and conditions for removal. In the case of Russian sanctions against Chechnya, none of these factors appeared to have been given full consideration. In conjunction with the imposition of sanctions, the Russian leaders further isolated Chechnya from the political center by failing to respond to their growing political crisis—while further contributing to their economic delinquency.

The variety of case studies presented in Part 2 of this work allow us to apply Breaking the Cycle's theoretical work across a spectrum of conflicts in order to draw out the parallels between lessons learned in various conflicts. In this last case, the Russian misuse of deterrent and coercive forces parallels those of the UN and others in a profoundly different use of deterrence and coercion against a military junta in the Haiti case study.

In the chapter on Haiti, Esther Brimmer reinforces the caution for clear consideration of the effects of sanctions. Against Haiti, economic sanctions were insufficiently focused to deter the actions of those elites who were key supporters of the military junta, nor were these elites given a stake in the outcome of the condition for sanction removal: the return of Aristide portended a decline in their political influence. Further, Haiti's long history of political and economic dysfunction indicated that the need for intervention was growing, not diminishing, as sanctions further impoverished and isolated the majority of its already poor population.

April Oliver points out that in Somalia, the early signs of disenfranchisement were ignored by the neocolonial policies of its Cold War patrons. The divisive policies and clan favoritism practiced by former president Siad Barré were clearly contributing to the political disenfranchisement of most Somalis. As geostrategic interests in Somalia waned, civil war tore apart the fabric of its society. External intervention came too late, and in the wrong form, to prevent the near-total destruction of Somalia's remaining infrastructure and civil society.

Similarly, Kori Schake's work on the former Yugoslavia strongly supports the Intervention Cycle's emphasis on the elements of prevention by noting that preventative opportunities were missed there too. Schake suggests that had the international community expressed its disapproval at the establishment of ethnic-based solutions to Yugoslavia's political turmoil and recognized the volatile mix of political and economic disenfranchisement inherited from its legacy of Tito and communism, the conflict may have been checked before reaching its overwhelmingly destructive proportions. A clear response to the divisive 1990 elections in the Slovenian, Serbian, and Croatian republics may have weakened the centrifugal forces being fed—had the international community (or some interested party) recognized that the rush toward nationalism had little to do with the embrace of democracy in this splintering federation.

Preventative measures, through the recognition of these disenfranchising trends, would have been the most effective and least costly form of intervention—as well as provided the greatest number of intervention options for those who sought to intervene to prevent Yugoslavia's violent collapse.

A thread common to many of the case studies developed in this work is the risk faced by post-Soviet states of suffering from a false perception of political and economic enfranchisement. While apparently stable in their former state of existence, release of the coercive forces of authoritarian rule—as well as the demise of the enfranchising forces of communist ideology—appears to lead to instability and violent conflict. The only way to break this cycle is through the application of preventative measures that foster greater political and economic enfranchisement rather than further polarize the society.

The legacies of Bosnia and Somalia may be that preventative types of intervention are realized to be most effective and least costly. The legacy of the

Intervention Cycle may be that it helps clarify the types of intervention options available, and why prevention is the key to success—both before intergroup conflict reaches violent proportions and after existing conflict has been resolved.

II. BREAKING THE CYCLE

Most of the interventions discussed in Part 2 were considered as "limited" in scope and duration at the time of their undertaking. In light of this work's discussion, one now sees that attempts at "limited" involvement equate to a commitment to act during one, but not all, of the phases of conflict intervention. Such a commitment may be, indeed, both realistic and helpful; however, few tools are available to the decision maker to help him or her decide how and when the application of limited resources will best affect the conflict at hand. The Intervention Cycle framework helps illustrate how the various types of intervening mechanisms available to the decision maker may be best applied to specific phases of an ongoing conflict.

The case studies presented here show that, even after the passage of years and the expenditure of billions of dollars, there clearly remains much more work to be done. For example, in Rwanda (as well as Burundi), Bosnia, and Gaza, mitigation has been temporary and violent outbreak remains a continued, near-term prospect. In other cases, such as Somalia, Chechnya, and Nagorno-Karabakh, the task of resolution remains unfinished, disenfranchisement unabated, and the cycle unbroken. And finally, in Tajikistan, El Salvador, and Haiti, only continued vigilance, developmental intervention, and preventative measures will keep political and economic disenfranchisement from rekindling the flames of intergroup conflict. The question remains, then: will the international community or interested parties remain engaged in these states? If so, how can they most effectively allocate their limited resources?

Especially in cases where parties feel compelled to remain involved due to "limited" interests—political, economic, or humanitarian—the limits of their resources demand the deliberate application of some principle of engagement, concept of operation, or guide by which the probability of their success may be determined. In a growing world of dwindling resources and a declining propensity to allocate precious natural, human, fiscal, or political assets toward the attainment of peace and prosperity beyond one's borders, an heuristic device such as the Intervention Cycle provides a clear point of departure.

Those who wish to maximize the effectiveness of the resources they commit to solving the problems associated with intergroup conflict, and breaking the cycle of violence and intervention, will find that this framework provides a tool with which to coordinate and prioritize their efforts and those of others who sponsor intervention initiatives.

Because the need to intervene is often precipitated by a sudden turn of events—a natural disaster, leadership crisis, or the like—response may require rapid coordination among a plethora of organizations, states, and agencies. Most emergency efforts will be conducted on an ad hoc basis, with little or no time for coordination. However, because the framework clearly delineates those phases of conflict in which the various follow-on efforts and mechanisms are more—and less—effective, rapid coordination may be achieved by using the Intervention Cycle as a conceptual guide for directing the response.

Some of the case studies provided above illustrate that regardless how urgent the need for assistance, without a conceptual basis for the conduct of conflict intervention precious resources can be squandered and lost. Further, the limited assistance available from economic or developmental organizations, for example, may be ineffective if applied prematurely as in Gaza; or the impact of vital security forces can be negated if utilized ambiguously as in the former Yugoslavia.

Absent a conceptual guide to intervention efforts, there is more than efficiency at stake. As illustrated in the case studies, a purely humanitarian intervention may actually contribute to the sources of conflict as in Somalia, or feed and succor belligerent parties as in Bosnia and Rwanda. While these results were certainly unintended and possibly unavoidable, those who understand the Intervention Cycle will be able to anticipate that purely humanitarian efforts conducted in the center of a conflict at the height of violence are likely to have no effect on conflict mitigation. Rather, such efforts may extend the fighting beyond the natural limits of the partisan's rations and stamina and draw out the conflict indefinitely.

While purely humanitarian types of limited intervention may be conducted on behalf of those innocents that can be helped, they often go further toward the application of moral salve to the conscience of those external to the conflict than toward actually mitigating the violence. Those responsible for conducting limited interventions must carefully limit the expectations of all parties concerned. Constituents at home should not be led to believe that feeding the victims will bring an end the images of continued violence. Nor should the recipients of the humanitarian aid be emboldened by the prospect of additional forms of support when such intentions do not exist.

This caution neither argues for expanded intervention nor against limited ones. Rather, it appeals for a clear match between intervention ends and means. Where the task at hand is the resolution of conflict after the cessation of hostilities, neither heavy armor nor hard currency alone will provide for resolution. The added security forces may assist with the diplomatic and developmental efforts to enact an enfranchising political solution and rebuild the foundation of civil society; the added economic resources may fund those efforts as well as assist in the purchase of food, capital equipment, and reconstruction supplies. However, what is more needed are police to help open the roads to food supplies and medicine, doctors to support and reopen hospitals, diplomats and lawyers to draft agreements and, perhaps, a new constitution, and farmers to reestablish agricultural programs.

Conversely, how often have police, doctors, diplomats, lawyers, and farmers been sent in harm's way when heavy armor was more appropriate or when emergency economic structural assistance was required? The framework provided by the Intervention Cycle helps clarify these needs by dividing conflict intervention into three major categories and providing a conceptual template for the application of intervention resources available.

Thus, when the National Security Council director sits down to consider the options for future actions in the Middle East, or the Medécins Sans Frontières disaster response coordinator considers the allocation of humanitarian relief efforts in Central Africa, or the Russian parliamentarian considers assistance efforts for Central Asia, a back-of-the-envelope tool such as the Intervention Cycle can provide a point of departure. The end result, we hope, will not only be a more effective and efficient use of the precious intervention resources available, but a more effective and efficient approach to mitigating, resolving, and, ultimately, preventing the recurrence of violent intergroup conflict.

Index

numbers in **bold** type denote introductory or defining occurrence
subheadings that appear in parenthesis refer to country chapters only

(Haiti), 185
(Nagorno-Karabakh), 225
Hungary, 222
Hutu, 30, 31, 57, 62, 149, 150, 151, 153, 155, 156, 159, 162, 164, 288, 289

Imamate of Shamil, 271
immigration, 21, 37, 82
Impuzamugambi, 159
India, 296
Ingushetia, 275
insecurity dilemma, 208-10
Inter-African Union of Human Rights (Ouagadougou), 156
InterAction, 135
Interahamwe, 159
intergroup conflict, 3, 7-8
    (Yugoslavia), 103, 107, 109, 110
    (Rwanda), 149, 151, 164, 166
    (West Bank and Gaza), 195, 202, 208, 210
    (Nagorno-Karabakh), 216
    (Chechnya), 272
International Atomic Energy Agency (IAEA), 70
International Center for Human Rights and Democratic Development (Montreal), 156
International Civilian Mission, 187, 190
International Committee of the Red Cross/Red Crescent (ICRC), 59, 60, 61, 70, 134, 143
International Court of Justice, 37
International Development Association (IDA), 155
International Federation of Human Rights (Paris), 156
International Finanicial Institutions (IFIs), 42, 51, 53, 64-5, 75
International Human Rights Commission, 157
International Monetary Fund (IMF), 63, 64, 77, 85, 150, 152, 154, 155, 159, 164, 241
International Rescue Commission (IRC), 61, 135
International War Crimes Tribunal, 108
intervention, 4
Intervention Cycle, 6-7
Intifada, 202, 203, 204, 205, 206
Iran, 217, 223, 224, 251, 253, 254, 255, 256, 257, 296
Iraq, 69, 86, 136, 185
Irish Republican Army, 264
Iskandoarov, Akbarsho, 253, 254
Islamic/Muslim fundamentalists, 196, 249, 252, 264
Islamic Renaissance Movement, 252
Islamic Renaissance Party, 252
Islamic Resistance Movement (HAMAS), 28
Israel, 18, 28, 195, 199, 200, 201, 202, 204, 206, 207, 208, 209, 210, 292, 293
Israeli Defense Force, 204

Italy, 97, 122, 221
Ivory Coast, 157
Izméry, Antoine, 184, 186

Jericho, 194, 207, 208
Jerusalem, 200
Jess, Omar, 127
jihad, 7
Johnston, Robert B., 138, 139
Joint Chiefs of Staff, 62, 133
Jordan, 198, 199, 201, 202, 210, 292
Judea, 200

Kabul, 260
Karabakh War, 218, 220, 226
Karadzik, Radovan, 108
Karimov, Islam, 255-56, 258
Karl, Terry Lynn, 236
Kazakhstan, 254, 270, 272
"Kennebunkport order," 179
Kenya, 123
KGB, 222
Khasbulatov, Ruslan, 274
Khmer Rouge, 149
Khojand. See Uzbek Fergana Valley
Khojand City, 261
Khrushchev, Nikita, 23
Kigali, 62, 158, 159, 160, 288
Kimmerling, Baruch, 198
Kingdom of Southern Slavs, 97
Kinyarwanda, 151
Kocharyan, Robert, 223
Koh, Harold Hongju, 178
Korea, 136
Kosovo, 97, 98, 103, 109
Kraijina, 100, 102, 111
Kremlin, 276-77, 278
Kulab, 251, 253, 261
Kurds, 3
Kurgan Teppe, 251
Kurgan-Tube, 262
Kuwait, 69
Kyrgyzstan, 254

Labazanov, Ruslan, 275
Labor Party (Israel), 28, 203
Lachin, 219
    Lachin Corridor, 226
La Fontant, Roger, 182
Lake Victoria, 151
Latin America, 230, 294
Latrell, Bruce, 182
Lebanon, 198, 208
Leninabad. See Uzbek Fergana Valley
Likud Party (Israel), 28
localism, 250, 261, 265